FOR DUMMIES

BUSINESS AND
GENERAL
REFERENCE
BOOK SERIES
FROM IDG

Cooking For Dummies™

Quick Reference Card

Common Conversions

Liquid volume equivalents

1 cup = 8 fluid ounces = 250 mL

2 cups = 1 pint or 16 fluid ounces = 500 mL

2 pints = 1 quart or 32 fluid ounces = 1 L

4 quarts = 1 gallon = 4 L

1/2 tablespoon = 1 1/2 teaspoons = 7.5 mL

3 teaspoons = 1 tablespoon = 15 mL

2 tablespoons = 1 fluid ounce = 30 mL

Dry equivalents

4 tablespoons = 1/4 cup = 50 mL

5 tablespoons plus 1 teaspoon = 1/3 cup = 75 mL

12 tablespoons = 3/4 cup = 175 mL

1/2 cup = 4 ounces or 8 tablespoons = 125 mL

1 cup = 16 tablespoons = 250 mL

2 cups = 1 pint = 500 mL

4 cups = 1 quart = 1 L

Note: Some metric equivalents are approximate.

Baking equivalents

1 cup minus 2 tablespoons sifted all-purpose flour = 1 cup sifted cake flour

1 cup plus 2 tablespoons sifted cake flour = 1 cup sifted all-purpose flour

1/4 teaspoon baking soda plus 1/2 teaspoon cream of tartar = 1 teaspoon double-acting baking powder

Miscellaneous equivalents

1 tablespoon prepared mustard = 1 teaspoon dried

1 cup stock or broth = 1 bouillon cube dissolved in 1 cup boiling water

1 square (1 ounce) baking unsweetened chocolate = 3 tablespoons cocoa powder plus 1 tablespoon butter

1 ounce semisweet chocolate = 3 tablespoons cocoa powder plus 2 tablespoons butter and 3 tablespoons sugar

Food equivalents

2 slices bread = 1 cup fresh bread crumbs

8 tablespoons butter = 1 stick

4 sticks butter = 1 pound butter

1 pound confectioners' sugar = 4 1/2 cups confectioners' sugar, sifted

1 pound granulated sugar = 2 cups granulated sugar

1/2 pound hard cheese = about 2 cups grated cheese

(continued)

The Ten Commandments of Cooking

- **Taste. Taste. Taste.** That's the only way to know whether your dish is coming out right.

- **Be patient.** Don't blow hot breath over a pot to make it boil faster.

- **Be flexible.** If something looks terrific in the market, be willing to modify your meal plans.

- **Be thrifty.** Don't throw anything away unless it's spoiled. Use bones and peelings for stocks, leftovers for next-day dishes, stale bread for croutons, and so on.

- **Be organized.** Do all preparation (chopping, mincing, measuring, and so on) before you begin cooking.

- **Develop a memory bank for flavors and how they work together,** particularly herbs and spices.

- **Don't be a slave to recipes,** even if you're a beginner. Always modify something if the change suits your tastes.

- **Make sure that your knives are sharp and your equipment is in good working order.** It's easy to cut yourself with a dull blade that requires you to use more force.

- **Use only the freshest ingredients.**

- **Remember that no dish, no matter how botched or burned, is a failure** — serve it to the kids or the dog.

Timesaving Tips

- Precook pieces of chicken, meat, or potatoes in your microwave before finishing them on the grill.

- Take steaks and other meats out of the refrigerator about 15 minutes before grilling so that they warm to room temperature. They'll cook faster and more evenly.

- Line the broiler pan with aluminum foil to ease clean-up when broiling hamburgers, fish, steaks, and chops.

- Whirl salad dressings that contain fresh herbs, onion, and garlic in a blender or food processor to save chopping time.

- Place a garlic clove on a cutting board and whack it with the flat side of a heavy knife or a cleaver to make removing the skin easier. The skin should split right off.

- Roll a lemon or orange under the palm of your hand on the countertop to make extracting the juice easier.

(continued)

1 cup heavy whipping cream =
   2 cups whipped cream

1 medium lemon = 3 tablespoons lemon
   juice; 2 to 3 teaspoons grated peel

3 medium apples = 1 pound

1 large onion = about 1 cup chopped
   onion

1 cup raw converted rice = 4 cups
   cooked rice

1 large tomato = about ¾ cup chopped
   tomato

1 pound all-purpose flour = 4 cups sifted
   flour

5 large whole eggs = 1 cup

(For additional listings, see Appendix B.)

Recipe-Reading Checklist

- ✔ Read through the recipe at least twice to make sure that you understand the directions.
- ✔ Make sure that you can perform all the techniques.
- ✔ Check that you have all the necessary equipment and ingredients.
- ✔ Make sure that you have enough time to prepare and cook the recipe.
- ✔ Check whether you can (or need to) make any part of the recipe ahead of time.
- ✔ Read through the ingredients to see whether you like them all, or the recipe has too much fat, sugar, or salt for your dietary needs.
- ✔ Check whether you need to use an ingredient, such as butter or oil, at different stages in the recipe so that you don't make the mistake of using that ingredient all at once.
- ✔ Find out whether you need to preheat the oven.
- ✔ Check the yield of the recipe.

Cooking For Dummies™

Quick Reference Card

BUSINESS AND GENERAL REFERENCE BOOK SERIES FROM IDG

First Aid for Cooking Blunders

Bread, burned: Scrape off the black part with a grater.

Butter, blackened in pan: Pour off the burned butter and wipe the pan. Use equal amounts butter and vegetable oil, which does not burn.

Cake, burned bottom: Cut away the black parts and fill the holes with frosting. Scrape surface burns with a grater.

Cake, sticks to pan: Let sit for 5 minutes and then try again.

Chicken, browning too fast: Cover the browned parts with foil, shiny side out; continue roasting until all the chicken is cooked.

Chicken, breast cooked, legs not: Remove the chicken from the oven. Cut off the legs at the thigh joint. Return only the legs to the oven and keep the rest of the chicken warm.

Eggshells, crack while hard-cooking: Add a teaspoon of salt or a few drops of lemon juice to the cooking liquid to prevent the white from running out of the shell.

Egg whites, won't whip: Try again with whites at room temperature. Use a copper bowl or add a pinch of cream of tartar before whipping.

Fat, splattering in pan: Add pinch of salt or cornstarch to the hot fat. Pour off the fat as soon as possible.

Fruits, discolored: If cut fruits such as bananas and apples start turning brown, sprinkle them with lemon juice and cover with plastic wrap.

Gravy, lumpy: Stir vigorously or whirl in a food processor.

Gravy, too thin: Raise heat and reduce until the gravy thickens. Or add a creamy paste of 1½ teaspoons cornstarch to ½ cup stock or water for every cup of gravy. Stir and cook for about 2 minutes over medium heat.

Gravy, too salty: Add a little brown sugar or currant jelly.

Rice, crunchy: Add a little water and continue cooking.

Soufflé, won't rise: Salvage as a dessert by placing it as attractively as you can on a serving dish. Garnish with ice cream and a sprig of mint.

Soup, too salty: Add water. Or add slices of potato, which soak up salt.

Soup, too thin: Add beurre manié (a 1 to 1 ratio of softened butter and flour molded in a ball). Add to soup and stir well over medium heat until it thickens. Arrowroot and cornstarch are other thickeners.

Soup or stew, lacks flavor: Add freshly grated lemon peel. Also try adding salt or a pinch of sugar.

Vegetables, overcooked: Puree in a blender, adding cream and seasonings to taste.

...For Dummies™ Bestselling Book Series for Beginners

Praise for Cooking For Dummies

"Cooking — like anything — must be fun and should not be taken too seriously. Seasoned with Bryan Miller's hilarious sense of humor, *Cooking For Dummies* helps us do just that."
> — Ferdinand Metz, President, The Culinary Institute of America

"Always a dummy, but with *Cooking For Dummies,* an enlightened one!"
> — Paul C.P. McIlhenny, Executive Vice President, McIlhenny Co. (Tabasco Brands Products)

"Most of all, cooking should be an adventure, and it should be fun. *Cooking For Dummies* is seriously informative with a big dash of humor."
> — Wolfgang Puck, Chef and Owner of Spago Restaurant

"No 'dummy' — the person who adds *Cooking For Dummies* to his or her cookbook collection. Come to think of it, so encyclopedic, practical, and unintimidating is . . . *Cooking For Dummies* could be the first and only book in your kitchen."
> — William Rice, food and wine columnist, the *Chicago Tribune* and author of *The Steak Lover's Cookbook*

"Too often cookbooks are sanctimonious, but in *Cooking For Dummies,* the table is a fun place. It will nourish your tummy as well as your humor."
> — Jacques Pépin, Chef and Author

"The recipes for 'Dummies' are so delicious I felt compelled to eat the book."
> — Robert Klein, Actor and Comedian

"Applause to Bryan Miller for dishing humor up with the serious subject of cooking."
> — Molly Chappelet, Proprieter, Chappelet Vineyards, Napa Valley

"Simple to use and full of helpful hints and tips, *Cooking For Dummies* is sure to become a must have for 'dummies' and experienced chefs alike."
> — Joachin Splichal, Chef/Owner, Patina and Pinot Restaurants

Praise for Marie Rama

"Talk show hosts are always looking for the perfect guest. I found one in Marie Rama. Beyond professional, she is focused, gives great information, and is truly entertaining. Maybe she should host her own program?"
> — Mark Summers, former talk show host of *Biggers and Summers* and *Double Dare*, and currently host of *Majority Rules*

"Marie Rama is one of my favorite guests on *Our Home*. Not only does she have marvelous recipes but she makes her instructions so clear and simple. Because of Marie I spend more time in my kitchen."
— Boni Montgomery, Host, Lifetime Television, *Our Home*

"I've had the opportunity to have Marie Rama as a guest on *Creative Living* several times through the years, and always look forward to working with her. Her professionalism as a food expert, as well as her delightful personality, make her the consummate guest."
— Sheryl Bordon, Producer/Host, *Creative Living*

"Marie has visited our TV kitchen on a number of occasions. She's shown us with her talent and expertise that she's no 'dummy' when it comes to cooking."
— David Smith, host, *The Exchange,* Connecticut

"Marie Rama, a.k.a. the Lemon Lady, was undoubtedly one of the most appealing guests we've ever had on the program. She knows everything you ever wanted to know about lemons. After her appearance our audience was puckered up for days."
— Barry Bernon and Rachel Platt, Anchors, *Good Morning Kentuckiana,* Louisville

"Marie Rama, the Lemon Lady, is a great interview. Upbeat, informative — and you gotta love a guest who brings food! She shared the best lemon poppy seed bread I've ever tasted. I look forward to our next meeting."
— Lia Chelenza, Host, *Sunday Magazine* and *Live From The Palace,* Syracuse

"One of the best interviews we've ever had for our morning show! Great tips on healthy cooking — plus a great response from our viewers!"
— Ginger Daril, Supervising Producer, *News 4 at Sunrise,* Little Rock, Arkansas

"Marie's a delight, and as at home in the kitchen as a banana in a bowl of pudding! Our viewers thought so too, and let us know that they want to see more of her, and soon."
— Marietta Hoover Caudill, Associate Producer, *Wave 3 News Sunrise,* Louisville

Praise for Bryan Miller

". . . the most influential food critic in the world. . . ."
— Nicholas Lander, *Financial Times,* London

"Everybody in the food business, and a lot who aren't, know Bryan Miller. . . ."
— Jim Quinn, *Town & Country* magazine

"Miller's lively writing style . . . is one of *The Times'* sparkiest features. . . ."
— James Reginato, *W Magazine*

"The most famous gastronomic critic in the world . . ."
— Luis Bettonica, El Pipiripao, Barcelona

TM

References for the Rest of Us! ™

BUSINESS AND GENERAL REFERENCE BOOK SERIES FROM IDG

Do you find that traditional reference books are overloaded with technical details and advice you'll never use? Do you postpone important life decisions because you just don't want to deal with them? Then our *...For Dummies*™ business and general reference book series is for you.

...For Dummies business and general reference books are written for those frustrated and hard-working souls who know they aren't dumb, but find that the myriad of personal and business issues and the accompanying horror stories make them feel helpless. *...For Dummies* books use a lighthearted approach, a down-to-earth style, and even cartoons and humorous icons to diffuse fears and build confidence. Lighthearted but not lightweight, these books are perfect survival guides to solve your everyday personal and business problems.

> *"More than a publishing phenomenon, 'Dummies' is a sign of the times."*
> — The New York Times

> *"A world of detailed and authoritative information is packed into them..."*
> — U.S. News and World Report

> *"...you won't go wrong buying them."*
> — Walter Mossberg, Wall Street Journal, on IDG's ...For Dummies™ books

Already, millions of satisfied readers agree. They have made *...For Dummies* the #1 introductory level computer book series and a best-selling business book series. They have written asking for more. So, if you're looking for the best and easiest way to learn about business and other general reference topics, look to *...For Dummies* to give you a helping hand.

TM

IDG
BOOKS
WORLDWIDE

COOKING FOR DUMMIES™

by Bryan Miller
and Marie Rama

Foreword by Wolfgang Puck

IDG Books Worldwide, Inc.
An International Data Group Company

Foster City, CA ♦ Chicago, IL ♦ Indianapolis, IN ♦ Southlake, TX

Cooking For Dummies™

Published by
IDG Books Worldwide, Inc.
An International Data Group Company
919 E. Hillsdale Blvd.
Suite 400
Foster City, CA 94404
www.idgbooks.com (IDG Books Worldwide Web Site)
www.dummies.com (Dummies Press Web Site)

Library of Congress Catalog Card No.: 96-77264

ISBN: 0-7645-5002-0

Printed in the United States of America

10 9 8 7 6 5 4

1E/RR/QY/ZX/IN

Distributed in the United States by IDG Books Worldwide, Inc.

Distributed by Macmillan Canada for Canada; by Transworld Publishers Limited in the United Kingdom; by IDG Norge Books for Norway; by IDG Sweden Books for Sweden; by Woodslane Pty. Ltd. for Australia; by Woodslane Enterprises Ltd. for New Zealand; by Longman Singapore Publishers Ltd. for Singapore, Malaysia, Thailand, and Indonesia; by Simron Pty. Ltd. for South Africa; by Toppan Company Ltd. for Japan; by Distribuidora Cuspide for Argentina; by Livraria Cultura for Brazil; by Ediciencia S.A. for Ecuador; by Addison-Wesley Publishing Company for Korea; by Ediciones ZETA S.C.R. Ltda. for Peru; by WS Computer Publishing Corporation, Inc., for the Philippines; by Unalis Corporation for Taiwan; by Contemporanea de Ediciones for Venezuela; by Computer Book & Magazine Store for Puerto Rico; by Express Computer Distributors for the Caribbean and West Indies. Authorized Sales Agent: Anthony Rudkin Associates for the Middle East and North Africa.

For general information on IDG Books Worldwide's books in the U.S., please call our Consumer Customer Service department at 800-762-2974. For reseller information, including discounts and premium sales, please call our Reseller Customer Service department at 800-434-3422.

For information on where to purchase IDG Books Worldwide's books outside the U.S., please contact our International Sales department at 415-655-3200 or fax 415-655-3295.

For information on foreign language translations, please contact our Foreign & Subsidiary Rights department at 415-655-3021 or fax 415-655-3281.

For sales inquiries and special prices for bulk quantities, please contact our Sales department at 415-655-3200 or write to the address above.

For information on using IDG Books Worldwide's books in the classroom or for ordering examination copies, please contact our Educational Sales department at 800-434-2086 or fax 817-251-8174.

For press review copies, author interviews, or other publicity information, please contact our Public Relations department at 415-655-3000 or fax 415-655-3299.

For authorization to photocopy items for corporate, personal, or educational use, please contact Copyright Clearance Center, 222 Rosewood Drive, Danvers, MA 01923, or fax 508-750-4470.

is a trademark under exclusive license to IDG Books Worldwide, Inc., from International Data Group, Inc.

About the Authors

Bryan Miller (Manhattan, NY) is a former *New York Times* restaurant critic whose column appeared every Friday in the weekend section of the *Times*. He currently is a food and feature writer covering restaurants and dining trends all over the world. He has written four editions of *The New York Times Guide to Restaurants in New York City* and is coauthor of *The Seafood Cookbook: Classic to Contemporary, Cuisine Rapide,* and *A Chef's Tale.* Miller is the recipient of the James Beard Who's Who Food and Beverage Award, which recognizes outstanding lifetime achievement in the field of food and wine.

Marie Rama (Bronxville, NY) is an independent food, beverage, and media consultant. She's worked as a professional pastry chef and recipe developer for several food companies and associations, including McIlhenny Company's Tabasco Pepper Sauce and the United Fresh Fruits and Vegetable Association. She serves as a spokesperson for Sunkist Growers as the "Lemon Lady" and has appeared on hundreds of TV and radio shows around the U.S. and Canada.

ABOUT IDG BOOKS WORLDWIDE

Welcome to the world of IDG Books Worldwide.

IDG Books Worldwide, Inc., is a subsidiary of International Data Group, the world's largest publisher of computer-related information and the leading global provider of information services on information technology. IDG was founded more than 25 years ago and now employs more than 8,500 people worldwide. IDG publishes more than 275 computer publications in over 75 countries (see listing below). More than 60 million people read one or more IDG publications each month.

Launched in 1990, IDG Books Worldwide is today the #1 publisher of best-selling computer books in the United States. We are proud to have received eight awards from the Computer Press Association in recognition of editorial excellence and three from *Computer Currents'* First Annual Readers' Choice Awards. Our best-selling *...For Dummies*® series has more than 30 million copies in print with translations in 30 languages. IDG Books Worldwide, through a joint venture with IDG's Hi-Tech Beijing, became the first U.S. publisher to publish a computer book in the People's Republic of China. In record time, IDG Books Worldwide has become the first choice for millions of readers around the world who want to learn how to better manage their businesses.

Our mission is simple: Every one of our books is designed to bring extra value and skill-building instructions to the reader. Our books are written by experts who understand and care about our readers. The knowledge base of our editorial staff comes from years of experience in publishing, education, and journalism — experience we use to produce books for the '90s. In short, we care about books, so we attract the best people. We devote special attention to details such as audience, interior design, use of icons, and illustrations. And because we use an efficient process of authoring, editing, and desktop publishing our books electronically, we can spend more time ensuring superior content and spend less time on the technicalities of making books.

You can count on our commitment to deliver high-quality books at competitive prices on topics you want to read about. At IDG Books Worldwide, we continue in the IDG tradition of delivering quality for more than 25 years. You'll find no better book on a subject than one from IDG Books Worldwide.

John Kilcullen
CEO
IDG Books Worldwide, Inc.

Steven Berkowitz
President and Publisher
IDG Books Worldwide, Inc.

Eighth Annual Computer Press Awards ≥1992

Ninth Annual Computer Press Awards ≥1993

Tenth Annual Computer Press Awards ≥1994

Eleventh Annual Computer Press Awards ≥1995

Authors' Acknowledgments

There are many people we would like to thank who helped make this book possible.

We would like to especially thank and acknowledge the excellent work of our illustrators Elizabeth Kurtzman and Lillian Masamitsu-Hartmann, and cartoonist Rich Tennant.

Special thanks also to Paul Freitas, Ann Persico, Michael Nott, and Adele Kurtzman, our friends and home cooks, who helped with recipe testing and tasting. Thanks also to Betty Amer, Charlie Lilly, and Jane Uetz for their insightful review work, and to Sharon Dale for providing metric information.

The following experts, companies, and associations provided us with invaluable insights and information: Andrea Boyle and Sunkist Growers, Inc.; the Thacker Group; Kimberly Park and the Rice Council; Donna Myers and the Barbecue Industry Association; Susan Lamb Parenti and the National Cattlemen's Beef Association; Robin Kline and the National Pork Producers Council; Priscilla Root and the American Lamb Council; Nancy Tringali and the National Broiler Council; Sherry Weaver and the National Turkey Federation; Elisa Maloberti and the American Egg Board; and kitchen equipment experts Jean Tibbetts and Karen Deutsch.

We also thank Stephanie Avidon and Barbara Hunter of Hunter and Associates and Stacy Collins and Jamie Klobuchar of IDG Books Worldwide, our marketing and publicity team. Others at IDG Books Worldwide who have our thanks and appreciation for making this book happen include Sarah Kennedy, Kelly Ewing, and our Project Editor Pam Mourouzis for her attention and devotion to every detail.

Thanks also to Debbie Grimm at International Management Group, and to our agent Mark Reiter for his support, advice, and encouragement from beginning to end.

Publisher's Acknowledgments

We're proud of this book; please send us your comments about it by using the Reader Response Card at the back of the book or by e-mailing us at feedback/dummies@idgbooks.com. Some of the people who helped bring this book to market include the following:

Acquisitions, Development, & Editorial

Project Editor: Pamela Mourouzis

Acquisitions Editor: Sarah Kennedy, Executive Editor

Copy Editor: Kelly Ewing

General Reviewers: Betty Amer, Sharon Dale, Charlie Lilly, Jane Uetz

Editorial Manager: Kristin A. Cocks

Editorial Assistant: Ann Miller

Production

Project Coordinator: Debbie Sharpe

Layout and Graphics: E. Shawn Aylsworth, Linda M. Boyer, Elizabeth Cárdenas-Nelson, J. Tyler Connor, Angela F. Hunckler, Todd Klemme, Tom Missler, Drew R. Moore, Anna Rohrer, Brent Savage, Gina Scott

Special Art: Elizabeth Kurtzman, Lillian Masamitsu-Hartmann

Proofreaders: Betty Kish, Nancy Price, Robert Springer, Carrie Voorhis, Karen York

Indexer: Sharon Hilgenberg

General and Administrative

IDG Books Worldwide, Inc.: John Kilcullen, CEO; Steven Berkowitz, President and Publisher

IDG Books Technology Publishing: Brenda McLaughlin, Senior Vice President and Group Publisher

Dummies Technology Press and Dummies Editorial: Diane Graves Steele, Vice President and Associate Publisher; Judith A. Taylor, Product Marketing Manager; Kristin A. Cocks, Editorial Director; Mary Bednarek, Acquisitions and Product Development Director

Dummies Trade Press: Kathleen A. Welton, Vice President and Publisher

IDG Books Production for Dummies Press: Beth Jenkins, Production Director; Cindy L. Phipps, Manager of Project Coordination, Production Proofreading, and Indexing; Kathie S. Schutte, Supervisor of Page Layout; Shelley Lea, Supervisor of Graphics and Design; Debbie J. Gates, Production Systems Specialist; Robert Springer, Supervisor of Proofreading; Debbie Stailey, Special Projects Coordinator; Tony Augsburger, Supervisor of Reprints and Bluelines; Leslie Popplewell, Media Archive Coordinator

Dummies Packaging and Book Design: Patti Sandez, Packaging Specialist; Lance Kayser, Packaging Assistant; Kavish + Kavish, Cover Design; Cover photo artwork Copyright 1997 Derik Allen/TIB

♦

The publisher would like to give special thanks to Patrick J. McGovern, without whom this book would not have been possible.

♦

Contents at a Glance

Cartoons at a Glance

By Rich Tennant • Fax: 508-546-7747 • E-mail: the5wave@tiac.net

page 169

page 49

page 7

page 265

page 353

Recipes at a Glance

Meat and Poultry

Fish and Shellfish

Meatless Main Dishes

Vegetables and Side Dishes

Sauces and Garnishes

Desserts

Table of Contents

· ·

Part II: Know Your Techniques 49

Chapter 3: Boiling, Poaching, and Steaming 51

Chapter 4: Sautéing 71

Foreword

· ·

Cooking For Dummies may seem at first glance to be just a lighthearted romp through the culinary meadow, but in fact, beneath all the fun it is a solid learning tool that introduces readers to an impressively wide range of skills. Wonderful ingredients and good technique are what good food is all about, and because knowing how to bring out the best in food is what makes a meal memorable, technique is the foundation of all good cooking, professional or amateur. Every great chef starts somewhere, and *Cooking For Dummies* shows you where.

At one of my restaurants, Spago in Los Angeles, we focus on grilling. Sure, we get our famous results partly by having a great staff and a professional kitchen, but *Cooking For Dummies* shows the home cook that superior grilling (as opposed to the average wham-bam backyard fare) lies in a number of easy-to-master techniques. Step-by-step recipes and illustrations walk you through different levels of sophistication, so you can see how all great food has the same beginnings.

Cooking is also about making wonderful food to share with family and friends, and *Cooking For Dummies* lets you do just that. Think of this book as a set of training wheels that prop you up as you learn all the twists and turns of the kitchen. Not only will you come away with plenty of exciting dishes, but you will also eventually take off the training wheels and set off on your own.

Cooking should be an adventure, a series of small discoveries that lead to a lifetime of great meals. *Cooking For Dummies* gives you all the information and direction you need to set out on that adventure, confident and ready to cook great food!

— Wolfgang Puck

Introduction

· ·

*W*hether you fancy yourself a hotshot home cook or someone who wouldn't know a whisk from a weimaraner, *Cooking For Dummies* can help you. For the novice, our technique-oriented approach teaches you the "whys" of cooking and not just the "whats" found in recipe books. That way, you can eventually throw away your training wheels and create dishes all on your own.

More experienced cooks may want to hone their basic skills, and the nearly 200 recipes in this book offer plenty of food for thought.

Unlike most cookbooks, this book is more than a compilation of tasty recipes. We also focus on cooking techniques such as broiling, steaming, braising, and roasting. After you learn these techniques, you are no longer a slave to recipes. You can cook with imagination and creativity — and that's the sign of a skilled cook.

The best part about discovering how to cook this way is that while you are practicing your techniques, you have all kinds of delightful food to eat. Sure beats trumpet lessons.

Furthermore, this book is structured around the way you live. For example, it includes information about cooking for guests when you have only one hour (or less!), cooking economically, and making a delicious meal when you don't have time to get to the market.

Most of all, you'll actually have fun as you explore the endless pleasures of cooking. And that, after all, is what food is all about.

The Good News

In the past decade, the food revolution has made available to home cooks products that they had never dreamed of: truffles, Chinese pea shoots, frozen stocks, rare Italian cheeses, and countless types of olive oil, to name just a few. At the same time, the technology of cooking equipment has narrowed the gap between home cooks and professional kitchens.

The Real News

Of course, new products and technology don't make a good cook. The requirements of a refined cook have not changed since the 17th century: a sensitive palate, an understanding of cooking techniques and products, strong knife skills, and patience. These are skills we want to help you develop.

How to Use This Book

We start at the very beginning: your kitchen and your equipment. What basic tools do you need? How do you use these things? Then we move on to cooking techniques to get you up and running as soon as possible. Doing simple things well offers great personal satisfaction, as you will see.

Depending on your needs and cooking skills, you can start at the beginning of the book and work your way through, or go straight to the chapters that interest you the most, or read the book Arab style, from the back forward.

How This Book Is Organized

This book is organized around cooking techniques and real-life situations. Major sections are called *parts*. Within each part are chapters that address specific subjects. Following is a rundown of each part and what you can read about there.

Part I: Go On In — It's Only the Kitchen

What is this strange room? It's the most popular room in the house, where friends hang out as they help themselves to your food and drinks; parties inevitably gravitate; and couples have their best arguments. This part is designed to help you get over your fear of cooking. It touches on kitchen design and organization, helping you to arrange your appliances, kitchen space, counters, and cabinets for maximum efficiency. It also covers in detail necessary equipment like pots, pans, knives, and all kinds of gadgets.

Part II: Know Your Techniques

Part II is where the fun begins. Each chapter includes recipes that illustrate an essential cooking technique: braising, sautéing, roasting, grilling, and more. From that starting point, we take you through a number of recipe variations that show you how to improvise with skill and confidence.

Part III: Expand Your Repertoire

Part III looks at pasta and eggs and at larger categories of dishes like soups, salads, and one-pot oven meals. Here, you can read about how to make the perfect omelet, how to mix a balanced vinaigrette, and how to make a pretty soup garnish. Also included are illustrations and charts — like the one identifying different types of pastas (so that you know tagliatelle from linguine) — and, of course, dozens of delicious recipes.

Part IV: Now You're Cooking! Real Menus for Real Life

Part IV injects another dose of reality into the cooking experience. Most glossy cookbooks assume that you have all the time in the world to prepare a dish. Some books also assume that price is no object — "now take that loin of veal and sprinkle it with black truffles" — and that everybody lives next door to a gourmet market. In the real world, you have 45 minutes, if you're lucky, to prepare dinner while a 2-year-old is clinging to your leg and the cat is coughing up hair balls. At the same time, the local supermarket may be closing in 5 minutes. Now that's real-life cooking. And that's what these chapters are all about.

Part V: The Part of Tens

Just when you thought that we had covered everything, we give you more! These quick lists include sundry observations about cooking, a few important reminders, plus a list of classic cookbooks you should know about.

Appendixes

This straightforward reference section gives you useful lists and charts and a glossary. Here, you can find the meaning of more than 100 common cooking terms. We also provide common equivalents and substitutions for those emergency situations when you discover at the last minute that you don't have the ingredient you need.

Icons Used in This Book

When there's an easier way to do something, a step you can take to save money, or a shortcut you can take to get yourself to the dinner table faster, we let you know by marking the tip with this icon.

The kitchen can be a dangerous place. This icon, like a flashing yellow light, steers you clear of potentially dangerous mishaps.

We hope that you remember *every* valuable piece of information in this book, but if your brain can hold only so much, make sure that you hang on to these tidbits.

We show you skills all along, but some skills are more important than others. This icon highlights fundamental skills and techniques that you should practice. Some are easy, such as zesting an orange. Others, like carving a roasted chicken, require more concentration.

This chef's toque, a symbol of culinary excellence, alerts you to the advice and secrets of some of the world's greatest chefs.

We anticipate possible problems with a recipe — you ran out of cooking liquid in the rice, the soufflé didn't rise, and so on — and offer solutions.

In many cases, we give you a recipe, say meat loaf, and then describe easy variations that use different ingredients, various sauces, and so on.

A Few Guidelines before You Begin

Before charging ahead to make any of the recipes in this book, you should know a few things about the ingredients we choose to use:

- ✔ Milk is always whole. You can substitute lowfat or skim milk, but it gives soups and sauces a thinner, less creamy consistency.

- ✔ Use unsalted butter so that you can control the amount of salt in a dish. We don't recommend substituting margarine, which has just as many calories per tablespoon (100) as butter and inferior flavor.

- ✔ Unless otherwise noted, all eggs are large.

- ✔ All dry ingredient measurements are level. Brown sugar is measured and firmly packed.

- ✔ All salt is common table salt and pepper is freshly ground. We seldom specify measured amounts of salt and pepper because every cook has a different palate. Sample the recipe several times during preparation to taste for seasoning and add salt and pepper to taste when we instruct you to do so.

And keep the following general tips in mind:

- ✔ Read through each recipe at least once to make sure that you have all the necessary ingredients and utensils, understand all the steps, and have enough preparation time. (We begin each recipe by listing the cooking utensils you need and the preparation and cooking times.)

- ✔ Be sure to use the proper size pan when a measurement is given.

- ✔ Preheat ovens, broilers, and grills at least 15 minutes before cooking begins. Place all food on the middle rack of the oven unless the recipe says otherwise.

- ✔ Most of the recipes in this book are written to serve four. You can reduce by half or double many of them to satisfy two or eight diners.

A Note about Metrics

For those of you who live in areas where the metric system is used in cooking, we have done our best to provide metric equivalents throughout the book. Generally, we give the equivalent volume measure: for example, 1 cup equals about 500 milliliters. Please note, however, that these equivalents aren't always exact. We tested all our recipes by using imperial measures, so if you use metrics, the consistency or texture of your dishes may end up being a little different. Take notes as you try recipes so that you'll know how you need to modify different dishes the next time you make them.

Cooking utensil sizes may differ from country to country, too. In each recipe, we give the equivalent metric size for each utensil, even though that particular size may not actually exist. If you don't have the exact size we call for, use the closest thing you can find.

Finally, as a rule of thumb, never mix metric and imperial measures — if you're going to measure one ingredient in milliliters and not cups, for example, do them all that way. For help in converting measurements to and from metrics, see Appendix B at the back of this book.

Part I
Go On In — It's Only the Kitchen

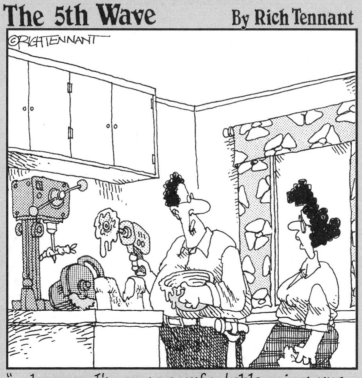

The 5th Wave   By Rich Tennant

"...because I'm more comfortable using my own tools. Now-how much longer do you want me to sand the cake batter?"

In this part . . .

There's no doubt about it: If you want to learn to cook, you have to go into the kitchen. If this idea seems frightening, try looking at photographs of your kitchen for a few weeks until you feel better; then stand just outside the kitchen until your nerves subside. Then make the final assault.

After you're inside, we can help you make it an enjoyable and efficient room in which to prepare all kinds of wonderful food. In this part, you'll find everything from kitchen design to cooking equipment, from lighting your cooking area to seating party guests on the kitchen counter when they insist on watching you work.

Chapter 1

Warming Up to Your Kitchen

- -

- -

*F*rom morning till night, sounds drift from the kitchen, most of them familiar *and comforting, some of them surprising and worth investigating. On days when warmth is the most important need of the human heart, the kitchen is the place you can find it; it dries the wet sock, it cools the hot little brain.*

— E. B. White

Whether you have a cramped apartment kitchen with counter space the size of a cereal box or a sprawling country kitchen with a commercial stove and a work island, this chapter can help you become a more productive cook. To be sure, space is great. But knowing how to use what you have efficiently is the real key. You would be surprised to see how small some restaurant kitchens are; they work, however, because everything is in its place and is easily accessible. Have you ever ricocheted around the kitchen desperately searching for a spatula while your omelet burned on the range? We want to ensure that you're never in that situation again.

Aside from discussing smart kitchen design, we look briefly at large appliances — refrigerators, stoves, microwaves, and such — just so you'll be armed with knowledge if you have to buy or replace anything in your kitchen.

And forgive us if we get a bit mushy about kitchens as being the soul of the home, where happy memories are made along with roasted chickens and golden apple pies. It just happens to be true.

To get started, here are ten good reasons why everyone should learn to cook:

▶ When you dine in restaurants, you can complain with authority that particular dishes are not made the way you make them.

- You get to use all kinds of bizarre implements — and actually know what to do with them.

- You can control your diet rather than depend on the dubious victuals churned out by carry-out places.

- At home, seconds and thirds are permissible.

- Feeding loved ones — or even your mother-in-law — is inherently more tolerable than going to a restaurant. At least you'll have leftovers.

- Establishing a connection with the food chain allows you to distinguish quality food from what's second rate. Who knows, you may even be inspired to plant a vegetable garden next spring.

- You start hanging around the cookbook section in bookstores, fertile terrain for opposite-sex encounters.

Freud and Foccacia: How Kitchens Exude Love

The aromas of childhood and carefree days cling to the walls of kitchens, those blissful days when your priorities in life were circumscribed by showing up at mealtime and not getting run over by a car. When you are anxious about something in the middle of the night and need comfort, where do you go? To the kitchen for a nibble. The kitchen is both the emergency room and chapel of the home.

Kitchens are warm. Kitchens are nurturing. And not that you don't trust your dinner host, but seeing your food before it's cooked is always reassuring.

As Joseph Conrad said, "We owe much to the fruitful meditation of our sages, but a sane view of life is, after all, elaborated mainly in the kitchen."

The Evolution of the Modern Kitchen

In the 1950s, domestic architecture hid the kitchen from the rest of the house — remember Rob and Laura Petrie's suburban digs in the 1960s television sitcom "The Dick van Dyke Show"? A swinging door concealed their kitchen. This setup allowed Rob endless opportunities for pratfalls, but it also made a statement about the home kitchen: It was a place you went only when you had to, a utilitarian room with no more allure than the garage.

Today, kitchens are often the most "designy" rooms in the house, complete with colorful Italian tile, antique tables, terra-cotta floors, work islands, skylights, and professional stoves. The Petries' swinging door (and maybe a wall as well) has been knocked down to open the kitchen to the living area. Food as theater! Cooking as camaraderie! Friends interact in the kitchen; strangers are greeted in the living room.

Today's more casual, personal style of entertaining allows what once would have been considered barbaric: watching food being prepared! Moreover, near-manic interest has made the kitchen the most interesting — not to mention the most fun — room in the house.

Friends now slump over the counters and watch you trim artichokes; they offer to peel tomatoes or dry the salad. They bring good wine and open it during the festivities. Even if you try to nudge them into the living room or den, they slide back to the kitchen as if pulled by a magnet.

Guests who offer to work save on labor costs. Do not discourage them.

Do You Need a Big Kitchen?

You don't need a fabulous kitchen to prepare fabulous food. But a well-designed work place sure makes cooking easier and more pleasurable. Catherine Beecher, an ardent feminist and cookbook author in the late 19th century, decried the cavernous Victorian kitchens of the day. She wrote that sprinting around a vast room was not only fatiguing but also inefficient. Beecher looked for models of a workable kitchen and found it in, of all places, a railroad dining car (this was before the days of Amtrak).

In the early 20th century, architects took Beecher's message and started designing spaces that required minimal movement to cook a meal. Ideally, you could be at the range and in a few steps reach over to the ice box, the bread box, and the produce bin.

In the 1980s, the pendulum began to swing back toward large, lavish kitchens with islands, skylights, and more chrome than a Chevrolet factory. Some of these rooms are highly functional; others are pure vanity.

Even the pros make fools of themselves

In the pressure cooker environment of a professional kitchen, slipups are inevitable — chefs incinerate ducks, drop cakes, and spill more than an Irish pub on St. Patrick's Day. Interviews with leading chefs reveal that you have to have a sense of humor about your mistakes. Look at blunders as learning experiences. Above all, don't get discouraged. Here are a few tales from the front:

- **Francesco Antonucci, Executive Chef at Remi in New York City:** "In 1975, I was a commi garde manager at the Hotel Las Vegas near Venice. The chef told me to get a 50-liter container of tomato sauce from the cooler. As I was carrying it out, the handle broke on the container, and all of the sauce poured out over the sawdust floor. I looked up at my boss. He stared at me. Then he said, 'Well, I guess we don't need Parmesan on the sauce tonight.'"

- **Andrew D'Amico, Executive Chef at The Sign of the Dove in New York City:** "In 1978, right after school, I got a job working at the Berkshire Place Hotel (Manhattan). The consultant there was Wolfgang Puck. The first week there I was learning how to make a beurre blanc. Wolfgang Puck came over to taste it . . . and he spit it out! Great way to start a career."

- **Charley Palmer, Executive Chef at Aureole Restaurant in New York City:** "As a student at the Culinary Institute of America, I was helping a Belgian chef cater a party. It was a spectacular menu — roasted veal racks and all the trimmings with two 10-inch chocolate soufflés for dessert. Well, I took one soufflé out and the chef took out the other, and then we bumped into each other, smashing both to the floor. We had nothing else to serve. We scooped them up (the floor of this house was really clean), saved what we could, and spooned them onto plates with a little sauce. Our host came back to tell us he was really pleased — except for the soufflé. It was delicious, he said, but there wasn't enough."

From Chaos to Confidence: Setting Up Your Cooking Space

Beecher had a good point. If you want to run, you can join a health club. Although nothing is wrong with a large eat-in kitchen, the design of the cooking area should be practical.

You should be able to move from your working counter space to the stove and the refrigerator in a smooth, unobstructed fashion. This working space actually has a name: the *kitchen triangle* (see Figure 1-1). If a table, plant, or small child is blocking the way, move it.

Figure 1-1:
An efficient
kitchen
triangle.

Countertops

Counter space is the single most overlooked item in many kitchens. The counter is where you set out and prepare food (on a cutting board), stack plates before serving, place kitchen machines, and lose car keys amid the clutter. Try to keep your counters neat and clean. So many kitchen counters are cluttered with paraphernalia and become nearly useless. Place only your most frequently used appliances on top of your counters — the coffee machine, toaster, and blender, for example. Put away all other appliances that consume precious work space.

You can place a hot pot or roasting pan straight out of the oven on a slab of granite or on a countertop made of ceramic tile. But when you place hot pots and pans on most other countertops, including those made of expensive Corian (a synthetic, solid-surface material), they can scorch the counter surface. As a general rule, set hot pots and pans on your stovetop or on a heat-resistant ceramic or metal trivet after removing them from the oven.

Lighting

It goes without saying that kitchens should be well lit — the stove and work spaces most of all. If you have a combination kitchen/dining area, you may want to put the lights on a dimmer, preferably in different zones. That way, you can keep the kitchen bright while the dining area is dim.

Another option is to have special lighting for the cooking area, either inset into overhead cabinets or in the ceiling. Nothing is worse than trying to watch your food in a dimly lit area. If your kitchen is poorly lit over the cooking area, the least expensive solution is a wall-mounted supplementary light.

Stove lights can be helpful, but in most cases they illuminate only the top panel of the unit and not the whole cooking area.

Storage

You can't have too much storage space in your kitchen. Of course, most of us have to make do by being creative with what we have.

Dry storage

Dry storage refers to anything that is not refrigerated or frozen. Many ingenious kitchen cabinets are on the market, such as those that have storage shelves on the swing-out doors as well as inside. If your cabinets don't have this feature, you can improvise by mounting racks on the inside of the doors. Roll-out cabinets under counters are also convenient options.

You can store dried beans, pasta, flour, tea, coffee, and the like in large glass jars and place them on a shelf. Store the items you use every day closest to your stove or work station. Look around your kitchen for any wall space where you can mount a shelf. Use the vertical space in your kitchen, too. Mount wall racks to the ceiling and use the space above your cabinets for storage.

Store your knives in a butcher block or on magnetic wall strips. Keeping knives in a drawer not only ties up space that could be used for other items but also dulls their blades quickly.

Kitchen islands are extremely efficient space in that they can have considerable storage space below. Moreover, they can double as a kitchen table. If you don't have an island, consider buying a butcher block table with shelving underneath.

Wet storage

You don't have much room to experiment when it comes to refrigeration. A refrigerator/freezer should be within steps of your work space. You can store a stand-alone freezer, however, in another room off the kitchen or even in the basement.

Countertop materials

If you are thinking of changing your countertops, consider these choices:

- **Hardwood** is attractive and good for your knives (although you should always use a cutting board, no matter what kind of countertop you have). The varnish seals tend to break down with steady use and little cracks and crevices can catch food particles, presenting a potential bacteria problem.

- **Marble** is cool, making it ideal for preparing pastry, which is less likely to stick to a cool, smooth marble surface. It's also beautiful and very expensive and can stain.

- **Stainless steel** is ideal in many ways, although somewhat harsh and industrial looking. Stainless steel does not break, rust, or tarnish, which is also why it is a good material for sinks.

- **Tile** is beautiful, rich looking, and functional as long as the surface is flat and unbroken. However, tile tends to chip and wear away, especially if you place hot pots and pans on it or install it incorrectly.

- **Synthetic surfaces** of all kinds are available, and they are highly functional. Corian is a synthetic material that has a deep opalescent quality. It can be cut and shaped in every which way without ever showing a seam. It is very hard and durable — and very expensive.

- **Plastic lamination,** such as Formica, has many advantages for the home kitchen. It is durable and relatively inexpensive, comes in various colors, and can be molded around edges. It should not be used as a cutting surface, however, or as a resting place for hot pots and pans.

Exhaust

Adequate exhaust is crucial to the comfort of a kitchen. Many exhaust systems for home ranges and microwaves are inadequate if you do a lot of cooking, especially sautéing and roasting. A separate exhaust system that has a grease filter and a pipe that vents smoke outside is a smart investment. Some units retract into the wall when not in use. Some cooks prefer downdraft exhaust systems — those that pull air down into the unit — because they save space. However, such units must fight warm air's tendency to rise, limiting their effectiveness.

Major Appliances

In this section, we discuss the various types of appliances available to home cooks today. Chances are that you are not in a position to make major changes in your appliances and will have to make do. Knowing each appliance's relative strengths and weaknesses can help you do so.

Ovens and stovetops

Kitchen technology is giving professional cooks space-age ovens and stoves — induction cooking based on a magnetic principle, gadgets that whip up ice cream to order, conduction and steam ovens, to name a few. All these inventions will likely filter down to the home before long, and some of them already have.

Following is a rundown on basic home stoves and ovens and what you should know about them.

Cooking with gas

Most serious cooks prefer gas stoves. You can turn a gas flame up and down quickly, which is important in sautéing and sauce-making. Commercial gas ranges are extremely powerful and can cut your cooking time by as much as one-fourth.

A gas range built within the last five years should not smell of gas from flaming pilots. Newer models no longer have standing pilots. They ignite electronically; therefore, gas does not flow through the system unless the range is turned on. If you do smell gas, you have a leak in your system. This situation is dangerous — call your gas company immediately. Do not use the stove or any other electrical appliances, even your lights, because doing so can spark an explosion.

Electric heat

Electric ranges became all the rage after World War II. They were considered clean, easy to use, and modern. The drawback to electric ranges is their slow response time. Reducing heat from high to low can take a minute; gas can do it in seconds. Today's new gas and electric ovens are equally calibrated to hold and maintain an oven temperature within a variance of about 5 degrees.

Induction

Induction is a new form of kitchen heat. Some professional chefs are so impressed with it that they predict it will supplant all other systems in ten years.

Whether or not that is true, induction cooking is impressive to watch. Basically, it works on a magnetic transfer principle — heat passes via magnetic force from the burner to the pan. If you place a paper towel between the burner and the pan, the towel does not get hot. A 2-quart (2-L) pot of water comes to a boil in about a minute. However, an induction cooktop uses only selected metal pans to which a magnet adheres, such as stainless steel. Copper and glass cookware, for example, do not work on this rangetop. An induction rangetop is expensive, priced at over $800 for four burners.

Halogen

Halogen is another innovation in stovetop cooking. Halogen glass bulbs heat the smooth glass rangetop. Range manufacturers say that halogen gives much more control than gas or electric, especially in lower temperature settings, making simmering and sautéing easier. Flat-bottomed metal pans work best. This rangetop is also relatively expensive, selling for about $700 for a 30-inch unit.

Convection ovens

Chefs have used convection ovens for years. If we were to recommend an addition to your kitchen, a convection oven might be the one. A small fan in the rear of the oven circulates air all around the food to cook it rapidly and evenly, much like a rotisserie. Cooking times and temperature settings are generally reduced by about 25 percent, so most manufacturers suggest that you reduce the cooking temperature given in the recipe by 25 degrees when baking. A built-in 30-inch convection wall oven of good quality starts at $900 to $1,000.

If a convection wall oven is over your budget right now, consider the smaller, less expensive convection toaster oven, especially if you're cooking for a household of one or two. It can toast, bake a cake, broil a burger, and roast a small chicken. And cooking times are shorter than in conventional ovens. A 15 x 12 x 9 inch unit costs about $160.

Microwave ovens

Microwave cooking is totally unlike conventional cooking. You must follow a different set of cooking rules. Although 92 percent of all American kitchens have a microwave, most people use the microwave only as a reheating and defrosting device. If this is your intention, purchase a simple unit with only one or two power levels. If you're short on counter or wall space, consider a microwave-convection oven combination that allows you to cook by using either method.

How does this thing cook?

Every microwave has an energy box called a *magnetron* that produces microwaves (from electricity). The microwaves pass through materials like glass, paper, china, and plastic and convert to heat when they come in contact with food molecules. The microwaves cause the water molecules in the food to rotate so rapidly that they vibrate, creating friction and heat.

A major notion is that microwaves cook from the inside out. They do not. Microwaves penetrate primarily the surface and no farther than 2 inches (5 cm) into the food. The heat spreads by conduction to the rest of the food.

Microwaves cannot pass through metal, so you cannot cook with traditional metal cookware. You can, however, use flameproof glass, some plastics, porcelain, paper, ceramic, and plastic cooking bags. Some microwaves permit you to use aluminum foil to cover dishes or keep the legs of a turkey from burning, as long as the foil doesn't touch the oven walls or the temperature probe. Check your operating manual to see whether your appliance allows using foil in this way. Cookware placed in the microwave should not get hot. If it does, it's probably not microwaveable.

A microwave is not a replacement for conventional cooking of grilled meats, baked breads, cakes and cookies, and other foods that need browning unless it has a browning unit. Use your microwave for what it does best and in combination with other appliances. For example, you can precook chicken in minutes in the microwave and finish it under the broiler or on an outdoor grill. Following are some other microwave tips:

- Recipes that require a lot of water, such as pasta, diminish the efficiency of the microwave and probably cook in less time on your stovetop.

- Foods must be arranged properly to cook evenly. Face the thickest parts, like broccoli stalks, outward toward the oven walls. Arrange foods of the same size and shape, such as potatoes, in a circle or square with space between them and no item in the center.

- Covering dishes cuts down on cooking time and splattering. Frequently stirring, turning, and rotating foods ensures an even distribution of heat.

- As with conventional cooking, cutting foods into smaller pieces shortens cooking time.

- Pierce foods with an outer skin, like potatoes, hot dogs, and sausages, with a fork before cooking to release steam that can lead to sudden popping and splattering.

- A number of variables, including the type of your microwave, can affect a recipe's given cooking time, so check for doneness after the *minimum* cooking time elapses. You can always cook food longer. Always observe the recipe's "standing" time, because microwaved food continues to cook after you remove it from the oven.

- Be sure to use the defrost power setting (30 to 40 percent of full power) when thawing food to ensure slow and even defrosting; otherwise, the outside of the food can start to cook before the inside is thoroughly thawed.

Read your microwave manual carefully before using the oven. One woman we know ruined her microwave oven because she used it as a kitchen timer, not realizing that you should never run an empty microwave, an instruction found in just about every manual.

Foods and dishes that cook well in the microwave

✔ **Bacon:** Cooks to perfect crispness quickly and without much attention. Cover with paper towels to catch splattered grease.

✔ **Custard and pudding fillings for pies and tarts:** Require a double boiler if you cook them conventionally.

✔ **Fish and shellfish:** Retain their juices, texture, and flavor. Be careful not to overcook. To open clams and oysters easily for stews and soups, microwave uncovered for a few seconds or until shells partially open; then pry them fully open with a knife.

✔ **Melted chocolate:** Most conventional recipes call for a double boiler to keep the chocolate from burning in the pan. Because microwaveable cookware does not get very hot, chocolate doesn't need a protective boiling water barrier as it melts.

✔ **Most vegetables:** Cooking vegetables in the microwave requires less water than conventional cooking and retains the vegetables' nutrients, color, and texture.

✔ **Potatoes:** Bake an 8-ounce (250 g) potato on high for 6 to 8 minutes. Two potatoes take from 8 to 10 minutes; four from 14 to 16 minutes. Let them stand for at least 5 minutes before serving.

✔ **Risotto and polenta:** These northern Italian dishes require constant stirring and watching during 20 to 30 minutes of stovetop cooking, but not as much if you microwave them.

Most major appliance companies, including General Electric (800-626-2000), Amana (800-843-0304), and KitchenAid (800-422-1230) have toll-free information numbers with appliance experts on hand to answer questions about using and caring for your microwave.

The refrigerator

Refrigerators are the black holes of the kitchen — objects drift in and are never seen again, at least until the next thorough cleaning. At that time, your leftovers may resemble compost. And what's in this little ball of aluminum foil? *Do not open!*

Refrigerators come in many sizes and shapes. A family of four needs a minimum of 16 cubic feet and should probably buy one that's at least 18 cubic feet (unless you have a teenage boy, in which case you need a second refrigerator). If you use the freezer a great deal, having the freezer compartment on the top, rather than the bottom, is more convenient. Make sure that the doors open in the most convenient way for your kitchen. Also check the door compartments and see whether there is space to place a bottle upright. The door should not be cluttered with little compartments that just eat up space.

Try not to pack the refrigerator too densely so that the cold air has sufficient space to circulate around and cool the food. Store foods in the same spot so that you don't have to search for that little jar of mustard or jelly every time you open the door.

The bottom drawers are usually the coldest and should be used for storing meat, poultry, and fish. Remove the package wrapping around uncooked meats, fish, or poultry before storing in the refrigerator and rewrap loosely in waxed paper or foil. Fresh vegetables are usually stored in the "crisper" drawer, which is often located just above the meat bin. Salad greens and leafy herbs can be washed, thoroughly dried, and wrapped in paper towels to extend their storage life. Other vegetables, like broccoli and cauliflower, should be washed just before serving. Excess water on any vegetable held in storage can hasten its deterioration.

It's also a good idea to rotate supplies, storing new ones behind old, and to place the most frequently used supplies — like milk, juice, and bottled water — in easy-to-reach spots. Package all leftovers in airtight containers or in foil or plastic wrap. Remove stuffing from meat, fish, or poultry and wrap it separately. Leftover canned foods can be safely covered and stored in the can three to four days or removed to airtight plastic containers. (Turn to Chapter 13 for more information about storing specific foods.)

Liberate old food from the refrigerator every two weeks or so, and give the fridge a good soap-and-water bath every few months. Invite your friends to the event, if you like. An open box of baking soda at the back of a shelf soaks up odors. Remember to replace the baking soda with a fresh box every few months.

The dishwasher

There are almost as many kinds of dishwashers as there are dishes. Be aware that more expensive machines generally require less prewashing or rinsing before loading. The other major difference among machines is that some dishwashers use the home's hot water supply, whereas others heat the water themselves. The latter is preferable; otherwise, you spend energy bringing household water to dishwasher temperature. Upper-end models usually come with more cycles and fancier racks. Buy a dishwasher with only as many cycles as you think you'll actually use. Most dishwashers are not safe for cleaning silver, but some have special cycles for washing fine crystal and china.

You should never put the following things in your dishwasher:

- Good knives
- Wooden bowls, spoons, cutting boards, and so on
- Hubcaps
- Electrical appliances
- Fragile glassware like crystal wine glasses

Kitchen Safety 101

You may think that the biggest danger in the kitchen is serving a meal that has guests roaring hysterically with laughter on their way home. As humiliating as that can be, home cooks should be aware of other perils as well.

Do you remember Dan Akroyd's classic skit on *Saturday Night Live,* in which he impersonates Julia Child? In the middle of his cooking demonstration, he pretends to accidentally cut off his fingers: "Just a flesh wound," he warbles and continues cooking. Then he severs his wrist, his hand falling to the ground. Blood spurts everywhere. Pretty funny, huh?

That wildly exaggerated scene carries a cautionary note about razor-sharp knives: Always pay attention to what you're doing because one slip can cause great pain. (Keep in mind that dull knives can be dangerous, too, because they force you to apply more pressure, and your hand may slip.) Other rules of safety include the following:

- Never cook in loose-hanging clothes that may catch fire.

- Never cook while wearing loose-hanging jewelry that can get tangled around pot handles.

- Professional chefs have hands of asbestos from years of grabbing hot pots and pans. You do not. Keep pot holders nearby and use them.

- Turn pot handles away from the front of the stove, where children may grab them.

- Don't let fragile foods sit out in your kitchen, especially in warm weather. Raw meat, fish, and certain dairy products can spoil quickly, so refrigerate or freeze them right away. Use the refrigerator to marinate or defrost.

- Wipe up spills and stains immediately so that no one slips and falls.

- Don't try to cook if your mind is elsewhere because your fingers may wind up elsewhere.

- Separate raw meat and poultry from produce and other items in your refrigerator to avoid cross-contamination of harmful bacteria from one food to another.

- Wash your hands before handling food. Hands can be a virtual freight train of bacteria, depending, of course, on what you do during the day.

- To avoid panic-stricken searches, always return utensils to where you got them. Always return a knife to its holder when you're finished with it.

✔ Clean up as you work. Obvious, no? Then why doesn't anybody do it? We know people who can make a tuna fish sandwich and leave the kitchen looking as if they had just catered a lunch for the United Nations. Put away dirty knives, wipe down counters, and return food to the refrigerator between steps in a recipe — doing so keeps you thinking clearly and discourages household pets from jumping onto countertops. Plus, cleaning up as you go frees up that spatula or those egg-coated mixer blades for the next step of the recipe.

✔ Every kitchen needs a fire extinguisher. It is inexpensive (about $15), easy to use, and mounts on the wall. This device may not do much for your cherries jubilee, but it can avert a disaster.

✔ The old wives' tale "Oil and water do not mix" happens to be true. Throwing water on a grease fire makes it worse by spreading it around. If the fire is contained in a pot or pan, cover it with a lid. For a fire in your oven or one that has spread to the floor, a few handfuls of baking soda or salt should cut off its oxygen supply.

A word about cleanliness

That you should keep your kitchen clean goes without saying. The warm, moist, food-filled kitchen is a virtual petri dish for bacteria. Food poisoning is more common that you may think. About 7 million cases of food-borne illness occur in the U.S. each year.

Vulnerable spots in the kitchen include cutting boards, countertops, sponges, dish towels, refrigerator bins, and soiled dishware. So what can you do? Simply wash these items well with soap and warm water. You can scrub cutting boards with lemon juice and salt to get rid of garlic and onion odors. As unattractive as plastic and polyethylene cutting boards can be, they are very easy to clean and have no cracks or joints where food can get lodged. Some can even go in the dishwasher.

Chapter 2

The Cook's Tools

*K*itchen equipment is sort of like a car. When you first get your driver's license, a dented ten-year-old Honda Civic is nirvana. But as you become a more experienced driver, you start dreaming of a better car, maybe a new Ford Taurus. When you begin exploring the wonderful world of cooking, you really can do with just few basic tools — the ride may not be as smooth as a new Ford Taurus, but you'll still get to the prom on time.

This chapter is all about understanding and using kitchen equipment. Knowing how to use a piece of equipment properly — say, a chef's knife — makes it work better and last longer.

If you are just getting started or are on a tight budget, you can find out which essential tools you need; as you become more proficient, you may want to expand your repertoire — and more luxurious equipment is here, too.

First, we outline the bare-bones-all-I-can-spend-now kitchen equipment (you can find more detailed descriptions of these items later in this chapter):

- ✔ **10-inch chef's knife:** You can perform more than 80 percent of all cutting and slicing chores with this knife.

- ✔ **Paring knife:** For peeling, coring, and carving garnishes from vegetables and fruits.

- ✔ **10-inch nonstick fry pan:** The all-around pan for sautéing, making egg dishes, braising small quantities of food, and more.

- ✔ **3-quart saucepan:** For cooking vegetables, rice, soups, sauces, and small quantities of pasta.

- ✔ **Expandable steamer attachment (to fit the 3-quart saucepan):** For steaming vegetables, fish, and shellfish.

- ✔ **10-quart stock pot with lid:** For making stocks or large quantities of soup, pasta, and vegetables. You'll be surprised by how often you use this pot.

- ✔ **Electric blender:** This machine does not slice and chop like a food processor, but it's terrific for making quick, healthful sauces (see Chapter 7), soups, purees, and drinks.

- ✔ **Heavy-duty roasting pan:** For all kinds of roasting.

- ✔ **Liquid and dry measuring cups:** So you don't botch up recipes by using too much or too little of something.

- ✔ **Strainer or chinois:** Essential for certain sauces, desserts, and soups.

- ✔ **Meat thermometer:** Why guess?

- ✔ **Vegetable peeler, pepper mill, hand grater, rubber spatula, and wooden spoons:** You could go off the deep end buying little kitchen gizmos, but you'll definitely need these tools.

In this chapter, we describe many items generically, occasionally mentioning well-known brands with good reputations. We also offer advice on which materials to look for — stainless steel, copper, aluminum, and so on — and what size of appliance to consider, as well as how to judge whether the equipment is well made. You should know the precise definitions and names of these items, especially if you plan to order equipment by mail.

Don't Get Skewered in Kitchen Shops

First, a word about price and availability. Listing specific prices is difficult because retail markups on kitchenware vary greatly from store to store, generally ranging from 50 to 100 percent of the wholesale price. For example, a quality heavy-gauge 10-inch stainless steel skillet with a base of sandwiched aluminum (or copper) can cost $100 or more at a major department store or small kitchenware shop, but the same item may cost 20 to 30 percent less in a well-known discount house in a major city or in a professional cookware outlet. In most cases, we give you a price range to use as a shopping guide, but our best advice is to shop around. Many of the prices we include are from major department stores, which tend to have high markups.

Cooking equipment is frequently discounted. Watch for special sales on kitchenware, tools, and gadgets. If a restaurant supply store is nearby, check it out. These places cater to professionals, so knives and other items may be cheaper than in regular retail stores. Also watch for sales in mail order catalogs.

A Rose Is a Rose, but a Pot Is Not a Pan: Cookware

If it has two opposite-set handles and a lid, it's classified as a *pot. Pans* have one long handle and come with or without lids. This section gives a rundown of important pots and pans and how to evaluate them.

Among major brands of retail cookware are All-Clad, Berndes, Borgeat, Calphalon, Chantal, Cuisinart, Demeyere, Farberware, Le Creuset, Mauviel, Paderno, Revereware, Sitram, and T-Fal. Most major companies offer limited lifetime warranties and will replace a pot, pan, or piece of equipment if a problem arises from normal wear and tear.

Chip Fisher, owner of Lamalle Kitchenware, New York, offers the following tips for buying cookware:

- Examine how you cook and how you will use equipment. For example, if you do a lot of fat-free and lowfat cooking, you'll want to invest in several nonstick pieces.

- Don't buy whole sets, even if they are on sale, unless you can use every piece. Sets are limited to one type of material and one style, whereas you may need various styles and materials.

- Grasp the handle of the pan in the store. It should sit comfortably in your hand. Ask yourself whether having a heat-resistant handle is important, or whether you always remember to cook with a pot holder.

- Consider the appearance of your cookware, which is important especially if you decide to hang your pots and pans for decoration.

- Buy the best equipment you can afford. Cheap, flimsy pots and pans need to be replaced after a few years of normal use.

Pots and pans have handles with varying degrees of heat resistance. Many pans with metal handles are purposely made to withstand extreme temperatures. Sometimes cooking starts on top of the stove and finishes in the oven or the broiler. Assume that every handle is roaring hot; never grab one without a *real* pot holder.

Heavy-gauge cast-iron skillet

cast-iron
skillet

The cast-iron pan, shown in Figure 2-1, has been a standard in American and European kitchens for hundreds of years and still outperforms contemporary cookware in some respects (for example, for browning, blackening, and searing). Better yet, a cast-iron pan is one of the most inexpensive pans you can find. Tag sales and antique shops are loaded with them.

If you treat a cast-iron pan well, it should last a lifetime. You must season the pan occasionally by wiping it with vegetable oil and then heating it on the range on a medium setting for about 2 minutes. In addition, you must thoroughly wipe the pan dry after washing it to prevent rust. Clean the pan gently with soap and water; never scour with metal pads. (Plastic pads are fine.) Look for a pan with a spout for pouring off fat.

Several companies, including General Housewares Corporation and Lodge, make cast-iron pans. Prices range from $12 to $15.

Omelet pan or skillet

10" omelet pan

A 10-inch omelet pan, shown in Figure 2-2, with curved sides is handy to have around, especially for beginners, who tend to cook a lot of eggs. Contrary to what manufacturers say, reserving the omelet pan exclusively for eggs is not necessary. An omelet pan is also excellent for sautéing potatoes and other vegetables. (See Chapter 4 for more information about sautéing.) But if you keep the pan (whether nonstick or untreated metal) in pristine condition and grease it well before cooking, you can make picture-perfect omelets. Prices range from $30 to $70.

Sauté pan or fry pan

Figure 2-3:
You can use
a sauté pan
or fry pan to
sauté foods
in little fat.

saute´ pan

You also need at least one straight-sided, stainless steel sauté pan (see Figure 2-3) that's at least 10 or 12 inches in diameter with a depth of 2 inches for sautéing, braising, frying, and making quick sauces. These pans have a lid so that food can be covered and simmered in small amounts of liquid. Good-quality sauté pans retail from about $75 to $150.

Nonstick coatings are the best aid to novice cooks since spaghetti sauce in jars. Nonstick pans have great appeal with today's emphasis on lowfat cooking. You can sauté potatoes, vegetables, fish, poultry, and meats in very little oil or butter. Nonstick pans do not brown as well as regular pans, but they are easier to clean, and the convenience is worth it.

In recent years, nonstick pans have improved tremendously, and the linings last longer than before (ten years and more) — as long as you don't use metal utensils with them. So many brands exist that keeping track of them all is hard. Look for well-known manufacturers, such as All-Clad, Calphalon, Cuisinart, and WearEver.

Don't buy an inexpensive pan that is thin and light — it will warp over time. Purchase pots and pans from a major manufacturer who stands behind its products and will quickly replace or repair damaged goods. Prices range from about $30 to $50.

Twelve-inch rondeau

A rondeau (pronounced *ron-DOE*) is great to have on hand when you entertain — and of course you will! A straight-sided pot with two handles and a lid, as shown in Figure 2-4, a 12-inch rondeau can hold enough food to serve eight people or more. (Its diameter ranges from 8 to $15^1/2$ inches.) If you just got a raise, splurge for heavy-gauge copper, which is expensive but beautiful to serve from. Stainless steel is good, too, but make sure that it has a copper or aluminum core for fast heat conduction. Stainless steel alone is not an efficient heat conductor. (See the following sidebar, "Pros and cons of different materials.")

A rondeau has many uses, among them braising, stewing, and browning large quantities of meat, poultry, or fish. Look for brands like All-Clad, Cuisinart, Sitram, Calphalon, Paderno, Magnalite, and the better-made imports. A good 12-inch stainless steel rondeau can cost well over $100, and one made of copper can cost over $300.

Sauteuse evasée

This Gallic mouthful refers to a little pan that is the workhorse of the French kitchen. If you ever splurge on a piece of copper cookware, we recommend a sauteuse evasée (pronounced *sew-TUHZ ay-va-SAY*), which is 8 to 9 inches in diameter with a volume of about 3 quarts. (See Figure 2-5.) A sauteuse evasée may be referred to as simply a saucepan, which is its major role. Its sloped sides (*evasée* refers to the sloped sides) make for easy whisking.

TIP

Pros and cons of different materials

When buying pots and pans, you should know a little about the heat conductivity of different metals. Following are descriptions for common cookware materials:

Copper is the best heat conductor of all commercial metals. It is 99 percent heat efficient, which enables it to heat up and cool down almost immediately. Chefs value this quality when making delicate sauces. Copper alone is too soft for cooking, so it always has a stainless steel, tin, or other lining.

Copper has several drawbacks, however. For one, the good stuff is very expensive. Many stores sell shimmering sets of light-gauge copper cookware, mostly suitable for placing on a sideboard as decoration. Good-quality copper is heavy — a big saucepan weighs about the same as a St. Bernard puppy. Finally, you can spend half your productive life cleaning and polishing the darn stuff — copper discolors whenever more than two people look at it. As for the linings, tin is old-fashioned. Professionals know how to use it, but amateurs may melt the tin by accident. Moreover, tin lining wears out and must be replaced. Don't bother; go with a stainless steel lining.

Note: Gauge refers to the thickness and weight of a utensil's bottom and sides.

Stainless steel may not conduct heat very efficiently, but it has many advantages. For one, stainless steel is easy to clean; it is also indestructible. To improve heat conductivity, manufacturers today put a copper or aluminum core in stainless steel pans, giving you the best of both worlds.

Aluminum pots and pans have gotten a bad rap in recent years. Certain scientists contended that aluminum cookware releases toxins that can have sundry bad health effects. Recent studies have found no hazards with aluminum, however. True, certain acidic foods, such as tomatoes, react to aluminum and turn the color of pond scum, but the transformation is no health hazard. (Besides, seeing the expression on your dinner guests' faces when you serve lime green pasta puttanesca has humorous benefits.)

Go into a restaurant kitchen; chances are that the cooks are using inexpensive and durable aluminum.

Chemically treated anodized aluminum cookware has become increasingly popular in recent years. *Anodization* is an electrolytic process that creates a hard, impenetrable oxide film over the aluminum, which prevents reaction to foods like eggs and tomatoes. Anodized aluminum pots and pans are always heavy-gauge, charcoal gray in color, and more expensive than regular aluminum cookware (but still cost less than stainless and copper). Calphalon is the major purveyor of anodized aluminum.

Cast iron is a good conductor of heat and retains heat better than other materials used in cookware. That quality makes cast iron ideal for searing steaks, hamburgers, or other meats at extremely high temperatures, or for browning stew meat before adding it to a casserole. Cast iron is inexpensive, durable, and versatile. It takes a long time to heat and cool, so we don't recommend it for making delicate sauces.

Copper (lined with stainless steel or tin) provides the best heat control of all metals and is priced from $100 to $200. That control is the secret of well-textured sauces. Stainless steel with copper or aluminum sandwiched in the base works very well, too. Stainless steel costs $80 to $100.

Two- or three-quart saucepan

Figure 2-6:
You use a saucepan to boil foods and make sauces.

This saucepan can be stainless steel with a copper or aluminum core, heavy-gauge aluminum, or a combination of metals. It is an all-round pan used for cooking vegetables, soups, rice, and sauces for pasta and other dishes. (See Figure 2-6.) Depending on their material and size, these straight-sided pans with lids run from about $50 to $100 each.

Enameled cast-iron casserole (or Dutch oven)

Figure 2-7:
An enameled casserole, or Dutch oven, is for cooking stews and soups.

This attractive, all-round casserole dish, also called a *Dutch oven,* is ideal for slow-cooking stews and soups and all sorts of hearty winter meals. (See Figure 2-7.) Enamel does not brown food as well as cast-iron or stainless steel, however. You may want to brown or sear meat before adding it to the casserole. A 4-quart version made by Le Creuset and a similar one from Copco are excellent, heavy-gauge casseroles with tight-fitting lids. Prices range from $65 to $150 for a 12-inch casserole.

Stock pot and steamer basket

Figure 2-8: In a stock pot, you make soups. With a steamer basket, it doubles as a steamer.

stock pot

These items are indispensable in any kitchen. If purchased separately, a stock pot, soup kettle, and steamer can take up enormous storage space, but one well-designed pot can do it all. Look for a tall, narrow, 10- to 14-quart heavy-gauge pot with a tight-fitting lid that can hold a steamer basket. Inexpensive circular steamers open and close like a fan to fit different size pots and pans. Heavy aluminum is fine for a stock pot; stainless steel costs twice as much — $150 and up for an 11- to 12-quart pot.

Pasta pot

A large, 8-quart stainless steel pot fitted with a lid is the perfect size for cooking $^1/_2$ to 1 pound of pasta (or you can use your stock pot instead). Prices range from $50 to $150.

Two roasting pans

A well-equipped kitchen should have one oval roasting pan, about 12 inches long, and a rectangular one, about 14 x 11 inches. An oval roasting pan is suitable for poultry and small roasts; a 14-inch rectangular one can handle two chickens or a large roast. The oval one should be enameled cast iron so that it can double as a gratin pan (see the following section); the rectangular pan can be heavy-gauge aluminum or stainless steel. A rectangular 14 x 11-inch stainless steel pan costs about $40, and a 12-inch-long oval enamel pan runs about $50.

A flat roasting rack made of chromed steel prevents meat and poultry roasts from sitting directly on the bottom of the pan and stewing in juices and fat (see Chapter 5 for more information). These racks cost less than $20.

Gratin pan

Figure 2-9: A gratin pan is handy for finishing one-pot dishes.

gratin pan

Novice cooks tend to make many one-pot dishes. To give these entrees a delicious finishing touch, often by oven broiling to crisp the top, you should have a gratin dish, shown in Figure 2-9. Unlike casseroles and Dutch ovens, gratin dishes are shallow, measure from 10 inches long and up, and do not have a lid. A 12-inch dish can feed six or more people. These pans are ideal for macaroni and cheese, turkey casserole, gratinéed shellfish, and many other simple dishes, and some are attractive enough to go from oven to table. Prices range from about $30 to $50 for a porcelain pan.

From Slicing to Dicing: Knives for All Occasions

Every department store carries kitchen knives these days, and some knives look quite impressive. But don't buy knives on appearance alone.

Hold a knife. If it is well constructed, it should feel substantial in your hand. The handle should be comfortable. The knife should be *balanced* — that is, the handle should not be significantly heavier than the blade or vice versa.

What you need

Knives are often sold in sets of six to eight, which can be a bargain when you compare them to individual purchases. But think twice. Do you really need a boning knife or a filleting knife right now? Sometimes buying what you need as you progress makes more sense.

Home cooks really need only four essential knives: an 8- to 10-inch chef's knife, a 6- to 8-inch utility knife, a 9- to 12-inch serrated knife, and a small paring knife. Investing in top quality yields dividends for years.

Look for carbon steel or high-carbon stainless steel blades with riveted wooden handles. Carbon-steel blades take the best edge and are easy to hone with a sharpening steel (another essential kitchen item that you should use each time you use a knife — see the sidebar at the end of this chapter). The disadvantage of carbon steel is that it rusts if not dried immediately after use.

The best knives have a single tapered blade that runs from the tip to the base of the handle — the technical term is *forged.* Among the most reputable brands are

- Henckels
- Wüsthof
- Sabatier
- International Cutlery
- Chef's Choice
- Friedr. Dick.

A *chef's knife* is generally 8 to 10 inches long and can be used for all sorts of chopping, slicing, dicing, and mincing. This knife is really the workhorse of the kitchen, so investing in a top chef's knife always pays. Expect to pay at least $70 for one of good quality. (See Figure 2-10.)

Figure 2-10:
A chef's knife is handy for all sorts of chopping chores.

chef's knife

A 6- to 8-inch narrow-blade *utility knife* has myriad uses: dicing small vegetables and herbs, such as garlic and shallots; cutting up or deboning chickens (although cutting through large bones may require the heavier chef's knife); and many other more delicate chores. Prices range from $60 to $70. (See Figure 2-11.)

Figure 2-11:
Use a utility knife for smaller cutting tasks.

A *serrated knife,* generally with an 8- to 10-inch blade, is essential as a bread knife. Hard-crusted French or Italian bread dulls a chef's knife quickly. Look for a serrated knife that has wide teeth. Prices range from $70 to $90. (See Figure 2-12.)

Figure 2-12:
A serrated knife is great for cutting crusty breads.

A *paring knife,* from 2 to 4 inches long, is for delicate jobs such as peeling apples and other fruits, trimming shallots, trimming the roots off garlic, removing stems from strawberries, or making vegetable or fruit decorations. A good 4-inch paring knife costs about $30 to $40. (See Figure 2-13.)

Figure 2-13:
Use a paring knife for delicate cutting tasks.

Using knives properly

According to the United States Consumer Product Safety Commission, 472,201 people made a trip to the emergency room to treat injuries caused by a kitchen knife (this figure does not include homicides) in 1994. Many injuries resulted from time-pressed, hungry people trying to pry apart frozen hamburgers or slice through hard bagels. Don't make their mistake! Slice away from your hand, keep your fingers clear of the blades, and don't ever use the palm of your hand as a cutting board.

Using a knife properly is just as important as choosing the right knife. In the following sections, we explain how the pros chop garlic and fresh herbs.

Chopping garlic

Chef, author, and cooking teacher Jacques Pépin has a slightly unconventional method for chopping garlic that works exceptionally well for novices and professionals alike. Follow these steps:

1. **Peel off the outer skin of the garlic, smash the garlic slightly with the side of your knife, and remove the rest of the skin.**

2. **Hold the garlic clove on a cutting board with the knuckles of your index finger and middle finger leaning against the side of the blade.**

   Keep your fingertips folded over inward to prevent cuts. (This chopping technique works for most vegetables.)

3. **Start working the chef's knife up and down, slowly moving your knuckles toward the other end of the garlic as you chop. (This technique takes a little practice.)**

When Pépin slices the whole garlic, he runs the side of his knife over the slices to flatten them and presses them to adhere to the cutting board. Doing so makes the second round of chopping easier because the garlic is not moving around the board.

Chopping parsley and other fresh herbs

Chef and author Pierre Franey recommends, "When you chop vegetables, you don't want to strain your wrists. With parsley, I chop it roughly and then go back over it with my chef's knife in a rocking motion, walking the blade all around as I do it." (See Figure 2-14.)

Chopping Parsley & Other Fresh Herbs

Figure 2-14: The correct way to chop parsley and other fresh herbs.

1. Rinse and dry well

2. chop roughly

*NOTE:
For herbs like rosemary and thyme, remove and chop leaves. Discard thick stem.

3. gather and chop some more

Use rocking motion

move knife around

Processors, Blenders, and Mixers

Food processor: A food processor, shown in Figure 2-15, is an extremely versatile tool. Robot-Coupe, Cuisinart, and KitchenAid make high-quality food processors that come with a full line of accessories for mixing, slicing, shredding, pureeing, kneading, and more. Food processors come in various sizes and are widely discounted. Prices range from roughly $125 for small models to $300 or more for larger models.

Figure 2-15:
Food processors can do a wide variety of tasks.

food processor

Blender: With good reason, a blender is up there with the coffee machine as one of the most popular small appliances in the kitchen. A blender's ultrafast blades can puree fresh fruits such as strawberries into a smooth sauce, whip milkshakes, crush ice, and more. (Turn to Chapter 7 for specific blender sauce recipes.) Waring made the first blender, which is still considered a classic, but other companies produce reliable machines as well. Some blenders come with 12 or more speeds, but we recommend simpler models because they are less likely to break down, and you probably won't need all those speeds anyway. Prices range from $90 to $130.

Figure 2-16:
A blender is an extremely useful tool.

blender

TIP

Why a blender is one of the most useful kitchen machines

Twenty years ago, the blender was a symbol of "modern" American kitchens, a shiny electric obelisk that could do it all — or at least all the tasks of that relatively ingenuous age, namely mixing batters, pureeing soups, and frothing drinks. Then along came the flashy foreign food processor, with its French accent, Porsche-like motor, and more blades than a lawn-mower factory. As home cooks became enamored of this exotic appliance, they consigned blenders to milkshake duty.

But don't sell your blender short. Old-fashioned one-speed blenders, as well as the new ones with up to a dozen or more settings, are finding a role in the light and healthful cooking style that so many people desire today. This type of cooking is based on colorful and intensely flavorful sauces that use minimal amounts of butter and cream, if any.

Although food processors are unsurpassed for chopping, slicing, and grating, blenders have an edge when it comes to liquefying and sauce-making. For example, the upcoming chapters show you how to make dishes like sautéed chicken breasts with a wonderful quick sauce of white wine, chicken stock, leeks, and herbs. The normal way to make this sauce is to cook down the leeks, stock, and other ingredients, maybe add a little butter for smoothness, and pass them through a strainer. With a blender, however, you just toss everything in the bowl and whizzzzzzz — instant sauce. The sauce is even more flavorful because the leeks and herbs dissolve into it. This technique does not work as well in a food processor, whose two-level slicing blade cuts through liquids instead of blending them.

Electric mixer: Electric mixers come in two basic types: hand-held and standing. Either type comes in handy for all kinds of batters, sauces, homemade mayonnaise (you won't believe how much better it is!), and various egg dishes. Whereas a hand-held beater is terrific for lighter jobs like beating heavy cream and egg whites, a heavy-duty, freestanding mixer is designed to accommodate the more serious cook.

Most standing mixers come with a 5-quart stainless steel bowl and multiple removable attachments that paddle, knead, and whisk. A heavy-duty standing electric mixer also frees your hands, allowing you to accomplish other tasks as it whisks away. Major brands of heavy-duty standing mixers include KitchenAid and Sunbeam. Models cost from $170 to $300 or more.

Bowls and Other Mixing Equipment

Stainless steel mixing bowls: Mixing bowls are among the most frequently used items in every kitchen. Buy bowls with flat bottoms for good balance in these sizes: 8 quarts, 5 quarts, 3 quarts, and 1$^1/_2$ quarts. You can use these bowls to mix salads and sauces, store leftovers, let bread dough rise, and send your kid down a snowy hill.

Whisks: Whisks (one stiff and one flexible) should be made of stainless steel. You use a stiff whisk, about 8 to 10 inches long, to blend sauces, such as béchamel and some cream sauces. You use a lighter one, sometimes called a *balloon whisk,* generally 10 to 12 inches long, for whipping egg whites and heavy cream.

Spoons, spatulas, long-handled forks, and tongs: Look for a variety of spoons. A solid, one-piece stainless steel spoon, about 12 to 15 inches long, and a large bowl fills most needs. Buy wooden spoons of various sizes for scraping food bits off the bottom of a simmering casserole and countless other tasks. A slotted, stainless steel spoon removes pieces of food that are cooking in hot liquid, such as tender ravioli.

You can use a long-handled, stainless steel ladle with a 4- to 6-ounce bowl to dole out soups and pour pancake batter onto a griddle. Buy at least two rubber spatulas and a square-tipped metal turner to flip burgers and other foods. You need metal tongs for turning over tender pieces of meat or fish. Inexpensive plastic spaghetti tongs are useful for serving cooked pasta.

Baking Equipment

The wide-ranging subject of baking equipment is difficult to compress into a few paragraphs. But following is our list of essentials for beginners, plus a few items that are just plain fun to own:

Baking (or cookie) sheet: For baking cookies, biscuits, and breads, a heavy-duty steel or nonstick baking sheet with $^1/_2$-inch flared edges that prevent butter and juices from spilling onto your oven is essential. Baking sheets come in different sizes. Buy two large ones that fit in your oven, leaving a 2-inch margin on all sides to allow an even flow of heat during baking.

Jelly roll pan: This 15 x 10-inch shallow rectangular baking pan holds cake batters and egg batters that are filled and rolled. If you ever saw a Yule Log and wondered how the filling ends up swirled into the center, this pan is the answer. Buy a heavy-quality aluminum pan.

Round cake pans: Standard layer cake recipes call for two 9 x 2-inch pans. Choose anodized or nonstick aluminum.

Square cake pan: For making brownies or gingerbread, you need an 8- or 9-inch square, 2-quart capacity pan. Anodized aluminum and other nonstick materials make removing the brownies easier.

Muffin tins: For baking quick breads and muffins, you need a 12-cup tray of nonstick or heavy-gauge aluminum. And buy a box of paper muffin liners so you don't have to grease and flour each metal cup.

Pie pan: A glass or aluminum pan that is 9 inches in diameter suits most standard recipes.

Rolling pin: You don't need an arsenal of rolling pins like professional pastry chefs do. For general home-baking tasks, get a two-handled, hardwood rolling pin that is about 15 inches long.

Cooling racks: Cookies and cakes removed from the oven and from baking sheets and pans need to cool. Racks allow air to circulate around them and steam to vent. They come in many sizes. Buy two large 12- to 14-inch racks made of chromed steel.

Loaf pan: For baking breads, terrines, and meat loaf, you want a sturdy 6-cup loaf pan. (See Figure 2-17.)

Figure 2-17:
You can bake all sorts of foods in a loaf pan.

loaf pan

Springform pan: With its hinged release and detachable bottom, a springform pan easily unmolds cheesecakes, delicate tarts, and cakes with crumb crusts. Get a 9- to 10-inch pan of heavy-gauge aluminum. (See Figure 2-18.)

springform pan

Flour sifter: Not all baking recipes call for sifted flour, but when they do, you need a sifter to aerate or incorporate air uniformly into the flour to remove lumps. A 3-cup stainless steel sifter with a rotating handle is a good choice.

If you don't have a sifter and need sifted flour for a recipe, you can use a strainer instead. (See Figure 2-19 for instructions.)

How to Sift Flour If You Don't Have a Sifter

Figure 2-19:
In a pinch,
you can sift
flour by
using a
strainer.

1. Pour flour into a strainer

2. Use your hand to lightly tap the strainer

— OR —
tap the strainer on the inside of the bowl

Pastry brush: To apply glazes and coatings to your breads and cakes, use an all-purpose 1¹/₂-inch pastry brush with natural bristles.

Cake tester: A cake tester helps you determine whether your cake is finished. You pierce the cake with the needle-thin tester; if the tester comes out free of sticky batter, the cake is done. In a pinch, you can use a toothpick instead.

Metal or plastic dry measuring cups: To follow recipes, you need a set of dry measuring cups — $^1/_4$ cup, $^1/_3$ cup, $^1/_2$ cup, and 1 cup, shown in Figure 2-20. Metal is much better than plastic, which can break or melt in the dishwasher.

Figure 2-20:
Every cook needs a set of dry measuring cups.

dry measure cups

Glass liquid measuring cup: Get one with a 2-cup capacity and a spout for pouring liquids, as shown in Figure 2-21. A 4-cup liquid measuring cup comes in handy, too.

Figure 2-21:
Use a glass measuring cup to measure and pour liquids.

liquid measure cup

Metal measuring spoons: Essential for many recipes, especially baking. Make sure that the set you purchase comes with $^1/_4$ teaspoon, $^1/_2$ teaspoon, 1 teaspoon, and 1 tablespoon capacities.

Half empty or half full: Measuring techniques

Measuring is important, especially for a beginning cook. Too much salt, and the stew is ruined. Too little baking powder, and the cake doesn't rise. Too much milk, and the pudding never sets.

But measuring does not replace tasting, and the more you cook, the less you need to measure. Experienced chefs are able to sense in their hands the feel of a tablespoon of salt or $1/2$ teaspoon of lemon peel. But this feel comes with years of practice. Here are some basic measuring guidelines:

✔ **Measure dry and liquid ingredients in different cups.** The dry measure is a metal or plastic cup with a handle. To measure flour or rice, dip the measure into the canister or bag, scooping out more than you need. Then use the straight edge of a knife to level off the excess. Work over a piece of waxed paper or the bag or canister to catch and save any excess.

You measure liquids in a glass or plastic cup with a spout for pouring; do not fill the cup while holding it at eye level. Place the cup on the counter (so that you're sure the liquid is level) and lower yourself to read the mark.

✔ **Measure very precisely when baking cakes, breads, and desserts.** A baking recipe is a formula that requires an exact proportion of dry to wet ingredients.

✔ **Use a kitchen scale to measure dry ingredients accurately when a recipe calls for ounces or pounds.**

✔ **Use measuring spoons for small amounts of liquid and dry ingredients,** such as a teaspoon of vanilla extract or $1/2$ teaspoon of baking soda. Don't use your table silverware — it's not equivalent to measuring spoons.

✔ **Do not measure over your working bowl, especially if it's filled with other ingredients.** You may accidentally add too much of an ingredient.

✔ **Pack solid fats and brown sugar into a cup.** For butter, use the measure marks on the wrapper to slice off a specific amount.

✔ **To easily remove sticky foods like honey, peanut butter, and molasses from a measuring cup, coat the cup first with a small amount of vegetable oil or spray.**

✔ **If the recipe calls for sifted flour, be sure to sift it.** Sifting incorporates air into the flour, and a cup of sifted flour is less — by 2 tablespoons or more — than a cup of unsifted flour. Using a dry measuring cup, scoop out the approximate amount of flour called for in the recipe and place it in the top of the sifter. Sift the flour into a large mixing bowl or over a piece of waxed paper. After sifting, so as not to lose the flour's new "lightness," gently spoon the flour into the appropriate measure cup, fill to overflowing, and then level it off with the straight edge of a knife.

✔ **If you feel a sneeze coming on, always turn your head away from measured, dry ingredients.** Sneeze onto the butter instead.

Miscellaneous Tools

Kitchen timer: Don't stand in front of the oven staring at the clock like a monk at the shrine of Buddha. Set a timer and go watch *Jeopardy.* The price is about $10.

Salad dryer: An inexpensive plastic salad spinner, shown in Figure 2-22, makes short work of drying lettuce. If lettuce is not completely dry, the dressing slides right off.

Figure 2-22: Salad spinners are useful for drying greens so dressing adheres to them.

salad spinner

Colander: Buy one made of stainless steel or plastic for draining pasta and rinsing salad greens, vegetables, and berries. (See Figure 2-23.)

Figure 2-23: Use a colander to drain pasta and rinse foods.

colander

Chinois: This cone-shaped sieve (so named because it is shaped like a Chinese hat) is well suited for straining sauces, stocks, and just about anything. (See Figure 2-24.) A chinois also looks funny when you put it on your head and chase the kids around the house with a rolling pin.

Figure 2-24:
Use a
chinois
to strain
liquids.

Cutting boards: Use cutting boards to save your counters from sharp knives and hot pots and pans. Plastic boards are easier to clean than wooden ones and can be washed in the dishwasher. Chefs clean their wooden boards with a solution of water and bleach or rub them with lemon juice. Excessive soaking or placing wooden boards in the dishwasher causes them to splinter and crack.

Use different cutting boards to accomplish different tasks. Reserve one for slicing only raw meat and poultry and another for slicing only breads and vegetables. (Bacteria from raw meat transferred to the surface of a cutting board can contaminate other foods.)

Meat thermometer: Unlike great chefs, most people can't tell that a roast has finished cooking by pressing its surface. You can use two types of meat thermometers to check: An instant read thermometer has a thin rod that lets you pierce into the roast periodically to test for doneness. An ovenproof thermometer remains inside the meat or poultry from beginning to end of cooking.

Figure 2-24:
Meat
thermo-
meters are
handy for
determining
whether a
roast is
done.

Bulb baster: Using this tool is the most convenient way to coat a roast with pan juices. A large spoon also works as a basting tool, but a bulb baster is quicker and safer for removing hot grease from the bottom of a roasting pan.

Following are ten more handy utensils to have around your kitchen (see Figure 2-26):

- ✔ Vegetable peeler
- ✔ Lemon and cheese grater
- ✔ Citrus juicer
- ✔ Pepper mill
- ✔ Potato masher
- ✔ Shrimp deveiner
- ✔ Multipurpose kitchen shears
- ✔ Oven thermometer
- ✔ Pie server

Figure 2-26:
Everyday utensils that every cook should own.

And following are ten utensils you don't need to buy . . . yet (see Figure 2-27):

- ✔ **Butter mold:** Shapes butter into a decorative oval.
- ✔ **Rillettes pot:** For serving *rillettes,* a pâté of shredded pork, pork fat, and seasonings (also made with rabbit).
- ✔ **Sugar pump:** Don't ask.

- **Pommes Anna pan:** Beautiful copper pan with a lid used to make — what else? — *pommes Anna,* a stack of sliced potatoes coated with butter. Doubles as an elegant ashtray.

- **Roquefort cutter:** Looks like a mini-high jump and works like a guillotine. (So what if the Roquefort crumbles a little?)

- **Sea urchin scissors:** Can also be used to clip toenails.

- **Truffle slicer:** For all those truffles cluttering your vegetable crisper.

- **Spade-shaped fish scaler**

- **Roller docker:** Used to prick pastry dough to check its rise.

- **Duck press:** To extract juice from a duck carcass.

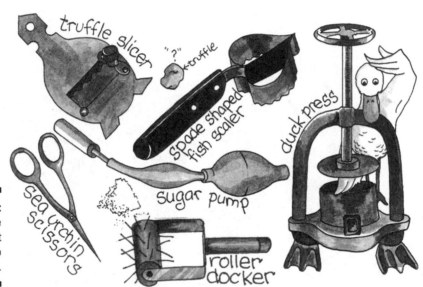

Figure 2-27: Some utensils that you can do without.

Care and Feeding of Your Beautiful Utensils

So you have forgone a trip to Disney World and bought all these kitchen supplies. If you follow our advice and buy good stuff, your supplies should last a lifetime. Of course, you need to take care of your utensils. The following sections give you a few tips.

Pots and pans

If you have a high ceiling, hanging pots and pans on a rack is a great way to go. The cookware is safe and easily accessible. A low ceiling, however, risks concussion. For an inexpensive alternative, mount a pegboard on a wall and hang utensils and pots and pans from hooks.

To remove burnt food from a pot, try boiling water in it until the food lifts off. Or sprinkle cleanser or a little dishwashing detergent onto the bottom, add water to cover, and let the pot soak for about an hour before scrubbing. If the burn is really severe, you'll have to repeat this process a couple of times. Or warm the burnt pot in your oven; then remove and place it on a piece of newspaper. Wearing rubber gloves, spray all burned areas with oven cleaner and after 15 minutes wash in hot, soapy water. Don't try oven cleaner with nonstick pans, however — they require gentle cleaning. Wash them with hot, sudsy water and a sponge or soft plastic cleaning pad. Avoid harsh abrasives and steel wool pads that can damage the interior coating.

Not all pots and pans can be put in a dishwasher. Be especially careful with those made with copper, anodized aluminum, and nonstick coatings; harsh dishwasher detergents may cause them to discolor. Read the care and cleaning guide for specific instructions for handling your equipment.

Knives

Everyone has a kitchen drawer filled with an awesome stash of junk, from old calendars and chopsticks to unidentified keys and dried-up tubes of glue. People often consider these drawers to be convenient spots to store knives. *Don't do it!* Get a wooden knife block to protect your knives' edges. Or you can get one of those magnetic strips that you mount on the wall for hanging knives. The advantage of the magnetic strip is that you know exactly which knife you are choosing, whereas in a wood block you see only the handles.

Home cooks may want to have their knives (especially high-carbon stainless, the most common type) professionally sharpened twice a year, because oversharpening wears down the blade. Check the Yellow Pages under "Sharpening" or "Cutlery" for sharpening services. A paring knife should cost about 50 cents to sharpen, a chef's knife $3 to $4. Your local butcher or gourmet retailer might sharpen them for free. Or get a good commercial home sharpener, like the Chef's Choice Electric Knife Sharpener, which costs about $85.

However, you should run your knife over a *steel* (a 12-inch-long steel shaft with a handle) every time you use it. Doing so realigns the molecules on your knife and restores the sharp edge. Not using a steel is like putting watered-down gasoline in a Maserati — performance suffers. See the sidebar "Sharpening a knife with a steel" for illustrated instructions.

Sharpening a knife with a steel

Grab the steel firmly and hold it slightly away from your body and at a slight angle as shown.

Then hold the knife firmly with the other hand and run the blade down the shaft at about a 30-degree angle. Start near the tip of the steel and, as you move down the steel, run the blade from near handle to tip.

Repeat on the other side of the blade. Keep alternating until you've sharpened each side of the blade (about ten times).

How to use a Sharpening Steel

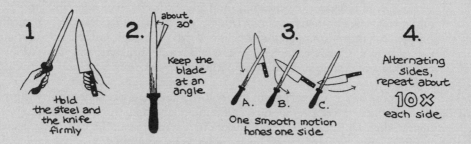

Never do these things with a good knife:

- ✔ Pry open tuna fish cans.
- ✔ Use as a screwdriver.
- ✔ Open packages.
- ✔ Try to walk through airport security.
- ✔ Shave like they did in old Westerns.

Never put good knives in the dishwasher, either. Knives are a cook's lifetime companions and should be cared for as such. Over time, a dishwasher bleaches and damages the handles. And reaching into a dishwasher with sharp knives inside is very dangerous. Whatever the kitchen utensil, read the washing instructions on its little tag (you know, the one that you usually throw away).

Part II
Know Your Techniques

The 5th Wave   By Rich Tennant

"QUIT MOPING—YOU WON FIRST PLACE IN THE MEATLOAF CATEGORY, AND THAT'S GOOD. I'M THE ONLY ONE WHO KNOWS IT WAS A CARROT CAKE YOU ENTERED."

In this part . . .

The focus of this book is cooking techniques — chopping, slicing, sautéing, braising, poaching, roasting, and a whole lot more. Granted, you have a lot to absorb, but you already exhibited superior intelligence by buying this book, so the rest should be a cakewalk.

The goal of this part — and indeed this book — is to give you the basic tools you need to cook from a recipe. We explain each technique from the ground up, giving you a variety of recipes to practice with. As you gain experience, you'll learn to improvise and maybe even invent some recipes yourself.

Chapter 3

Boiling, Poaching, and Steaming

• •

In This Chapter

▶ Water world: Simmering, boiling, and steaming defined

▶ Uncle Ben and friends: All about rice

▶ Surf's up: Poaching

• •

"**I** can't even boil water" is the would-be cook's lament. Well, grab a pot so we can tell you about this bubbly experience — and faster than you can say "instant coffee."

In this chapter, we cover three vital cooking techniques: boiling, steaming, and poaching. We concentrate here on vegetables because there are no better ways to enjoy their fresh flavors and textures. We also tell you about the different types of rice, an incredibly versatile staple, and how to cook and season them. And who can forget potatoes? Finally, we talk about two important stocks, those flavor-packed liquids that fuel so many great dishes.

Into the Pool: The Techniques Defined

Relax; even Home Ec. dropouts can figure out these basic techniques. *Boiling* is bringing water to 212° F (100° C) for cooking. You don't need a thermometer. Let the water come to a full *rolling boil* (bubbles are rapidly breaking the surface). Covering the pot speeds the process by trapping surface heat. And watching the pot indeed slows down the boiling process. Why? We have no idea.

In *simmering,* tiny bubbles break the surface gently — like a soft summer shower on a still lake. (Sorry for going overboard with these similes.) Simmering occurs at a lower temperature — just below a boil — and is used for long, slow cooking and braising. (Chapter 5 talks more about braising.)

A soup or stock recipe often combines the techniques of boiling and simmering, instructing you to bring the liquid to a full boil and then to lower the heat and simmer, sometimes for a long time. Sauce recipes may ask you to *reduce* the stock or liquid. Reducing means boiling again to thicken and intensify the flavor of the cooking liquid by decreasing its volume. The result is often a delicious sauce.

How would you like your meat boiled?

Boiling is an ancient method of cooking. Thank your lucky starts that you didn't live in medieval times, when they boiled just about everything. Meat was boiled to kill germs that flourished in food that sat out on a counter for days. Boiling also washed off salt, which was used heavily to preserve meat. Before preparing the meat, cooks had to rinse off the salt or else diners would be worshipping the town well all night.

In case you ever want to have a medieval feast on your front lawn — where guys wearing metal vests and helmets mount horses and try to knock each other down — here is a medieval picnic recipe. This excerpt comes from the fascinating book *Food in History,* by Reay Tannahill:

"Take and boil a good piece of pork, and not too lean, as tender as you may; then take it up and chop it as small as you may; then take raisins of Corinth; then take it and roll it as round as you may, like to small pellets, at two inches about, and then lay them on a dish by themselves; then make a good almond milk, and blend it with flour of rice, and let it boil well, but look that it be quite runny; and at the dresser, lay five pumpes* in a dish, and pour the pottage thereon. And if you will, set on every pumpe a flower, and over them strew on sugar enough and mace: and serve them forth. And some men make the pellets of veal or beef, but pork is best and fairest."

*The word *pumpes* appears frequently in medieval cooking. We have absolutely no idea what it means.

Poaching and *simmering* are virtually identical; cookbook writers use the terms interchangeably just to confuse you. *Steaming* is the gentlest way to cook and is better than boiling or poaching for retaining a food's color, flavor, texture, shape, and most important, its nutrients. Steaming involves placing food over simmering water on a perforated rack in a covered pot.

So which foods do you boil, simmer or poach, and steam? For starters, you can poach eggs, fish, and chicken breasts. Lobster and artichokes are often boiled. You can simmer rice and certain cuts of meat and poultry, and one of the best ways to cook fresh vegetables is to steam them.

Making Rice

Before we get into recipes that demonstrate boiling, simmering, poaching, and steaming techniques, we'll say a few words about rice, an incredibly versatile food that is usually boiled and then simmered. Rice has an affinity with countless boiled and steamed foods, and you can season it to create exciting taste sensations.

The world is home to thousands of strains of rice. India alone has more than 1,100 types, which must make shopping a real pain. Fortunately, the rest of us can get away with remembering five types of rice:

✔ **Converted or parboiled rice:** Basic white rice used for home cooking in much of the Western world; medium to long grain

✔ **Long-grain rice:** Includes the Indian basmati

✔ **Short-grain rice:** The family of Italian Arborio

✔ **"Wild rice":** Not really rice at all (We'll get to that.)

✔ **Brown rice:** Healthful, unrefined rice with a slightly nutty flavor

Each type has its textural and flavor differences, as the following sections explain.

Converted or parboiled rice

You've probably seen converted rice in the supermarket. The term *converted* is not apostolic but rather refers to a process by which whole grains of rice are soaked in water, steamed, and then dried. This precooking makes milling easier and also conserves nutrients that are otherwise lost. Steaming also removes some of the rice's sticky starch, leaving each grain smoother in texture. (If this sounds like Madison Avenue hype, just take a look at Uncle Ben on the rice box. His skin practically shines!)

Rice absorbs its cooking water while simmering, so getting your proportions right is important — too much water leaves the rice soupy, and too little water leaves it dry. To practice, try the following simple recipe for converted rice.

Converted Rice

Tools: *Medium (3-quart/3L) saucepan fitted with a lid*

Preparation time: *About 5 minutes*

Cooking time: *About 25 minutes*

2¹/₄ cups (550 mL) water

1 cup (250 mL) converted rice

1 tablespoon (15 mL) butter

¹/₂ teaspoon (2 mL) salt, or to taste

1 Bring the water to a boil in a medium saucepan. Add the rice, butter, and salt. Stir and cover.

2 Reduce the heat to low and simmer for 20 minutes.

3 Remove from the heat and let stand, covered, until all the water is absorbed, about 5 minutes. (If you have excess water, strain it off; if the rice is too dry, add a little boiling water and stir. Let sit for 3 to 5 minutes.) Fluff the rice with a fork; check the seasoning, adding more salt and pepper to taste, if desired; and serve.

(continued)

Yield: *3 to 4 servings.*

This basic rice accompanies many dishes, including spicy shrimp (see Chapter 15) and Salmon Marinated in Ginger and Coriander (see Chapter 15).

Basically, the more flavor in the cooking liquid, the better the rice tastes. The flavors permeate the grains, making them a superb complement to steamed vegetables or sautéed meats or poultry. You can use chicken or vegetable stock, seasoned herbs, a dash of saffron, lemon peel or juice, or any combination of herbs and spices you like to flavor the liquid. If adding fresh herbs, do so in the last 10 minutes of cooking.

Long-grain and short-grain rice

Because rice goes with almost everything, making it well is a very important skill to master. Follow these tips for perfect long-grain rice:

- ✔ Always read package cooking directions.
- ✔ Always measure the amounts of rice and liquid.
- ✔ Time your cooking.
- ✔ Keep the lid on tightly to trap steam.
- ✔ At end of cooking time, test for doneness. If necessary, cook for 2 to 4 minutes more. Rice is cooked when the liquid is absorbed and you see small spaces between the cooked grains.
- ✔ Fluff cooked rice with a fork to help separate the grains.

The technique for cooking long-grain rice and short-grain rice is essentially the same, except when using Arborio rice (available in gourmet markets) to make *risotto,* the creamy, long-stirred specialty of northern Italy. Don't panic if you can't find Arborio — regular old converted rice, although texturally different, is a fine substitute.

When making risotto, you want the short-grain Arborio rice to slowly absorb enough of the hot broth to form a creamy blend of tender yet still firm grains. Giving an exact amount of liquid for making risotto is difficult. The key is to keep stirring the rice over low heat, adding only enough liquid (a little at a time) so that the rice is surrounded by but never swimming in broth.

Make this basic recipe once or twice until you have the technique down and then alter it by using the suggestions that follow the recipe or by improvising on your own.

Risotto

Tools: *Chef's knife, skillet or sauté pan, small saucepan with lid, wooden spoon*

Preparation time: *About 15 minutes*

Cooking time: *About 35 minutes*

1 teaspoon (5 mL) olive oil

3 strips lean bacon, cut into 1-inch (2.5-cm) pieces

½ cup (125 mL) peeled and chopped shallots (or onions)

About 5 cups (1.25 L) chicken or vegetable stock

1½ cups (375 mL) Arborio rice

Salt and freshly ground pepper to taste

1 Place the olive oil and bacon in a large skillet or sauté pan and cook over medium heat, stirring occasionally until the bacon is brown, about 2 to 3 minutes. Add the chopped shallots (or onions) and lower the heat to medium-low. Cook the shallots until golden but not browned, stirring occasionally.

2 While the shallots are cooking, bring the stock to a boil in a small, covered saucepan. Reduce the heat to a simmer.

3 When the shallots are golden, add the rice to the skillet. Raise the heat to medium and cook 1 to 2 minutes, stirring, until the rice is well coated with the cooking fat.

4 Add ½ cup (125 mL) hot stock to the rice and stir it in with a wooden spoon. When most of the liquid is absorbed (and it will be absorbed quickly), add another ½ cup (125 mL) stock to the rice, stirring constantly. The rice should be surrounded by liquid but never swim in the stock. Be sure to loosen the rice from the bottom and sides of the pan to keep it from sticking.

5 Continue cooking, stirring and adding ½ cup (125 mL) stock after most of the broth is absorbed. (You may not need all of the broth.) The risotto should be creamy and tender but still firm to the bite after about 25 to 30 minutes. During the last 10 minutes, add only ¼ cup (50 mL) broth at a time so that most of the cooking liquid is absorbed when the rice is done.

6 Remove from the heat. Taste for seasoning and add salt and pepper, if desired. Serve immediately.

Yield: *4 servings.*

Risotto can be a course on its own or served as a side dish with entrees like Grilled Flank Steak with Rosemary and Sage (see Chapter 15), Braised Chicken Legs in Red Wine (see Chapter 5), or Roast Loin of Pork (see Chapter 6).

Mise en place

The French term *mise en place* means to have all the ingredients that you need to prepare a dish ready to go: Onions and herbs are chopped, garlic is minced, vegetables are rinsed, ingredients are measured, and so on. This preparation is very important, because it allows you to cook efficiently and without interruption. Practice mise en place and have all your prep work completed right up to the point of cooking.

You can add an endless variety of ingredients to risotto. About 5 minutes before it's done, try stirring in 1 cup (250 mL) fresh or frozen peas or ¹/₂ cup (125 mL) chopped fresh parsley for more color and flavor. For vegetarian risotto, omit the bacon and increase the oil to 4 tablespoons (60 mL). Or add chopped, fresh kale, spinach leaves, or broccoli rape to the pan after browning the shallots. You also can add 1 cup (250 mL) chopped carrots, asparagus, zucchini, or mushrooms; be sure to sauté or parboil these vegetables to soften them before adding to the rice mixture.

For a risotto that's more of a main dish, add 1 cup (250 mL) cooked ground pork, veal, or beef to the pan with the shallots. Or stir in ¹/₂ cup (125 mL) or more grated Parmesan cheese just before serving. You can even substitute ¹/₂ cup (125 mL) dry white wine for an equal amount of the broth, or butter for the olive oil.

Wild rice

Wild rice is a remote relative of white rice and is actually a long-grain, aquatic grass. The wild version (it is now cultivated) grows almost exclusively in the U.S. Great Lakes region and has become quite expensive because of its scarcity. You can reduce the expense by cooking and combining it with brown rice. Wild rice is especially good with robust meat dishes, game, and smoked foods.

Basic Wild Rice

Tools: *Colander, medium saucepan fitted with a lid*

Preparation time: *About 15 minutes*

Cooking time: *About 50 minutes*

1 cup (250 mL) wild rice

2¹/₂ cups (625 mL) water

2 tablespoons (30 mL) butter

Salt and freshly ground pepper to taste

1 Wash the wild rice thoroughly before you cook it. Place the rice in a pot filled with cold water and let stand for a few minutes. Pour off the water and any debris that floats to the surface. Drain well in a colander.

2 Bring the 2¹/₂ cups (625 mL) water to a boil in a medium covered saucepan over high heat. Add the rinsed rice, butter, and salt and pepper to taste. Stir once. Reduce the heat to low and simmer, covered, for 45 to 55 minutes or until the rice is tender.

3 Fluff the rice and add more salt and pepper, if desired, before serving.

Yield: *4 to 6 servings.*

If the rice is cooked but the cooking liquid is not completely absorbed, place it in a colander to drain off any excess liquid. If the liquid is completely absorbed before the rice is cooked, add a little more water or stock, about ¹/₄ cup (50 mL) at a time, and continue to cook until the grains are tender.

Brown rice

If you associate brown rice with bare-wood, macrame-festooned health food cafes, think again. Brown rice can be cool; brown rice can be elegant.

The term *brown rice* refers to rice that has not been "polished"; that is, nothing but the tough, outer husk has been removed. With its bran layer intact, brown rice is superior in nutrition to polished rice and is also a little more expensive. Brown rice has a faintly nutty flavor and a shorter shelf life than white rice. You can store white rice almost indefinitely, but brown rice should be consumed within 6 months of purchase.

Flavored Brown Rice

Tools: *Chef's knife, wooden spoon, sauté pan or saucepan with a lid*

Preparation time: *About 15 minutes*

Cooking time: *About 45 minutes*

2 tablespoons (30 mL) olive oil

1/2 cup (125 mL) peeled and finely chopped onion, about 1 medium onion

2 teaspoons (10 mL) peeled and minced garlic, about 2 cloves (optional)

1 cup (250 mL) brown rice

2 1/2 cups (625mL) chicken or vegetable stock or water

Salt and freshly ground pepper to taste

1 Heat the oil in a medium sauté pan or saucepan. Add the onion and garlic (if desired) and cook very slowly over low heat until the vegetables are just golden. (Do not brown the garlic.) Add the brown rice and cook for another 1 to 2 minutes, stirring often.

2 Add the stock or water, raise the heat to high to bring to a boil, and cook, uncovered, for 2 minutes. Lower the heat, add salt and pepper to taste, cover, and simmer for about 45 minutes or until the liquid is absorbed and the rice is cooked but still firm to the bite.

3 Keeping the pan covered, set aside for 5 minutes to let the flavors meld. If desired, add more salt and pepper before serving.

Yield: *4 servings.*

Brown rice's nutty flavor complements hearty roasts as well as seasoned vegetables. Try it with Broiled Skirt Steak, Cajun Style (see Chapter 15), Roasted Chicken (see Chapter 6), or Grilled Summer Vegetables with Basil Marinade (see Chapter 6).

Substitute 1 chopped leek (use the white section only) for the onion and add a bay leaf to the cooking liquid. Be sure to remove the bay leaf before serving. You also can stir 1/2 to 1 cup (125 to 250 mL) cooked, sliced carrots or other vegetables into the cooked rice.

Boiling, Parboiling, and Blanching Vegetables

Sometimes a recipe calls for *parboiling* vegetables. Certain dense vegetables, such as carrots, potatoes, and turnips, are sometimes parboiled, or cooked briefly in boiling water, to soften them slightly before another method finishes cooking them. This technique guarantees that all the ingredients in the dish finish cooking at the same time. You might, for example, parboil green peppers before you stuff and bake them. Or you might parboil pieces of broccoli, carrots, and cauliflower before tossing them into a stir-fry of egg noodles and shrimp. (See Roasted Winter Vegetables in Chapter 6 for a recipe that uses this technique.)

Blanching is the technique of briefly plunging vegetables or fruits into boiling water for a few seconds and then into cold water to stop the cooking process. Cooks blanch tomatoes, almonds, nectarines, and peaches to remove their skins easily. (See Chapter 11 for instructions for removing the skins of tomatoes.) Some vegetables, like green beans, are blanched before they are frozen or canned to help retain their color and flavor.

Everyone's favorite boiling recipe

Though it sounds like a contradiction, "baking" potatoes (often referred to as Idaho potatoes) actually make fluffier, lighter mashed potatoes than "boiling" potatoes (see Figure 3-1). Boiling potatoes get dense and gluey when they are mashed but are great for recipes in which they need to hold their shape — such as in potato salad.

Figure 3-1:
Common types of potatoes.

When it comes to mashing potatoes, the slow way is the best. Mashed potatoes are much better when mashed by hand with a potato masher or fork or when pressed through a *ricer* (a round, metal device with small holes through which foods are pressed). Blenders and food processors whiz too fast and can leave you with excellent wallboard paste. Even when mashing by hand, don't overdo it. Mash just enough to get rid of the lumps.

Mashed Potatoes

Tools: *Chef's knife, medium saucepan fitted with a lid, potato masher or ricer, colander*

Preparation time: *About 15 minutes*

Cooking time: *About 20 minutes*

4 large Idaho potatoes, about 2 pounds (1 kg)

1/2 teaspoon (2 mL) salt, or to taste

3 tablespoons (45 mL) butter

1/2 cup (125 mL) milk

Freshly ground pepper to taste

1 Peel the potatoes and cut them into quarters.

2 Place them in a medium saucepan with cold water to barely cover and 1/2 teaspoon (2 mL) salt, or to taste.

3 Cover and bring to a boil over high heat. Reduce heat to medium and cook, covered, for about 15 minutes or until you can easily pierce the potatoes with a fork.

4 Drain the potatoes in a colander and then return them to the saucepan. Shake the potatoes in the pan over low heat for 10 to 15 seconds to evaporate excess moisture, if necessary.

5 Remove the pan from the heat. Mash the potatoes a few times with a potato masher, ricer, or fork. (You can use a hand-held mixer to mash them on low speed if you don't have a potato masher, but be careful not to overdo it!) Add the butter, milk, and salt and pepper to taste and mash again until smooth and creamy.

Yield: *4 servings.*

Mashed potato fiends think that they go with everything short of oatmeal. Try these potatoes with Broiled Skirt Steak, Cajun Style (see Chapter 15), Mustard-Brushed Barbecued Chicken Breasts (see Chapter 6), or Pork Loin Braised in Milk and Onions (see Chapter 15).

For garlic mashed potatoes, wrap a whole, medium head of garlic in aluminum foil and roast it in a 350° F (180° C) oven for 1 hour. Remove the foil, allow the cloves to cool slightly, and then press the soft cloves free of their crispy skins. Mash them into the potatoes with the butter and milk; then season with salt and pepper to taste. You can mash other cooked vegetables, such as broccoli, carrots, turnips, or sweet potatoes, into white potatoes to add flavor and color.

You need to monitor dishes that are boiled, simmered, steamed, or poached to make sure that the water or broth doesn't steam away. (Otherwise, your pot will not be a pretty sight.) If necessary, add a little more liquid to prevent the food from burning.

Simple tips for boiling and steaming a dozen fresh vegetables

Boiling other vegetables is as easy as boiling potatoes. Following are specific instructions for boiling and steaming common vegetables:

- **Artichokes:** Place trimmed artichokes in a deep pot with cold water to cover. (They should fit snugly to keep them from bobbing in the water.) Add salt and pepper and lemon juice to taste and bring to a boil. Boil gently for 30 to 40 minutes, depending on size. When the artichokes are done, you should be able to pierce the bottom with a fork or easily pull off a leaf. Use tongs to remove the artichokes and drain upside down on a plate or in a colander. Serve hot with a sauce of lemon juice and melted butter. Or marinate for several hours in a vinaigrette dressing (see Chapter 10) and serve at room temperature.

- **Asparagus:** Snap off the thick, woody stem ends at the natural breaking point. (If very coarse, use a vegetable peeler to remove some of the outer green layer at the thick end of each spear.) Rinse the stalks under cold water or soak them for about 5 minutes if they seem especially sandy. Place the spears in a large skillet or wide, shallow pan in one layer, if possible (and never more than two). Add boiling water to cover and salt to taste. Cover and boil gently until crisp-tender, about 8 minutes for medium spears. Cooking time varies with the thickness of the stalks. Drain and serve immediately with butter, lemon juice, salt and pepper, and, if desired, a generous grating of Parmesan cheese.

- **Beans:** Trim by snapping off the stem ends. Add the beans to lightly salted boiling water to cover and cook for 8 to 10 minutes, or until crisp-tender. They should retain their bright green color.

  To steam, place steaming basket over about 1 inch (2.5 cm) of boiling water. Add beans, cover the pot tightly, and check for doneness after 5 minutes. Serve hot beans with a simple butter sauce or toss in a vinaigrette dressing and chill before serving.

✔ **Brussels sprouts:** Trim off the outer yellow leaves. Using a paring knife, trim a very thin slice off the stem end. Then cut an X in the stem end to ensure even cooking of stem and leaves. To boil, add sprouts to about 1 inch (2.5 cm) of boiling water in a saucepan. Cover and boil gently for about 8 to 10 minutes or until crisp-tender. Test for doneness by tasting. Drain and serve with a simple lemon-butter sauce.

To steam brussels sprouts, place trimmed sprouts in a steaming basket over about 1 inch (2.5 cm) of boiling water. Cover the pot and steam for about 8 minutes, depending on size.

✔ **Cabbage:** Cut the head into quarters and cut out the core. Add the quarters to a large pot of lightly salted boiling water, cover, and boil gently for about 12 minutes. Cabbage should remain somewhat crisp.

To steam, place the quarters in a large skillet or saucepan with about $1/2$ inch (12 mm) of water and cook, covered, over low heat until crisp-tender. Cabbage is also quite delicious when braised. (See Chapter 15 for a recipe for Braised Cabbage with Apple and Caraway.)

✔ **Carrots or parsnips:** Trim off the ends and scrape with a vegetable peeler. Place them sliced or whole into a pot with lightly salted water to just cover. Cover the pot and boil gently for about 12 to 15 minutes. Or place in a steaming basket and steam in a covered pot over about 1 inch (2.5 cm) of boiling water. Sliced carrots or parsnips steam in 5 minutes; whole and large, 2- to 3-inch (5- to 8-cm) pieces need about 12 minutes. Serve with butter sauce flavored with lemon juice and grated lemon or orange peel or a sauce of melted butter and minced fresh dill.

✔ **Cauliflower:** To boil, cut a whole head into florets and boil gently in lightly salted water to cover for about 8 to 10 minutes or until crisp-tender. Adding the juice of half a lemon to the cooking water helps to retain cauliflower's whiteness.

To steam, place florets in a steaming basket over about 1 inch (2.5 cm) of boiling water. Cover pot and steam for about 5 minutes or until desired doneness. Toss in a sauce of melted butter, lemon juice, and chopped fresh parsley.

✔ **Corn:** Don't husk or remove the ears from the refrigerator until you're ready to boil them. (The sugar in corn rapidly turns to starch at room temperature. To retain sweetness, keep ears cold and cook the same day of purchase.) Heat a large pot filled with enough water just to cover the corn, add husked corn, cover the pot, and boil for about 5 minutes. Remove with tongs and serve immediately with butter.

✔ **Pearl onions:** Peel and boil in a covered pot with lightly salted water to just cover for about 15 minutes or until tender but still firm. Don't overcook, or they will fall apart. Serve smothered in a sauce or gravy, or mixed with other vegetables.

✔ **Snow peas:** Rinse the peas, snap off the stem ends, and slide the string across the top to remove it. Place in boiling water to cover and cook for 2 minutes. Drain in a colander and run cold water over them to stop the cooking and retain their green color. (See the Roasted Pepper and Snow Pea Salad recipe in Chapter 10.)

✔ **Sweet potatoes:** Scrub the potatoes well, trim the tapered ends, and cut out any bruised spots. (Cut very large sweet potatoes in half crosswise or quarter them.) Place in a large pot, add cold water to cover, cover the pot, and boil gently for about 35 to 40 minutes for whole potatoes or 20 to 25 minutes for halved or quartered potatoes. Potatoes are done when you can pierce them easily with a knife. Don't overcook, or they will fall apart in the water. Drain and cool slightly before peeling. Mash or serve in large chunks with butter, salt and pepper, and ground ginger or nutmeg to taste, if desired.

✔ **Yellow squash and zucchini:** Scrub clean and trim the ends. Place in a steaming basket over about 1 inch (2.5 cm) of boiling water and steam in a covered pot for about 5 minutes or just until crisp-tender. These tender vegetables are also delicious sautéed. (See Chapter 15 for Quick Vegetable Sauté, a recipe that combines yellow squash, asparagus, tomatoes, and herbs.)

How do you season to taste? Many recipes say to "taste for seasonings" or "add seasonings to taste," which is a critical part of a cook's discipline. No matter how well a recipe is written, it often needs a slight adjustment before serving — more salt, more pepper, and so on. To season "to taste" means just that. Adjust the seasoning by adding as much or as little as it needs, according to your taste. (Remember, while cooking, always taste, taste, taste!) But proceed gingerly at the beginning. You can't remove seasonings after adding them.

Creating Two Great Stocks: Chicken and Vegetable

Scores of recipes call for either chicken stock or vegetable stock in lieu of water. By learning to make these building blocks of cuisine, which involve a simple simmering technique, you can vastly enhance many dishes.

After you roast a chicken, for example, save the carcass and toss it in the freezer (wrap it first in foil or freezer paper). When you accumulate three or four, you'll have to make a stock because the freezer door won't shut.

Chicken Stock

Tools: *Stock pot or other large pot, slotted spoon, colander*

Preparation time: *About 15 minutes*

Cooking time: *About 2 hours*

3 to 4 chicken carcasses, with wings, back, neck, and legs (skin removed)

3 quarts (3 L) water

2 stalks celery, rinsed and halved crosswise

2 carrots, scraped, trimmed, and halved crosswise

4 sprigs parsley

2 bay leaves

10 black peppercorns

Salt to taste

1 Place everything in a large, deep pot and bring to a boil. Reduce heat; simmer and cook, uncovered, for 2 hours, skimming foam off the surface with a slotted spoon as necessary. Taste the stock and add more salt and pepper if desired.

2 Strain the stock through a large colander set over a large pot or bowl to separate the broth from the chicken parts and vegetables. Let the strained stock cool slightly and then refrigerate. After the stock is completely chilled, scrape off any fat that has solidified on the surface. If desired, freeze the stock in small containers or in ice cube trays for later use.

Yield: *About 2 quarts (2 L) of stock.*

When you are making stock, some scum or particles from animal bones, vegetables, or dried beans may float to the surface. Remove them with a slotted spoon. An easy way to remove the fat from a meat stock is to let it cool down and congeal. Then simply lift the fat off the surface and throw it away.

If you don't have chicken bones for making stock (or the time to deal with them), a flavorful vegetable stock is a wonderful substitute. It's traditionally used for poaching seafood: salmon, halibut, sole, flounder, fluke, grouper, and more. (A recipe for Poached Salmon comes later in this chapter.) You also can use vegetable stock as the base for all kinds of soups and sauces.

Vegetable Stock

Tools: *Stock pot or other large pot, vegetable peeler, cheesecloth, slotted spoon, colander, large bowl*

Preparation time: *About 25 minutes*

Cooking time: *About 1¹/₂ hours*

1 small bunch parsley, rinsed

10 black peppercorns

5 sprigs fresh thyme, or ¹/₂ teaspoon (2 mL) dried

1 bay leaf

Dash of cayenne pepper

10 cups (2.5 L) water

1 bottle dry white wine (see note)

5 carrots, scraped and cut into 2-inch (5-cm) pieces

5 stalks celery, rinsed and cut into 2-inch (5-cm) pieces

2 medium onions, peeled and each pierced with a clove

2 leeks, washed and coarsely chopped (including dark green parts)

1 Tie the parsley, peppercorns, thyme, bay leaf, and cayenne in a sheet of cheesecloth or a patch of white cotton. (You can even use part of an old white shirt.)

2 Combine with all remaining ingredients in a stock pot or other large pot and bring to a boil. Reduce heat to a simmer and cook, uncovered, for 1¹/₂ hours, stirring occasionally and skimming foam off the surface with a slotted spoon as necessary.

3 Strain the stock through a colander or sieve placed over a large bowl or pot to catch the broth. Let cool. Discard the solids.

Yield: *About 1¹/₂ quarts (1.5 L).*

Note: *Dry white wines are made from many grapes; you can use Chardonnay, Pinot Gris, Chenin Blanc, and Sauvignon Blanc, to name a few. There is no need to spend more than $8 to $10 on a bottle of wine for cooking. (See* Ed McCarthy and Mary Ewing-Mulligan's Wine For Dummies *for more information about how wines complement food.)*

To make a fish stock for soups or for poaching seafood, simply add fresh fish bones and heads (gills removed) to the preceding vegetable stock at the outset. Ask your fishmonger for bones and heads — he or she is probably up to the ears in them and would be happy to get rid of some. For more on meat stocks, which are generally used in sauce-making, take a look at Chapter 7. Some soups use specialized stocks that involve these techniques, also; you can find those stocks in Chapter 9.

Poaching Seafood in Stock

Poaching seafood is a fabulous way to preserve its flavor and texture. You just have to watch the clock to prevent overcooking and keep the poaching liquid to a gentle simmer. Vigorous boiling breaks up the fish's tender flesh.

Classic vegetable stock imparts a subtle, herby flavor to seafood. The carrots and onions give a touch of sweetness, and even the dash of cayenne plays an important role in the overall balance. Poaching works best with firm-fleshed fish: salmon, tuna, black sea bass, halibut, and the like.

In the following recipe, you simmer the salmon steaks in the vegetable stock for only about 5 minutes; they continue cooking gently off the heat for another 5 minutes in the hot stock. (See why a kitchen timer is so important?)

The accompanying sauce is a vinaigrette seasoned with chervil, which is abundant in summer. (In winter, use fresh or dried dill.) You can whisk the sauce by hand or, for a smoother sauce, place the ingredients in a blender or small food processor.

TOQUE TIP

Is that fish done or just resting?

One traditional guideline to tell whether fish is cooked is the so-called Canadian Fish Rule. Measure the whole fish steak or fillet at its thickest point and cook it (whether you are boiling, steaming, baking, broiling, or poaching) for precisely 10 minutes per inch (2.5 cm). Use this rule only as a general guideline, however. We've found that in some cases it leads to slightly overcooked fish. We recommend 8 to 9 minutes per inch (2.5 cm); then check for doneness. If the thickest part of the fish is ¾ inch (18 mm) thick, for example, cook it for 6 to 7 minutes.

The fish should flake easily when pricked with a fork. If it doesn't, cook it a little more. Whole fish is easiest to check. If the dorsal fin comes out easily, it is done. If not, it needs more cooking. Scallops turn opaque, and shrimp, which takes only a couple of minutes to cook, turns pink. Salmon and tuna are darkish pink at the center when medium. White fish should be glistening and wet looking *only* at the innermost core. Unless the recipe instructs you to do otherwise, remove all cooked fish from the heat or the poaching liquid immediately.

"One of the surest ways to tell if fish is cooked is to pierce its flesh using a very thin needle (like a cake tester) or a sharp knife. If it goes through, the fish is cooked," says Eric Ripert, Executive Chef of Le Bernardin in New York City.

Mussels, clams, and oysters give you a clear indication that they are cooked: Their shells open when they are done, no matter how you cook them.

Poached Salmon Steaks with Herbed Vinaigrette Sauce

Tools: *Chef's knife, large skillet or small fish poacher, blender or food processor*

Preparation time: *About 25 minutes*

Cooking time: *About 10 minutes*

Salmon Steaks

1¹/₂ quarts (1.5 L) vegetable stock

4 salmon steaks, 4 to 6 ounces
(112 to 168 g), each with skin

Water (if necessary)

1 Bring the vegetable stock to a boil over high heat in a large skillet or fish poacher. Submerge the salmon steaks in the vegetable stock. Add more water only if there is not enough stock to cover the steaks by about 1 inch (2.5 cm).

2 Return to a boil; then lower the heat to a simmer and poach, uncovered, for about 5 minutes. As the salmon cooks, make the following vinaigrette sauce.

3 Turn off the heat and let the steaks stand in the poaching liquid about 5 minutes longer or until done. Be careful not to overcook. Cut into the center delicately to check for doneness. (See the sidebar "Is that fish done or just resting?" for details.) Remove the poached steaks to a platter.

Vinaigrette Sauce

3 tablespoons (45 mL) coarsely chopped
fresh chervil or parsley

2 tablespoons (30 mL) red wine vinegar
or lemon juice

2 small cloves garlic, peeled

1 tablespoon (15 mL) peeled and thinly
sliced shallots

1 tablespoon (15 mL) Dijon-style mustard

¹/₃ cup (75 mL) olive or vegetable oil

2 tablespoons (30 mL) water or vegetable
stock, if necessary

Salt and freshly ground pepper to taste

1 Place the chervil, vinegar or lemon juice, garlic, shallots, and mustard in a blender or food processor and begin blending.

(continued)

2 As the mixture blends, slowly pour the oil through the opening of the cover. Blend well. If the sauce is too thick, add 2 tablespoons (30 mL) water or vegetable stock and blend again. Adjust the seasonings with salt and pepper to taste.

3 Drizzle some vinaigrette over each salmon steak and serve immediately.

Yield: 4 servings.

Serve this delicate, light dish with Braised Endive (see Chapter 5), Red and Green Pepper Rice (see Chapter 10), or Grilled Summer Vegetables with Basil Marinade (see Chapter 6).

Steamy Stuff

Steaming is the gentlest way to cook vegetables and seafood. It is also one of the most healthful because nutrients are not lost in the cooking liquids. This method is a particularly good way to cook delicate seafood, especially shellfish.

You can steam in two ways: in a perforated steamer set over simmering water (and covered) or in a deep, covered pot or saucepan holding about 1 to 2 inches (2.5 to 5 cm) of water. The latter method works especially well for large vegetables like broccoli and asparagus.

If you steam foods often, you may want to invest in some sort of steamer. The conventional steamer model is a pair of pots, the top one having a perforated bottom and a lid. (See Chapter 2 for more information about steamers.)

Try the following recipe for steamed broccoli. You also can substitute large vegetables like cauliflower, kale, and tall asparagus. Make sure that you trim and slice the vegetables into equal-sized pieces so that they cook evenly.

Fresh vegetables have more flavor and retain their nutrients better if you cook them only until *crisp-tender,* or firm to the bite. (The B vitamins and vitamin C are water soluble and leach into the cooking water as the vegetables cook.) Save the vitamin-packed liquid, in which you boil vegetables, to fortify soups and stews.

Steamed Broccoli

Tools: *Paring knife, deep 3- or 4-quart (3- or 4-L) saucepan fitted with a lid, tongs, small saucepan*

Preparation time: *About 15 minutes*

Cooking time: *About 10 minutes*

1 head of broccoli

Water

Salt and freshly ground pepper to taste

3 tablespoons (45 mL) butter or margarine

Juice of half a lemon

1 Wash the broccoli thoroughly. Trim off only the thickest part of the stems and the large leaves. Divide the larger florets by slicing through the base of the flower and straight down through the length of the stem. All pieces should be roughly the same size.

2 Place the broccoli in a deep 3- or 4-quart (3- or 4-L) saucepan holding about 2 inches (5 cm) of water. (The stalks should stand on the bottom with the florets facing up.) Add salt and pepper to taste and cover the pan.

3 Bring to a boil over high heat; then reduce the heat to low and simmer, covered, for about 8 minutes or until the stalk is tender but not soft. When done, the stalks should be firm but easy to pierce with a sharp knife.

4 While the broccoli steams, melt the butter in a small saucepan and add the lemon juice. Stir to blend.

5 Using tongs, carefully remove the broccoli to a serving dish. Pour the lemon-butter sauce over the broccoli and serve.

Yield: 4 servings.

Fresh broccoli adds color and flavor to innumerable meals, including Roasted Fillet of Beef (see Chapter 6) and Glazed Leg of Lamb with Pan Gravy and Red Currant Glaze (see Chapter 6).

Chapter 4

Sautéing

*T*he common technique of sautéing, or *pan-frying,* as many hip restaurants call it today, is generally associated with French cuisine. But in fact, many other nationalities sauté routinely to sear steaks, cook fillets of fish, glaze vegetables, and quick-cook shellfish.

Sautéing is nothing more than cooking food in a hot pan, usually with a little fat (butter or oil, for example) to prevent sticking. Sautéing, which uses just enough fat to prevent sticking, imparts a crispy texture to foods and brings out all sorts of flavors from herbs and spices.

The French word *sauté* translates literally as *to jump.* Chefs shake the sauté pan back and forth over the heat, tossing the food without using utensils, to keep the food from burning and to expose all sides to the intense heat. Practice this technique in an empty cold skillet by using small candies, such as M&Ms.

Because sautéing is done at high or medium-high heat, you have to be careful not to leave food in the pan too long. For example, if you drop a steak onto a roaring-hot pan (maybe with a little oil to prevent sticking), it develops a dark crust in a few minutes. This effect is desirable because you want to trap the juices inside the steak. If you do not flip the steak quickly to sear the other side, however, it may blacken and burn.

After your steak is browned on both sides, you should turn down the heat to medium to finish cooking. Doing so gives you the best of both worlds — a crispy outside and juicy inside.

Seafood benefits from sautéing in the same way; sautéing gives it texture and flavor. Sautéed vegetables become glazed with butter and absorb seasonings — that is, the seasonings are cooked into the vegetable, not added at the table.

Oil or Butter?

The type of fat in which you sauté foods makes a big difference. Regular butter is flavorful but can burn at too high a heat. Oils don't burn, but they don't add much flavor unless they're seasoned.

We asked our friend Andre Soltner, former owner and chef of the celebrated Lutèce in Manhattan, about sautéing. He tells us, "You have to understand the heat. If the sauté pan is not hot enough, the pores of your meat will not close and the juices will run out.

"The next most important factor is the type of fat you use. Oil is best for meat; it can get very hot without burning. Butter is fine for vegetables and pasta. I also like rapeseed oil (also called canola oil) because of its high smoke point," Soltner says.

Oil should be sizzling but not smoking in the pan before you add food. Butter should foam at its edges but not brown. Some chefs insist on using only *clarified* butter when sautéing.

To clarify, you melt butter in a saucepan to separate its milk solids, which sink to the bottom of the pan. You then skim off the top layer of foam and save only the clear (or clarified) yellow liquid in the middle to use for sautéing. Without milk solids, clarified butter has a higher smoke point and is less likely to burn. To avoid clarifying butter but still impart some of butter's delicious flavor, you can use a combination of equal parts butter and oil.

Deglazing

A very hot sauté pan begins to cook meat, poultry, or fish right away, browning the juices that flow from it and leaving bits of food sticking to the bottom of the pan. These browned bits are loaded with flavor. If *deglazed* (moistened and scraped up) in the pan, they transform into a delicious sauce.

To deglaze, remove the meat, poultry, or fish from the pan onto a serving platter. Immediately add liquid — you can use water, wine, broth, or a combination. The liquid should be twice the amount of sauce you want to make. Raise the heat to high, bringing the liquid to a boil while you stir and scrape the browned bits off the bottom of the pan until they dissolve into the sauce. Boil until the sauce is reduced by half the volume. Season to taste and maybe stir in a teaspoon (5 mL) or more of butter for flavor and to add a smooth texture. Then spoon it over the cooked meat, poultry, or fish and serve. (See Figure 4-1.)

Deglazing a Pan

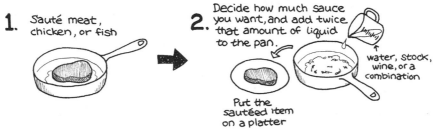

1. Sauté meat, chicken, or fish

2. Decide how much sauce you want, and add twice that amount of liquid to the pan.

water, stock, wine, or a combination

Put the sautéed item on a platter

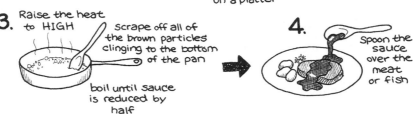

Figure 4-1:
Deglazing a pan enables you to add the flavorful browned bits to your sauce.

3. Raise the heat to HIGH

Scrape off all of the brown particles clinging to the bottom of the pan

boil until sauce is reduced by half

4. Spoon the sauce over the meat or fish

As a rule, the wine you use for deglazing depends on what you're sautéing: Use white wine for poultry and seafood, and red wine for meat.

Versatile Sautéing

Notice how the following recipes use the same basic sautéing technique and change only the types of fat and seasonings.

Vegetables

Vegetables are excellent when boiled or steamed until about 90 percent done and then transferred to a pan to be finished in butter and maybe fresh herbs. Many classic recipes for potatoes call for sautéing; thinly sliced raw potatoes are delicious when cooked this way. In the following recipe, you cut the potatoes into fine cubes and toss them in a hot pan until crispy.

These potatoes, an excellent accompaniment to steak or veal chops, are similar to the French *pommes de coin rue,* which are cubed potatoes sautéed in oil and butter until well browned. Here, the potatoes are cubed even finer and thus cook faster. By using a combination of butter and oil, you give them a rich flavor and eliminate the risk of burning.

Sautéed Cubed Potatoes

Tools: *Vegetable peeler, chef's knife, colander, large nonstick skillet, slotted spoon*

Preparation time: *About 15 minutes*

Cooking time: *About 15 minutes*

2 large baking potatoes, about 1¹/₂ pounds (750 g)

¹/₃ cup (75 mL) vegetable or corn oil

2 tablespoons (30 mL) butter

Salt and freshly ground pepper to taste

1 Peel the potatoes and cut each into cubes of ¹/₄ inch (6 mm) or smaller. Place the cubes in cold water to prevent discoloration.

2 When ready to cook, drain the cubes in a colander. Run very hot water over them for about 10 seconds. (The hot water rinses off the starch so that the potatoes don't stick together in the pan.) Drain well and dry on paper towels.

3 Heat the oil in a large nonstick skillet over high heat until it sizzles. Add the potatoes and cook, shaking the skillet and stirring the potatoes (to keep them from sticking to the pan) for about 6 to 8 minutes or until lightly browned. With a slotted spoon, remove the potatoes from the pan to a platter. Pour all the fat out of the pan and wipe out the skillet with paper towels.

4 Heat the butter in the skillet over medium heat. Do not let it burn. Add the potatoes and salt and pepper. Cook, shaking and stirring, for 5 to 6 minutes or until the cubes are browned and crisp. Serve immediately, removing the potatoes with a slotted spoon.

Yield: *3 to 4 servings.*

These potatoes are a delicious side dish to omelets (see Chapter 8), Roasted Fillet of Beef (see Chapter 6), or Grilled Brochettes of Pork with Rosemary (see Chapter 6).

Be very careful when you put rinsed vegetables (or other foods) into a pan of hot fat. The water that clings to the vegetables makes the fat splatter, which can cause serious burns. Be sure to dry the vegetables thoroughly, as instructed here, or cover the pan after you add the vegetables to trap the splattering grease.

Following is a quick and healthy side dish that is a fine match with the Salmon Steaks with Sweet Red Pepper Sauce recipe later in this chapter.

Sautéed Spinach Leaves

Tools: *Large sauté pan or skillet fitted with a lid*

Preparation time: *About 15 minutes*

Cooking time: *About 4 minutes*

1 1/2 pounds (750 g) fresh spinach	*1/4 teaspoon (1 mL) ground nutmeg*
1 tablespoon (15 mL) olive oil	*Salt and freshly ground pepper to taste*
1 tablespoon (15 mL) butter	

1 Cut away and discard any tough spinach stems and blemished leaves. Wash spinach thoroughly in cold water and drain well. (See Chapter 10 for complete instructions for rinsing and trimming greens.)

2 Heat the oil and butter in a large sauté pan or skillet over medium heat. Add the spinach, nutmeg, and salt and pepper.

3 Stir the spinach leaves to coat with the oil. (The spinach wilts so fast that you may think you barely have enough for one portion — don't worry, you do.) Cover and cook over medium-high heat for about 2 to 3 minutes or until the spinach leaves wilt thoroughly. Remove from heat and serve.

Yield: *4 to 6 servings.*

Spinach also makes a fine meal with Grilled Swordfish Steaks with Lemon and Thyme (see Chapter 6) or Mustard-Brushed Barbecued Chicken Breasts (see Chapter 6).

Shellfish

You sauté shellfish, which is incredibly delicate, for just minutes. Scallops are tricky because they become rubbery if undercooked and rubbery if overcooked.

Beware when buying so-called bay scallops in the fish market or restaurants. The real thing is scarce and expensive, coming from certain bays on the East Coast of the U.S., from the Carolinas to Maine. They generally measure no more than 3 inches (8 cm) across the shell and are distinguished by their buttery texture and sweet flavor. The rather bland and larger Calico scallop, which comes from southern Atlantic waters, is sometimes foisted off as a bay scallop.

Sea scallops, which are excellent in their own right, can measure 5 inches (13 cm) across the shell. In Europe, the tender and exquisite orange roe that is attached to sea scallops is prized; in the U.S., for some reason, it is discarded.

The natural sweetness of scallops makes them ideal for a Provençal dish made with capers, lemon, garlic, thyme, and tomatoes. If you have all the ingredients at hand, you can make this dish in about 10 minutes. The scallops cook in about 3 minutes and must be served immediately.

Sea Scallops Provençal

Tools: *Chef's knife, large skillet, large nonstick skillet*

Preparation time: *About 15 minutes*

Cooking time: *About 10 minutes*

2 medium sweet red peppers

2 tablespoons (30 mL) olive oil

1 tablespoon (15 mL) peeled and chopped garlic, about 3 large cloves

6 small, ripe plum tomatoes, cored and cut into ¹/₂-inch (12-mm) cubes

10 pitted and coarsely chopped black olives (optional)

¹/₄ cup (50 mL) drained and rinsed capers

1 teaspoon (5 mL) chopped fresh thyme leaves, or ¹/₂ teaspoon (2 mL) dried

Salt and freshly ground pepper to taste

2 tablespoons (30 mL) butter

1¹/₂ pounds (750 g) bay or sea scallops, cut in half crosswise if very large

Juice of 1 lemon

¹/₄ cup (50 mL) coarsely chopped fresh basil or parsley

1 Core and remove the seeds of the red peppers and cut into pieces that are about ¹/₄ inch (6 mm) thick and about 1 inch (2.5 cm) long. (See Figure 4-2.)

2 Heat the oil in a large skillet over medium heat. Add the garlic and cook briefly. (Do not let the garlic brown.) Add the red peppers, tomatoes, olives (if desired), capers, thyme, and salt and pepper to taste. Cook, stirring, for about 5 minutes. Remove from the heat and cover to keep warm.

(continued)

3 In a large nonstick skillet, melt the butter over medium-high heat. When the butter is bubbling, add the scallops. Season with salt and pepper to taste and cook, stirring, for about 3 minutes or until done. (Be careful not to overcook the scallops.) Sprinkle the lemon juice and basil or parsley over the scallops, stir briefly, and remove from the heat.

Remember, when we tell you to season with salt and pepper to taste, apply the seasoning cautiously. You can always add more salt and pepper after the dish is done, but going in reverse is not easy.

4 Spoon a portion of the tomato mixture onto each of four serving plates. Distribute the scallops evenly over the mixture and serve immediately.

Yield: *4 servings.*

Note: *Only the precise amount of cooking yields the buttery, succulent texture for which scallops are known. The best way we know to test scallops is to cut off a little piece when you think they are done and taste it. Cooked scallops look white and opaque in the center; uncooked ones have a translucent look.*

How to Core and Seed a Pepper

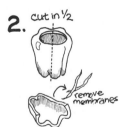

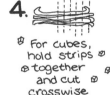

Figure 4-2: Removing the seeds and core from a pepper.

1. cut out stem — twist and pull out

2. cut in ½ — remove membranes

3. Cut into lengthwise strips

4. For cubes, hold strips together and cut crosswise

Other fruits and vegetables that may require coring or seeding include apples, pears, avocados, tomatoes, hard-shell squash, pineapple, citrus fruits, and mangoes. To remove the large pit of an avocado, slice the fruit in half lengthwise and pull apart the halves. One half should contain the whole pit. Firmly and carefully strike the exposed pit with a chef's knife. The blade should sink into the pit, enabling you to lift it out with a gentle twist.

Shrimp are more forgiving than scallops, especially if you sauté them in the shell. If you remove the shells before sautéing, removing the bitter black vein that runs along the inside is a good idea. You can buy an inexpensive tool to do that — see Chapter 12.

Dark-fleshed fish

Dark-fleshed fish, such as salmon, tuna, and bluefish, can be exceptionally good when sautéed. And you can enhance them with countless sauces that you can make in 15 minutes or less. Because these fish have relatively high fat contents (but the kind of fat that's good for you), they also stand up to spicy sauces.

The Japanese demonstrate this idea with their fiery *wasabi,* which is used like horseradish and combined with soy sauce to make a dipping sauce for sushi and sashimi.

However, a spicy sauce paired with a delicate fish, like sole or snapper, can be a culinary train wreck. In general, firm-fleshed fish (or rich, darker-fleshed fish) stand up to spiciness.

The same rules apply to sweetness. In the newly voguish Caribbean-style cooking, tropical fruits such as mango and papaya are incorporated into sauces, sometimes combined with a counterpoint of hot pepper. This business is tricky, so you may want to wait until you have your sea legs before trying it.

In the following easy recipe, which is faintly sweet from sautéed red peppers and shallots, note that you first sear the salmon to seal in moisture and then remove it from the pan. You make the quick sauce in the same pan, and then you return the fish to the sauce for the rest of the cooking. This technique helps to keep the salmon moist and infuses it with some of the sauce flavors. Note that this recipe calls for $1/2$ cup (125 mL) of heavy cream (or half and half) at the end to bind the sauce, which works out to only 2 tablespoons (30 mL) of cream per person.

Binding a sauce means simply to pull together sauce ingredients in the pan and create a smoother texture by stirring in butter, cream, yogurt, or other dairy product. Binding is done at the very end of the sauce-making process, just before serving.

The following salmon dish goes well with sautéed spinach accented with nutmeg; snap peas; rice; green beans; or asparagus. (We include a recipe for Sautéed Spinach Leaves earlier in this chapter.)

Salmon Steaks with Sweet Red Pepper Sauce

Tools: *Paring knife, chef's knife, large nonstick skillet or sauté pan*

Preparation time: *About 15 minutes*

Cooking time: *About 15 minutes*

2 medium sweet red peppers

4 salmon steaks, each about 6 to 7 ounces (168 to 196 g) and ³/₄ inch (18 mm) thick

Salt and freshly ground pepper to taste

2 tablespoons (30 mL) butter

¹/₄ cup (50 mL) peeled and finely chopped shallots

¹/₄ teaspoon (1 mL) cayenne pepper

¹/₄ cup (50 mL) dry white wine

¹/₂ cup (125 mL) heavy cream or half and half

2 tablespoons (30 mL) finely chopped fresh dill and dill sprigs for garnishing

1 Core and remove the seeds from the red peppers and then cut them into ¹/₄-inch (6-mm) cubes. (Refer to Figure 4-2.)

2 Season both sides of the salmon steaks with salt and pepper. Melt the butter over medium-high heat in a nonstick skillet or sauté pan large enough to hold the steaks in one layer.

3 Place the steaks in the pan and cook over medium-high heat until lightly browned on both sides, about 3 to 4 minutes per side. The cooking time varies with the thickness of the fish and the doneness desired.

4 Transfer the steaks to a warm platter and cover with foil. Leave the cooking butter in the skillet and scrape the bottom of the pan with a wooden spoon to loosen the browned bits clinging to the pan. Add the shallots, cayenne pepper, and red peppers. Cook over medium-high heat, stirring, for about 4 to 5 minutes or until the vegetables are wilted (or softened).

5 Add the wine, turn up the heat to high, and cook until about half the liquid in the pan evaporates. (This step intensifies the flavor of the sauce.) Lower the heat to medium-high, add the cream, and cook, stirring, until the liquid reduces again by about half.

6 Add the salmon steaks, chopped dill, and any juices that have accumulated around the steaks and bring to a simmer. Cook for about 1 minute more or until warmed through. Do not overcook. Check the seasoning and add salt and pepper if desired. Serve immediately with dill sprigs for decoration.

Yield: *4 servings.*

Chicken

Sautéing is probably the best method to impart flavor to chicken. The following simple recipe combines chicken with the sweet flavors of onions and tomatoes. This recipe is an easy one to modify.

Sautéed Chicken Breasts with Tomatoes and Thyme

Tools: *Chef's knife, large sauté pan or fry pan, meat mallet or heavy pan*

Preparation time: *About 20 minutes*

Cooking time: *About 10 minutes*

4 boneless, skinless chicken breast halves

Salt and freshly ground pepper to taste

2 tablespoons (30 mL) olive oil

$^1/_2$ cup (125 mL) peeled and chopped onion, about 1 medium onion

1 teaspoon (5 mL) peeled and chopped garlic, about 1 large clove

$1^1/_2$ cups (375 mL) peeled, seeded, and chopped tomatoes, about 2 medium tomatoes (see Chapter 11 for instructions)

1 teaspoon (5 mL) chopped fresh thyme, or $^1/_4$ (1 mL) teaspoon dried

2 tablespoons (30 mL) chopped fresh basil (optional)

$^1/_3$ cup (75 mL) white wine or chicken broth

1 Place the chicken breasts on a cutting board, cover with waxed paper, and pound them lightly so that they are of equal thickness. (Use the bottom of a heavy pan or a meat mallet.) Salt and pepper each piece well.

2 Heat the olive oil in a large sauté pan or fry pan over medium heat. Add the chicken and sauté for about 4 to 5 minutes per side or until done. (To test for doneness, make a small incision in the center of each piece. The meat should look white, with no trace of pink.) Remove the pieces to a platter and cover with aluminum foil to keep warm.

3 Add the onions to the pan over medium heat. Stir for 1 minute, scraping the bottom of the pan. Add the garlic, stirring for another minute. Add the chopped tomatoes, thyme, basil (if desired), and salt and pepper to taste. Stir for 1 minute. Add the white wine or broth, increase the heat to high, and cook, stirring, for about 2 to 3 minutes or until most of the liquid evaporates. (The mixture should be moist but not soupy.)

4 Place the chicken on 4 plates. Spoon equal portions of sauce over each piece.

Yield: 4 servings.

You can serve the chicken with side dishes of Mashed Potatoes (see Chapter 3) or Ginger Rice with Fresh Coriander (see Chapter 15).

 You can modify this recipe in many ways. For example, you can use turkey breasts or slices of veal instead of chicken; add 1 cup (250 mL) fresh, frozen, or canned corn kernels with the chopped tomatoes; add 2 tablespoons (30 mL) heavy cream with the broth or wine; substitute tarragon, marjoram, or other herb of choice for the thyme; or grate some Parmesan cheese over the top of each serving.

Steak

One of the most popular beef dishes in restaurants is what the French call *steak au poivre,* in which beef is coated liberally with cracked black pepper before it is cooked in a hot pan. The sauce is usually made with beef stock, shallots, red wine, and maybe a little brandy. The combination is compelling if the cook skillfully balances the hot pepper with sweet elements.

Sautéed Peppered Fillet of Beef

Tools: *Chef's knife, large cast-iron pan or other heavy-bottomed pan*

Preparation time: *About 20 minutes*

Cooking time: *About 15 minutes*

3 to 4 tablespoons (45 to 60 mL) black peppercorns

2 boneless sirloin steaks, trimmed, each about 1 pound (500 g) and 1¹/₄ inches (3 cm) thick

2 tablespoons (30 mL) vegetable oil

3 tablespoons (45 mL) peeled and minced shallots

2 tablespoons (30 mL) peeled and minced onion (see following sidebar for instructions)

2 tablespoons (30 mL) butter

³/₄ cup (175 mL) dry red wine

2 tablespoons (30 mL) brandy

¹/₄ cup (50 mL) fresh or canned beef or chicken broth

1 teaspoon (5 mL) tomato paste

(continued)

1 Crush the peppercorns by using a mortar and pestle or on a hard surface (such as a wooden cutting board) with the bottom of a heavy pan, as shown in Figure 4-3. Doing so shortly before cooking gets the most potency from the pepper.

2 Press the steaks into the peppercorns, covering both sides evenly. (If you come up short of peppercorns, crush some more.)

3 Coat a cast-iron pan (or other large, heavy-bottomed pan) with the oil and place over high heat. When the pan is very hot, lay the steaks in and cook for about 3 to 4 minutes per side to sear, and then another 4 to 5 minutes, flipping periodically to finish. Cooking times vary with the thickness of the meat, so make a small incision in the meat and check for the desired degree of doneness. Medium doneness has a slightly pink center with soft-brown edges.

4 Remove the steaks from the pan and set aside on a plate. Cover the plate with foil to keep the steaks warm. Let the cooking pan cool slightly and remove any little burnt particles, but do not rinse under water!

5 Return the pan to medium heat and add the shallots, onions, and 1 tablespoon (15 mL) butter. Cook for about 1 minute, stirring. Add the red wine and brandy. Raise the heat to high and let the sauce evaporate, or *reduce,* to about half its original volume, stirring often. Add the broth and tomato paste. Reduce the sauce again until it is about ¹/₂ cup (125 mL) total, stirring. Lower the heat to medium.

6 Add the remaining 1 tablespoon (15 mL) butter and stir well until it melts to *bind,* or pull together, the sauce. Spoon the sauce over the steaks and serve immediately.

Yield: *4 servings.*

If you'd like to flambé the steaks, bring the steaks and the pan to the table. Pour 2 tablespooons (30 mL) of brandy over the steaks and ignite them with a match. Even if you don't taste the difference, your guests will be impressed. After the flame dies out, distribute the sauce over the sliced or unsliced steaks.

How to Crush Peppercorns

Figure 4-3: Crushing peppercorns with a heavy pan.

1. Gather whole peppercorns in the middle of a cuttingboard

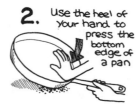

2. Use the heel of your hand to press the bottom edge of a pan

3. Repeat steps 1 & 2 until peppercorns are crushed to desired size.

ESSENTIAL SKILL

Mincing onions and garlic

A sliced onion releases intense flavor and juice, which is why so many recipes call for chopped, minced, or diced onion. To avoid tears, the best strategy is a sharp knife that reduces cutting time. Follow these steps (also illustrated below) to mince an onion:

1. Cut the onion in half lengthwise through the bulbous center. Peel back the papery skin and chop off the top, but leave the root end intact. (As you slice through the onion, the intact root end helps you to keep the slices from slipping out from under the knife.) Place each half cut side down.

2. With your knife tip just in front of the root end, slice the onion as thinly as possible.

3. Turning the knife so that it is horizontal to your cutting board, slice through the onion from top to bottom, again leaving the root end intact.

4. To finish the mince, slice down through the onion from end to end, making a grid pattern. Cubes should fall onto the cutting board.

Just as with onions, slicing, chopping, and mincing garlic releases its pungent juices. The more you chop it, the stronger its flavor becomes. Raw, mashed garlic carries the biggest punch, while whole roasted garlic cloves release a nutty, slightly sweet flavor. See the "Using knives properly" section in Chapter 2 for famous chef Jacques Pépin's method for chopping garlic.

How to Mince an Onion

1. Cut off stem / Cut in half through the root / Peel off skin

2. Make parallel lengthwise cuts / don't cut through root end!

3. Cut horizontal slices from top to bottom / not all the way through!

4. Now cut crosswise

Chapter 5

Mom Food: Braising and Stewing

. . . .

In This Chapter

▶ Braising and stewing: Twin tenderizers

▶ Sniffing your way through the herb garden

▶ Bang for the buck: Homey recipes for braising and stewing

. . . .

*I*f you're like most people, you have precious little time, especially during the week, to stand over a pot. This chapter is for you. Braising and stewing are slow cooking methods that allow you to put all the ingredients in a pot, turn the heat to low, and do something else for an hour or two — maybe dust the TV or return the neighbor's newspaper that your dog retrieves every day.

Because braising and stewing dishes take so much time, they are best cooked the day before and reheated — the flavors are actually more pronounced that way. They are also great for parties because they are easily made in large batches and are inexpensive (usually using less expensive cuts of meat).

Most meat dishes in this chapter use the less expensive front cuts of the animal: the chuck, brisket, shank, and plate. (See Chapter 13 for an illustration of the various cuts of beef.) These more muscular cuts do not make much of a steak, but when you braise them for hours, their fibers break down and they become succulent. In some ways, these cuts are more flavorful than expensive filet.

Braising versus Stewing

Both braising and stewing involve long, slow cooking in liquid. The major difference is that braised foods lie in a puddle of liquid, not quite submerged, so that they stew and steam at the same time.

Stewing involves submerging ingredients in a liquid and simmering the mixture for a long time. Larger cuts of meat — and the very toughest — tend to be braised, whereas cut-up meat is stewed.

Where does a fricassee fit in?

A *fricassee* is a variation on stew. A traditional fricassee is made with poultry, usually chicken. Moreover, the poultry in a fricassee is not seared and browned first, as in a stew. The lack of browning makes the sauce whiter than that of a stew.

Exotic Flavors to Fill Your Pantry: Herb and Spice Charts

Herbs and spices energize virtually every type of cooking. Change the herb or spice, and the dish takes on entirely different tastes and aromas. Herbs and spices are particularly important in braising and stewing, where a last-minute addition of the right herb and spice combination can make a dish soar.

Purchasing and storing herbs and spices

Purchase dried herbs and spices in small quantities, keep them in tightly sealed containers away from heat and light, and try to use them within 10 to 12 months. The flavor of dried herbs fades quickly.

You also can cultivate fresh herbs in a window box. Rinse fresh herbs thoroughly, wrap them in damp paper towels, and store them for up to a week in the refrigerator.

Cooking with herbs and spices

Elizabeth Terry is one of the South's most acclaimed chefs, owing to the pure and unfussy regional fare she turns out at Elizabeth on 37th in Savannah, Georgia. Fans of family-style Southern food come from hundreds of miles away to experience this unpretentious and unforgettable place.

Terry says, "Use fresh herbs rather than dried whenever possible. The full flavor of the fresh herb or spice is best released if you add it to the dish just before serving."

Following are some of Chef Terry's favorite ways to add fresh herbs and spices to food:

- **Basil and mint combined:** Delicious with tomato sauces and salads, potato salads, and marinated vegetable salads.

- **Rosemary and thyme:** Go well with oven-roasted potatoes and roasted chicken. Rub the rosemary into the poultry before roasting it and then sprinkle it with the fresh thyme when it comes out of the oven. One herb is roasted, the other is fresh, and the flavors are perfect together.

- **Lemon grass, hot chili peppers, garlic, and rosemary:** For flavored oils. Be sure to refrigerate to keep them from spoiling. Refrigerated oils harden to a solid state but liquefy if left to stand at room temperature for about 5 minutes.

- **Curry powder and sautéed onions:** Add curry powder to sautéed onions for a wonderful cold vegetable garnish.

- **Cumin:** Use in soups and sauces. Especially good sautéed with red cabbage, apple, and a little cream.

- **Fresh ginger, sweet red peppers, and onions:** Make a sauce for fish, shrimp, and grilled vegetables by pureeing fresh ginger, sweet red peppers, and onions in a blender.

- **Cinnamon, allspice, finely chopped red pepper, fresh crushed garlic, and oil:** Make a paste for coating and marinating shrimp before cooking it on the grill.

- **Whole mustard seeds and salmon:** Rub whole mustard seeds on the outside of salmon and sear in a pan of hot oil until the seeds form a crunchy crust and the fish is cooked.

Table 5-1 can help you decide which herbs go best with which kinds of dishes. (Also see Figure 5-1.) After you become familiar with the properties of these flavor enhancers, you can toss the chart and navigate on your own.

Table 5-1	A Few Fresh Herbs You Should Know
Herb	*Description*
Basil	Pungent, sweet flavor. Most fresh varieties are dark green, except for the purple-leafed opal basil. Available as fresh sprigs or crumbled dried. Essential to Mediterranean cooking, especially Italian and French cuisine. Excellent with tomatoes, eggs, pasta, poultry, fish, and green salads, and in vinaigrettes.

(continued)

Table 5-1 *(continued)*

Spice	Description
Bay leaf	Strong, herbaceous taste. Sold as a whole, dried leaf. Excellent in long-cooking dishes like soups, stews, poaching liquid, marinades, pot roasts, rice casseroles, stuffings, and barbecue sauces. Remove the leaf before serving the dish.
Chervil	Quite aromatic, with delicate licorice-like flavor. Available as fresh sprigs (available mostly in summer) or crumbled dry. Use with fish and shellfish, eggs, chicken, tomatoes, asparagus, summer squash, eggplant, herb butters, sauces, green salads, and soups.
Chives	Delicate mild-onion flavor. Sold in thin, fresh stalks, chopped, dried, or frozen. Wonderful in cream sauces or soups, with chicken, eggs, shellfish, or marinated salads, or as a plate garnish.
Cilantro or Chinese parsley	Extremely pungent and aromatic. Sold in fresh, curly-leafed bunches. Use leaves only. Found in Mexican and Asian dishes and works well with rice, fish, pork, ham, salsa, avocado, and tomato.
Dill	Delicate caraway flavor. Sold in feathery, fresh bunches or as dried seeds. Use seeds in pickling recipes; use fresh leaves with fish and shellfish, omelets, chicken, turkey, dressings and vinaigrettes, cold salads and marinades, fish mousses, and pâtés.
Marjoram	A little like oregano in taste, but much milder and sweeter. Sold fresh or crumbled dry. Extremely versatile herb. Add to almost any vegetable dish, especially good with sweet potatoes, squash, tomatoes, corn, stuffings, stews, omelets, soups, herb butters, rice, pork, lamb, beef, poultry, or any fish.
Mint	Fresh scent and a sweet, pungent flavor. Most common varieties are peppermint and spearmint. Sold in fresh bunches or crumbled dry. Terrific in cold grain and rice salads, with fresh fruit, in cold fruit soups and sauces, and with marinated vegetable salads of cucumber or tomato; also good with grilled chicken, pork, lamb, and shellfish and in cold drinks like iced tea.
Oregano	Intense flavor. Sold fresh or crumbled dry. An essential ingredient in Italian and Greek cooking. A little goes far with poultry, tomato sauces, egg dishes, vegetable stews, and stir-fries.

Herb	Description
Parsley	Fresh-flavored and crisp-textured. Available year-round in fresh bunches or crumbled dry. Two common fresh varieties are the stronger-flavored Italian flat leaf and the curly leaf. An all-purpose herb; use in savory soups or stocks in bouquet garni, stews, dressings, stuffings, and frittatas, with fish, poultry, beef, pork, lamb, veal, game, and all vegetables. Also a pretty plate garnish.
Rosemary	Quite aromatic, needle-shaped leaves smell a little like lemon and pine. Sold as fresh sprigs or dried. Use sparingly with vegetables and in stuffings, rice dishes, and stews. Excellent with game, meats (especially grilled), chicken, halibut, salmon, tuna, in herb breads, or to flavor oils and marinades.
Sage	Green-gray oval leaves with a slightly bitter mint taste. Available in fresh sprigs, crumbled dried, and ground. Use sparingly. Excellent in poultry stuffings, pâtés, fish and chicken stews, chicken salads, meat loaves, and herb butters, with halibut and sole, and to season meat and poultry roasts.
Savory	Full-bodied herb that some people say tastes like a cross between mint and thyme. Fresh sprigs available in two varieties: winter savory and milder summer savory. Crumbled dried available year-round. Excellent with fresh or dried bean salads, most fish and shellfish dishes, omelets, soufflés, rice dishes, stuffings, meat and poultry, tomatoes, potatoes, artichokes, and onions.
Tarragon	Aromatic herb with assertive, licorice-like flavor. Sold as fresh whole sprigs, crumbled dried, and whole dried leaves. Fresh French tarragon has the most subtle flavor. Use with chicken, pork, lamb, veal, fish, shellfish, omelets and other egg dishes, dips and dressings, mayonnaise, vegetable casseroles and salads, herb butters, and as flavoring for white vinegar and hot or cold potato dishes.
Thyme	Tiny leaves with minty aroma and tea-like taste. Sold as fresh sprigs and crumbled dried. Fresh varieties include lemon, orange, and French. Add to vegetables, meat, poultry, fish, egg dishes, soups, stews, cream sauces, meat loaf, pâtés, chowders, stuffings, and bouquet garni.

Spices, which are almost always sold dried, have been a vital element in international cooking since Byzantine times. Most spices come from the East, where they were introduced to Europe during the Crusades.

Figure 5-1:
Types of herbs.

Dried spices are generally more concentrated than dried herbs, so use them carefully. After you become familiar with the qualities of different spices, your cooking repertoire expands exponentially.

The flavor of freshly ground spices is much more potent than those sold already ground. Whenever possible, buy whole spices, like nutmeg and pepper-corns, and grate or grind them yourself before using them. You can purchase a small spice grater for just this purpose.

Whole spices also can be wrapped and tied in a piece of cheesecloth, added to soups and stews, and then removed before serving. Cloves are often stuck into an onion and then added to a stew.

Store spices in a cool, dry place and try to use them within 6 to 10 months. Table 5-2 lists the more common spices (also pictured in Figure 5-2).

Figure 5-2: Types of spices.

Table 5-2	A Few Spices You Should Know
Spice	*Description*
Allspice	Spice berries of the evergreen pimiento tree with tastes of cinnamon, nutmeg, and cloves — hence the name. Sold as whole, dried berries or ground. Excellent in both sweet and savory dishes — pâtés, stews, chilies, poached fish, meat loaf and meatballs, pumpkin and fruit pie fillings, barbecue sauce, stuffed cabbage, meat glazes, winter squash, chutneys and preserves, and gingerbread.
Caraway	Has a nutty, faint anise flavor and is most commonly used in German cooking. Sold as dried seeds. Found in rye bread and also in cakes, stews, and some European cheeses.
Cardamom	Pungent, spicy-sweet flavor. Sold as whole dried seeds and ground. Excellent in baked goods, fruit salads, pumpkin pie, and Indian curries.
Cayenne or red pepper	A hot, powdered mixture of several chili peppers. Sold ground. Use sparingly. Especially good in dishes with egg, cheese, rice, fish, chicken, or ground beef.
Chili powder	A hot and spicy mixture of dried chilies, cumin, oregano, garlic, coriander, and cloves. Sold ground. A multipurpose hot seasoner; use sparingly in stews, soups, chili, egg dishes, dressings, guacamole and bean dips, barbecue sauces, and rice and bean casseroles.
Cinnamon	Sweet and aromatic spice from the bark of a tropical tree. Sold whole, in dry sticks or ground. Primarily a baking spice in cakes, cookies, and pies, but also adds a savory touch to stews, curries, baked sweet potatoes, and yellow squash.
Clove	Sharp and deeply fragrant. Sold as whole dried buds or ground. Use much like cinnamon, but more judiciously. Excellent in stocks, vegetable soups, and glazes.
Coriander	From fragrant seeds, similar in flavor to caraway. Sold as whole dried and ground seeds. Seeds used for pickling; powder used for curries, lamb, pork, sausage, and baked goods.
Cumin	Slightly acidic aroma; nutty-flavored seed. Sold as whole dried and ground seeds. Essential to Middle Eastern and Asian cooking. Use in curries, chili, and bean dips and with fish, lamb, poultry, and beef.

Spice	Description
Curry powder	A spice blend of more than a dozen different herbs and spices, often including cinnamon, cloves, cardamom, chilies, mace, nutmeg, turmeric (which gives curry its distinctive color), red and black pepper, and ground sesame seeds. Commercial blends tend to lose their flavor fast and should be used within 2 months of purchase. Use to season lamb, pork, chicken, rice, stuffings, and sautéed vegetables like onions, cabbage, and baked squash.
Ginger	Sharp and faintly sweet flavor; intensely aromatic. Sold dried ground, dried whole, crystallized, preserved, and fresh. Use ground sparingly in curries, spice cakes, and marinades and with pork, chicken, and seafood. Use crystallized (candied) in fruit syrups and glazes and with pies and cakes. Grate fresh ginger into stir-fries of pork, chicken, beef, and fresh vegetables.
Nutmeg	Pleasing aroma; slightly sweet and nutty taste. Sold as whole seeds and ground. Delicious in white sauces, sweet sauces, and glazes, pureed vegetables and soups, eggnog, fruit pies, spice cakes, and pumpkin pie. Best freshly grated.
Paprika	Beautiful red powder; varieties range from faintly spicy to hot. Sold ground (the Hungarian variety is considered the best). Accents dips, creamy salads, dressings, stews (like goulash), sautéed meats, chicken, and fish. Imparts red color to creamed dishes and sauces.
Peppercorn	Intense, hot flavor and aroma. Sold cracked, finely ground, or as whole peppercorns in black, white, and green, with black being the strongest. Black pepper is perhaps the world's most popular spice, used to accent nearly every savory dish. Use freshly ground peppercorns for best effect — ground pepper quickly loses its intensity. Use white pepper to enrich cream sauces and white dishes if you don't want the pepper specks to show.
Saffron	The world's most expensive spice. Made from dried stigmas hand-picked from purple crocus flowers. Available as powder or whole, red threads (which are of better quality). A little goes a long way. Essential to classic dishes like bouillabaisse and paella, but also delicious in rice casseroles, creamed dishes, risotto, and with seafood. Imparts a pale yellow color to cream sauces and rice dishes.
Turmeric	Yellow-orange powder that is intensely aromatic and has a bitter, pungent flavor; gives American-style mustard its color. Sold as a powder. Essential ingredient in curries; use in rice and chili and with lamb and winter squash.

Learning your herbs and spices

Because the rainbow of herbs and spices available to home cooks is so exciting, you may tend to overdo it. The best way to get to know herbs and spices is to cook dishes that contain only one herb or spice — learn how it interacts with different foods, watch how it intensifies with cooking, and find out whether you really like it.

For example, with rosemary, you can make a quick sauce for sautéed or grilled chicken breast by combining 3 parts chicken stock to 1 part white wine in a saucepan. Then add a generous amount of rosemary (preferably fresh), some slices of garlic, and salt and freshly ground pepper to taste. Cook down the liquid until it is reduced by three-quarters. Then strain the sauce and serve it over the chicken.

This dish gives you a pure rosemary flavor. If you like it, you can refine it by adding more or less rosemary or even by adding a complementary herb, such as thyme, tarragon, or chives.

Brawny Beef Stew

Dollar for dollar, beef stew goes a long way. Lean, boneless chuck is one of the least expensive cuts of beef, and the root vegetables (carrots and turnips) that surround it are as economical as they are healthful. Other good cuts to ask for are neck, brisket, and shank.

The following recipe serves 8 to 10 and is a perfect make-ahead meal for a small party. To reduce the yield to serve 4 or 5, use half the ingredients. But remember, stews are always better the next day, after the seasonings have a chance to permeate the meat. If you make too much, you'll have delicious leftovers.

You also can store meat stews in the freezer in tightly covered containers for up to six months.

Old-Fashioned Beef Stew

Tools: *Chef's knife, stew pot (cast iron is best), large spoon, long tongs*

Preparation time: *About 25 minutes*

Cooking time: *About 1 hour and 40 minutes*

(continued)

¹/₄ cup (50 mL) olive or vegetable oil

4 pounds (2 kg) lean, boneless chuck, cut into 2-inch (5-cm) cubes

2 cups (500 mL) peeled and coarsely chopped onions, about 2 large onions

2 tablespoons (30 mL) peeled and chopped garlic, about 6 large cloves

6 tablespoons (90 mL) flour

Salt and freshly ground pepper to taste

3 cups (750 mL) dry red wine

3 cups (750 mL) beef or chicken stock

2 tablespoons (30 mL) tomato paste

4 whole cloves

2 bay leaves

4 sprigs parsley, tied together (see following note)

4 sprigs fresh thyme, or 1 teaspoon (5 mL) dried

1 tablespoon (15 mL) minced fresh rosemary, leaves only, or 1 teaspoon (5 mL) dried and crumbled

1 pound (500 g) small purple turnips, trimmed of ends and cut into 2-inch (5-cm) pieces

6 large carrots, trimmed, scraped, and cut into 1-inch (2.5-cm) lengths

1 Heat the oil in a large stew pot over medium-high heat. Then add the beef cubes (see following What If icon). Cook, stirring and turning the meat as necessary, for 5 to 10 minutes or until evenly browned. ***Warning:*** Meat or poultry browned in hot oil or fat of any kind splatters hot grease. Use long tongs to turn the meat carefully. If the oil becomes too hot, lower the heat to medium for the remainder of the browning.

2 Add the onion and garlic and cook over medium heat, stirring occasionally for about 8 minutes. Sprinkle the flour and salt and pepper and stir to coat the meat evenly.

3 Add the wine, stock, and tomato paste and stir over high heat until the cooking liquid thickens as it comes to a boil. Add the cloves, bay leaves, parsley, thyme, rosemary, and turnips. Cover and reduce the heat to low. Simmer for 1 hour, occasionally stirring and scraping the bottom of the pot. Add the carrots and cook until meat and carrots are tender, about 20 minutes more. Remove the herb sprigs and bay leaves before serving.

Yield: *8 to 10 servings.*

Note: *Tie the sprigs of parsley and other fresh herbs together with a little kitchen twine (or a piece of unwaxed flossing string). Doing so makes removing the herb sprigs easier, and you get the benefit of parsley flavor without stringy stems.*

You can serve this stew with country bread and a tomato, red onion, and basil salad (see Chapter 10).

Before adding a dried herb, like rosemary, to a stewing pot, crush the brittle leaves with your fingers into smaller, more palatable pieces. Doing so also releases more of the herb's flavor.

If you don't have a stew pot big enough to brown the meat in one layer, cook the meat a little at a time, moving the browned pieces to a platter. Return the pieces to the pot after they are all browned.

Hanging Out at Home? Try Pot Roast

Pot roast is a good dish to make when you intend to be around the house all afternoon. The braising technique is the same as in the preceding recipe. First you brown the piece of meat well on both sides; then you braise it in its juices and the cooking liquids for about one football game, or almost 3 hours.

The best cut of beef for a pot roast is the *first-cut* brisket. Sometimes referred to as the *flat cut,* the first-cut brisket has just the right amount of fat and is neither too greasy nor too dry after it's cooked for a long time. Ask your butcher for the first cut.

Pot roast is also relatively inexpensive. Our testing determined the cost of all the ingredients in this recipe at under $20, with an individual serving costing about $2.50. This rich and satisfying dish is excellent served hot or cold with Dijon-style mustard or a horseradish sauce.

Pot Roast with Vegetables

Tools: *Large Dutch oven, chef's knife, carving board*

Preparation time: *About 20 minutes*

Cooking time: *About 3 hours*

2 tablespoons (30 mL) vegetable oil

4 pounds (2 kg) first-cut beef brisket

2 cups (30 mL) peeled and chopped onions, about 2 large onions

1 tablespoon (15 mL) peeled and chopped garlic, about 3 large cloves

1/2 cup (125 mL) dry white wine

1/2 cup (125 mL) water

1 bay leaf

1/4 teaspoon (1 mL) dried thyme

Salt and freshly ground pepper to taste

1/2 to 1 cup (125 to 250 mL) water, if necessary

4 large Idaho potatoes, peeled and cut into bite-size chunks

3 large carrots, scraped and sliced crosswise into 2-inch (5-cm) pieces

3 tablespoons (45 mL) chopped fresh parsley

1 Heat the oil in a large Dutch oven (cast iron is best) over high heat; add the brisket and brown on both sides, about 7 to 8 minutes. Allow the meat to sear to a golden brown without burning. Remove the brisket from the pot and set aside on a large plate.

(continued)

2 Reduce the heat to medium; add the onions and garlic and sauté until the onions are lightly browned, stirring frequently. (Do not let the garlic brown.)

3 Return the brisket to the pot. Add the wine, water, bay leaf, thyme, and salt and pepper. Cover, bring to a boil, reduce heat, and simmer for 2 ³/₄ to 3 hours, turning the meat several times and adding ¹/₂ to 1 cup (125 to 250 mL) water as necessary if the liquid evaporates.

4 About 10 minutes before the end of the cooking time, add the potatoes and carrots to the saucepan.

5 When the meat is so tender that you can pierce it easily with a fork, carefully remove it to a carving board; cover with foil and let it rest for 10 to 15 minutes. Continue cooking the potatoes and carrots in the covered saucepan, for about 10 to 15 minutes more, or until tender.

6 To assemble the meat and vegetable platter, slice the brisket across the grain, as shown in Figure 5-3. (If you cut *with* the grain — see the following tip — you'll shred the meat.) Arrange the slices on a serving platter.

7 Remove the cooked potatoes and carrots from the gravy and spoon them around the meat. Skim off the fat from the surface of the remaining juices, heat the juices through, and spoon over the meat and vegetables. Sprinkle with the chopped parsley. Serve the extra gravy in a sauceboat.

Yield: 6 to 8 servings.

Pot roast is delicious served with a mixed green salad and country bread.

Most meat has a *grain,* or visible layers of muscle tissue that hold it together. As Figure 5-3 shows, you should cut *across* the grain.

Leftover terminology

The term *leftover* is unfortunate in some cases. Its unsavory connotation — something you "left" like your briefcase — hardly does justice to foods that can be just as good, or better, the next day, such as stews, soups, and certain one-pot dishes.

We invite you to join our campaign to find a new term for *leftovers*. Possibilities include

✔ previously prepared

✔ tested

✔ enjoyed again

Cutting Across the Grain

Figure 5-3:
Cut across the grain to avoid shredding the meat.

Downright Regal Chicken Legs

A dinner of chicken legs may not sound like reason to get excited, but slow braising can turn them into something special. This technique makes the legs tender and succulent (it also works with tough duck legs), and the red wine sauce is packed with flavor. Chicken legs, with the thighs, are the most flavorful part of the bird, much better than breast meat. When braised, the legs loosen up and absorb some of the red wine sauce.

We were amazed to discover upon preparing this dish that the cost of all the ingredients came to about $4. Serve this dish with rice, egg noodles, or instant couscous (see Chapter 14).

Braised Chicken Legs in Red Wine

Tools: *Large sauté pan with lid, chef's knife, vegetable peeler*

Preparation time: *About 25 minutes*

Cooking time: *About 45 minutes*

4 chicken legs with thighs attached, about 2¹/₂ to 3 pounds (1.25 to 1.5 kg) total

Salt and freshly ground pepper to taste

About ¹/₄ cup (50 mL) flour

2 tablespoons (30 mL) vegetable oil

8 small white onions, peeled

¹/₂ pound (250 g) small white mushrooms, cleaned and trimmed, about 20 mushrooms (optional)

2 teaspoons (10 mL) peeled and finely chopped garlic, about 2 cloves

(continued)

4 sprigs fresh thyme, or 1 teaspoon (5 mL) dried

1 bay leaf

1¹/₂ cups (375 mL) dry red wine, preferably Burgundy style

8 baby carrots, trimmed and scraped

2 whole cloves

4 parsley sprigs

2 tablespoons (30 mL) finely chopped fresh parsley

1 Rinse the chicken legs under cold running water and pat dry. Trim the legs of all excess flaps of skin and fat. Sprinkle with salt and pepper on both sides. Coat the legs lightly with flour (see the following tip).

2 Heat the oil in a heavy pan that is large enough to hold the chicken legs in one layer. Place the legs in the pan and cook over medium-high heat until they are nicely browned on one side, about 5 minutes. Turn the chicken legs over and continue cooking about 5 minutes more or until browned. Remove the legs to a large platter.

3 Add the onions to the pan and cook about 4 to 5 minutes, turning occasionally. Add the mushrooms (if desired) and cook about 3 minutes more or until nicely browned, turning occasionally.

4 Remove the onions and mushrooms from the pan to the large platter and carefully pour off all the fat — but not down the sink! (You can pour fat into an old coffee can. After the fat cools and hardens, throw the can away.)

5 Return the chicken and vegetables to the pan over medium heat. Add the garlic, thyme, and bay leaf and cook for 1 minute, stirring. Do not brown the garlic. Add the wine, carrots, cloves, and parsley sprigs; then raise the heat and bring to a boil.

6 Cover tightly, reduce heat, and simmer for 25 to 30 minutes or until the chicken and vegetables are tender.

7 Transfer the chicken, onions, mushrooms, and carrots to a serving dish. Discard the thyme and parsley sprigs, bay leaf, and cloves. Turn up the heat to high and reduce the sauce, if necessary, for 2 to 3 minutes or until slightly thickened. Adjust the seasoning with salt and freshly ground pepper to taste. Pour the sauce over the chicken and sprinkle with the chopped parsley.

Yield: *4 servings.*

Cooking with wine

An adage goes, "If you wouldn't drink it, don't cook with it." That is really the only rule you need to remember when you cook with wine. If you see a bottle in the store labeled *cooking wine,* keep walking.

Fortified wines, such as Madeira, port, sherry, and marsala, can add a lovely touch to stews and braised dishes. All have their places in certain recipes.

Note: In an episode of *The Honeymooners,* Alice Kramden says that her husband, Ralph, has so little tolerance to alcohol that he gets tipsy eating rum cake. Although some residual alcohol may be found in rum cake, none survives in a long-cooked stew. What you get are the flavors from the wine or spirit and maybe some added body. If you want to have a wild and crazy night, you'll have to drink lots of wine along with the stew. (See *Wine For Dummies* for more information about which wines go with which foods.)

To seal in the moisture of meat, fish, or poultry before sautéeing, you *dredge,* or coat, with flour and shake off the excess. Simply drag or roll the food in flour to coat all sides.

To give the chicken dish a rich, smooth texture, stir in 2 to 3 tablespoons (30 to 45 mL) light cream after reducing the sauce and heat through. To reduce the number of calories in this dish, remove the skin from the chicken legs before cooking.

The Best Lamb You've Ever Had

Lamb and white beans are a classic combination in many of the world's cuisines. This wonderful, rustic dish uses a shoulder of lamb, which is lean and sinewy but exceptionally tasty.

Braised Lamb with White Beans

Tools: *Large saucepan, wooden spoon, chef's knife, nonstick pan, heavy stovetop casserole*

Preparation time: *About 20 minutes, plus soaking time for beans*

Cooking time: *About 2 hours*

(continued)

Beans

1 pound (500 g) dried lima beans or any small white beans

7 cups (1.75 L) water

4 large carrots, trimmed of ends and scraped

1 medium onion stuck with 2 whole cloves (see following note)

4 sprigs fresh thyme, or l teaspoon (5 mL) dried

1 bay leaf

Salt and freshly ground pepper to taste

1 Soak the beans in cold water for 8 to 10 hours, or overnight. (To shorten the soaking process, boil the beans in enough water to cover in a saucepan for 3 minutes; then let soak, covered, for 1 to 2 hours.)

2 Drain the beans, transfer them to a large saucepan, and add the 7 cups (1.75 L) water, carrots, onion with cloves, thyme, bay leaf, and salt and pepper to taste. Bring to a boil, reduce heat, and simmer for 45 minutes or until the beans are tender, skimming the surface frequently to remove any foam. As the beans cook, prepare the lamb.

Lamb

3 pounds (1.5 kg) lean shoulder of lamb, cut into 2-inch (5-cm) cubes, including the bones

1 cup (250 mL) peeled and chopped onion, about 1 large onion

1 tablespoon (15 mL) peeled and chopped garlic, about 3 cloves

28-ounce can (about 796 mL) crushed tomatoes

1 cup (250 mL) dry white wine

1 cup (250 mL) water

4 sprigs fresh thyme, or 1 teaspoon (5 mL) dried

1 bay leaf

Salt and freshly ground pepper to taste

1 Heat a nonstick pan large enough to hold the meat in one layer. Add the meat and cook, stirring, about 10 to 15 minutes or until well browned on all sides.

2 Transfer the meat to a heavy pot or stovetop casserole. Add the chopped onion and garlic. Cook and stir over medium heat for 3 minutes. Add the tomatoes, wine, 1 cup (250 mL) water, thyme, bay leaf, and salt and pepper to taste. Stir well, cover, and simmer for about 1^1/$_2$ hours, or until the lamb is tender.

3 After the lamb is cooked, drain the cooked beans, reserving 1 cup (250 mL) of the cooking liquid. Remove the thyme sprigs, bay leaf, onion with cloves, and carrots from the pot of cooked beans. Remove the cloves from the onion. Cut the onion and carrots into small cubes and add them and the beans to the lamb casserole. Stir well. Simmer for 5 minutes, stirring occasionally. If the dish seems too thick, add some of the reserved bean liquid. Remove thyme sprigs and bay leaf before serving.

(continued)

Yield: *8 servings.*

Note: *Clove adds a lovely perfume to dishes like this one. However, you must remove the clove before serving — chomping on it is like biting a nail.*

This one-dish meal needs no side dish — just good bread.

A Fish in Every Pot

This fish stew combines different compatible flavors in one pot. Like other stews, you can prepare it several hours ahead of serving time. Simply complete the recipe up to step 3. Five minutes before you want to serve the stew, add the fish and finish cooking.

Note that you add cilantro to this dish at the very last minute — that is because fresh herbs are at their most fragrant when they are raw. Cooking delicate chervil, cilantro, or parsley mutes its flavors. Moreover, herbs are more colorful when added at the last minute.

Mediterranean Seafood Stew

Tools: *Large sauté pan or skillet, chef's knife, shrimp deveiner (optional)*

Preparation time: *About 30 minutes*

Cooking time: *About 25 minutes*

3 tablespoons (45 mL) olive oil

2 large leeks, white and light green parts only, washed and cut into ¹/₂-inch (12-mm) pieces

2 teaspoons (10 mL) peeled and finely chopped garlic, about 2 large cloves

1 cup (250 mL) cored, seeded, and diced sweet red pepper, about 1 red pepper

³/₄ teaspoon (3 mL) ground cumin

¹/₂ teaspoon (2 mL) red pepper flakes

1¹/₂ cups (375 mL) cored and diced ripe plum tomatoes, about 3 tomatoes

1 cup (250 mL) dry white wine

1 cup (250 mL) water

Salt and freshly ground pepper to taste

1 pound (500 g) medium shrimp, shelled and deveined

³/₄ pound (375 g) sea scallops, cut in half

¹/₄ cup (50 mL) coarsely chopped fresh cilantro or Italian parsley

(continued)

1 Heat the oil in a large sauté pan or skillet over medium heat. Add the leeks and cook, stirring, about 4 minutes or until they wilt. Add the garlic and stir for another 2 minutes or until just golden. (Don't let the garlic get brown.)

2 Add the sweet red pepper, cumin, and red pepper flakes and cook over low heat or until the peppers are tender, about 8 minutes.

3 Add the tomatoes, wine, water, and salt and pepper to taste. Bring to a boil, reduce heat to medium, and cook for 6 to 8 minutes.

4 Add the shrimp and scallops and cook about 5 minutes more, or just until the fish is done (or until the shrimp is no longer pink and the scallops are opaque). Remove from heat, stir in the cilantro or parsley, and serve with noodles or rice.

Yield: 4 servings.

A salad and good bread are all you need with this dish.

You can make fish stew with any number of different species, such as cod, blackfish (also known as *tautog*), porgy, squid, tilefish, and weakfish, some of which are quite inexpensive. Think of the texture and flavor of different fish. In stew, you want a relatively firm-fleshed fish that does not fall apart. Sole, for example, would be too delicate. Dark-fleshed fish, like mackerel, would overpower the stew.

Solving cooking woes

What do you do if a stew or a braised dish is . . .

✔ **Flat-tasting?** Add salt and pepper. Or try a little sherry or Madeira.

✔ **Tough?** Cook it longer. Sometimes more cooking breaks down the sinew in muscular cuts of meat. You may want to remove the vegetables in the dish with a slotted spoon to prevent them from disintegrating.

✔ **Burned on the bottom?** Tell your guests that the odd smell is your son trying to prove nuclear fission. Then carefully transfer the unburned portion of the stew into a separate pot. Add water or stock to stretch it if necessary, and add sherry and a chopped onion. (The sweetness in an onion can mask many mistakes.)

✔ **Too thin?** Blend 1 tablespoon (15 mL) flour with 1 tablespoon (15 mL) water. Mix this mixture with 1 cup (250 mL) stew liquid and return to the pot with the rest of the stew. Stir well. Heat slowly until thickened.

Braising Vegetables

Braising is not only for tough cuts of meat. It also is a fine way to add flavor to certain firm vegetables, such as cabbage, artichokes, endive, rutabagas, turnips, potatoes, and kale. The principle is exactly the same as with meat.

Endive, as shown in Figure 5-4, has many uses in addition to being a salad ingredient. It is delicious gratinéed, steamed, and, in this case, baked and then braised with a bit of butter and lemon juice. For another tasty braised vegetable dish, Braised Cabbage with Apple and Caraway, turn to Chapter 15.

Braised Endive

Tools: *Dutch oven, slotted spoon*

Preparation time: *About 10 minutes*

Cooking time: *About 35 minutes*

8 heads medium-size Belgian endive	*2 tablespoons (30 mL) butter*
¹/₃ cup (75 mL) water	*Salt and freshly ground pepper to taste*
Juice of 1 lemon	*2 tablespoons (30 mL) finely chopped parsley*
¹/₂ teaspoon (2 mL) sugar	

1 Preheat the oven to 450° F (230° C).

2 Trim off the stems and any discolored leaves of the endive, leaving the heads intact. Wash the endive by plunging it into a large pot of cold water. Drain well.

3 Place the endive in a large Dutch oven. Add the water, lemon juice, sugar, butter, and salt and pepper to taste. Cover and bring to a boil on the range; then bake in the preheated oven for 20 to 30 minutes or until the endive is tender. Drain well or remove to a plate using a slotted spoon. Serve sprinkled with the chopped parsley.

Yield: *4 to 6 servings.*

Endive goes well with Grilled Flank Steak with Rosemary and Sage (see Chapter 15) or Roast Loin of Pork (see Chapter 6).

Chapter 6

Grate Possibilities: Roasting and Grilling

*H*ere's where we get to the meat of the matter, so to speak. In theory, if you had only an oven with a broiler, you could survive quite well — you might get a hankering for pasta once in a while, but it would pass. Similarly, if you lived in a sunny spot with little rain, you could probably make do with just a barbecue grill. In this chapter, we take a look at both.

Roasting

The strict definition of *roasting* is cooking in an oven in which heat emanates from the walls and air circulates slowly around.

When it comes to ease and simplicity, roasting is a valuable technique. You simply buy a big hunk of meat or a variety of vegetables, crank up the oven, and toss it in (well, almost). Whole fish are sublime when seasoned well and roasted. And root vegetables — carrots, onions, and beets, for example — become particularly sweet and succulent when you cook them in the oven.

Note this most important roasting rule: *Roasting speeds up in direct proportion to your distance from the house.* In other words, if you drive down to the 7-Eleven to buy ice cream, the roast may resemble a blow-torched walnut when you get back.

The art of roasting is 90 percent timing and 10 percent patience. And if you use a meat thermometer when roasting meats, fouling up is almost impossible. After you understand timing, you can focus on the finer points.

Seasoning a roast

Have you ever eaten a superb, charbroiled steak that lingers on the palate like an aged wine? Part of its appeal comes from being salted lightly before cooking. Salt is a flavor enhancer that brings out the best in many foods. For that reason, salting meat, fish, poultry, and vegetables before roasting is usually a good idea. However, because some people are advised to limit salt in their diets because of high blood pressure or other reasons, you should keep this consideration in mind.

To sear or not to sear?

Searing refers to the technique of exposing meat or fish to extreme heat at the outset of cooking in order to seal the surface and add flavor by browning. You often sear steaks and fish fillets by placing them in a very hot pan and then turning them all around until a crust forms on the surface.

"Searing a roast helps to caramelize the juices and sugars on the roast's surface and give it a nice, flavorful crust," says Waldy Malouf, chef of the Rainbow Room in Manhattan, New York. "Be sure to reduce the oven temperature to an even 350 or 325 degrees (Fahrenheit) after the surface of your roast has some color so that it doesn't shrink or dry out."

Unless a recipe says otherwise, it's usually best to place the roast on a rack in a roasting pan so that it doesn't touch the roaring-hot surface of the pan. Otherwise, the roast may burn because hot air cannot circulate under it, or it may get soggy from sitting in the pan juices.

Basting

Many recipes call for *basting* the roast, which means brushing or pouring pan juices over it during cooking. To baste, use a large spoon, bulb baster, or basting brush to coat the roast's surface with the pan juices, oil, or melted butter. Basting keeps the meat or vegetables moist, prevents shrinkage, and gives the crust or skin an even brown color.

Flip that roast

An oven, like the San Francisco Bay area, contains different microclimates. If the roast sits close to the oven wall, it cooks in very dry heat. If it sits on the bottom of a roasting pan instead of on a rack, it simmers in its juices. Turning the roast ensures even cooking.

As a rule of thumb, divide the cooking time by four and rotate the roast a quarter turn at each interval, letting it sit for the last interval.

Before turning a roast, remove the roasting pan carefully from the oven to the stovetop or other flat, heatproof surface. Turn meat or poultry gently.

Chill out: Resting

If you are like us, by the time a roast of any sort emerges from the oven you are so hungry that you could tear at it like a dog. Instead, go have some Cheez Whiz and crackers and let the roast sit out, covered, for 15 to 20 minutes or so (if the cut of meat is large). Even a roast chicken or duck should sit for 10 minutes out of the oven before you carve it. Sitting lets the meat *rest:* that is, to loosen up a bit and allow the internal juices to distribute more evenly.

Chef Malouf has a different technique. He says, "I like to slightly undercook the roast and then turn my home oven off and let it rest undisturbed (in the oven) about 20 minutes before carving. The roast will continue to cook, with its internal temperature increasing about 10 degrees during this time."

Roasting times and temperatures

Tables 6-1 through 6-4 give approximate cooking times and temperatures for various roasts and weights. Remember to remove a roast when its internal temperature is 5 to 10 degrees *less* than final internal temperature, and then let it rest for 15 to 20 minutes. During the resting time, the roast cooks 5 to 10 degrees more. None of this is exact science, though; you have to use a meat thermometer to get the results you like. See Figure 6-1 for illustrated instructions for using a meat thermometer.

Note: When inserting a meat thermometer in a roast, do not let the metal touch the bone — the bone is hotter than the meat and registers a falsely higher temperature.

Where to put a Dial (or Oven-proof) Meat Thermometer

Figure 6-1:
How to insert a meat thermometer in various roasts.

Boneless Roast

Insert to core

Poultry

Insert inside of the thigh

Meat with bone

Insert into the thickest part of the meat

✳ For an accurate reading, do NOT touch the bone, fat, or bottom of the pan with the thermometer

Table 6-1			Beef Roasting Chart	
Beef Roast	*Oven Temperature (Preheated ° F)*	*Weight*	*Approximate Total Cooking Time*	*Remove from Oven at This Meat Temperature (° F)*
Boneless rib-eye roast (small end)	350°	3 to 4 pounds	Medium rare: $1^1/_2$ to $1^3/_4$ hours	135°
			Medium: $1^3/_4$ to 2 hours	150°
		4 to 6 pounds	Medium rare: $1^3/_4$ to 2 hours	135°
			Medium: 2 to $2^1/_2$ hours	150°
		6 to 8 pounds	Medium rare: 2 to $2^1/_4$ hours	135°
			Medium: $2^1/_2$ to $2^3/_4$ hours	150°
Bone-in rib roast (chine bone removed)	350°	4 to 6 pounds (2 ribs)	Medium rare: $1^3/_4$ to $2^1/_4$ hours	135°
			Medium: $2^1/_4$ to $2^3/_4$ hours	150°
		6 to 8 pounds (2 to 4 ribs)	Medium rare: $2^1/_4$ to $2^1/_2$ hours	135°
			Medium: $2^3/_4$ to 3 hours	150°
		8 to 10 pounds (4 to 5 ribs)	Medium rare: $2^1/_2$ to 3 hours	135°
			Medium: 3 to $3^1/_2$ hours	150°
Round tip roast (sirloin tip)	325°	3 to 4 pounds	Medium rare: $1^3/_4$ to 2 hours	140°
			Medium: $2^1/_4$ to $2^1/_2$ hours	155°

Beef Roast	Oven Temperature (Preheated ° F)	Weight	Approximate Total Cooking Time	Remove from Oven at This Meat Temperature (° F)
Round tip roast (sirloin tip)	325°	4 to 6 pounds	Medium rare: 2 to 2¹/₂ hours	140°
			Medium: 2¹/₂ to 3 hours	155°
		6 to 8 pounds	Medium rare: 2¹/₂ to 3 hours	140°
			Medium: 3 to 3¹/₂ hours	155°
Tenderloin roast	425°	2 to 3 pounds	Medium rare: 35 to 40 minutes	135°
			Medium: 45 to 50 minutes	150°
		4 to 5 pounds	Medium rare: 50 to 60 minutes	135°
			Medium: 60 to 70 minutes	150°

Medium rare doneness: 145° F final meat temperature after 10 to 15 minutes standing time
Medium doneness: 160° F final meat temperature after 10 to 15 minutes standing time
Source: National Cattlemen's Beef Association

Table 6-2	Poultry Roasting Chart		
Bird	**Weight**	**Preheated Oven Temperature (° F)**	**Cooking Time**
Chicken, broiler/fryer (unstuffed)	2¹/₂ to 4¹/₄ pounds	350°	1¹/₄ to 1¹/₂ hours
Chicken, roaster (unstuffed)	5 to 7 pounds	350°	2 to 2¹/₄ hours
Whole turkey (thawed and unstuffed)	8 to 12 pounds	325°	3 to 3¹/₂ hours
	12 to 16 pounds	325°	3¹/₂ to 4 hours
	16 to 20 pounds	325°	4 to 4¹/₂ hours
	20 to 24 pounds	325°	4¹/₂ to 5 hours
Duck (whole, unstuffed)	4 to 5¹/₂ pounds	325°	2¹/₂ to 3 hours

Allow 15 to 30 minutes additional cooking time if stuffed. Internal temperature for stuffing should be 165° F. Internal temperature for meat should be minimum 180° F in the thigh.
Source: National Broiler Council

Table 6-3	Pork Roasting Chart		
Cut	*Thickness/Weight*	*Final Internal Temperature (° F)*	*Cooking Time*
Loin roast (bone-in)	3 to 5 pounds	160°	20 minutes per pound
Boneless pork roast	2 to 4 pounds	160°	20 minutes per pound
Tenderloin (roast at 425° to 450°)	1/2 to 1 1/2 pounds	160°	20 to 30 minutes
Crown roast	6 to 10 pounds	160°	20 minutes per pound
Boneless loin chops	1 inch thich	160°	12 to 16 minutes
Ribs		Tender	1 1/2 to 2 hours

Roast in a shallow pan, uncovered, at 350° F.
Source: National Pork Producers Council

Table 6-4	Lamb Roasting Chart		
Roast	*Weight*	*Final Internal Temperature (° F)*	*Approx. Cooking Time Per Pound*
Leg (bone-in)	5 to 7 pounds	Medium rare: 145° to 150°	15 minutes
		Medium: 155° to 160°	20 minutes
Boneless (rolled and tied)	4 to 7 pounds	Medium rare: 145° to 150°	20 minutes
		Medium: 155° to 160°	25 minutes
Sirloin roast (boneless)	3 to 5 pounds	Medium rare: 145° to 150°	25 minutes
		Medium: 155° to 160°	30 minutes
Top round roast	1 1/4 to 1 3/4 pounds	Medium rare: 145° to 150°	45 minutes total
		Medium: 155 ° to 160°	55 minutes total

Preheat oven to 325° F and remove from oven about 10° below desired temperature.
Allow 1/4 to 1/3 pound of boneless lamb per serving and 1/3 to 1/2 pound of bone-in lamb per serving.
Source: American Lamb Council

Every oven is different, no matter how much or how little you spend for it. Some ovens are off by as much as 50 degrees, which can be like trying to make gourmet coffee with tap water. Baking can be a disaster without precision. Investing in an oven thermometer to know exactly how your oven works is worthwhile. This way, if you annihilate a dish, you can blame it on the blasted oven.

Don't keep opening the oven door to see whether the roast is done. Your kitchen will get hot, and the meat or vegetables will get cold.

Roasting poultry

Contrary to what beginning cooks may think, roasting a chicken is not just a matter of tossing it in the oven and mixing a gin and tonic. Roasted chicken is a classic American meal, and attention to fine details yields a memorable result.

The most common mistake home cooks make when roasting chicken is using an insufficiently hot oven. The following recipe calls for a 425° F (220° C) oven, which yields a brittle, golden-brown skin.

Again, use a meat thermometer! (When you feel feverish, which would you prefer: a doctor who places a hand on your forehead or one who uses a thermometer?) Whatever the type of thermometer you use, instant-read or ovenproof (see Chapter 2 for information about the different types), insert it deep into the flesh between the bird's thigh and breast. If you don't have a thermometer, insert a knife into the thick part of the thigh; if the juices run clear, the bird is thoroughly cooked. If they run pink, let the meat cook for about another 15 minutes before testing for doneness again. Then go buy a thermometer so that you have one next time!

Before you roast a chicken, remove the packaged giblets (the neck, heart, gizzard, and liver) inside the cavity and save them. Rinse the bird thoroughly, inside and out, under cold running water. Then pat the skin dry with paper towels and season. The following recipe uses the giblets to make a delicious pan gravy.

If you want your chicken to hold its shape perfectly while roasting, you can truss it. You can do without this step if you're in a hurry, but we'll explain the technique anyway. See Figures 6-2 and 6-3 for illustrated instructions.

Trussing a Chicken

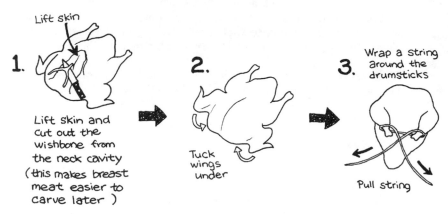

1. Lift skin

Lift skin and cut out the wishbone from the neck cavity (this makes breast meat easier to carve later)

2. Tuck wings under

3. Wrap a string around the drumsticks

Pull string

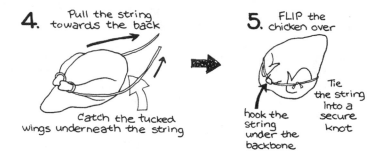

4. Pull the string towards the back

Catch the tucked wings underneath the string

5. FLIP the chicken over

hook the string under the backbone

Tie the string into a secure knot

Figure 6-2: Trussing helps chicken keep its shape.

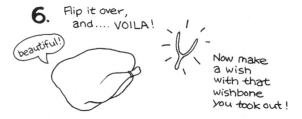

6. Flip it over, and.... VOILA!

beautiful!

Now make a wish with that wishbone you took out !

Even Quicker... Truss Me!

Figure 6-3: How to truss a chicken the fast way.

1. Tuck wings under, as in step 2, "Trussing a Chicken"

2. Cross drumsticks and tie together

3. Tie another string around the bird at its wings

Eat your chicken liver

A cardinal rule of many chefs (who hate to throw out food of any kind) is to never discard the giblets. You can add giblets to homemade soup or to canned stock to enrich its flavor.

Sautéed in a little butter, chicken liver is a nutritious, tasty treat. Be sure to sauté the liver gently but thoroughly until its edges are brown and not a trace of pink remains. We know a woman who saves and freezes chicken livers until the winter holidays, when she defrosts them to make an exquisite chicken liver pâté flavored with apples, brandy, and spices.

Roasted Chicken

Tools: *Chef's knife, large metal roasting pan, roasting rack, meat thermometer, tongs or large fork*

Preparation time: *About 15 minutes (or 20 if trussing)*

Roasting time: *About 1 hour and 15 minutes, plus 15 minutes resting time*

1 chicken, 4 to 4^1/$_2$ pounds (2 to 2.5 kg), with giblets

Salt and freshly ground pepper to taste

1 lemon, pricked several times with a fork

2 sprigs fresh thyme, or ^{1}/$_2$ teaspoon (2 mL) dried

1 clove garlic, peeled

2 tablespoons (30 mL) olive oil

1 medium onion, peeled and quartered

2 tablespoons (30 mL) butter

^{1}/$_2$ cup (125 mL) chicken stock

^{1}/$_2$ cup (125 mL) water, or more as necessary

1 Preheat the oven to 425° F (220° C). Remove the giblets from the chicken's cavity; rinse and reserve. Rinse the chicken under cold running water, inside and out, and pat dry with paper towels.

2 Sprinkle the chicken inside and out with salt and pepper. Insert the lemon, thyme, and garlic into the cavity of the chicken. Rub the outside of the chicken all over with olive oil.

3 Truss the chicken with string, if desired. (See Figures 6-2 and 6-3 for instructions.)

4 Place the chicken on its side on a rack in a shallow metal roasting pan. Scatter the neck, gizzard, liver, and onions on the bottom of the pan.

5 Place the chicken in the oven and roast for 25 minutes. Using large forks or tongs, gently turn the chicken onto its other side, being careful not to pierce the skin. Roast for another 25 minutes, basting once with the pan juices.

(continued)

6 Carefully remove the roasting pan from the oven and close the oven door. Using a large spoon, skim any surface fat from the roasting pan juices. Turn the chicken on its back. Add the butter, chicken stock, and ½ cup (125 mL) water to the pan. Roast for another 25 minutes, basting once with pan juices.

When cooked, the chicken should be golden brown all over, and no red juice should flow when you pierce the joint between the thigh and leg with a fork. A meat thermometer in the thigh should read 180° F (80° C) (refer to Figure 6-1) before you remove the bird from the oven. Lift up the chicken to let the cavity juices flow into the pan. Transfer to a carving board or serving platter and let rest for 10 to 15 minutes.

7 Meanwhile, place the roasting pan on top of the stove. Remove and discard any very burnt pieces of giblets or onion. Add water or broth if necessary to make about 1 cup liquid. Bring to a boil and reduce for 1 to 2 minutes (letting the sauce evaporate and condense as it cooks over high heat), stirring and scraping the bottom of the pan. If desired, add fresh parsley, rosemary, tarragon, or other fresh herbs to taste. Turn off the heat when the sauce is reduced to about ¾ cup (175 mL).

8 Untruss the chicken (if necessary), cutting the string with a sharp knife or kitchen shears. Remove and discard the lemon and thyme sprigs.

9 Carve the chicken into serving pieces, as shown in Figure 6-4, and serve with the hot pan juices.

Yield: *4 servings.*

Serve this dish with any of the following side dishes: White Beans with Tomato and Thyme, Baby Carrots with Cumin Butter, Couscous with Yellow Squash, Homestyle Kale (all in Chapter 14), or Potatoes Layered in Cream and Cheese (see Chapter 13).

Now that you know how to roast a chicken, you should have no problem tackling a duck. Roasting a duck is about the same as roasting a chicken, but keep in mind that duck is much fattier than chicken and has a lower percentage of meat. But the flavor is richer and more distinctive in many ways. Duck goes beautifully with all sorts of fruit sauces or even a slathering of good jelly. For that reason, duck is a nice special occasion or holiday dish. Serve with wild rice, yams, mashed potatoes (see Chapter 3), or roasted winter vegetables (later in this chapter).

Jean-Jacques Rachou, esteemed chef of La Côte Basque in New York City, has an effective technique for *rendering,* or melting away, much of the fat from a duck. Before preparing it for cooking, he sears the duck in a hot pan for about 2 minutes, turning it all around. This technique melts away much of its excess fat and slightly browns the skin. Chef Rachou then roasts the duck at 500° F (260° C).

Carving a Chicken

1. Place the chicken, breast side up, on a carving board

Remove the leg by pulling it away from the body and cutting through the ball joint

2.

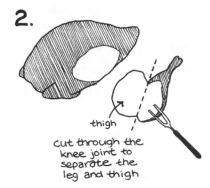

thigh

Cut through the knee joint to separate the leg and thigh

3.

Remove the wing, cutting as close to the breast as possible, through the joint that attaches it to the body. (cut off the wing tips, if desired)

4.

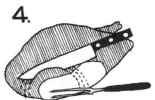

Carve the breast meat parallel to the ribs, slicing towards the top of the breast. Keep the slices as thin as possible.

(Now get someone else to carve the other side, exactly the same way.)

Figure 6-4: How to carve a chicken.

"Duck is better if you cook it hot and fast because you get a nice skin without making it dry," Rachou says.

The rich, moist meat of duck's sweet skin goes particularly well with sweet sauces — hence the famous duck à l'orange. In the following recipe, the bird is glazed with honey while cooking, giving it a lovely sweet skin. Because ducks don't have as much meat as chicken, we cook two to feed four people.

Roasted Duck with Honey Glaze

Tools: *Chef's knife, large skillet, meat thermometer, large roasting pan, roasting rack, basting brush, small saucepan, carving board, sieve*

Preparation time: *About 25 minutes*

Roasting time: *About 1 hour and 25 minutes*

Two 5^1/$_2$-pound (2.75 kg) ducks, trussed if desired

Salt and freshly ground pepper to taste

2 tablespoons (30 mL) vegetable oil

2 medium onions, peeled and coarsely sliced, about 2 cups (500 mL)

3 medium carrots, trimmed, scraped, and coarsely sliced, about 1^1/$_2$ cups (375 mL)

3 large stalks celery, coarsely chopped, about 1^1/$_2$ cups (375 mL)

2 sprigs fresh thyme, or 1 tablespoon (15 mL) dried

^{1}/$_4$ cup (50 mL) honey

1^1/$_2$ cups (375 mL) red wine

1 tablespoon (15 mL) butter

1 Preheat the oven to 450° F (230° C).

2 Place a large skillet or fry pan over high heat. Sear the ducks in the hot pan, one at a time, all around (about 8 minutes per duck). Place them on a rack in a shallow roasting pan large enough to hold both ducks (or use two small roasting pans).

3 Generously salt and pepper the duck cavities and skin. Brush with oil and arrange the ducks breast side down. Roast in the preheated oven for 15 minutes. Remove the pan from the oven. Place the ducks on a platter and carefully pour off and discard any fat in the pan. (Drain the fat into an empty tin can. Do not pour fat down the sink — it can clog the drain.)

4 Return the ducks to the roasting pan breast side up and roast for 30 minutes more. Remove them from the oven and again pour off any fat in the pan in the manner described in step 3.

5 Scatter the onions, carrot, celery, and thyme around the ducks. Increase the oven temperature to 500° F (260° C). Return the ducks to the oven and cook 15 minutes more. Using a basting brush, brush the duck breasts and legs with honey. Cook for 15 minutes or until done, brushing on more honey from time to time. (To test for doneness, make an incision at the joint where the leg meets the thigh. If the juices run clear, the duck is done. Internal temperature should register 180° F/82° C on a meat thermometer.)

(continued)

6 Remove the ducks from the oven, place them on a platter, and cover with aluminum foil to keep them warm. Strain the roasting pan juices and vegetables over a saucepan. Discard the vegetables. Skim off any fat from the surface of the liquid. Add the wine and bring to a boil, stirring occasionally. Reduce the sauce (let some liquid evaporate) by about one-quarter volume. Add salt and pepper to taste. Swirl in the butter and set sauce aside until serving time.

7 To serve, carve the breast meat and legs from the ducks, as Figure 6-5 illustrates. In the center of four dinner plates, place a slice of breast meat and a leg. (Reserve the rest of the duck for stocks, soups, or other uses. See Chapters 3 and 7 for stock recipes.) Pour the sauce evenly over the meat.

Yield: 4 servings.

Serve with Basic Wild Rice or Risotto (see Chapter 3) and Braised Endive (see Chapter 5).

 This duck also goes well with any kind of root vegetable, either sliced or pureed. Turnip puree, which has a faintly tart flavor, contrasts nicely with the honeyed duck. To make that, you simply boil trimmed turnips in lightly salted water until tender and then place them in a food processor with cream or milk, salt and pepper, and butter. Then let it rip. Add more seasonings and/or milk until you get the desired texture and flavor.

 If you are cooking a duck or other fatty cut of meat and find that your kitchen has more smoke than the stairwell in *Towering Inferno,* pour off any grease that has accumulated in the roasting pan. If you have oven vents, they should be on. You also might take this time to drop in on a neighbor for a leisurely chat.

The techniques we discuss for chicken and duck work with other birds as well, such as Cornish hens, pheasant, and quail. If the bird is lean, follow the chicken technique. If it is rich and fatty, like duck, follow the duck technique.

Carving a Duck

1. Remove trussing.

Figure 6-5: How to carve a duck.

Cut through the joints that attach the leg to the body on both sides

2. Cut on both sides of the breast bone

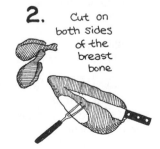

3. Carve the breast meat into diagonal slices

Impressing the clan at Thanksgiving

If you can grapple successfully with roasted chicken and roasted duck, you're definitely up for the heavyweight division — Big Tom Turkey. The roasting technique is essentially identical; just remember that turkey has a tendency to get dry easily, so you must baste often. All you need for a full holiday feast is this tasty turkey and enough side dishes to feed the army you invited over.

Thanksgiving Roasted Turkey

Tools: *Chef's knife, large roasting pan*

Preparation time: *20 minutes*

Cooking time: *3 hours and 15 minutes*

12- to 13-pound (about 6 kg) turkey with neck

1 onion, about ¹/₂ pound (500 g), peeled and cut into eighths

1 tablespoon (15 mL) peeled and finely minced garlic, about 3 large cloves

¹/₄ pound (250 g) carrots, coarsely chopped, about 4 to 5 medium carrots

Salt and pepper to taste

3 tablespoons (45 mL) corn, peanut, or vegetable oil

3 cups (750 mL) rich turkey or chicken broth

¹/₄ cup (50 mL) peeled and finely chopped onion

1 Preheat the oven to 450° F (230° C).

2 Cut off and discard the wing tips of the turkey.

3 Rinse the turkey cavity well and pat dry. Stuff the cavity of the turkey with the onion pieces, garlic, carrot, and salt and pepper to taste. Sprinkle the outside of the turkey with salt and pepper and rub the turkey all over with 2 tablespoons (30 mL) of the oil.

4 Rub the bottom of a large roasting pan with the remaining 1 tablespoon (15 mL) oil.

5 Place the turkey on one side in the roasting pan. Place in the oven and roast for about 40 minutes. Turn the turkey onto its opposite side. Return it to the oven and roast for another 45 minutes, basting often.

6 When a meat thermometer registers 180° F in the thigh, remove the turkey and set it aside briefly. Pour off and discard the fat from the pan.

7 Return the turkey to the pan, breast-side up, and return to the oven. Pour 2 cups (500 mL) of the broth around the turkey. Bake for about 30 minutes, turning the pan laterally so that the turkey cooks evenly. Continue baking, basting occasionally, for about 1 hour and 15 minutes. Remove the turkey from the pan and cover it loosely with aluminum foil.

(continued)

8 Scoop out the vegetables from the cavity of the turkey and add them to the liquid in the roasting pan. Add the remaining 1 cup (250 mL) of broth and the chopped onions, bring to a boil, and then remove from the heat. Strain the sauce and season well.

Yield: *12 to 16 servings.*

For a twist on tradition, serve this turkey with Roasted Winter Vegetables (later in this chapter) or Homestyle Kale (see Chapter 14). And don't forget that old favorite, Mashed Potatoes (see Chapter 3). Open a can of cranberry sauce and you're ready to go!

Roasting your veggies

Roasting works well for vegetables, too, and it saves work because roasting eliminates pots and pans to clean. Sometimes, as in the following recipe, you parboil (partially boil) potatoes, carrots, squash, and other "hard" vegetables on top of the stove before roasting them crisp. Parboiling simply cuts down the roasting time.

Roasted Winter Vegetables

Tools: *Chef's knife, saucepan, colander, shallow baking dish*

Preparation time: *About 15 minutes*

Roasting time: *About 30 minutes*

4 medium baking potatoes, peeled

2 medium onions, peeled

3 large carrots, scraped and trimmed

1 tablespoon (15 mL) olive oil

2 tablespoons (30 mL) chopped fresh tarragon, or ¹/₂ teaspoon (2 mL) dried

Salt and freshly ground pepper to taste

2 tablespoons (30 mL) butter, cut into 4 to 5 pieces

1 Preheat the oven to 375° F (190° C).

2 Quarter the potatoes and onions, cutting any very large quarters in half. Cut carrots in half lengthwise and then into 2-inch-long (5-cm) pieces.

3 Place potatoes, carrots, and onions in a medium saucepan with cold water to just cover. Cover the pan and bring to a boil over high heat. Reduce heat and simmer for 1 minute; drain immediately and thoroughly in a colander.

(continued)

4 Place the vegetables in a shallow baking dish. Add the olive oil, tarragon, and salt and pepper. Mix well to coat. Dot with butter and roast for 15 minutes, basting and turning once. Raise oven temperature to 450° F (230° C) and roast 15 minutes more or until potatoes are tender and lightly browned, basting and turning once.

Yield: *4 servings.*

These sweet, browned vegetables enhance all kinds of dishes, including Roasted Duck with Honey Glaze (earlier in this chapter) and Grilled Flank Steak with Rosemary and Sage (see Chapter 15).

The Big Guns: Beef, pork, and lamb

Americans have two immutable love affairs: automobiles and meat. And little the government says about them seems to change that.

In the past decade, the American pork industry has made great strides in breeding leaner animals without sacrificing tenderness. What's more, pork remains a relative bargain. You can assemble this uncomplicated dish in about half an hour and then pop it in the oven.

Roast Loin of Pork

Tools: *Chef's knife, vegetable peeler, large roasting pan, roasting rack, meat thermometer*

Preparation time: *About 30 minutes*

Roasting time: *About 1 hour and 20 minutes, plus 15 minutes resting time*

Center-cut, boneless loin of pork, 2¹/₂ to 3 pounds (1.25 to 1.5 kg)

3 tablespoons (45 mL) olive oil

Salt and freshly ground pepper to taste

2 tablespoons (30 mL) chopped fresh thyme, or 1 teaspoon (5 mL) dried

8 medium red potatoes, peeled and cut in half

3 medium onions, peeled and quartered

3 cloves garlic, peeled

1 bay leaf

¹/₂ cup (125 mL) water

¹/₄ cup (60 mL) chopped fresh parsley

1 Preheat the oven to 400° F (200° C).

2 Place the pork on a rack in a large roasting pan and brush or rub the meat with the oil. Season well with salt and pepper and thyme. Roast for 20 minutes.

(continued)

3 Gently turn the roast. Add the potatoes, onions, garlic, and bay leaf to the bottom of the pan. Using a spoon, coat the vegetables in the cooking juices. Roast for 15 minutes or until meat is browned.

4 Add ¹/₂ cup (125 mL) water and cover the pan with aluminum foil. Reduce the heat to 350° F (180° C) and roast for 40 to 45 minutes or until a meat thermometer registers 155 to 160° F (68 to 71° C).

5 Remove the meat from the oven and let it rest for 15 to 20 minutes. Slice the roast in the pan. Present the meat on a platter surrounded by the potatoes and onions. Using a large spoon, skim the fat from the pan juices. Pour the juices over everything and sprinkle with chopped parsley.

Yield: 4 to 6 servings.

Serve this hearty dish with wintery vegetables like Homestyle Kale (see Chapter 14) or Braised Cabbage with Apple and Caraway (see Chapter 15).

The best butchers are also knowledgeable cooks. They can offer recipes and tips and prepare your roast so that it is "oven ready." An oven-ready roast is trimmed of excess fat and sometimes tied with butcher's string to make it as uniform as possible for even cooking. For example, a leg of lamb should have its fat and shank bone removed. The skin and rind of a smoked ham are trimmed away, leaving just a thin layer of fat that you can score (to make a diamond pattern on the meat's surface) for a pretty effect.

Following is a basic recipe for leg of lamb. Feel free to add root vegetables such as carrots, onions, and potatoes to the pan during the last hour of cooking.

Pork paranoia

Cooks used to believe that if you ate pork cooked under 185° F (85° C), you could contract *trichinosis.* The average person didn't know what that was — or how many days of school kids could miss because of it — but it sure sounded unpleasant. Thus for years, everyone ate over-cooked pork. About a decade ago, scientists discovered that trichinae are killed at 135° F (57° C). Cooking pork to 160° F (70° C) is considered plenty safe and yields a much juicier result.

Glazed Leg of Lamb with Pan Gravy and Red Currant Glaze

Tools: Paring knife, roasting pan, roasting rack, basting brush, meat thermometer

Preparation time: About 15 minutes

Roasting time: About 1 hour and 40 minutes, plus 20 minutes resting time

One 6- to 7-pound (3 to 3.5 kg) leg of lamb, well trimmed and ready for roasting

3 cloves garlic, peeled and sliced thinly

1 tablespoon (15 mL) vegetable oil

$^1/_2$ teaspoon (2 mL) ground ginger

Salt and freshly ground pepper to taste

Red Currant Glaze (see following recipe)

1 Preheat the oven to 425° F (220° C).

2 With a paring knife, make small incisions along the leg and then insert the garlic slivers.

3 Rub the lamb with the olive oil and place it on a rack in a shallow roasting pan, fat side up. Sprinkle the meat with the ginger and salt and pepper.

4 Roast the lamb for 20 minutes; reduce heat to 350° F (180° C) and roast for about 1 hour and 20 minutes or until a meat thermometer registers 145° F (63° C) in the thickest part of the leg for medium rare or 155° F (68° C) for medium. (See the What If icon following this recipe for more information.) As the lamb roasts, make the Red Currant Glaze.

5 During the last 30 minutes of roasting, brush the top and sides of the lamb every 10 minutes with Red Currant Glaze and pan juices. (Start brushing when meat thermometer in lamb registers about 115° F/46° C.)

6 Remove from the oven and let rest for 20 minutes. Carve (see Figure 6-6) and serve with some natural pan juices spooned over the top of the slices. Serve with Roasted Winter Vegetables (earlier in this chapter) and a tossed green salad (see Chapter 10).

Yield: Serves 8 to 10.

Red Currant Glaze

Tools: Small saucepan, basting brush

Preparation time: About 10 minutes

Cooking time: About 1 minute

$^1/_4$ cup (50 mL) seedless red currant jelly

Juice and grated peel of $^1/_2$ lemon

$1^1/_2$ teaspoons (7 mL) Dijon-style mustard

Salt and freshly ground pepper to taste

Combine all ingredients in a small saucepan and heat until jelly is melted. Use as a basting sauce for a leg of lamb, brushing every 10 minutes during the last 30 minutes of roasting.

(continued)

Carving a Leg of Lamb

1.

Cut out a narrow wedge of meat

2.
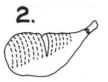
Carve the meat from either side of the wedge, down to the bone.

3.

Slice through cuts to form pieces

4.

Turn the leg over. Trim off the fat and carve off slices parallel to the bone

Figure 6-6:
The proper technique for carving a leg of lamb.

Yield: *About ¹/₄ cup (50 mL).*

Leg of lamb is best with a sweetish side dish, such as Grilled Peppers (later in this chapter), or a rich dish like Creamed Spinach (see Chapter 7).

If you enjoy your lamb cooked medium to well, just roast it a little longer until the internal temperature reaches 155° F (68° C) or more. But you may not need to. A roasted leg of lamb offers meat of varying degrees of doneness. The meat at the thin, shank end, very close to the bone, is browned and well done, and the meat at the thicker end ideally is quite pink and medium rare. Use the drier meats for hash or to train your dog to separate the sports section of the newspaper and bring it to you.

If you're lucky, a whole leg of lamb will leave you with delicious leftovers. You can make cold lamb sandwiches, Shepherd's Pie (see Chapter 12), or Lamb Barley Soup (see Chapter 9).

The following extravagant dish, although on the pricey side, is fast, simple and always delicious — a real last-minute party saver. Serve it with simple dishes like garlic-flavored mashed potatoes and fresh-steamed asparagus (see Chapter 3).

Roasted Fillet of Beef

Tools: *Roasting rack, roasting pan, meat thermometer*

Preparation time: *About 10 minutes*

Roasting time: *About 45 minutes, plus 10 minutes resting time*

1 beef tenderloin roast, oven-ready from the butcher, about 4 pounds (2 kg)

Salt and freshly ground pepper to taste

2 tablespoons (30 mL) vegetable oil

1 Preheat the oven to 425° F (220° C).

2 Sprinkle the fillet of beef with salt and pepper to taste.

3 Place the meat on a rack in a heavy roasting pan and brush or rub it with oil. Roast for about 45 minutes for medium rare or until desired doneness. A meat thermometer should read 135° F (57° C) to 140° F (60° C) for medium rare and 150° F (67° C) to 155° F (68° C) for medium. In the middle of roasting, invert the meat and baste once with the pan juices.

4 Transfer to a carving board, cover with aluminum foil, and let stand for 10 minutes before carving.

5 Carve the fillet into approximately ¹/₂-inch-thick (12-mm) slices and serve immediately, perhaps topped with a pat of herb butter. (See Chapter 7.)

Yield: *6 to 8 servings.*

You can serve filet mignon with almost anything, from a simple avocado and tomato salad to Couscous with Yellow Squash (see Chapter 14).

You overcooked the roast beef

Unfortunately, ovens do not have reverse gears. But you can salvage overcooked roast beef in many tasty ways. You can always make roast beef hash or beef croquettes made with onions, beef broth, bread crumbs, and seasonings. Beef pot pie. Various soups. Beef Stroganoff. Any recipe that calls for liquid or a cream-based sauce is good, too.

Coals and Coils: Grilling and Broiling

The beauty of cooking is that a single food can be exposed to various cooking techniques and take on different characteristics. This is most dramatically seen in charcoal grilling and oven broiling, which impart very different flavors to foods than roasting does.

Since time immemorial, men have been drawn to open fire, namely the barbecue. Even in macho countries like Spain, where many men would no sooner enter their home kitchens than don a pair of leotards at high noon, they get all giddy and puffed up over their grilling responsibilities.

Here are a few axioms of outdoor grilling:

- The fire is always at its peak 15 minutes after you finish cooking the food.
- If you overhear the cook say, "No problem, I'll just dust it off," it's time to visit the salad bowl.
- The chances of getting good food at a home barbecue is in inverse proportion to the silliness of the chef's apron. If the apron is plain and solid in color, you have reason for hope; if it says, "Who Needs Mom?" or sports hot dogs with legs and says, "Dog Catcher," hit the onion dip fast.
- Barbecues benefit from the "Hot dogs taste better at the ball park" syndrome. That is, ambiance makes everything taste better.

Grilling today has become extraordinarily hip and theatrical, as anyone who has been to a California trattoria or American bistro can attest. Whereas people used to confine grilling to hot dogs, hamburgers, and steaks, today chefs consider anything that can be held down without falling through the grates suitable for charcoal cooking — tiny quails, leeks, fennel bulbs, radicchio, lobsters, clams, mussels, and wild mushrooms, to name a few. In Italy, they even grill pasta — now that you have to see!

Wolfgang Puck, owner and chef of Spago, Los Angeles, and a preeminent authority on the subject of grilling, says, "Just about anything can be grilled, and it's probably a more healthy way to cook because the food isn't swimming in oil. But it doesn't have to be steak or hamburgers. It can be a simple grilled olive bread, drizzled with oil, or roasted vegetables — even pieces of corn bread can be toasted on the grill. Americans think of grilling as BBQ or spicy, southwestern foods — but you can grill even the most refined piece of fish for wonderful flavor."

Whatever you grill, the cardinal principles are the same.

If you can grill, you can broil

Strictly speaking, the terms *grilling* and *broiling* are interchangeable. In grilling, which is done on a barbecue grill, the heat source is below; in oven broiling, it's above. Because both methods involve intense heat, they are best reserved for relatively thin pieces of meat, poultry, or vegetables — thick cuts of meat can burn on the outside before cooking sufficiently in the middle. The advantage of grilling or broiling is that the surface of the food being cooked, especially meat, turns dark brown and develops a characteristic "charcoal" flavor.

You do most broiling about 4 inches (10 cm) from the heat source. It is always best to put the food, whatever it is, on a broiling pan, which has a grated top that allows juices to fall into a pan below. And watch out for flare-ups, either in the oven or on the grill. Flare-ups not only pose a fire danger, but they also can burn meat and give it an acrid flavor. Keep a spray bottle with water in it nearby to douse grilling flare-ups, and keep a box of baking soda or salt handy in the kitchen for broiler flare-ups.

When grilling over either charcoal or gas, the goal is to sear the food all over. Then cook it, turning occasionally so that it cooks evenly, until done. You can use a meat thermometer or simply cut into the meat to see whether it is done: Poultry and game, when pierced in the thigh, should have clear (not pink) juices. Beef is best judged visually, but a meat thermometer is better for pork and lamb. As with a roast, let grilled meat rest for a few minutes before carving.

The barbecue recipes in this chapter work for broiling as well. Because you cannot see food that is broiling as readily as food on a grill, check it more often until you get used to the timing. Just watch and vary your cooking times because broiler heat is slightly more intense and the food generally cooks more quickly.

Gas versus charcoal

About 80 percent of all American households do some kind of grilling at home or on vacation, whether it is with a $12 hibachi or a $500 "grilling unit" that is roughly the size of a Fiat and sports everything from gas burners (for sauce-making and so on) and cutting boards to rotisseries and satellite TV (just kidding). The following sections explore the specifics of gas and charcoal grills.

Charcoal grills

The key to successful charcoal barbecuing is the same as for stovetop cooking: a powerful, even source of heat. Probably the most common failing of amateur chefs is trying to work with a charcoal fire that is too cool. If you're using charcoal, load the grill nearly to capacity and let the coals turn 75 percent white before cooking. A weak fire fails to sear food; the result is a steak that is grayish-brown rather than cross-hatched with black streaks.

Shopping for a grill

When shopping for a grill, think of your realistic needs. Will you be grilling often, and for how many? Can you do with a relatively inexpensive unit, or do you want the luxury of a big gas-sucking Cadillac model? Starting out with a modest charcoal unit before moving up may be wise. If all you want to do is grill small pieces of meat or vegetables without a smoky effect, a little hibachi will do; however, gas units offer conveniences such as heat controls, instant lighting, and minimal waiting.

Weber-Stephen, Sunbeam, Char-Broil, Thermos, Ducane, and Fiesta are major manufacturers of charcoal and gas grills. Charcoal grills range in price from $60 to $135 or more. Gas grills can fetch $1,000 and more for elite, top-of-the-line cooking systems. The most popular gas grills range from about $199 to $399.

Before you choose a gas or charcoal grill, you should know that there is a bit of a controversy in the grilling world about what imparts that delicious "barbecue" flavor to food. One camp contends that it is not the coals or wood that flavor the food, but rather the flare-ups that occur when fat drips from the meat into the fire. Of course, if you do not control the flare-ups, the meat will taste burned. But a little bit of flaring up, they say, is essential.

The contesting group says that, no, the charcoal or wood imparts the flavor. So what can the consumer do? Experiment yourself. If you have a gas grill that operates with lava stones (molded pieces of lava that get very hot, standard in today's gas grills), try grilling a steak just with that; another time, add some wood chips (hardwood such as apple, hickory, or oak; never soft wood such as pine or spruce) and see whether you can tell the difference.

If you are cooking a large quantity of food and the fire begins to fade before you finish, add a small amount of fresh charcoal from time to time to keep the fire alive. And store your charcoal in a dry place to help it light faster and burn more quickly.

Real charcoal, which looks like blackened shards of wood, is preferable to charcoal briquettes. You can find real charcoal in many wood stove shops as well as at lumberyards. The self-starting briquettes are treated with a flammable fluid that can give off a chemical smell that permeates food. For the same reason, try to avoid lighting cooking fires with kerosene or other chemicals. Dry newspaper and a little patience work wonders. A good alternative is the *plug* — an electric rod that you place in the center of a charcoal pile until it ignites.

Gas grills

The gas-powered grills that have become increasingly popular in recent years have an advantage over charcoal in that they maintain high heat without fading. Some gas grills use lava rocks to simulate charcoal, which works exceedingly well. The cooking technique is the same as for charcoal grills.

If you add wood chips to a barbecue, soak them first in water for about 15 minutes. Doing so makes them smolder and smoke rather than burn up in a flash.

Charcoal igniting made easy

Here's another quick and simple way to ignite charcoal without using fluid lighters or electric devices. Buy a piece of stovepipe about 8 inches (20 cm) in diameter and about 15 inches (38 cm) long, or buy a commercial lighter that is a stovepipe with handles. Remove the grill grate and place the pipe in the base. Stuff a few sheets of crumpled newspaper in the bottom of the pipe. On top of that, place four or five handfuls of charcoal so that they are resting on the newspaper. When you ignite the newspaper from below by tilting it slightly, the flame is concentrated and directed toward the charcoal, lighting it within a few minutes. When the coals begin to whiten (usually in 5 to 7 minutes), lift the pipe carefully, using thick kitchen mitts or pot holders, allowing the charcoal to scatter on the bottom of the grill. Pour fresh charcoal over it and wait for it to turn white before cooking.

The coals are ready when they are 75 percent or more white — usually 20 to 30 minutes after you light them. Keep a water bottle with a spray nozzle nearby to douse grease flare-ups — you also can use it to keep away annoying kids (or adults!).

Using a grill's lid

Many barbecue grills come with lids, which, when secured, create an oven that can exceed 450° F (230° C). Certain foods that take a relatively long time to cook — chicken legs, thick slices of steak, and so on — grill faster and better with the lid on. Essentially, you are grilling and roasting at the same time. A lid traps much of the smoke, directing it into the food rather than allowing it to blow away. The lid also creates a smoky effect that can be used with apple, hickory, or mesquite chips.

Grilling tips

- ✔ Clean the grill grate well with a wire brush between uses. Before igniting the fire, brush some vegetable oil over the grates to prevent food, particularly fish, from sticking.

- ✔ If possible, all foods should be at room temperature before you grill them. This cuts cooking time and allows for even heating.

- ✔ Combining microwave cooking with outdoor barbecuing significantly reduces the grilling time of poultry by partially cooking it.

- ✔ Trim meat of excess fat to avoid grease flare-ups that blacken the meat and give it a burned flavor.

- ✔ Cooking times in outdoor grill recipes are approximate; don't throw the meat on and jump in the pool for 15 minutes. Many variables affect cooking time: wind, intensity of coals, thickness of meat, and your fondness for dancing every time a Supremes song comes on.

- ✔ Do not apply sweet barbecue sauces to meat until the last ten minutes or else the sugar in them may burn.

- ✔ Be sure to shut off the valve that leads gas into your grill after you turn off the burners. On a charcoal grill, close all the vents after grilling to extinguish the hot coals.

Marinating myths and facts

A common misperception is that marinades tenderize meat. They don't. A marinade barely penetrates the outer ⅛ inch (3 mm) of meat, poultry, or game. What a marinade *can* do is add flavor to the surface, which is, of course, the first thing you taste.

We could write a whole book about marinades. Suffice to say that most marinades involve an acidic ingredient (vinegar, lemon, or some kinds of wine), oil, herbs, and perhaps a base flavor ingredient (beef or chicken stock or broth, for example). You want to end up with a marinade that is well balanced and flavorful. The only way to know what you have made is to taste it.

Consider this example: You have a T-bone or New York strip steak. Ask yourself whether you want to add a hot, medium, or sweet flavor. Much of this depends on the main ingredient. You might not want a sweet flavor on fish, for example. With pork, though, you might.

Say for now that you want a hot marinade for the steak. You want to give the steak some zip. Start with red chili flakes (carefully!). Then what? You need a liquid that goes with beef as well as chilies. You can use beef stock (homemade or canned beef broth) or red wine. Try red wine. So here you have the foundation of your hot marinade. Now you can jazz it up. What goes well with hot things? Minced garlic and black peppercorns, maybe. Chopped fresh coriander adds flavor, too. (As you begin to cook, you will learn more about ingredients in the supermarket and how to blend them.) Depending on your taste, you may want to add a little dried cumin or coriander seed. Then at the end, add salt and freshly ground pepper.

So there you have your basic hot marinade for steak, which you can vary as you go along to make it hotter, milder, or whatever.

You may wonder why many cookbooks call for freshly ground pepper and not the stuff that comes already ground in a can. The reason is that whole peppercorns begin to lose their potency the minute you grind them, so grinding them at the last minute only makes sense. (Get yourself a quality pepper grinder, such as the one made by Peugeot.) If you want proof, grind some pepper on the kitchen counter. Pour some commercial ground pepper on the counter. Then smell them (but not too vigorously!). Notice the difference?

You can go through the same exercise for sweetness: fruit preserves, acid (like lemon), maybe some wine, or sweet herbs such as fennel seed and chervil. Another sweet marinade can begin with wine or stock and then be sweetened with soy sauce, mirin wine (a Japanese sweet wine), sugar, Madeira (a fortified wine to which alcohol is added), fortified wine, or even papaya or orange juice. A marinade in the middle is seasoned mainly with herbs, with perhaps a white wine base.

Fresh lemon juice and grated lemon peel are also good additions. And some marinades, especially those for game, are cooked first to extract the most flavor from the ingredients. A typical combination might include red wine vinegar, rosemary, juniper berries, cloves, peppercorns, celery, carrots, onions, and salt and pepper.

Be sure to marinate meats, fish, poultry, and vegetables in the refrigerator. Bacteria forms on the surface of room-temperature food very quickly. And don't re-use marinade from pieces of raw chicken or fish unless you bring it to a boil first.

Barbecue time

Following are some recipes to get you started grilling. Novice cooks should follow the recipes exactly before modifying them to fit personal tastes.

The basics: Burgers and chicken breasts

We start with the most basic of American foods: the burger. The classic all-American hamburger — said to be invented at Louis' Lunch in New Haven, Connecticut — is usually made with ground chuck or sirloin. You can get more extravagant if you like, but more expensive cuts of beef have less *marbling* (visible veins of fat that run throughout a piece of raw sliced or chopped meat). You need marbling to keep the burger moist. Generally, more marbling means higher fat content and richer flavor and texture.

Hamburgers for the grill should be plump and well seasoned. The flavors you can add are limitless. If you like it hot, add Tabasco sauce or one of the scores of hot sauces on the market. Soy sauce makes hamburgers salty-sweet. In this recipe and the chicken breat recipe that follows, Dijon-style mustard, exquisite with grilled foods, is used as the principal seasoning ingredient. And you don't even have to stick to beef; lamb and turkey burgers, or blends of all three, are super, too.

Barbecued Hamburgers

Tools: *Mixing bowl*

Preparation time: *About 5 minutes, plus time to preheat grill*

Grilling time: *About 15 minutes*

$1^1/_2$ *pounds (750 g) ground beef, chuck, or chuck and sirloin mix*

2 tablespoons (30 mL) finely chopped fresh parsley

2 tablespoons (30 mL) Dijon-style mustard (optional)

Salt and freshly ground pepper to taste

1 Preheat a charcoal fire or gas grill.

2 Place the meat in a mixing bowl and add the parsley, mustard (if desired), and salt and pepper. Blend well with your fingers. Divide the mixture into four equal portions and shape each portion into a patty, about $^1/_2$ inch (12 mm) thick.

(continued)

3 Place the burgers on a grate 4 to 5 inches (10 to 13 cm) from the coals. Cook for about 8 to 10 minutes per side for medium-done burgers. (Medium has no trace of pink in the center of the patty.)

Yield: *4 servings.*

Note: *When you cook meat, poultry, or seafood over charcoal, the grate should be 4 to 5 inches (10 to 13 cm) from the coals. Any closer, and you risk burning the outside while leaving the center raw; too far away, and your guests will start bickering.*

Serve your burgers with lowfat but flavorful French Potato Salad (see Chapter 10).

Quick and tasty burger toppings include thinly sliced red or yellow onions, tomato slices marinated in a basil vinaigrette dressing, flavored mustards, mango or tomato chutney, tomato-based salsa, grilled peppers, and garlic-grilled mushrooms. (The last two recipes come later in this chapter.)

Chicken breasts are also a cinch on the grill, and you can liven them up in countless ways. In this version, you swab them with Dijon mustard and then perfume them with a little fresh rosemary.

Mustard-Brushed Barbecued Chicken Breasts

Tools: *Brush for basting*

Preparation time: *About 15 minutes, plus time to preheat grill*

Grilling time: *About 20 minutes*

8 chicken breast halves, with skin and bones, about 3¹/₂ pounds (1.75 kg) total weight

2 tablespoons (30 mL) Dijon-style mustard

2 tablespoons (30 mL) chopped fresh rosemary, or 1 tablespoon (15 mL) dried

Salt and freshly ground pepper to taste

1 Preheat a charcoal fire or gas grill.

2 Brush chicken breasts with mustard and sprinkle them with rosemary and salt and pepper.

3 Place the breasts on the grill, skin side down. Cook for about 10 minutes, shifting them as necessary to prevent burning by flames caused by fat dripping on the coals.

(continued)

4 Turn the breasts skin side up and continue cooking about 8 to 10 minutes more, moving them around the grill as necessary, until the juices run clear and the chicken is done.

Yield: 4 servings.

Note: Keep a keen eye on the fire as you cook. If it appears to be fading, carefully move the grate (without dropping the food on the patio) and add more charcoal. Charcoal should extend out about 2 inches beyond the perimeter of the food.

Grilled chicken with piquant mustard is good with a Cucumber-Dill Salad and French Potato Salad (see Chapter 10).

You can substitute boneless, skinless chicken breasts in the preceding recipe, but marinate them first for about 30 minutes in a 3-to-1 oil and lemon juice marinade seasoned with the rosemary, mustard (if desired), and salt and pepper. Grill the breasts on a lightly oiled grate for about 5 minutes per side or until done. Grilling time varies with the thickness of the breasts and the heat of the grill.

You also can grill chicken legs and thighs. Before cooking chicken legs or legs of duck or other fowl, run a knife along both sides of the thigh bone and the leg bone on the skinless side to separate the meat from the bone slightly. Doing so allows the legs to cook faster and more evenly. Slicing three-quarters of the way through the bottom of the joint that connects the thigh and the leg also helps. The leg lies flatter on the grill and cooks faster.

Grilling vegetables

When it comes to vegetables, even those that you're not wild about can taste terrific when grilled. Charcoal imparts an alluring texture and smoky essence that is irresistible. Moreover, preparation is easy and quick. Here are some examples:

- **Eggplant and zucchini:** Cut them lengthwise into 1-inch-thick (2.5-cm) slices before grilling. Brush with oil, season to taste, and grill for 15 to 20 minutes or until charred and tender, turning occasionally. Using small eggplants, about 4 to 5 ounces (110 to 140 g) each, is best. For additional flavor, marinate first in a three-to-one oil/vinegar mixture with salt and pepper and maybe Dijon-style mustard (put in a bowl first) for about 1 hour before grilling.

- **Corn:** Pull back the husks to remove the silk, but leave husks attached to the base of the ear. Wrap the husks back around the corn and tie at the top with string or a strip of husk. (Do not oil.) Soak wrapped ears in cold water for about 1 hour. Grill 20 minutes or until tender, turning frequently. Serve with melted butter flavored with herbs and fresh lemon juice.

- **Potatoes, carrots, onion, and turnips:** Peel and slice into uniform pieces and precook in boiling water until almost tender. Rinse in cold water to stop the cooking and drain well. Wrap in aluminum foil with seasonings such as olive oil, lemon juice, fresh herbs, and salt and pepper to taste and grill for 10 to 15 minutes or until tender. (You can thread them onto skewers before grilling.)

- **Tomatoes:** Slice firm, ripe tomatoes into $1/2$-inch-thick (12-mm) slices. Brush with olive oil; sprinkle with dried basil or parsley and salt and pepper. Grill until heated through.

You can grill or roast red, green, or yellow peppers under the broiler until the intense heat blackens and blisters their skin. You peel back and discard the charred skin, leaving a satiny underlayer with exquisite roasted flavor. Serve them with any grilled meat or poultry, slice them into a salad of mixed greens, or add them to antipasto (see Chapter 15).

Grilled Peppers

Tools: Paper bag, paring knife, mixing bowls, wire whisk

Preparation time: About 5 minutes, plus time to preheat grill or charcoal

Marinating time: About 15 minutes

Grilling time: About 20 minutes

4 medium bell peppers (any color or combination of colors)	Grated peel of half a lemon
$1/4$ cup (60 mL) olive oil	1 teaspoon peeled and minced garlic, about 1 large clove
2 tablespoons (30 mL) fresh lemon juice	Salt and pepper to taste

1 Roast whole peppers on a preheated grill or under the broiler about 4 inches (10 cm) from the heat for 15 to 20 minutes or until the skins are blackened all over, turning the peppers about every 5 to 10 minutes during cooking. Transfer peppers to a paper bag and close the bag tightly so that the peppers can steam for 10 minutes.

2 Using a paring knife and working over the bowl to catch their juice, peel, core, and seed the peppers. (If the blackened skin does not slip off easily, grill the peppers for a few more minutes.) Slice the peppers into 2-inch (5-cm) strips.

3 Whisk together olive oil, lemon juice, lemon peel, garlic, and salt and pepper and pour the dressing over the pepper strips. Allow to marinate for at least 15 minutes. Serve chilled or at room temperature, as a side dish or a condiment to grilled meats or chicken.

Yield: 4 to 6 servings.

(continued)

Note: Most barbecue grills have hot spots. You should move pieces of food around periodically while they cook to ensure even exposure to heat.

Charred sweet peppers are excellent as an accompaniment to hamburgers (earlier in this chapter) or Grilled Swordfish Steaks with Lemon and Thyme (later in this chapter).

Peppers are also terrific in a mixture of grilled vegetables, as in the following recipe.

Grilled Summer Vegetables with Basil Marinade

Tools: *Chef's knife, colander, mixing bowls, brush for basting, wire whisk*

Preparation time: *About 45 minutes, plus time to preheat grill*

Marinating time: *About 1 hour*

Grilling time: *About 10 minutes*

2 medium eggplants, about 2 pounds (1 kg) total, trimmed and sliced crosswise into $^1/_2$-inch-thick (12-mm) rounds

2 medium yellow summer squash, ends trimmed and cut in half lengthwise

3 medium zucchini, ends trimmed and cut in half lengthwise

1 tablespoon (15 mL) salt

Basil Marinade (see following recipe)

2 medium red bell peppers, cored, seeded, and quartered

1 medium red onion, peeled and sliced into $^1/_2$-inch-thick (12-mm) rounds

1 Place the eggplant, squash, and zucchini in a colander over the sink. Add the salt, which causes the vegetables to shed water. Toss and let drain for 30 minutes. Make the Basil Marinade as the vegetables drain.

2 Rinse the eggplant, squash, and zucchini. Pat dry with paper towels and place in a large bowl. Add the peppers. Pour the basil marinade over the vegetables and toss well. Let sit for up to 1 hour, refrigerated, before grilling.

3 Before the vegetables have finished marinating, heat a charcoal fire or gas grill.

4 Brush the red onion slices with marinade from the vegetable bowl. Shake off any excess marinade on the other vegetables. Reserve the remaining marinade.

5 Grill the vegetables about 5 minutes per side or until tender but not mushy. Place them on a serving plate and drizzle the reserved marinade over them.

Yield: *4 to 6 servings.*

(continued)

Basil Marinade

6 tablespoons (90 mL) extra-virgin olive oil

3 tablespoons (45 mL) minced fresh basil

2 tablespoons (30 mL) red wine vinegar

1 clove garlic, peeled and minced

Salt and freshly ground pepper to taste

Combine all ingredients in a small mixing bowl and whisk well. Taste for seasoning. (You can add other herbs or spices of choice.) Store in a covered container in the refrigerator until you're ready to use it.

Yield: About $1/2$ cup (125 mL).

Serve these vegetables with anything from a hamburger to Grilled Brochettes of Pork with Rosemary (both in this chapter).

Getting fancy: Pork, mushrooms, and swordfish

In this savory recipe for brochettes of pork, you cube the meat and marinate it in olive oil, red wine vinegar, garlic, rosemary (preferably fresh), cumin, salt, and hot pepper. Cumin is a lovely match for pork (and lamb, too). Rosemary gives it a sunny Provençale flavor.

Grilled Brochettes of Pork with Rosemary

Tools: Chef's knife, mixing bowl, wooden or metal skewers

Preparation time: About 25 minutes, plus time to preheat grill

Marinating time: About 30 minutes

Grilling time: About 20 minutes

$1^1/4$ pounds (625 g) lean boneless pork loin, cut into 1-inch (2.5-cm) cubes

2 tablespoons (30 mL) olive oil

2 tablespoons (30 mL) chopped fresh rosemary, or 2 teaspoons (10 mL) dried

1 tablespoon (15 mL) red wine vinegar

1 teaspoon (5 mL) peeled and finely chopped garlic, about 1 large clove

1 teaspoon (5 mL) ground cumin

$1/4$ teaspoon (1 mL) red pepper flakes

Salt and freshly ground pepper to taste

Vegetable for oiling grill grate

1 Place the pork in a mixing bowl. Add the remaining ingredients and mix well. Cover with plastic wrap and allow to marinate in the refrigerator for at least 30 minutes.

2 Preheat a charcoal fire or gas grill.

(continued)

3 Arrange the pork cubes on four skewers. If you use wooden skewers, soak them for half an hour in cold water and cover the tips with foil to prevent burning.

4 Place the meat on a grate that you have lightly brushed with oil. Grill about 4 inches (10 cm) from the fire for about 20 minutes or until done, turning often. Serve immediately.

Yield: 4 servings.

Add color to these brochettes by serving them with Grilled Summer Vegetables with Basil Marinade (earlier in this chapter) or Couscous with Yellow Squash (see Chapter 14).

Porous vegetables, such as mushrooms and sliced eggplant, need not be marinated. You simply brush them with a flavorful liquid, as in the following recipe.

Garlic-Grilled Mushrooms

Tools: *Chef's knife, small bowl, brush for basting*

Preparation time: *About 10 minutes, plus time to preheat grill*

Grilling time: *About 5 minutes*

1 pound (500 g) mushrooms with large caps (portobello or shiitake)

¹/₃ cup (85 mL) extra-virgin olive oil

3 tablespoons (45 mL) lemon juice (preferably freshly squeezed), about 1 large lemon

2 teaspoons (10 mL) peeled and minced garlic, about 2 large cloves

Salt and freshly ground pepper to taste

2 tablespoons (30 mL) minced fresh parsley (optional)

1 Preheat a charcoal fire or gas grill.

2 Clean the mushrooms with a damp paper towel. Remove the stems, as shown in Figure 6-7. (You can save them to put in soups or stocks.)

3 In a small bowl, combine the oil, lemon juice, and garlic. Brush the caps with the flavored oil and season with salt and pepper.

4 Place the caps on the grill, top side down, and grill for about 3 minutes. (Do not let them burn.) Turn the caps over and grill for another 2 to 3 minutes or until you can easily pierce the caps with a knife and the mushrooms are nicely browned.

5 Remove the mushrooms to a platter. Garnish with parsley and serve with grilled hamburgers, steak, chicken, or fish.

(continued)

Figure 6-7:
Trim the stems off the mushrooms before grilling the caps.

How to Trim and Slice Mushrooms

1. wipe away dirt using a paper towel or a dish towel

2. Cut off stem

3. slice

Yield: *4 servings.*

Steak — such as the Roasted Fillet of Beef (earlier in this chapter) or Broiled Skirt Steak, Cajun Style (see Chapter 15) — is the natural accompaniment to these savory mushrooms.

 Cleaning mushrooms thoroughly is important. The wild varieties especially can be full of sand and dirt. But if you soak or rinse mushrooms too long, they can become water-drenched and mushy. Using a damp paper towel to gently brush off any dirt is best. If the mushrooms are very dirty, rinse them quickly with cold water and drain in a colander, wiping away excess moisture with a cloth or paper towel. Peeling mushrooms isn't advisable unless they are extremely soft and in need of a lot of trimming.

Fish and shellfish lend themselves particularly well to grilling, too. Use firm-fleshed fish that holds together on the grill, such as salmon, halibut, swordfish, mako shark, or monkfish. Delicate fish such as sole tends to flake and fall apart. Species with relatively oily flesh, such as bluefish and mackerel, also grill well.

 This swordfish dish could not be easier or more delicious. (Salmon, tuna, halibut, and mako shark also work well with this recipe.) Notice that the marinating time is limited to 1 hour. If you leave the fish in the marinade any longer than that, the acid in the lemon begins to "cook" the fish.

Wild mushrooms

Finding wild mushrooms at supermarket and specialty stores year-round is becoming increasingly common. Though they are more expensive than cultivated mushrooms, you need to purchase only a few to add intense flavor to a dish. Wild mushrooms are generally not eaten raw and can be sautéed, broiled, grilled, or roasted. In some cases, you can substitute dried wild mushrooms for fresh, especially in risottos, soups, sauces, and other dishes that simmer or stew for a relatively long time. Just reconstitute them in very hot water to barely cover for about 20 minutes or until soft. Then drain and add to the dish. Save the mushroom water for sauces, soups, or stews.

You want to choose mushrooms with plump, unshriveled caps that look fresh. Following are a few of the types of wild mushrooms that you can purchase, some of which are pictured in the following figure:

- **Chanterelle:** Beautifully trumpet-shaped with bright yellow to orange color and delicate flavor. Available fresh in summer and winter.

- **Cremini:** Similar to white button mushrooms but darker colored, with rich, earthy flavor. Available year-round.

- **Morels:** Dark brown with a honeycombed, cone-shaped cap. Meaty texture and a nutty, woodsy taste. Darker morels have the most flavor. Available mostly in the spring months, from April through June. Wonderful simply sautéed in butter and a little garlic.

- **Oyster:** Beige colored and fan-shaped with silky texture. Can be eaten raw or cooked. Excellent in creamed dishes and sauces. Sold cultivated or wild and available year-round.

- **Porcini (cèpe):** Range in size from one ounce to a pound. Umbrella-shaped cap with thick stem and pale brown color. Deep, rich, woodsy flavor. Available in the fall months, but hard to find fresh in the U.S.

- **Portobello:** Big, brown mushroom with juicy, meat-like texture and a woodsy taste. Excellent basted with olive oil and grilled, or stuffed and baked. Available year-round.

- **Shiitakes (Golden Oak):** Both cultivated and wild. Relatively thin, tan to brown umbrella-shaped caps. Tender and full-flavored flesh. Can be sautéed, broiled, stir-fried, or baked. Available year-round.

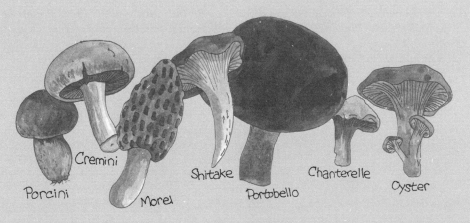

Grilled Swordfish Steaks with Lemon and Thyme

Tools: *Large metal roasting or broiling pan, brush for basting*

Preparation time: *About 10 minutes, plus time to preheat grill*

Marinating time: *About 1 hour*

Grilling time: *About 10 minutes*

4 swordfish steaks, each about 1 inch (2.5 cm) thick, about 1¹/₂ pounds (750 g) total

Salt and freshly ground pepper to taste

2 to 3 tablespoons (30 to 45 mL) corn or vegetable oil

Juice of one large lemon

2 sprigs fresh thyme, chopped, or ¹/₂ teaspoon (2 mL) dried

2 tablespoons (30 mL) butter at room temperature

1 One hour before cooking, sprinkle the swordfish steaks on all sides with salt and pepper. Mix together the oil, lemon juice, and thyme in a large metal roasting or broiling pan. Add the fish steaks, turning them in the marinade to coat. Cover with plastic wrap and refrigerate for no more than 1 hour.

2 Preheat a charcoal fire or gas grill.

3 Remove the swordfish from the pan, reserving the marinade. Grill the swordfish steaks for about 4 to 5 minutes per side or until done, depending on their thickness and the grill's temperature. Then return the fish to the metal pan with the marinade. Add the butter and place the dish on the grill to just simmer the marinade and melt the butter. Coat the fish with sauce and serve.

Yield: *4 servings.*

You can enliven swordfish like this with Lentils with Balsamic Vinegar (see Chapter 14) or Orzo Medley (see Chapter 10). Gazpacho beforehand would be great, too (see Chapter 9).

Chapter 7

Sauces

A *great meal without a sauce is like a beautiful woman without clothes. It can provoke and satisfy the appetite, but it lacks the coating of civilization that would arouse our fullest interest.*

— Raymond Sokolov, from *The Saucier's Apprentice*

Probably no aspect of cooking sends a kitchen novice running for a restaurant like sauce-making. All this reducing and blending and seasoning and adjusting seems about as arcane as DNA testing.

In fact, sauce-making is within the reach of the absolute cooking rookie. Some sauces require nothing more than cooking several ingredients in a pan and tossing them in the blender. We tell you how to do that in this chapter. From there, you can progress to some of the more important basic sauces in American and European cooking, with all kinds of variations.

Don't think of today's sauces only as those old triple-bypass cream-and-butter concoctions. Most sauces in restaurants today are Mediterranean or Californian in style, made with olive oil, aromatic herbs, vegetables, and maybe wine. The gelatin-like demi-glace, essentially a heavy concentrated veal stock, also adds wonderful flavor to many lowfat sauces today.

Not only are these Mediterranean sauces easier to make than the classic sauces (although we explain the classics because they can be superb in moderation), but they also keep you light on your feet.

Who came up with this saucy idea anyway?

The earliest use of sauces, dating at least as far back as classical Rome, was primarily to disguise food that was, shall we say, not exactly at peak freshness. The Romans concocted a salty sauce called *liquamen* that could presumably make a putrid, long-deceased rabbit taste just dandy. We give you the recipe just in case you are planning a toga party and would like to serve authentic Roman food. (Of course, this being the 20th century, you would have to buy whole rabbits and ducks and leave them in the spare bedroom for a few weeks.)

Roman Liquamen

1. Place sprats, anchovies, or mackerel in a baking trough (because troughs are hard to find these days, you can substitute a child's "flying saucer" or your bathtub) and cover with salt. Let sit for a day.

2. Transfer to an earthenware vessel and set out in the sun for two or three months, stirring occasionally with a stick. (The narrow end of a baseball bat will do. Don't expect to use the bat again.) Remove to a covered container and add old wine. Serve with old fish or any other foul-smelling, unrefrigerated creature.

Throughout the Middle Ages and the Renaissance, *gravies,* or thickened pan juices, were served with meat, game, and fowl; they were not sophisticated sauces as we know them today. But what would you expect from people who ate with their hands, tossed bones under the table, and tortured criminals on racks? It wasn't until the 18th century that modern sauces entered the cooking vocabulary. By 1800, a celebrated French chef known as Carême had compiled more than a dozen classical recipes for sauces, each of which could be modified in different ways. These recipes include some of the most famous of French sauces today: *ravigote* (highly seasoned white sauce), *Champagne* (white sauce made with Champagne), *bourguignonne* (red wine with mushrooms and onions), *poivrade* (red wine sauce with black pepper), tomato (red sauce), *raifort* (horseradish and cream), mayonnaise (egg yolks and oil emulsion), and *Provençale* (usually tomatoes along with other ingredients and fresh herbs).

Today, the French cooking repertoire includes several hundred sauces. (Annoyingly, most of these sauce recipes are written in French.) Add to those the sauces of Spain, Italy, and America, and the list is mind-boggling. But don't fret. Most cooks use no more than a dozen sauces and their variations, and those are within the grasp of anyone who can boil a hot dog and carry on a conversation at the same time.

What Is a Sauce?

Think of a sauce as a primary liquid (chicken stock, beef stock, fish stock, or vegetable stock, for example) flavored with ingredients (sautéed shallots, garlic, tomatoes, and so on) and seasoned with salt and pepper and herbs of choice.

Before it's served, a sauce is often *reduced*. Reduced simply means that the sauce is cooked and evaporated over high heat so that it thickens and intensifies in flavor. Sometimes you strain a sauce through a sieve to eliminate all the solids. Other times you puree everything in a blender.

The Family Tree of Sauces

The best way to understand sauces is to become familiar with their foundations:

- ✔ *White sauces* usually contain milk or cream.
- ✔ *White butter sauces* are based on a reduction of butter, vinegar, and shallots.
- ✔ *Brown sauces* are based on dark stocks like lamb or veal.
- ✔ *Vinaigrettes* are made up of oil, vinegar, and seasonings.
- ✔ *Hollandaise* is based on cooked egg yolks.
- ✔ *Mayonnaise* is based on uncooked egg yolks and oil.

For the purposes of this book, a subcategory might include compound butters, which we discuss later in this chapter, and tomato sauces.

Classic White Sauce or Library Paste? Béchamel

For centuries, béchamel has been the mortar that supports the house of French cuisine. With its buttery, faintly nutty flavor, béchamel is also the base of hot soufflés and such homey dishes as macaroni and cheese. You can modify béchamel in many ways to suit the dish it garnishes. For example, if you are cooking fish, you can add fish stock to the sauce. If you are cooking poultry, you can add chicken stock. Like most white sauces, béchamel is based on a *roux*, which is nothing more than butter melted in a pan and then sprinkled with flour (equal quantities of each) and stirred into a paste over low heat. See how in the following recipe, béchamel begins with a roux.

Béchamel and its variations go with all kinds of foods, including poached and grilled fish, chicken, veal, and vegetables like pearl onions, brussels sprouts, broccoli, and cauliflower. (See Chapter 3 for information about steaming and boiling these vegetables.)

Béchamel

Tools: *Small saucepan, medium saucepan, wire whisk*

Preparation time: *About 5 minutes*

Cooking time: *About 8 minutes*

(continued)

1¹/₄ cups (300 mL) milk

2 tablespoons (30 mL) butter

2 tablespoons (30 mL) flour

¹/₄ teaspoon (1 mL) ground nutmeg, or to taste

Salt and freshly ground pepper to taste

1 Heat the milk over medium heat in a small saucepan until almost boiling. (If the milk is hot when you add it to the butter and flour, there's less chance that the béchamel will be lumpy.)

2 Meanwhile, in a medium saucepan, melt the butter over medium heat. Add the flour and whisk constantly for 2 minutes. (You are cooking the loose paste, or *roux,* made from the butter and flour.) The roux should reach a thick paste consistency.

3 Gradually add the hot milk while continuing to whisk the mixture vigorously. When the sauce is blended smooth, reduce heat and simmer for 3 to 4 minutes, whisking frequently. The béchamel should have the consistency of a very thick sauce. Remove from heat, add the nutmeg and salt and pepper, and whisk well.

Yield: *About 1 cup (250 mL).*

If the butter burns or even gets too brown, you should probably start over, or your white sauce will have a brown tint.

Variations on béchamel

Mornay sauce: Add grated cheese, like Gruyère or Parmesan, to the simmering béchamel, along with fish stock (optional) and butter.

Horseradish sauce: Add freshly grated horseradish to taste. Serve with game, fish such as river trout, or long-braised sinewy cuts of beef from the shoulder and neck.

Soubise: Boil or steam yellow onions until they are soft; puree them in the blender and add to the sauce, seasoning to taste with salt and pepper. Slightly sweet from the onions, soubise sauce is suitable for many types of game, poultry, and meat.

Caper sauce: After the béchamel has finished cooking, add some chopped, drained capers.

You can use dozens of other ingredients commonly found in a well-stocked pantry or refrigerator to easily and dramatically alter the flavor of béchamel. A short list of possibilities include fresh tomatoes (skinned and finely chopped); sautéed mushrooms, shallots, onions, garlic, or leeks; ground ginger or curry powder; chopped fresh tarragon, dill, parsley or marjoram; paprika; grated lemon peel; white pepper; and Tabasco sauce. Add them to taste when the béchamel has almost finished cooking.

Whipping up some creamed spinach (or creamed vegetables in general) is a good way to try out your béchamel-making skills.

If creamed spinach conjures dark memories of school cafeterias, try the real thing. Because this dish is very rich — as is anything based on béchamel — serve it with something lean, like roast chicken, lowfat fish, or maybe just saltines and a Dr. Pepper.

Creamed Spinach

Tools: *Large pot, colander, food processor or electric blender, two saucepans, wire whisk*

Preparation time: *About 15 minutes*

Cooking time: *About 8 minutes*

8 cups (2 L) fresh, trimmed spinach, about 10 ounces (280 g)

1 cup (250 mL) milk

1 tablespoon (15 mL) butter

1 tablespoon (15 mL) flour

¹/₂ teaspoon (2 mL) ground nutmeg

Salt and freshly ground pepper to taste

2 tablespoons (30 mL) grated Parmesan cheese

1 Wash spinach well. (Do not dry.) Immediately place spinach with the water that clings to its leaves in a large pot. Cover and cook over medium-low heat for about 2 minutes, or until the leaves are wilted.

2 Place the cooked spinach in a colander and, using a wooden spoon, press down on the spinach to extract most of the water.

3 Put the spinach in a food processor or electric blender container and blend thoroughly. You should have about ³/₄ cup (175 mL) processed spinach.

4 Heat the milk almost to boiling in a small saucepan over medium heat.

5 Meanwhile, melt the butter in a medium saucepan over medium heat; add the flour, stirring with a wire whisk. Add the warmed milk, whisking rapidly. Add the nutmeg and salt and pepper to taste. Cook, whisking, about 3 to 4 minutes or until the sauce thickens. Reduce heat to low, stir in the spinach and Parmesan cheese, and cook just until heated through.

Yield: *2 to 3 servings.*

You can substitute frozen chopped spinach for the fresh ingredient. You need about ³/₄ cup (175 mL), cooked and drained.

Velouté: A Variation on Béchamel

A *velouté* is essentially a béchamel made with a clear stock (fish or chicken), which gives it extra flavor. Sometimes you enhance a velouté before serving by adding a little cream (for a smoother texture) or some fresh lemon juice (for a little tartness). It is wonderful with poached fish, poultry, veal, vegetables, and eggs. Following is a simplified version of a classic velouté; variations are endless after you get this technique down.

Velouté

Tools: *Saucepan, wire whisk, waxed paper*

Preparation time: *About 10 minutes*

Cooking time: *About 8 minutes*

2 tablespoons (30 mL) unsalted butter

3 tablespoons (45 mL) flour

1¹/₂ cups (375 mL) hot chicken or vegetable broth (fresh or canned)

¹/₃ cup (75 mL) heavy cream or half and half

Salt and freshly ground white pepper to taste

1 Melt the butter over medium heat in a medium saucepan. Add the flour and whisk until blended smooth. Reduce heat to low and cook for about 2 minutes, whisking constantly.

2 Raise the heat setting to medium and gradually add the hot chicken broth (watch out — it splatters!), whisking for about 1 minute or until the sauce thickens. Raise the heat and bring to a boil; immediately lower the heat to simmer and cook for about 2 minutes, whisking often.

3 Add the cream and salt and pepper to taste. Raise the heat and whisk constantly while bringing the mixture back to a boil. When it boils, immediately remove the saucepan from heat and cover with waxed paper (to prevent a thin film from forming on the surface) until served.

Yield: *About 1³/₄ cups (425 mL).*

If you forget to cover the velouté with waxed paper and a thin film or skin forms on the sauce's surface, simply whisk it back into the sauce. If the sauce cooks a little too long and gets too thick, add a little more broth or cream.

Brown Sauces

One major difference between white and brown sauce is that brown sauce is harder to get off your silk tie. The basic brown sauce derives from the 19th century Espagnole sauce, so called because a major ingredient was Spanish ham. It took two or three days to make, which is probably one reason why women's liberation did not catch on faster in Spain. That's all you need to know about the traditional Espagnole sauce — most modern chefs don't bother with it.

Most brown sauces today are based on a reduced stock of beef, veal, or lamb. When we use the term *stock,* we mean a liquid that results from boiling bones, water, vegetables, and seasonings. The more you reduce the liquid, the stronger the flavor.

If you reduce veal stock to a jelly consistency, it is sometimes called *demi-glace.* If you reduce the liquid so much that it coats a spoon, it is called simply *glace.* Note that you can cut demi-glace and glace into small pieces and freeze them for later use.

Making stock

Following is a standard recipe for veal stock, the single most important stock in French cuisine and the base for dozens of sauces. If veal stock is too much for you to tackle now, keep it in mind. Chances are you will make it someday.

Granted, making stocks is time-consuming, but after you're finished you have a delicious base that you can use to enhance all kinds of dishes. Some cookbooks skip stocks altogether, assuming that they are too tedious to make; instead, they recommend bouillon cubes, which is like comparing a cow to nondairy creamer.

Save all leftover veal bones and chicken carcasses in your freezer. When you have enough, you can make stock. You also can ask your butcher for spare bones. (Veal bones from the neck have the most gelatin, which is desirable.)

Veal Stock

Tools: *Large roasting pan, metal spatula, large stock pot, wooden spoon, sieve*

Preparation time: *About 20 minutes*

Cooking time: *About 12 hours*

8 pounds (4 kg) veal bones

1 pound (500 g) (about 3 medium) onions, quartered (skins left on)

1 pound (500 g) carrots, washed, trimmed, and cut in thirds crosswise

1 whole head garlic, flaky outer skin removed and cloves separated

1 large bunch parsley, washed

6 stalks celery, washed and halved crosswise

5 bay leaves

1 tablespoon (15 mL) dried thyme

1 tablespoon (15 mL) black peppercorns

5 whole ripe tomatoes or 28-ounce can (about 796 mL) Italian plum tomatoes

1 Preheat the oven to 400° F (200° C).

2 Distribute the bones over a large roasting pan and place in the oven for 1¹/₂ hours, moving the bones around occasionally.

3 Add the onions and carrots to the bones and cook 45 minutes longer, moving the bones around occasionally.

4 Remove the bones and vegetables from the oven and, using a metal spatula, transfer them to a large stock pot (20 quarts/20 L or more). If you do not have a stock pot this large, divide ingredients into 2 smaller pots. Discard fat that has accumulated in the roasting pan.

5 Place the pan on the stovetop over low heat and pour in enough water to cover the bottom. With a wooden spoon, scrape away all the pieces of meat that are sticking to the bottom of the pan (that are not burned) and add them to the stock pot.

6 Fill the stock pot with water almost to the top. Bring to a boil (which may take over an hour). Add remaining ingredients and return to a boil. Simmer overnight uncovered (no need to watch overnight unless you are an insomniac).

7 In the morning, strain the liquid through a sieve into a large pot or bowl, discarding the solids. Let cool.

8 After the stock cools, skim fat from the surface and discard. What you have left is your stock.

Yield: *8 to 10 quarts (2 to 2.5 L).*

Store-bought frozen stocks

Frozen stocks are becoming easier to find in specialty grocery stores and markets. Perfect Additions and D'Artagnan are two companies that manufacture frozen stocks and demi-glace, which you can use when you can't find time to make your own. Perfect Additions makes a complete line of frozen stocks — vegetable, beef, veal, chicken, and fish — packaged in half-pint plastic containers for about $3.75. D'Artagnan, located in New Jersey, produces a frozen veal and duck demi-glace in a 4-ounce container. Many specialty markets also sell their own brand of fresh stocks.

You can freeze and store stocks. To make demi-glace, reduce the stock to about 2¹/₂ quarts (2.5 L) and let cool. The liquid should be very gelatinous. Freeze in plastic bags or in ice cube trays.

Cooking with demi-glace

The following typical Parisian bistro dish, which is based on a demi-glace, can warm you right down to your Reeboks in fall and winter. If you cannot make or buy the demi-glace that this recipe calls for, you can substitute canned beef broth, but not bouillon cubes, please!

Beef Braised in Beaujolais

Tools: *Chef's knife, Dutch oven*

Preparation time: *About 25 minutes*

Cooking time: *About 3 hours and 15 minutes*

1 tablespoon (15 mL) vegetable oil

4 pounds (2 kg) brisket of beef, well trimmed and cut into 1¹/₂-inch (4-cm) cubes

2 cups (500 mL) peeled and chopped onions, about 2 large onions

2 large carrots, cleaned and sliced into ¹/₂-inch (12-mm) rounds

1 tablespoon (15 mL) peeled and chopped garlic, about 3 large cloves

4 sprigs fresh thyme, or 1 teaspoon (5 mL) dried

4 sprigs minced fresh rosemary (leaves only), or 1 teaspoon (5 mL) dried

¹/₄ cup (50 mL) flour

1 cup (250 mL) Beaujolais (light, dry fruity red wine) or other dry red wine

³/₄ cup (175 mL) melted demi-glace or fresh or canned beef or chicken stock

1 bay leaf

2 whole cloves

Salt and freshly ground pepper to taste

(continued)

1 Heat the oil in a heavy, cast-iron Dutch oven large enough to hold the meat in one layer (or do it in two batches). Add the cubed beef and cook over medium-high heat, turning occasionally until well browned on all sides, about 10 minutes.

2 Add the onions, carrots, garlic, thyme, and rosemary. Cook and stir for about 5 minutes. Add the flour. Blend well, stirring for 1 minute. Add the wine, demi-glace (or stock), bay leaf, cloves, and salt and pepper to taste. Blend well and bring to a simmer. Cook, covered, over low heat for $2^1/_2$ hours; then uncover and cook for $^1/_2$ hour more or until the meat is tender. Remove the bay leaf, cloves, and thyme sprigs before serving. Serve with mashed potatoes, noodles, or rice. (See Chapter 3 for recipes.)

Yield: *8 servings.*

Deglazing: Picky, picky, picky

Do you ever have a casserole of macaroni and cheese and, when dinner is over, go over and pick at the little semi-burned nuggets of cheese and pasta that cling to the dish? Aren't they the best part?

Well, think of deglazing as more or less the same thing. When you sauté a steak or chicken in a hot pan, it leaves behind little particles that stick to the pan. These bits are packed with flavor, and you want to incorporate them into any sauce you make.

For example, when you remove a steak from the pan, you might deglaze the pan with red wine (you generally do deglazing with wine or stock of some sort). As the stock sizzles in the pan, you scrape the pan's bottom (preferably with a spatula or wooden spoon) to release those tasty little particles. That process is called *deglazing.* After you do that, you finish the sauce and serve.

Restaurant cooks use this technique all the time to make sauces over high heat in the same pan in which the meat was cooked. This à la minute technique makes a lot of sense if you have somebody (for example, a waiter or small child) to grab the dish and run as soon as it is ready.

The following two recipes use the deglazing technique. You make the sauce quickly in the same pan you use to brown the pork and chicken.

Pork Chops with Chervil Sauce

Tools: *Chef's knife, large skillet or sauté pan, wooden spoon or rubber spatula*

Preparation time: *About 15 minutes*

Cooking time: *About 25 minutes*

4 loin pork chops, each about 8 ounces (250 g)

Salt and freshly ground pepper to taste

1 tablespoon (15 mL) olive oil

2 tablespoons (30 mL) butter

2 large shallots, peeled and minced

$^1/_2$ cup (125 mL) demi-glace or beef broth

$^1/_2$ cup (125 mL) dry red wine

2 tablespoons (30 mL) chopped fresh chervil or rosemary leaves, or 2 teaspoons (10 mL) crumbled, dried

1 Season the pork chops with salt and pepper. Heat the olive oil over medium-high setting in a pan or skillet large enough to hold the chops in one layer. Cook the chops for about 20 minutes or until done, turning them occasionally. (Watch them carefully and reduce the heat to medium if they brown too quickly.) Set the chops aside on a platter and cover with foil to keep warm.

2 Pour off any accumulated fat and scrape off and discard only the very burned bits of food sticking to the bottom of the pan. Return the pan to medium heat. Add the 2 tablespoons (30 mL) butter. When it melts, add the shallots, stirring and scraping the pan until they wilt, about 2 to 3 minutes. Add the demi-glace (or beef broth) and stir. Add the red wine; stir for 1 minute. Add the chervil or rosemary.

3 Reduce the sauce over high heat, stirring until it evaporates slightly and thickens. Taste for seasoning, adding more salt and pepper, if desired. Add the chops to the pan and heat a few seconds until warmed through, spooning the sauce over the chops. Serve with buttered rice, noodles, or mashed potatoes. (See Chapter 3 for recipes.)

Yield: *4 servings.*

As we indicate, you can make this recipe with either demi-glace or beef broth. Demi-glace produces a richer, thicker sauce. You also can substitute more expensive veal chops for the pork.

Shallots

To paraphrase Mark Twain, shallots are onions with a college education. Buy them regularly, as you do onions and garlic. Shallots resemble garlic, growing in clusters with individual bulbs. They are generally available year-round, although they are freshest in the spring. They have a flavor that is more delicate than onions and are less acidic, which makes them ideal for subtle sauces, raw vegetable salads, and vinaigrettes. To use shallots, remove their papery skin and thinly slice or mince the pale purple flesh of each bulb.

Sautéed capers give this dish a lively saline accent that is counterbalanced by the garlic, rosemary, and vegetables. Capers are the flower buds of a Mediterranean plant that are dried and then pickled in a vinegar and salt solution. You should rinse and drain them before adding them to a recipe. Capers can be found in any major supermarket or specialty food store.

Chicken Breasts with Garlic and Capers

Tools: *Chef's knife, large sauté pan, spatula or wooden spoon*

Preparation time: *About 25 minutes*

Cooking time: *About 20 minutes*

4 boneless, skinless chicken breast halves, about 1¹/₄ pounds (625 g) total

Salt and freshly ground pepper to taste

2 tablespoons (30 mL) olive oil

¹/₂ cup (125 mL) peeled and chopped onion, about 1 medium onion

1 tablespoon (15 mL) chopped fresh rosemary leaves, or 1 teaspoon (5 mL) crumbled, dried

1 teaspoon (5 mL) peeled and chopped garlic, about 1 large clove

²/₃ cup (150 mL) fresh or canned chicken broth

1 tablespoon (15 mL) red wine vinegar

3 tablespoons (45 mL) capers, rinsed and drained

1 tablespoon plus 1 teaspoon (20 mL) tomato paste

2 tablespoons (30 mL) chopped fresh parsley

(continued)

1 Sprinkle the chicken breasts lightly with salt and pepper.

2 Heat the oil in a large sauté pan over medium-high setting. Add the chicken and sauté, turning occasionally, until lightly browned on both sides, about 7 minutes. Remove the chicken to a platter.

3 Over medium heat, add the onion, rosemary, and garlic to the pan. Cook, stirring, for 1 to 2 minutes or until the onion is wilted. (Be careful not to brown the garlic.)

4 Add the chicken broth and vinegar. Deglaze the pan by stirring and scraping with a wooden spoon or spatula for about l minute to dissolve the brown particles clinging to the bottom.

5 Add the capers and tomato paste and blend well. Return the chicken breasts and any juices on the plate to the pan. Bring to a boil, cover, and reduce heat to simmer 5 to 7 minutes or until cooked, turning the chicken once.

6 Stir in the parsley and serve, if desired, with Couscous with Yellow Squash or White Beans with Tomato and Thyme (see Chapter 14).

Yield: *4 servings.*

Vinaigrette Sauces

Vinaigrette sauces, which are low in saturated fat, are worth knowing about. They are also quick. After you get the technique down, the possible modifications are endless.

You can make quick, sprightly sauces for grilled fish or meat by using oil and vinegar as a base. Swordfish is ideal for this type of cooking, even though it may cost as much as a month's health-club membership. The following recipe is a variation (read: stolen) on one of our favorite recipes from Wolfgang Puck's Spago Restaurant in Los Angeles.

Dried versus fresh herbs

Unless you live in one of the southern or western regions of the United States, fresh herbs are not always available. Dried herbs will generally do in these circumstances, but you must remember that they are three times as concentrated as fresh ones. So if a recipe calls for 1 tablespoon (15 mL) of fresh thyme, for example, use 1 teaspoon (5 mL) of the dried herb. (See Chapter 5 for herb and spice charts.)

Grilled Swordfish with Cilantro and Cherry Tomatoes Vinaigrette

Tools: Baking sheet, mixing bowl, wire whisk, blender or food processor, chef's knife

Preparation time: About 20 minutes, plus 1 hour to marinate fish

Cooking time: About 25 minutes

Cherry Tomato Vinaigrette

³/₄ pound (375 g) cherry tomatoes, stems removed (or ripe plum tomatoes, cored and quartered)

6 sprigs cilantro

2 cloves garlic, peeled and crushed

¹/₂ teaspoon (2 mL) seeded and chopped jalapeño pepper (optional)

¹/₂ cup plus 2 tablespoons (155 mL) olive oil

Salt and freshly ground pepper to taste

2 tablespoons (30 mL) red wine vinegar

1 Preheat the oven to 400°F (200° C).

2 On a baking pan, arrange the cherry tomatoes, cilantro, garlic, and jalapeño pepper. Sprinkle 2 tablespoons (30 mL) of the olive oil over them and add salt and pepper to taste. Bake for 20 minutes. (The cherry tomatoes should begin to break apart.)

3 Scrape everything into the bowl of a food processor or electric blender container and puree well. Pour into a bowl.

4 Whisk in the vinegar and remaining olive oil. Taste for seasoning, adding salt and pepper, if desired. Cover and set aside.

Grilled Swordfish Steaks

2 pounds (1 kg) swordfish, cut into 4 equal portions

¹/₄ cup (50 mL) olive oil

Salt and freshly ground pepper to taste

3 tablespoons (45 mL) chopped fresh chervil (or savory, tarragon, dill, or thyme)

1 Place the swordfish steaks on a baking sheet. Rub all over with olive oil and season generously with salt and pepper. Sprinkle chervil evenly over the tops of the steaks. Refrigerate for 1 hour.

2 Preheat a charcoal or gas grill.

3 When the grill is hot, cook the swordfish for about 2 to 3 minutes per side (depending on thickness) or until done. Transfer to warm plates. Spoon some of the vinaigrette onto the plate and set the fish over it. If desired, garnish with chervil, basil, or other herb of choice.

(continued)

Yield: 4 servings.

Note: If you'd rather, you can cook the entire recipe in your oven. After roasting the cherry tomato mixture for about 12 minutes, simply turn on the oven broiler to cook the swordfish for about 4 minutes per side or until done.

Serve this swordfish with Baby Carrots in Cumin Butter (see Chapter 14), Couscous with Yellow Squash (see Chapter 14), or Grilled Peppers (see Chapter 6).

Egg-Based Sauces: Hollandaise and Mayonnaise

Hollandaise is the most common of all egg-based sauces. Your first introduction to hollandaise probably came at a fancy brunch with your parents where they served Eggs Benedict — hopefully not from the steam table.

Hollandaise is a good exercise for beginners because if you blow it, you can repair it easily (see following What If icon). The rich, lemon-tinged hollandaise has chameleonic qualities: Add tarragon and chervil, and you have Béarnaise; add tomato, and you have Choron (good with steak); fold in heavy cream, and you have Chantilly; add dried mustard, and you have a fine accompaniment to boiled vegetables.

Hollandaise

Tools: Whisk, bowl, double boiler, rubber spatula

Preparation time: About 10 minutes

Cooking time: About 10 minutes

4 egg yolks, separated (see illustrated instructions for separating an egg in Chapter 8)

1 tablespoon (15 mL) cold water

¹/₂ cup (8 tablespoons/125 mL) room-temperature butter, cut into 8 pieces

2 tablespoons (30 mL) lemon juice

Salt and freshly ground white pepper to taste

(continued)

1 In a bowl, whisk the egg yolks for about 2 minutes or until they are thick and yellow. (See Chapter 8 for what to do with the leftover egg whites.) Add the water, whisking for about another minute, until the sauce easily coats a spoon. Transfer the contents to the top of a double boiler and set over water that is almost boiling. Heat until just warm, about 3 minutes, stirring constantly with a rubber spatula.

2 Add the butter 2 tablespoons (2 pieces) at a time, stirring vigorously until each batch is incorporated completely. Continue cooking, stirring and scraping the sides of the pot, until the sauce thickens enough to coat the back of a metal spoon. Add the lemon juice and salt and pepper to taste and cook about 1 minute more, or until the sauce is smooth and heated through.

Yield: *About ³/₄ cup (175 mL).*

The most common foul-up that beginners make when making hollandaise is to leave it on the heat until it curdles or breaks down. If that happens, or if the sauce becomes too thick, beat in 1 to 2 tablespoons (15 to 30 mL) boiling water. Stir until the sauce becomes smooth. To avoid lumpy hollandaise, be sure to lower the heat if the water starts to boil.

If your blender is not tied up on daiquiri patrol, you might try the following quick and quite satisfactory method of turning out hollandaise.

Blender Hollandaise

Tools: *Blender, double boiler (optional)*

Preparation time: *About 10 minutes*

4 egg yolks

2 tablespoons (30 mL) lemon juice

Pinch of salt

Freshly ground white pepper to taste

¹/₂ cup (125 mL) hot, melted butter

In a blender container, combine the egg yolks, lemon juice, and salt and pepper; cover and blend for about 30 seconds at low speed. With the motor still running, add the hot butter in a very thin drizzle (use the blender's feed tube, if you have one). As the sauce thickens, increase the volume gradually. Continue until the sauce is thick and smooth textured. Use immediately or keep warm in a double boiler until ready to serve.

Yield: *About ²/₃ cup (150 mL).*

Recipes that use raw eggs run a small risk of transmitting salmonella bacteria. Please review Chapter 8 for more information.

Did you ever wonder why a jar of mayonnaise has a refrigerator life longer than the life of the average golden retriever? Does that seem natural to you? Of course not. All the more reason to make your own mayonnaise, which is infinitely better, not to mention that it costs a fraction of the price of the commercial product. Try the following recipe and compare for yourself.

Mayonnaise

Tools: *Wire whisk, mixing bowl*

Preparation time: *About 10 minutes*

1 egg yolk

1 tablespoon (15 mL) fresh lemon juice

1 teaspoon (5 mL) Dijon-style mustard

Salt and freshly ground pepper to taste

1 cup (250 mL) olive oil

1 Place the egg yolk, lemon juice, mustard, and salt and pepper in a medium mixing bowl. Beat well with a wire whisk.

2 While continuing to whisk, add the oil in a thin drizzle. Continue until you use all the oil. (If you do not use the mayonnaise immediately, whip in 1 tablespoon/15 mL water to *stabilize* it, or to hold together all ingredients to form a smooth sauce.)

Yield: *About 1 cup (250 mL).*

You can season mayonnaise in all sorts of ways as an accompaniment to cold vegetables, meats, and appetizers; add dill, chervil, basil, capers, lemon juice, anchovies, chopped watercress, mashed avocado (maybe with Tabasco sauce), and more. Fresh mayonnaise lasts several days when sealed tightly and refrigerated.

The American Egg Board has developed the following recipe for a mayonnaise that gently cooks the egg yolks over very low heat (thus eliminating potential health hazards).

The American Egg Board's Cooked Mayonnaise

Tools: *Small saucepan, wooden spoon, blender, rubber spatula*

Preparation time: *About 10 minutes*

Cooking time: *About 2 minutes, plus 4 minutes standing time*

2 egg yolks

2 tablespoons (30 mL) vinegar or fresh lemon juice

2 tablespoons (30 mL) water

1 teaspoon (5 mL) sugar

1 teaspoon (5 mL) dry mustard

¹/₂ teaspoon (2 mL) salt

Dash pepper

1 cup (250 mL) vegetable oil

1 In a small saucepan, stir together the egg yolks, vinegar or lemon juice, water, sugar, mustard, and salt and pepper with a wooden spoon until thoroughly blended. Cook over very low heat, stirring constantly, until the mixture bubbles in 1 or 2 places.

2 Remove from the heat and let stand for 4 minutes. Pour into a blender container. Cover and blend at high speed.

3 While blending, very slowly add the oil. Blend until thick and smooth, occasionally turning off the motor to scrape down the sides of the container with a rubber spatula. Cover and chill if not using immediately.

Yield: *About 1¹/₄ cups (300 mL).*

Blender Sauces

For cooks in a hurry, the blender can be an invaluable tool. You can make blender sauces literally in minutes. And they are more healthful, too, because they can be bound with vegetables, lowfat cheeses (like ricotta), yogurt, and the like.

Although food processors are unsurpassed for chopping, slicing, and grating, blenders have an edge when it comes to liquefying and sauce-making. Their blades rotate faster, binding (or pulling together) liquids better. The two-level slicing blade on a food processor cuts through liquids instead of blending them, and its wide, flat work bowl is too large for mixing small quantities of sauce.

Blender sauces can be so quick that your dinner guests will suspect that Julia Child is hiding in the pantry. You can transform simple poached fish into something special by combining some of the poaching liquid with wine, fresh

TOQUE TIP

Even the pros use blenders these days

It may seem a minor historical irony that blenders have gained new respectability in the hands of leading French chefs and their American counterparts — the same people who abandoned the appliance two decades ago. Jean Banchet, chef and owner of the acclaimed Riviera restaurant in Atlanta, uses a blender to add smoother texture and subtle color to many of his sauces. "I first saw this when I was in France a few years ago visiting some restaurants, and I liked the way it worked," Banchet says. "Now I do most of my sauces in a blender."

watercress, seasonings, and just a dab of cream or ricotta cheese. When mixed in the blender with several pats of butter, these ingredients create a savory and exceptionally smooth sauce. (Read more about the blender in Chapter 2.)

Certain fruit sauces for desserts also work better in a blender than in a food processor, whether it's a puree of raspberries spiked with *framboise* (French raspberry brandy) or of mango with lime and rum. The same blending principles that apply to sauces for meat and fish succeed with dessert sauces, such as crème à l'Anglaise and sabayon (flavored custard sauces) to pour over poached fruit.

Following are two quick and terrific blender recipes.

Watercress sauce

This watercress sauce works with any smoked fish or meat, fresh vegetables, and omelets, or even as a thin and delicious sandwich spread.

Smoked Trout with Watercress Sauce

Tools: *Blender*

Preparation time: *About 15 minutes*

1¼ cups (300 mL) sour cream

1 cup (250 mL) rinsed and dried watercress (including stems)

½ teaspoon (2 mL) Dijon-style mustard (optional)

Salt and freshly ground pepper to taste

2 smoked trout, skinned and filleted into 4 pieces

1 lemon, quartered

(continued)

1 Place the sour cream, watercress, and, if desired, the mustard in a blender container. Blend at low speed until the sour cream liquefies and begins to incorporate the watercress.

2 Turn the blender to high for several seconds; then shut off the motor. Adjust seasoning with pepper and only enough salt to bring out the flavor of the watercress. (Smoked trout is already slightly salty.) Spoon 2 to 3 tablespoons (30 to 45 mL) of sauce over each serving of trout. Garnish with lemon wedges.

Yield: *4 servings.*

Pesto sauce

Pesto is a favorite summertime sauce that you can make easily in the blender. It goes beautifully with pasta, cold meats, and crudités. Try swirling a bit of pesto into a sauce of summer tomatoes as a topping for broiled fish or chicken or pasta.

Pesto Sauce

Tools: *Blender, cheese grater, rubber spatula*

Preparation time: *About 15 minutes*

2 cups (500 mL) fresh basil leaves, stems removed, about 2 ounces (56 g)

¹/₂ cup (125 mL) extra virgin olive oil

3 tablespoons (45 mL) pine nuts or walnuts

1 tablespoon (15 mL) peeled and coarsely chopped garlic, about 3 large cloves

Salt and freshly ground pepper to taste

¹/₂ cup (125 mL) grated Parmesan cheese

1 tablespoon (15 mL) hot water

1 Rinse and pat dry the trimmed basil leaves.

2 Put the basil leaves in the container of a food processor or blender. Add the oil, pine nuts or walnuts, garlic, and salt and pepper. Blend to a fine texture but not a smooth puree, stopping the motor once to scrape the down the sides of the blender container and to force the ingredients down to the blades.

3 Add the Parmesan cheese and water and blend just a few seconds more. Chill until served.

Yield: *About 1 cup (250 mL).*

TIP

Compound Butters

Take fresh herbs, chop them, and then squish them in your hands into room-temperature butter, and you have what chefs call *compound butter.* You can make these butters ahead of time and take them out of the refrigerator as you need them. Compound butters are great with all sorts of foods.

A dollop of herb butter atop a piece of grilled meat or fish makes a sprightly garnish that is more appropriate to warm weather than a heavy sauce. Herb butters also bring out the best in steamed vegetables. (See Chapter 3 for steamed and boiled vegetable recipes.) And in combination with white wine or stock, herb butters are the foundations of quick, flavorful sauces for all kinds of foods.

You can prepare many herb butters without using a blender or food processor. Simply let the butter soften in a bowl until it's malleable but not too soft and then work in the seasonings with your hands. Scoop the mixture onto a sheet of plastic wrap and cool the mixture slightly until you can mold it with your hands. Then roll the herb butter into a cylinder and wrap well. It lasts for months in the refrigerator.

Herb butter combinations are as varied as the gardens to which you have access. A bouquet garni butter made with finely minced bay leaf, parsley, and thyme is a versatile garnish to have around the house. It is so tasty that you can use it as a table butter for toast and sandwiches. Tarragon, sorrel, basil, chives, garlic, sage, chervil, shallots, and even spinach work well in various combinations. Try sorrel and parsley with fish, sage and shallots with fowl or game, and basil with tomatoes. Probably the best-known compound butter is *maitre d'hôtel,* which combines parsley, lemon juice, and salt and pepper. Maitre d'hôtel generally accompanies chicken or fish.

Compound butter sauces

With compound butters, you can make many quick butter sauces right in the pan in which you cook meat or fish. For example, if you sauté a fillet of swordfish that you have seasoned and rubbed with oil, after you take it out of the pan you can add half a stick of melted butter (for 4 portions) and 2 tablespoons (30 mL) rinsed and drained capers, working over medium heat. When the butter turns golden, add 1 tablespoon (15 mL) fresh lemon juice and a pinch of salt. Stir well, letting the butter sizzle but not turn too dark. Pour over the swordfish fillet.

After you learn to make this quick pan sauce, you can do all sorts of variations. Instead of capers, add fresh dill, basil, thyme, minced garlic, mustard, shallots, grated orange rind, or tomato paste. The list is endless.

Orange butter?

As a cook, you can have great fun experimenting with vegetable butters in all colors of the garden. A recent test with carrots elevated dishes of fresh vegetables into something both whimsical and delicious. After you discover this simple technique, you may be tempted to make your refrigerator dairy section look like a Crayola box.

Simple carrot butter can be the highlight of a dinner party when served over steamed red new potatoes.

Carrot Butter

Tools: *Saucepan, blender or food processor*

Preparation time: *About 5 minutes*

Cooking time: *About 15 minutes*

1 large carrot, scraped and cut into 6 pieces

1 stick (¹/₂ cup/125 mL) unsalted butter at room temperature

Dash of ground nutmeg

Salt and freshly ground white pepper to taste

1 Cook the carrot pieces in lightly salted boiling water until tender. Drain and put them in a blender or food processor container.

2 Add the butter, nutmeg, and salt and white pepper. Puree the mixture, stopping to scrape down the sides of the container if necessary. Put the mixture in a serving dish and chill until needed.

Yield: *About ¹/₂ cup (125 mL).*

Dessert Sauces

Most dessert sauces are so easy that you can make them during TV commercials. And you can vary almost all of them in innumerable ways.

Dessert sauces come in two basic types: cream based and fruit based. Cream-based recipes usually require cooking, but you can often make the fruit sauces right in a blender. In this section, you'll find some popular sauces and ways to modify them.

The following smooth and creamy vanilla sauce dresses up ice cream, fresh strawberries, pound cake, poached pears, soufflés, and cold mousses.

Keep in mind that when you're making this sauce, as well as custards and yeast breads, you scald milk primarily to shorten the cooking time. Without bringing it to a boil, cook the milk (or cream) in a saucepan over medium-low heat until it foams.

Be careful not to cook the following vanilla sauce too long. Also, maintain a low to medium-low heat setting to prevent the sauce from curdling. If the sauce curdles, whisk it quickly or whirl it in a blender container to cool it rapidly.

Vanilla Sauce

Tools: *Electric mixer, heavy saucepan, mixing bowl, wire whisk, sieve*

Preparation time: *About 15 minutes*

Cooking time: *About 25 minutes*

1 cup (250 mL) heavy cream	*4 egg yolks*
1 cup (250 mL) milk	*¼ cup (50 mL) granulated sugar*
2 vanilla beans, split lengthwise	

1 Place the cream, milk, and vanilla beans in a heavy medium saucepan. Scald the milk-cream mixture (bring to foam but not to boiling). Remove from heat and let sit for 15 to 20 minutes.

2 In a mixing bowl, beat the egg yolks and sugar for several minutes (a hand-held mixer or standup mixer makes beating easier). The mixture should be pale yellow and thick.

3 Return the cream mixture to the heat and scald it again. Pour about one-quarter of the hot cream mixture into the egg yolks and whisk vigorously. Pour the egg mixture into the saucepan that is holding the rest of the cream. Cook over low heat, stirring, about 4 to 5 minutes or until it thickens enough to coat the back of a metal spoon. Strain through a sieve into a bowl, cover, and chill.

Yield: *2 cups (500 mL).*

Note: *Many recipes call for vanilla extract. Vanilla extract is convenient, but using a whole, split vanilla bean is far preferable, especially for sauces and custards. You simply take a sharp knife and make an incision lengthwise to expose the crumbly black seeds before adding the bean to the recipe. Look for vanilla bean in the spice section of your supermarket. You can substitute 2 teaspoons (10 mL) vanilla extract for 1 whole vanilla bean.*

Variations: Add flavorings of your choice: rum, Grand Marnier, kirsch, or brandy. Three to 4 tablespoons should suffice. Or add 2 to 3 teaspoons instant coffee.

Cracklin' Hot Fudge Sauce is a twist on regular chocolate sauce and is ideal for ice cream. Because it has butter in it, the sauce turns hard when poured over ice cream and forms a thin, cracklin' crust.

Cracklin' Hot Fudge Sauce

Tools: *Sifter, saucepan, chef's knife, wooden spoon*

Preparation time: *About 15 minutes*

Cooking time: *About 5 minutes*

1 cup (250 mL) powdered sugar, sifted (see Chapter 2 for sifting instructions)

¹/₂ cup (125 mL) unsalted butter (1 stick)

¹/₂ cup (125 mL) heavy cream

8 ounces (224 g) bittersweet chocolate, chopped (see following Improvise icon)

2 teaspoons (10 mL) vanilla extract

1 In a heavy saucepan over medium-low heat, combine the powdered sugar, butter, and cream. Stir with a wooden spoon until smooth.

2 Remove the pan from the heat and add the chocolate, stirring until smooth. Then add the vanilla and stir to blend.

Yield: *About 2 cups (500 mL).*

You can prepare this sauce up to a week ahead of time and keep it covered and refrigerated. Rewarm in a double boiler or in the microwave.

If you can't find bittersweet chocolate, substitute the more common semisweet chocolate and reduce the powdered sugar by 2 tablespoons (30 mL).

Chop chocolate into pieces on a cutting board with a sharp knife or whirl the chocolate in the container of a blender or food processor for a few seconds until coarsely chopped.

You have no excuse to serve chemical tasting, aerosol whipped cream. The real thing is so easy and so good that everyone should know how to make it. Spoon sweetened, flavored whipped cream over pies, pudding, cakes, mousses, poached fruit, your cat's nose — anything!

Whipped Cream

Tools: *Chilled bowl, whisk or electric hand mixer*

Preparation time: *About 5 minutes*

1 cup (250 mL) well-chilled heavy cream

3 teaspoons (15 mL) sugar, or to taste

1 teaspoon (5 mL) vanilla extract, or to taste

In a chilled bowl, combine the cream, sugar, and vanilla. Beat with a whisk or electric mixer on medium speed until the cream thickens and forms peaks. (Do not overbeat, or the cream will become lumpy.)

Yield: *About 2 cups (500 mL).*

Add 1 tablespoon (15 mL) unsweetened cocoa powder before mixing; add 1 tablespoon (15 mL) instant coffee; or add 1 or 2 tablespoons (15 to 30 mL) Grand Marnier, Kahlua, Cointreau, Crème de Menthe, or other liqueur.

Caramel forms when the moisture is cooked out of sugar and the sugar turns dark golden. Caramel sauce is simply caramel thinned out with a little water, lemon juice, and cream so that it pours easily and has more flavor. It is delicious as a coating on meringue, ice cream, and fruit compotes.

Caramel Sauce

Tools: *Medium saucepan, whisk, wooden spoon*

Preparation time: *About 5 minutes*

Cooking time: *About 10 minutes*

1 cup (250 mL) granulated sugar

$^1/_3$ cup (75 mL) water

$^1/_2$ teaspoon (2 mL) lemon juice

$^2/_3$ cup (150 mL) heavy cream

1 Combine in a saucepan over medium-low heat the sugar, water, and lemon juice. Stir with a wooden spoon, about 3 minutes, until the sugar dissolves.

2 Increase the heat to medium-high and cook, stirring occasionally, until the mixture reaches an amber color, about 3 to 4 minutes. (The mixture boils rather rapidly.)

(continued)

3 If you want a medium-colored caramel, remove the mixture from the heat when it is still light golden because it continues to cook and darken off the heat. For dark caramel, remove when medium golden-brown. Remove the pan from the heat and gradually pour in the heavy cream, stirring with a wire whisk. (Be careful: The cream bubbles wildly as you do so.)

4 When all is incorporated, return the saucepan to medium-low heat and stir for 2 to 3 minutes or until the mixture is velvety. To reconstitute it after it cools, reheat it in a microwave or over medium heat on the stove.

Yield: *1 cup (250 mL).*

Quick sauces made with fresh, seasonal fruit could not be easier. The following technique also works for blueberries, raspberries, and lingonberries. (When making raspberry sauces, strain the sauce through a fine sieve before serving to remove the seeds.) These sauces are wonderful as toppings for ice cream, fresh fruits, custards, and puddings.

Fresh Strawberry Sauce

Tools: *Paring knife, food processor or blender*

Preparation time: *About 10 minutes*

1 quart (1 L) fresh strawberries, hulled (stems removed) and washed

1 tablespoon (15 mL) fresh lemon juice

2 tablespoons (30 mL) confectioners' sugar, or to taste, depending on fruit's ripeness

Place all ingredients in the bowl of a blender or food processor; puree until smooth. Taste for sweetness and add more sugar, if desired. Serve over ice cream, pound cake, or a big bowl of mixed berries.

Yield: *About 2 cups (500 mL).*

For extra flavor, add rum, kirsch, flavored vodka, or other liqueur of choice.

Part III

Expand Your Repertoire

In this part . . .

Here's where the music starts. You grab your culinary baton and start off slowly, executing the basics. From there, we tell you how to jazz things up — always in a harmonious way.

This part covers various categories of food — from sauces to soups and salads to one-pot meals. We explain the foundations of each category and also give you some ideas for improvising.

After a little bit of practice, you'll be ready to invite volunteer diners over for a meal. Solicit their opinions, always starting with their praise. And keep an open mind.

Chapter 8
The Amazing Egg

. . . .

In This Chapter

▶ The fresh egg test

▶ Cooking eggs the "hard" way

▶ Scrambling around

▶ The Big Three: omelets, frittatas, and soufflés

▶ Don't throw out those extra whites

. . . .

*N*othing helps scenery like ham and eggs.

— Mark Twain

Eggs are the Michael Jordan of the food world — they can do it all. What other food carries its main ingredient (the yolk) and a lightening agent (the white) all in the same convenient package?

Moreover, the repertoire of egg cooking embraces most of the techniques we stress in this book. Making eggs is a great way to start out, especially if your family is big on breakfast. And believe us, the first time a golden-brown soufflé comes out of the oven, with a golden puffed lid and an aroma that makes you weak-kneed, you'll be hooked.

Selecting Fresh Eggs

Freshness is of paramount concern for egg eaters. As an egg ages, the white breaks down and the membrane covering the yolk deteriorates. So if you cook an older egg, chances are greater that the yolk will break.

A short history of egg cookery

Egg cookery goes back at least to the Egyptians, who used eggs in bread-making, among other things. Western Europe didn't become acquainted with eggs on a wide scale until the 19th century.

In the mid-20th century, chicken-raising in the United States became high tech. Chickens weren't too keen on spending most of the day in a dark barn, but egg production exploded. The average chicken today produces from 250 to 300 eggs per year. (Talk about a Type A personality.)

Concern about cholesterol in the diet has curtailed egg consumption slightly in the U.S., but egg-eating is by no means nearing extinction.

Consumers rely on the expiration date on the carton and on the *Julian date,* which indicates the day the eggs were actually packed in their carton. A Julian date of 002, for example, means that the eggs were packed on January 2, or the second day of the year. As a standard, you should use eggs within 4 to 5 weeks of their packed date. But you can use other methods, like the cold water test described in the sidebar "Egg freshness: The cold water test," to determine the freshness of an egg.

Egg grading, sizing, and coloring

In the supermarket, you generally see two grades of eggs: AA and A. The differences between the grades are hardly noticeable to the average home cook. Purchase either grade.

Egg size is based on a minimum weight per dozen: 30 ounces (840 g) per dozen for jumbo eggs, 27 ounces (756 g) for extra large, 24 ounces (672 g) for large, and 21 ounces (588 g) for medium. Most recipes call for large eggs.

Shell color is not related to quality. Brown and speckled eggs are produced by a particular breed of chicken. Free-range eggs are laid by chickens that are allowed to roam outdoors under less controlled conditions than caged birds.

Egg freshness: The cold water test

If you want to have a little fun at home, pour cold water into a bowl and place a raw egg (in the shell) in the water. The fresher the egg, the faster it sinks to the bottom. If the egg floats, have cornflakes for breakfast instead.

Dollars for eggheads

Here's one to remember in case you are ever on a quiz show and the host says:

"For $500: By spinning an egg on a countertop, you can determine what?"

Tick ... tick ... tick ...

"Okay, Vern! What's your answer?"

"Uh, the gravity in the room?"

"Sorry, Vern, the correct answer is whether it's cooked: A hard-cooked egg, which has a solid center, spins quickly and easily; a raw egg, because it has liquid swishing around inside, does not."

Blood spots

Contrary to what most people believe, blood spots on an egg are not a sign that the egg was fertilized. They are usually the result of a blood vessel rupturing on the surface of the yolk. The spot does not affect flavor, and the egg is perfectly edible. You can remove the blood spot with the tip of a knife.

Raw Eggs

The American Egg Board, a marketing and research organization for the egg industry, does not recommend the consumption of raw eggs, yet many recipes call for them. Salmonella, one of several types of bacteria that can cause food poisoning, has been found inside a small number of raw eggs. Although the likelihood of an egg being infected is small — about .005 percent, or 1 in every 20,000 eggs — eating an infected egg can certainly put a damper on your golf game.

You can't tell by looking whether an egg is infected. Bacteria is completely destroyed when the egg reaches a temperature of 160° F (70° C). To be safe, you should avoid recipes that call for uncooked egg whites and yolks. And never eat an egg whose shell is cracked or broken. Cracked eggs become vulnerable to other types of bacteria, so you should throw them away.

Hard-Cooked Eggs

Eggs should never be boiled in their shells, but rather hard-cooked; boiling causes eggs to jostle and crack. The correct technique is to place the eggs in cold water, bring the water to a boil, and then immediately remove them from the heat, as in the following steps:

1. **Place the eggs in a saucepan large enough to hold them in a single layer. Add cold water to cover by about 1 inch.**

2. **Cover the saucepan and bring the water to a boil over high heat as fast as possible. Then turn off the heat.**

   If your stove is electric, remove the pan from the burner.

3. **Let eggs stand in the pan for 15 minutes for large eggs, 18 minutes for jumbo, and 12 minutes for small.**

4. **Drain the eggs in a colander in the sink and run cold water over them until completely cooled.**

Hard-cooked eggs have numerous uses. Slice them into tossed green salads or potato salads, make deviled eggs from them, mash them for egg salad sandwiches, or plan egg-decorating parties with your kids.

Peeling a hard-cooked egg

The fresher the egg, the more difficult it is to peel. Hard-cook eggs that have been refrigerated for a week to ten days or less. Then follow these steps to peel the eggs as soon as they are cool enough to handle:

1. **Tap each egg gently on a table or countertop to crackle the shell all over.**

2. **Roll the egg between your hands to loosen the shell.**

3. **Peel off the shell, starting at the large end of the egg.**

   Holding the egg under running water as you work makes peeling easier.

Egg salad for grown-ups

Egg salad is a classic for picnics and brown-bag lunches. And after you get the basic formula down, you can vary it in countless ways.

Let your taste buds and what's available in your refrigerator determine how you dress up this basic egg salad. You can add any number of ingredients to taste, such as flavored mustard, chopped pickles, minced onion, diced celery, fresh or dried herbs such as parsley, dill, or tarragon, sweet relish, or Tabasco sauce.

Easy Egg Salad

Tools: *Medium mixing bowl, fork*

Preparation time: *About 5 minutes*

Cooking time: *About 15 minutes*

4 hard-cooked eggs, peeled

2 tablespoons (30 mL) mayonnaise

Salt and freshly ground pepper to taste

Mash the hard-cooked eggs in a medium mixing bowl with a fork. Add the mayonnaise and season to taste with salt and pepper. Cover and refrigerate until ready to use.

Yield: *Enough for 2 sandwiches or servings.*

Scrambling Eggs

Keep this tip in mind if you want to make excellent scrambled eggs: Don't overbeat the eggs before you cook them.

Some scrambled egg recipes call for cream, which adds a nice smoothness to the eggs; others call for water, which increases the volume by stimulating the whites to foam. You can use either ingredient for the following recipe — try it both ways and see which you prefer.

Scrambled Eggs

Tools: *Medium bowl, fork, 10-inch (25-cm) skillet or omelet pan, spatula*

Preparation time: *About 5 minutes*

Cooking time: *About 1 minute*

6 eggs

2 tablespoons (30 mL) light cream, lowfat milk, or water

2 tablespoons (30 mL) chopped chives (optional)

Salt and freshly ground pepper to taste

2 tablespoons (30 mL) butter

(continued)

1 Break the eggs into a bowl. With a fork, beat the eggs until they are blended, but no more. Add the cream, chopped chives (if desired), and salt and pepper and beat a few seconds to blend well.

2 Melt the butter in a 10-inch (25-cm) skillet over medium heat. (Do not let it burn.) Pour in the egg mixture. As the mixture begins to set, use a spatula to pull the eggs gently across the bottom and sides of the pan, forming large, soft curds. The eggs are cooked when the mixture is no longer runny.

Yield: *3 servings.*

 You can dress up this basic scrambled eggs recipe by adding different season-ings to the liquid egg mixture, such as a dash of Tabasco sauce, a sprinkling of dry mustard or ground ginger, 2 tablespoons (30 mL) of chopped fresh parsley or basil, or a teaspoon (5 mL) or so of freshly grated lemon peel.

Making Omelets in a Flash

Supposedly, the first omelet was made by the ancient Romans, who sweetened it with honey and named it the *ovemele.* A plain omelet is quick and easy and cooked on top of the range, whereas a soufflé omelet combines stiff whites and beaten yolks and is finished in the oven.

You can serve the following basic omelet cooked on the range for breakfast, brunch, lunch, or dinner. If you're in a rush (and who isn't?), you can't beat it. Various garnishes, such as watercress, parsley, tarragon, or chives, make the omelet more eye-appealing.

If you cook the omelet properly, the skin is very smooth and the center is a little moist. You can change the herbs to suit seasonality or personal tastes. And fillings are unlimited: cheese, cooked vegetables, ham, hot peppers, and much more. (See the sidebar "Ten omelet variations" for suggestions.)

Omelet with Herbs

Tools: *Chef's knife, mixing bowl, fork, 10-inch (25-cm) omelet pan or skillet, rubber spatula*

Preparation time: *About 10 minutes*

Cooking time: *Less than 1 minute*

3 eggs

1 teaspoon (5 mL) chopped fresh tarragon, or ¹/₄ teaspoon (2 mL) dried

2 teaspoons (10 mL) chopped fresh parsley, or ¹/₂ teaspoon (2 mL) dried

1 tablespoon (30 mL) chopped chives

Salt and freshly ground pepper to taste

2 teaspoons (10 mL) butter

1 Place all ingredients except the butter and 1 teaspoon (5 mL) of the fresh herbs (reserve for garnish) in a mixing bowl and beat with a fork — just enough to combine the whites and yolks. (If you're using dried herbs, chop extra chives for garnish.)

2 Melt the butter in a prewarmed 10-inch (25-cm) omelet pan or skillet over medium-high heat. Make sure that the butter is hot and foaming, but not browned, before you add the eggs. Pour in the omelet mixture. It should begin to set at the edges immediately.

3 Using a rubber spatula, gently pull the cooked edges toward the center to expose the liquid mixture to the bottom of the pan, tilting the pan if necessary. When the mixture solidifies, remove the pan from the heat and let it rest for a few seconds. The center should be a little moist because the omelet continues to cook in the hot pan. (If you are making an omelet with a filling, add the filling at this point.)

4 Holding the pan so that it tilts away from you, use the spatula to fold about one-third of the near side of the omelet toward the center.

5 Firmly grasping the pan handle with one hand, lift the pan off the stove, keeping it tilted slightly down and away from you. (Be sure to use a pot holder!) Leave a little bit of the handle tip exposed. With the other hand, strike the handle tip two or three times with the side of your fist to swing up the far side of the pan. Doing so causes the far edge of the omelet to fold back on itself, completing the envelope. Use the spatula to press the omelet closed at the seam. Roll the omelet onto a warm dish, seam side down. Sprinkle the remaining herbs on the top. (See Figure 8-1 for illustrated instructions.)

Yield: *1 serving.*

For lunch or a light dinner, serve this omelet with a tossed green salad and Sautéed Cubed Potatoes (see Chapter 4), or the French Potato Salad in Chapter 10. Serve with a chilled Beaujolais.

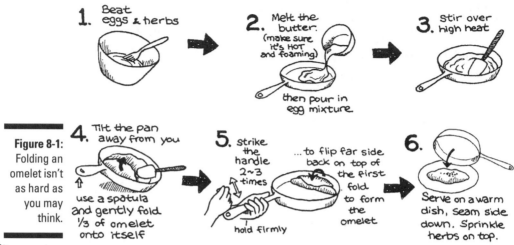

Folding an Omelet

1. Beat eggs & herbs

2. Melt the butter. (make sure it's HOT and foaming) then pour in egg mixture

3. Stir over high heat

Figure 8-1: Folding an omelet isn't as hard as you may think.

4. Tilt the pan away from you — use a spatula and gently fold 1/3 of omelet onto itself

5. strike the handle 2~3 times — hold firmly — ...to flip far side back on top of the first fold to form the omelet

6. Serve on a warm dish, seam side down. Sprinkle herbs on top.

IMPROVISE

Ten omelet variations

To alter the basic omelet recipe, omit the herbs and chives and use 1/2 cup (125 mL, more or less) of any of the following ingredients. There's no limit to the type and combination of ingredients, herbs, or seasonings that you can use to fill and flavor an omelet. Be sure to prepare your fillings before you start cooking the eggs and add them just before folding the omelet.

- **Cheese:** Grated hard cheese, such as cheddar, Swiss, or Gruyère, and soft and semisoft cheese, such as mozzarella, goat, or Brie

- **Spanish:** Any combination of chopped tomatoes, green peppers, onions, and hot sauce, or a couple of tablespoons of bottled salsa

- **Vegetarian:** Cooked, chopped asparagus, artichoke hearts, mushrooms, white or sweet potatoes, spinach, broccoli, or cauliflower; slices of avocado; grilled, sliced eggplant; and red peppers

- **Mediterranean:** Feta cheese, tomatoes, spinach, and onions

- **Seafood:** Smoked salmon or trout, crab meat, or cooked shrimp

- **Meat:** Cooked, crumbled bacon or sausage, diced cooked ham, or salami

- **Leftovers:** Chinese food, grilled hot dogs, mashed potatoes, cooked rice, or anything else to help clean out the refrigerator

- **Mixed greens:** Watercress, arugula, or spinach, with a dollop of sour cream

- **Mushrooms:** Sautéed button, portobello, crimini, or oyster mushrooms

- **Fruit fillings:** Sliced strawberries, grated apple, or sautéed peaches or pears

Keep in mind that fresh herbs and dried herbs are similar in flavor but different in potency. Fresh herbs are more delicate; dried herbs are more concentrated. When a recipe calls for, say, 1 teaspoon (5 mL) of fresh thyme and you have only dried thyme, use roughly a third to a half of the quantity.

If the butter burns before you add the egg mixture, carefully wipe the pan clean with paper towels and start again, being careful this time not to let the butter brown. If the folding is too difficult or the omelet gets stuck in the pan, serve the omelet folded in half or pancake style, unfolded, and keep practicing.

Frittatas: All Dressed Up in No Time at All

The Italian frittata can get time-pressed cooks out of a jam in no time. Making a frittata is simple, yet you can dress it up so that it looks great. The fundamental difference between an omelet and a frittata is that an omelet is made with eggs and seasonings and then filled with sundry ingredients; a frittata incorporates the ingredients in the egg mixture. The result is sort of like a cake, slightly thicker and more firm than an omelet. Moreover, an omelet is cooked completely on top of the stove, while a frittata, according to most versions, is finished under the broiler.

You can use an omelet pan or a nonstick, ovenproof skillet for this recipe.

Frittata with Sweet Peppers and Potatoes

Tools: Chef's knife, mixing bowl, 12-inch (30-cm) ovenproof skillet with lid

Preparation time: About 20 minutes

Cooking time: About 20 minutes

8 eggs

2 tablespoons (30 mL) finely chopped fresh basil or parsley, or 2 teaspoons (10 mL) dried

Salt and freshly ground pepper to taste

1/4 pound (125 mL) Gruyère or Swiss cheese (or any hard, aged cheese), cut into small cubes

2 tablespoons (30 mL) vegetable oil

2 small red potatoes, thinly sliced, about 1/2 pound (250 g)

1 1/2 cups (375 mL) sweet red pepper, cored, seeded, and cut into 1/2-inch cubes, about l medium pepper

1 1/2 cups (375 mL) green pepper, cored, seeded, and cut into 1/2-inch cubes, about l medium pepper

1/4 cup (60 mL) peeled and chopped onion, about l small onion

1 tablespoon (15 mL) olive oil

(continued)

1 Beat the eggs in a medium mixing bowl with the basil or parsley and salt and pepper. Add the cheese and set aside.

2 Heat the 2 tablespoons (30 mL) vegetable oil in a 12-inch (30-cm) nonstick skillet over medium heat. Add the potatoes in a single layer and cook for about 4 minutes, turning them over and shaking the pan occasionally. Add the peppers and onion and cook for 5 to 7 minutes or until the vegetables are tender, stirring occasionally.

3 Raise the heat to medium-high. Add the tablespoon (15 mL) of olive oil and the egg-cheese mixture to the skillet and cook for about 1 minute, running a rubber spatula around the edges to make sure it does not stick. Cover and reduce the heat to medium. Cook for about 5 minutes or until the bottom is set and golden brown. The top should still be wet.

4 As the frittata cooks, preheat the oven broiler.

5 Uncover the skillet and place it under the broiler on the highest oven rack. Broil (with the oven door open) for about 1 minute or until the top is cooked solid and golden.

6 To serve, run a rubber spatula around the outside of the frittata. Invert a large, round serving plate over the pan and invert the pan and plate again quickly, letting the frittata fall onto the plate. It should be golden brown. Serve immediately or at room temperature.

Yield: *4 servings.*

Note: *To core and seed a pepper, first cut a circle around the stem with a paring knife and then twist and pull out the stem and core in one piece. Cut the pepper in half lengthwise and remove any remaining white fibers and seeds. (See Figure 4-2 for illustrated instructions.)*

For a brunch or lunch serve this frittata with the Watercress, Endive and Orange Salad or the Roasted Pepper and Snow Pea Salad, both from Chapter 10.

Soufflé Savvy

Most home cooks are intimidated by soufflés, believing that if they look at one the wrong way, it will collapse like a house of cards, causing snickers among their guests. The truth is that soufflés are no more challenging than poached eggs.

After you learn the technique of making a soufflé — either sweet or savory — you can take off in many directions. All you do is decide on a main ingredient (in the first recipe, cheese) and combine it with egg yolks and seasonings, and then you fold in whipped egg whites. Savory soufflés often have a roux base (flour, butter, and milk) to give them muscle.

Soufflés are usually baked in round, straight-sided, ovenproof soufflé dishes. The straight sides allow the mixture to rise above the rim of the dish as it bakes. But you can substitute a straight-sided casserole dish as long as it is the correct size. If the dish is too big, the soufflé may not rise sufficiently above the rim. If the container is too small, the mixture may spill over onto the oven floor.

To make a soufflé, you need even, uninterrupted heat in the oven. So avoid the temptation to keep opening the door to peek in the oven.

Separating an egg

Soufflés require separated egg whites and yolks. Don't worry; separating an egg really isn't as difficult as it looks. Follow these steps, as illustrated in Figure 8-2, to separate an egg without breaking the yolk. (You don't want any yolk in your whites, or the whites will not beat stiff.)

1. **Hold the egg in one hand over two small bowls.**

2. **Crack the shell on the side of one bowl — just enough to break through the shell and the membrane without piercing the yolk.**

   This step might take a little practice. Repeat on the other side if necessary.

3. **Pry open the eggshell with both thumbs and gently let the bulk of the white fall into one of the bowls.**

4. **Pass the yolk back and forth from one shell cavity to the other, each time releasing more white.**

5. **When all the white is in the bowl, carefully transfer the yolk to a separate bowl or container and refrigerate, covered.**

Figure 8-2: Recipes often call for separated egg yolks or whites. Follow these steps to get only the part you want.

How to Separate an Egg

1. Hold the egg in one hand over two small bowls

2. Crack the shell on the side of one bowl

3. Let the white fall into one of the bowls

4. Pass the yolk back & forth, each time releasing more white

5. When all the white is in the bowl, drop yolk in the other bowl.

The copper connection

We won't go into the scientific details of why copper bowls are best for whipping egg whites — just believe us. As far back as the mid-18th century, cooks took this tradition for common knowledge. Just remember that if you are making a meringue or other dish that requires whipped whites, whipping the whites in a copper bowl with a whisk yields a creamier, more stable foam.

A 10-inch (25-cm) copper bowl for whisking costs about $60. If you don't have a copper bowl, a pinch of cream of tartar also can stabilize the foam.

Beating egg whites

Beaten egg whites make soufflés rise. Before beating egg whites, make sure that your mixing bowl and beaters are clean and dry. Even a speck of dirt, oil, or egg yolk can prevent the whites from beating stiff. Beat the whites slowly until they are foamy; then increase the beating speed to incorporate as much air as possible until the whites form smooth, shiny peaks. (If you use a whisk, the same principle applies.) If you're making a sweet soufflé, start beating in the sugar after the whites form soft peaks.

If any of the yolk breaks and falls into the separated whites before you beat them stiff, be sure to remove the yolk with a piece of paper towel. Also avoid using plastic bowls when beating whites. Fat and grease adhere to plastic, which can diminish the volume of the beaten whites.

Folding egg whites into a soufflé base

To fold egg whites into a soufflé base, begin by stirring about one-quarter of the beaten whites into the yolk mixture. (This step lightens the batter somewhat.) Then pile the remaining egg whites on top. Use a large rubber spatula to cut down through the center of the mixture to the bottom of the bowl. Pull the spatula toward you to the edge of the bowl, turning it to bring some of the yolk mixture up over the whites. Give the bowl a quarter-turn and repeat this plunging, scooping motion about 10 to 15 times (depending on the amount of batter) until the whites and yolk mixture are combined. Be careful not to overblend, or the beaten whites will deflate. See Figure 8-3 for illustrated instructions of this technique.

How to Fold Egg Whites into a Soufflé Base

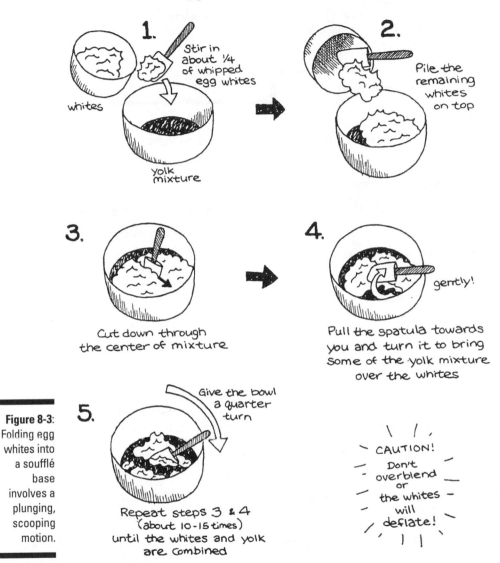

Figure 8-3: Folding egg whites into a soufflé base involves a plunging, scooping motion.

If you overbeat the egg whites so that they lose their shine and start to look dry and grainy, add another egg white and beat briefly to reconstitute. If any egg yolk falls into the separated egg whites, remove the yolk with the tip of a knife or a piece of paper towel before beating.

Basic cheese soufflé

Here is a recipe for a basic cheese soufflé (known as a *savory* soufflé, or one that is not sweet), with some variations.

Gruyère Soufflé

Tools: *6-cup (1.5-L) soufflé dish, chef's knife, mixing bowls, medium saucepan, rubber spatula, electric mixer or wire whisk, cheese grater, baking sheet*

Preparation time: *About 45 minutes*

Baking time: *About 30 minutes*

4 tablespoons (60 mL) butter

6 large eggs

2 tablespoons (30 mL) cornstarch

3 tablespoons (45 mL) water

2 cups (500 mL) milk

3 tablespoons (45 mL) flour

$1/8$ teaspoon (0.5 mL) ground nutmeg

Pinch of cayenne pepper (optional)

Salt and freshly ground white or black pepper to taste

4 ounces (125 g) Gruyère or Swiss cheese (or any hard, aged cheese), cut into small cubes

2 tablespoons (30 mL) grated Gruyère or Swiss cheese

1 Preheat the oven to 400° F (200° C).

2 Place a 6-cup (1.5-L) soufflé dish into the refrigerator to chill. When it's cool, take 1 tablespoon (15 mL) of the butter and thoroughly grease the bottom and sides of the dish, paying special attention to the sides. Return the dish to the refrigerator.

3 Separate the eggs, placing the yolks in one bowl and the whites in a larger bowl. (Refer to Figure 8-2 for instructions for separating eggs.)

4 Blend the cornstarch into the water and set aside. Heat the milk just to the point of boiling and then remove it from the heat.

5 Melt the remaining 3 tablespoons (45 mL) butter in a medium saucepan over medium heat. Add the flour, stirring with a wire whisk. Blend well, but do not brown the flour. Gradually add the warmed milk, stirring rapidly with a wire whisk. Add the nutmeg, cayenne, and salt and pepper. Bring to a boil and cook for 30 seconds, stirring constantly.

(continued)

6 Stir the cornstarch-water mixture into the bubbling sauce and cook for about 2 minutes over medium heat. Add the egg yolks, stirring vigorously. Cook, stirring, for about 1 minute.

7 Spoon and scrape the mixture into a large mixing bowl. Add the cubed Gruyère, blend well with a wire whisk, and set aside.

8 With a flexible balloon-shaped wire whisk or an electric beater, beat the egg whites in a large mixing bowl until stiff and thick. (See "Beating egg whites," earlier in this chapter, for more information.) Add about one-quarter of the whites to the soufflé mixture and mix thoroughly. Add the remaining whites, folding them in quickly but gently with a rubber spatula. (See Figure 8-3 for illustrated instructions for folding whites into batter.)

9 Gently transfer the mixture into the buttered soufflé dish. The mixture should fit inside the dish to about ¼ inch (6mm) from the top. With your thumb, create a channel around the periphery of the dish to allow for expansion. Sprinkle the top with the grated Gruyère or Swiss cheese.

10 Place the dish on a baking sheet on the bottom rack of the oven and bake for about 30 to 35 minutes or until the soufflé rises above the rim of the dish. Serve immediately.

Yield: 4 servings.

For dinner, serve with Baby Carrots in Cumin Butter or Lentils with Balsamic Vinegar, both in Chapter 14.

Or try one of these variations:

- **Salmon soufflé:** Add ¼ pound (125 g) smoked, diced salmon to the beaten egg mixture while it is simmering and being seasoned.

- **Spinach soufflé:** Add 1 cup (250 mL) chopped fresh spinach to the beaten egg mixture while it is simmering and being seasoned.

- **Ham soufflé:** Add ¼ pound (125 g) minced boiled ham or leftover baked ham to the egg mixture while it is simmering and being seasoned.

Basic sweet soufflé

After you master the simple savory soufflé, you can make all kinds of impressive dessert soufflés. Notice the variations for coffee and chocolate soufflés that follow this basic recipe.

Basic Sweet Soufflé

Tools: *Medium saucepan, mixing bowls, wire whisk, electric mixer, rubber spatula, four 1¹/₂-cup (375-mL) soufflé dishes*

Preparation time: *About 45 minutes*

Baking time: *About 12 minutes*

1 cup (250 mL) milk

¹/₂ cup (125 mL) sugar

¹/₃ cup (75 mL) flour

1¹/₂ tablespoons (22 mL) butter

4 large eggs, separated

2 tablespoons (30 mL) vanilla extract

Butter and sugar for greasing and dusting soufflé dishes

Confectioner's sugar

1 Reserve 3 tablespoons (45 mL) milk and place the remaining milk in a saucepan. Bring to a boil.

2 In a medium mixing bowl, combine ¹/₄ cup (50 mL) of the sugar and all the flour. Add the 3 tablespoons (45 mL) reserved cold milk and blend well with a wire whisk. Add a little of the boiling milk and mix well. Pour the mixture into the saucepan with the remaining milk. Blend well, boil for 1 minute, and then remove from heat.

3 Add the butter, blend well, cover, and allow to cool for 15 minutes. Stir in the egg yolks and vanilla extract with a wire whisk. Mix well. (See the following variations to change the flavoring.)

4 Beat the egg whites until they form soft peaks. Gradually add the remaining ¹/₄ cup (50 mL) sugar while continuing to beat until stiff. (See "Beating egg whites," earlier in this chapter, for more information.)

5 Using a rubber spatula, fold half the beaten egg whites into the yolk mixture; then gently fold in the rest. (See Figure 8-3 for illustrated instructions for folding whites into the yolk mixture.)

6 Preheat the oven to 425° F (220° C).

7 Gently spoon and scrape the mixture equally into four individual soufflé dishes (1¹/₂ cups/375 mL each) that you have coated with butter and dusted with sugar. With your thumb, create a channel around the periphery of the dish to leave room for expansion.

(continued)

8 Place the soufflé dishes on a baking sheet and bake for 10 minutes. Lower the oven heat to 400° F (200° C) and bake 2 to 3 minutes longer. Serve sprinkled with powdered (confectioners') sugar or top with cookies or fresh fruit marinated in liqueur of your choice.

Yield: *4 servings.*

To make a coffee soufflé, dissolve 1 tablespoon (15 mL) instant espresso coffee powder (or any strong instant coffee) in the hot milk. Add only 1 tablespoon (15 mL) vanilla extract to the egg yolk mixture.

To make a chocolate soufflé, omit the vanilla extra. Cut 5 ounces (140 g) semisweet chocolate into small bits. Add the chocolate to the mixture immediately after adding the heated milk.

Fun with Leftover Egg Whites and Yolks

From time to time, you'll find yourself with extra egg whites or yolks because some recipes call for only one, or more of one than the other. Do not discard these extras — they have many uses.

With extra yolks, you can do the following:

- ✔ Make a custard or any number of creamy dessert puddings.
- ✔ Use in a cake recipe.
- ✔ Use as a coating for foods dredged in flour or coated with bread crumbs.
- ✔ Use as a natural hair conditioner. (Be sure to rinse well.)

With extra whites, you can do the following:

- ✔ Make a soufflé (but not until you read our instructions).
- ✔ Lighten up the texture of other egg dishes.
- ✔ Make a meringue for a pie.
- ✔ Spread them over your head and upper body and go to a costume ball as Embryo Man.

Chapter 9

Soups

● ●

In This Chapter

▶ Clean the crisper: Improvising soups

▶ The stock market: Whizzing up stock-based soups

▶ Solving soup woes

▶ Garnishing soups

● ●

*N*o offense to the gastronomic wizards at major commercial soup companies, but most seven-year-olds with a recipe and a ladder can make soup that is superior to the canned version. For one, canned soups are always overcooked — overcooking usually occurs in the sterilization process. What's more, the seasonings are toned down so as to offend the smallest number of people — sort of like American beer.

Homemade soups are worth the minimal effort they take for many other reasons, too. For one, homemade soups can be awesomely nutritious. Secondly, they can be stunningly delicious. A soup can be a complete meal or a savory appetizer. In the winter months, a steaming bowl of soup can have a comforting, stick-to-the-ribs quality. In the summer heat, soup can be cold and refreshing. Need we say more?

Soups come in several categories: namely *clear,* as in consommé, certain vegetable soups, and broths; and *creamy,* as in New England-style chowder, vichyssoise (a creamy leek and potato soup), cream of tomato, cream of mushroom, cheesy soups, and so on. Soups that fall in-between include the cloudy Rhode Island Style Chowder, certain vegetable soups, onion soup, and so on. And then you have purees like gazpacho.

What am I eating? Soups defined

Bisque is a thick, rich, pureed soup usually made from seafood or shellfish.

Broth is a clear, flavored liquid made from simmering together any combination of water, vegetables, herbs, meats, poultry, and fish. All the solids are strained out. Broth is often served as an appetizer with a garnish floating on the surface. The French word for broth is *bouillon*.

Chowder is a fish soup with chunky pieces of fish and vegetables.

A *court bouillon* is a broth, usually strained, that simmers for only a short time — no more than 30 minutes — but enough to draw out the flavor in the vegetables, meat, or fish. It's used as a poaching liquid for fish, seafood, and vegetables.

Gumbo is a soup that combines assorted meat, fish, vegetables, a long-cooked dark brown roux of flour and oil, okra, and filé powder (a seasoning made from ground sassafras leaves), which thicken and flavor the soup as it cooks. *Gumbo* is the African word for okra.

A *consommé* is the "consummate" broth that is strained of solids and impurities so that it's clear.

A *fumet* is a strained stock of fish bones, water, vegetables, herbs, and often cloves. It cooks for about 30 minutes and is used as a flavoring base for soups and sauces.

In a *pureed* soup, solid ingredients are whirled in a blender or food processor or forced through a potato masher or food mill. Sometimes the puree is coarse, as in gazpacho (see the recipe later in this chapter). Other times the puree is creamy and velvety, as with a puree of cooked potatoes and leeks. Broth, stock, cream, or a velouté is often added to the vegetable mixture for extra texture and flavor.

Stock is the foundation of countless sauces. (Chapter 3 includes recipes for basic stocks.) It is usually more reduced and intense than broth. In a brown stock (see Chapter 7 for a recipe), meat bones are browned in the oven before being added to a simmering pot of liquid, vegetables, and herbs. This browning gives the stock a rich caramel color and flavor.

Clean the Crisper and Make Some Soup

You may have the makings of a terrific soup at home and not realize it. Start by looking in the vegetable crisper. Do you have carrots and celery? Toss them in a pot of water along with a bay leaf and black peppercorns. If you have parsley, toss that in. An onion? All the better. What you've made is a vegetable stock. The longer you cook and reduce it, the more flavorful it becomes.

To this stock, you can add pieces of cooked chicken, turkey, or beef; noodles; rice; or whatever you have on hand. Just as with sauces, as long as you have a good base, you can build upon it. This chapter includes a cross-section of easy soup bases that show you how to carry on by yourself and improvise to your heart's content.

Making the following soup is a great way to use the remaining meat and bones of a turkey carcass that looks as if a pack of dogs fought over it. Adding inexpensive turkey is a good way to turn a soup into a nutritious meal. The coriander garnish is a flourish that gives the soup an exotic Oriental accent.

Turkey (or Chicken) Vegetable Soup

Tools: *Large saucepan or pot, chef's knife, vegetable peeler*

Preparation time: *About 25 minutes*

Cooking time: *About 30 minutes*

2 tablespoons (30 mL) butter

1 large onion, peeled and chopped, about 1 cup (250 mL)

4 leeks, about 1 pound (500 g), white and pale green parts only, cleaned and sliced into $^1/_4$-inch (6-mm) cubes

3 carrots, scraped and cut into $^1/_4$-inch (6-mm) rounds, about $1^1/_2$ cups (375 mL)

1 parsnip, scraped and cut into $^1/_4$-inch (6-mm) cubes, about $^1/_2$ cup (125 mL)

3 potatoes, about 1 pound (500 g), peeled and cut into $^1/_4$-inch (6-mm) cubes

4 cups (1 L) fresh or canned chicken broth

4 cups (1 L) water

Salt and freshly ground pepper to taste

1 pound (500 g) boneless, skinless turkey or chicken breast (or 1 pound/500 g leftover cooked turkey or chicken), cut into $^1/_2$-inch (12-mm) cubes

3 tablespoons (45 mL) chopped fresh coriander leaves (optional)

1 In a large saucepan or pot over medium heat, melt the butter and add the onion, leeks, carrots, parsnip, and potatoes. Cook, stirring, until the onions and leeks wilt, about 5 minutes.

2 Add the chicken broth, water, and salt and pepper. Cover and bring to a boil; reduce heat and simmer, uncovered, for 30 minutes.

3 Add the turkey or chicken breast cubes and simmer for 20 to 30 minutes more, skimming the surface as necessary. Garnish each serving with fresh coriander, if desired.

Yield: *4 to 6 servings.*

For a light lunch, serve this soup with a Cherrry Tomato and Feta Salad (see Chapter 10).

For a curry flavor, add 1 tablespoon (15 mL) curry powder to the sautéing vegetables in step 1.

Skimming soups and stocks

When making soups or stocks, especially those that contain legumes, meat, or poultry, you often need to use a long-handled spoon to skim the surface of the simmering liquid to remove and discard any scum or foam that rises to the surface.

Try to skim the surface as soon as the foam forms. If you allow it to boil back into the broth, it affects the flavor. Also skim off any fat floating on the surface or refrigerate the soup to chill it and then lift off the congealed fat.

Sometimes you want to thicken your soup so that it looks more luxurious and tastes richer. You can thicken soup in several ways:

✔ Take 1 tablespoon (15 mL) slightly softened butter and work it together with 1 tablespoon (15 mL) all-purpose flour. (The French call this a *beurre manié*, but don't worry about that — they have a different word for everything.) Form the mixture into a ball. Scoop out a cup (250 mL) or so of soup liquid and mix in the flour-butter ball. Walk to the other side of the kitchen and make a free throw into the soup. If you miss, make another ball and try again. When you succeed, stir in the flour-butter ball to thicken the soup.

✔ Blend 1 tablespoon (15 mL) all-purpose flour with 2 tablespoons (30 mL) soup broth. Stir, add about 1 cup (250 mL) more broth, stir again, and add to the soup.

Pureed Soups

Pureed soups use a blender or food processor to whirl the ingredients into a smooth texture. After you understand the pureeing technique, the variations you can make on this cooking theme are limitless. Asparagus, broccoli, corn, cucumber, mushrooms, parsnips, spinach, rutabaga, winter squash, pumpkin, turnip, and watercress are among the vegetables that puree to a rich and smooth consistency.

Pureed soups often combine two or more compatible vegetables — for example, sweet with tart or intense with mild. In the classic, creamy potato-leek soup, pureed potatoes contribute body and texture and are a wonderful foil to the incomparable flavor of sautéed leeks. On a hot summer day, nothing is more refreshing than a bowl of this lovely cold soup.

Cream of Leek Soup

Tools: *Chef's knife, large saucepan or pot, wooden spoon or wire whisk, blender or food processor*

Preparation time: *About 20 minutes*

Cooking time: *About 25 minutes*

4 medium leeks, cleaned and trimmed (see following sidebar)

1 tablespoon (15 mL) butter

2 teaspoons (10 mL) olive oil

1 teaspoon (5 mL) peeled and finely minced garlic, about 1 large clove

3 tablespoons (45 mL) flour

2²/₃ cups (650 mL) chicken or vegetable broth

¹/₂ cup (125 mL) milk

Generous dash of nutmeg (optional)

Salt and freshly ground pepper to taste

¹/₂ cup (125 mL) heavy cream or half and half

4 small chervil sprigs, or 1 tablespoon (15 mL) chopped chives (optional)

1 Quarter the leeks lengthwise and cut into ¹/₂-inch-long (12-mm) pieces. You should have about 2¹/₂ cups (625 mL).

2 In a large saucepan or pot, melt the butter with the olive oil over medium heat. Add the leeks and garlic. Cook for about 2 minutes, stirring often.

3 Add the flour, blending well with a wooden spoon or wire whisk. Add the chicken or vegetable broth, milk, nutmeg, and salt and pepper. Stir well and bring to a simmer. Cook for about 15 to 20 minutes, stirring occasionally. Cool slightly. (See following warning.)

4 Spoon and scrape the mixture into a blender or food processor container and puree well.

5 To serve hot, warm the cream or half and half. Just before serving, add it to the soup and stir well. To serve cold, chill the soup and add the cold cream or half and half before serving. Always check seasonings before serving. Garnish each serving with chervil sprigs or chopped chives, if desired.

Yield: *Makes about 3¹/₂ cups (875 mL), or enough for 3 to 4 appetizer servings. Serve with country bread and a vinaigrette-based salad like Roasted Pepper and Snow Pea Salad (see Chapter 10).*

WARNING!

If you're going to puree a soup in the blender, let it cool first. Otherwise, the trapped steam could explode and redecorate your ceiling.

IMPROVISE

For a lower-calorie cream of leek soup, use 2 percent or skim milk and omit the cream or half and half in step 5.

Cleaning and trimming leeks

Leeks look like overgrown scallions but taste nothing like them. Leeks are milder in flavor than sweet onions and can be added to soups and stews or sautéed in butter with tender vegetables like mushrooms.

The fine grains of sand trapped between the root layers must be thoroughly washed away before the leek is cooked. On a cutting board with a sharp knife, trim off the little roots shooting out from the bulb end. Then cut off the dark green portion of the tops, leaving about 2 inches (5 cm) of pale green stem. (The dark green portion of the stems should be discarded. You use only the white and pale green part of the leek.) Then slice the trimmed leeks in half lengthwise and rinse them under running cold water, opening up the layers with your fingers to wash away the grit and sand.

Dill is a natural sidekick to carrots. The following pureed soup usually calls for heavy cream at the end; instead, we use lowfat ricotta, which works just as well at a fraction of the calories. Port adds a touch of sweetness.

This soup is as bland as an accountants' convention!

If your soup is bland, you may want to toss in a bouillon cube (chicken, beef, or vegetable, depending on the soup). But remember that bouillon cubes are loaded with salt. Maybe the soup simply lacks salt and pepper. Or perhaps herbs can give it zip: Try chervil, rosemary, sage, savory, tarragon, or thyme. You also can add a little lemon juice or dry sherry.

Carrot Soup with Dill

Tools: *Deep saucepan or pot, chef's knife, paring knife, colander, blender or food processor*

Preparation time: *About 15 minutes*

Cooking time: *About 35 minutes*

2 tablespoons (30 mL) butter

³/₄ cup (175 mL) peeled and finely chopped onion

1¹/₂ pounds (750 g) carrots, peeled and sliced into 1-inch (2.5-cm) pieces, about 4 cups (1 L)

4 cups (1 L) fresh or canned chicken or vegetable broth

2 cups (500 mL) water

Salt and freshly ground pepper to taste

¹/₂ cup (125 mL) lowfat ricotta cheese

2 to 3 tablespoons (30 to 45 mL) port (optional)

2 tablespoons (30 mL) chopped fresh dill, or 2 teaspoons (10 mL) dried

1 In a large, deep saucepan or soup pot over medium heat, melt the butter. Add the onions and cook, stirring often, until the onions wilt. Add the carrots, broth, water, and salt and pepper. Cover and bring to a boil. Reduce the heat and simmer, uncovered, for 30 minutes, skimming off any foam that rises to the surface. Cool slightly.

2 Strain the mixture through a colander set over a second deep pan or pot and reserve the cooking liquid. Puree the remaining solids in a food processor or blender container along with the ricotta and 1 cup (250 mL) of the reserved cooking liquid. Add the puree to the pot holding the remaining cooking liquid. Blend well with a wooden spoon.

3 Bring the soup to a boil and add the port (if desired) and dill. Serve hot or serve cold.

Yield: *6 servings.*

This soup makes a smashing lunch with sandwiches or Smoked Trout with Watercress Sauce (see Chapter 7).

Always add fresh herbs to soups or sauces at the last minute before serving. That way, the herbs remain vibrant and alive with flavor.

You also can use ground ginger as the seasoner in this creamy carrot soup. Ginger is more intense than dill, so you need less. Omit the dill and instead add ¹/₂ to ³/₄ teaspoon (2 to 3 mL) ground ginger.

To turn this soup into a vegetable side dish, simply proceed as instructed, pureeing the cooked vegetables with the ricotta but adding only as much of the cooking liquid as necessary to produce a thick puree.

The following soup of chicken broth, spinach, and eggs, derived from the Italian classic Stracciatella, is ready in minutes for a quick lunch and is especially easy if you use canned chicken broth. For special occasions, this soup makes an elegant introduction to a rich meal, but without question you'll want to prepare or purchase fresh stock. (Turn to Chapter 3 for our homemade chicken stock recipe.)

Spinach Cloud Soup

Tools: *Medium saucepan or pot, blender or food processor*

Preparation time: *About 10 minutes*

Cooking time: *About 5 minutes*

6 cups (1.5 L) fresh or canned chicken or vegetable broth

4 eggs

²/₃ cup (150 mL) chopped fresh spinach, rinsed and trimmed of stems

¹/₄ cup (50 mL) grated Parmesan cheese

2 tablespoons (30 mL) fresh lemon juice

Salt and freshly ground pepper to taste

1 Bring the broth to a boil in a covered medium saucepan over high heat.

2 As the broth heats, combine the eggs, spinach, Parmesan cheese, l tablespoon (15 mL) of the lemon juice, and salt and pepper to taste in a blender or food processor container. Whirl for a few seconds to puree smooth.

3 When the broth comes to a boil, stir in the remaining l tablespoon (15 mL) lemon juice and the spinach-egg mixture. Turn off the heat. Little cloudlike lumps of spinach and egg form immediately on the surface. Serve with extra grated Parmesan cheese.

Yield: *6 servings.*

Like the carrot soup, this soup is superb with sandwiches or salads like the garbanzo bean toss (see Chapter 10).

Add ¹/₂ cup (125 mL) cooked carrots, sliced into thin rounds, in step 1.

Stock-Based Soups

"You can tell a good cook from a great cook by how they make a soup," says Bob Kinkead, chef and owner of Kinkead's in Washington, D.C. "The single most important factor for a great soup is a great stock. If you can't make one from scratch, then buy it at a specialty market. College Inn is good quality canned stock, but buy the low-salt version and always enrich it with raw chicken or vegetables."

Kinkead adds that soups can be a last-minute meal if you have stock or canned broth on hand. "You can make a bowl of soup to order in a matter of minutes — we do it all the time at the restaurant — by adding any number and variations of sautéed vegetables, chicken, pork products (like sautéed bacon), fish, herbs, and spices."

Lamb or beef soup

Lamb or beef soups derive much of their flavor from bones added to the cooking liquid. Notice how the lamb bones are cooked in the broth in this easy recipe — in a sense, you are making your stock at the same time you make this soup. Because you remove the meat from the bone, cut it into small pieces, and put it in the soup, nothing is wasted, and the soup absorbs every bit of flavor. Be sure to use cold water to cook the ingredients — doing so helps the bones and meat give up their juices. This rich and hearty soup stands on its own as a main dish for a cold winter day.

Lamb Barley Soup

Tools: *Large pot, chef's knife, tongs or slotted spoon*

Preparation time: *About 20 minutes*

Cooking time: *About 2 hours*

2 lamb shanks, cracked (or a meaty bone from a leg of lamb, sometimes available from the butcher)

1 cup (250 mL) pearl barley, washed (see following note)

1 cup (250 mL) green split peas, washed (see following note)

1¹/₂ cups (375 mL) peeled and chopped onion, about 2 medium onions

1 tablespoon (15 mL) peeled and chopped garlic, about 3 large cloves

3¹/₂ quarts (3.5 L) water

3 to 4 teaspoons (15 to 20 mL) salt

Freshly ground pepper to taste

2 cups (500 mL) carrots, peeled and sliced into ¹/₂-inch (12-mm) rounds, about 5 carrots

1 Place all ingredients except the carrots in a large soup pot. Cover and bring to a boil. Reduce the heat and simmer for 1 hour and 40 minutes partially covered, stirring occasionally and skimming the surface as necessary.

2 Add the sliced carrots and simmer for another 20 minutes.

3 Taste for seasoning. Remove the bones with tongs or a slotted spoon and let them cool slightly. When the bones are cool enough to handle, trim off the meat and add it to the soup.

Yield: *8 to 10 servings.*

(continued)

Note: Rinse grains and dried beans thoroughly in a large pot of cold water to wash off soil particles and other impurities. Discard any small stones or stray pieces that rise to the surface before adding the grains or beans to the cooking water or broth.

Soups that contain grains, dried beans, or legumes have relatively long cooking times, so you can add them near the beginning of cooking. Add any "garnish" vegetables, like the carrots in the preceding recipe, toward the finish of the dish so that their flavors do not completely cook away before the soup is done.

When simmering thick soups like the preceding one, occasionally stir and scrape the bottom of the pot with a wooden spoon to prevent the mixture from sticking and burning. If you do burn food, make sure that you scoop it out and discard it.

Black bean soup

The secret to good black bean soup is a strong stock to give it that lingering flavor. Here we recommend fresh chicken stock, but if you don't have time, use a good brand of canned broth. The vegetables and slab bacon — available at butcher counters — provide a lot of flavor.

You can make the soup as spicy as you like. Black bean soup is best if made a day ahead of time, chilled, and then reheated. The recipe makes about $3\frac{1}{2}$ quarts (3.5 L) of soup, enough for a small army, but you can freeze leftovers for another day.

Note: The recipe is a little labor intensive, but trust us: This soup is worth the effort.

Freezing and reheating soup

If you cook up a big batch of soup and find that you can't eat it all at once, chill it in the refrigerator and skim off any fat that rises to the surface before freezing. You also can freeze soup in an airtight plastic container. Freezing cream- or egg-based soups may cause separation or curdling, so you need to add any cream or eggs listed in the ingredients when you reheat the soup. If the soup does separate upon reheating, try whirling it in a blender container for a few seconds to blend the ingredients smooth.

Reheat frozen soups in the microwave in a microwaveable container or in a heavy saucepan over low heat on the stovetop. Heat only until warmed through to avoid overcooking starchy ingredients, such as potatoes, pasta, and rice.

Always check the seasoning of a reheated soup. Underseason if you know that you'll eventually be freezing the mixture.

Black Bean Soup

Tools: *Chef's knife, large pot or heavy saucepan, colander, ladle*

Preparation time: *About 30 minutes if using canned broth*

Cooking time: *About 2 hours and 15 minutes*

$^1/_2$ *pound (250 g) smoked slab bacon with rind (see following note)*

$1^1/_2$ *cups (375 mL) peeled and finely chopped onion, about 2 medium onions*

$1^1/_2$ *cups (375 mL) finely chopped celery, about 2 stalks*

$1^1/_2$ *cups (375 mL) scraped and finely diced carrots, about 2 large carrots*

1 bay leaf

1 tablespoon (15 mL) peeled and minced garlic, about 3 large cloves

$1^1/_4$ *teaspoons (6 mL) dried thyme*

2 tablespoons (30 mL) ground cumin

1 teaspoon (5 mL) freshly ground pepper

2 tablespoons (30 mL) finely chopped fresh oregano leaves, or 2 teaspoons (10 mL) dried

3 tablespoons (45 mL) tomato paste

4 quarts (16 cups/4 L) chicken broth, preferably homemade and concentrated (canned broth may be substituted)

1 pound (500 g) dried black beans, about 3 cups (750 mL)

6 tablespoons (90 mL) freshly squeezed lime juice, about 4 limes

$^1/_4$ *teaspoon (1 mL) Tabasco sauce, or to taste*

$^1/_4$ *teaspoon (1 mL) cayenne pepper, or to taste*

Salt to taste

$^1/_2$ *cup (125 mL) finely chopped fresh coriander leaves*

Salsa for garnish (see following recipe)

Sour cream for garnish (optional)

1 Slice off and reserve the rind of the bacon. Cut the bacon into $^1/_4$-inch (6-mm) cubes. You should have about $1^1/_2$ cups (375 mL).

2 Put the bacon cubes and the rind into a stock pot or large, heavy saucepan and cook over medium-high heat, about 10 to 12 minutes, stirring often, until brown and crisp.

3 Add the onions, celery, carrots, bay leaf, garlic, thyme, 1 tablespoon (15 mL) of the cumin, black pepper, and oregano. Stir to blend and cover the pot. Cook for about 5 minutes over moderately low heat. Do not allow the mixture to burn.

4 Add the tomato paste and stir briefly. Add the chicken broth, increase the heat to high, and bring to a boil.

5 Rinse and drain the beans and add them to the soup. Reduce the heat and simmer, uncovered, for about 2 hours, skimming the surface occasionally to remove fat as it rises to the top. The soup is ready when the beans are soft and some of them have disintegrated because of the heat and stirring.

(continued)

6 Stir in the lime juice, Tabasco sauce, cayenne pepper, salt, coriander leaves, and remaining cumin. Remove and discard the bacon rind and bay leaf.

7 Ladle the soup into soup bowls. Serve salsa and sour cream, if desired, on the side.

Yield: 8 to 12 servings.

Note: Slab bacon comes in thick rectangles and has less fat than regular American bacon. If you use fatty bacon, trim most of the fat.

Black Bean Soup can be a meal in itself with bread. It also goes well with Barbecued Hamburgers (see Chapter 6) or Turkey Burgers with Quick Caper Sauce (see Chapter 16).

If the soup boils too rapidly when it's supposed to be simmering, be sure to lower the heat. You need to monitor and adjust long-simmering soups, stews, and casseroles to maintain an even temperature.

You can use this salsa fresh, but it tastes better after it marinates in the refrigerator for about an hour.

Salsa

Tools: Chef's knife, small mixing bowl

Preparation time: About 20 minutes

2 cups (500 mL) peeled and seeded tomatoes, cut into ¹/₄-inch (6-mm) cubes, about 2 large tomatoes

¹/₂ cup (125 mL) peeled and finely chopped onion, about 1 medium onion

¹/₄ cup (50 mL) finely chopped fresh coriander leaves

2 tablespoons (30 mL) freshly squeezed lime juice

1¹/₂ teaspoons (7 mL) or more seeded, finely chopped jalapeño peppers

Salt to taste, if desired

Combine all the ingredients in a mixing bowl and blend well. Refrigerate until ready to serve. Taste for seasoning before serving.

Yield: About 2¹/₂ cups (625 mL).

You can add one ripe, chopped avocado to the salsa and serve as an appetizer with soft tacos or blue corn chips.

Jalapeño pepper seeds can burn your eyes as badly as tear gas. Take care not to accidentally rub your eyes after chopping and seeding them. You may want to wear rubber gloves when working with them. To seed and chop a jalapeño, slice the pepper lengthwise in half, discarding the stem and core. Scrape away the seeds; then mince or dice. (Then go wash your hands!)

The best way to ream or extract the juice from limes, lemons, oranges, and other citrus fruits is to use a manual or electric juicer that separates the juice from the seeds. Rolling the fruit on a counter, or between your palms, for a few seconds helps to break up the juice sacks and makes juicing easier.

Flavor from pork fat

Pork products, like the slab bacon in the preceding Black Bean Soup recipe, are often used to flavor soups, stews, and long-simmering casserole dishes. Chef Bob Kinkead of Kinkead's in Washington, D.C., says that the most important step in making a great soup is to first "render the bacon fat," which means cooking it until the fat melts away.

Here's a list of common cooking products available from pork:

- **Back fat** is taken right from under the pig's skin, has no meat at all, and is sold fresh and salted as a cooking fat. Sometimes it is also tied around roasts or used to line meat terrines.

- **Canadian bacon** is made by curing the boneless center-cut loin of pork in the same fashion as bacon. It needs no cooking but is delicious warmed in a fry pan with eggs or chopped into scrambled eggs and omelets. It's also lower in fat than other pork products.

- **Crispy pork skin, or cracklings,** produced from fried or roasted pork skin, is considered a delicacy by some. In the southern U.S., it is used to flavor corn bread and vegetable dishes.

- **Fresh pork belly** is an important ingredient in sausages and for flavoring vegetables. If salted or cured, it becomes **salt pork**. **Bacon** is pork belly that has been both smoked and salted. Most bacon is sold presliced, but some independent butcher shops still carry unsliced or slab bacon that you can cut into chunks or cubes for flavoring soups, stews, and chowders. Slab bacon comes with the rind or skin intact and has a smoky-salty character all its own.

- **Lard** is pure, clarified pork fat — free of all skin or other protein. It is especially good as a shortening for biscuits and baked goods because it produces a very light and flaky pastry.

- **Pancetta** is Italian bacon, cured with salt and spices, but not smoked like American bacon. It usually comes in a sausage-shaped roll and is thinly sliced for flavoring sauces, pasta dishes, stuffings, breads, and omelets.

Seafood Soup

Seafood soups of all kinds are quick and easy to make. Fish cooks in minutes, so you have to have your timing right. The following version adds mussels, but you also can use clams or scallops. This recipe is especially delicious if you make it the day before you serve it, allowing the anise seed to permeate the fish and vegetables with their licorice-like flavor.

Seafood Soup

Tools: *Chef's knife, large, heavy saucepan or pot*

Preparation time: *About 35 minutes*

Cooking time: *About 25 minutes*

1 pound (500 g) nonoily fresh fish, such as monkfish, blackfish, tilefish, or any combination

2 tablespoons (30 mL) olive oil

¹/₂ cup (125 mL) peeled and chopped onion, about l medium onion

1 cup (250 mL) trimmed, rinsed, and finely chopped leeks, white and pale green parts only, about l large leek

³/₄ cup (175 mL) cored and seeded sweet red pepper, cut into small cubes, about 1 medium pepper

³/₄ cup (175 mL) cored and seeded green pepper, cut into small cubes, about 1 medium pepper

1 tablespoon (15 mL) peeled and finely chopped garlic, about 3 large cloves

2 cups (500 mL) water

1 cup (250 mL) dry white wine

1 cup (250 mL) canned crushed tomatoes

1 sprig fresh thyme, or ¹/₂ teaspoon (2 mL) dried

1 bay leaf

1 teaspoon (5 mL) anise seed

¹/₄ teaspoon (1 mL) red pepper flakes (optional)

Salt and freshly ground pepper to taste

20 mussels, well scrubbed and with beards removed (see following sidebar)

¹/₄ cup (50 mL) finely chopped fresh basil or parsley

1 Cut the fish into 1-inch (2.5-cm) cubes and remove any small bones.

2 Heat the oil in a heavy pot over medium heat. Add the onions, leeks, red and green peppers, and garlic. Cook, stirring often, until the onions and peppers wilt, about 8 minutes.

3 Add the water, wine, tomatoes, thyme, bay leaf, anise seed, red pepper flakes (if desired), and salt and pepper to taste. Bring to a boil and then reduce heat to simmer for 10 minutes.

4 Add the fish and the mussels, stir gently, and bring to a boil. Cover and simmer over low heat for about 5 to 10 minutes or until the mussels steam open. (Discard any mussels that do not open.) Check for seasoning.

(continued)

5 Remove the thyme sprig (if you used a fresh sprig) and bay leaf. Sprinkle with the basil or parsley and serve with chunks of Italian or French bread.

Yield: 4 servings.

Fish soup makes a fine lunch with a side dish of Watercress, Endive, and Orange Salad (see Chapter 10).

Be sure to remove any small bones before adding the fish to the stew.

If you goofed with the salt, don't dump the soup. If the soup tastes too salty, the simple solution is to add water. If you don't want to add water and thin the soup, try adding paper-thin slices of potato. Cook them until translucent — they tend to soak up salt. Leave them in the soup if you like.

Tomatoes, either fresh or canned (but unsalted!), do the same thing.

Cleaning mussels

See the following figure for an illustration of each step.

1. Using a clam knife or scouring pad, scrape any barnacles off the shells.

2. Pull off the beardlike strands. (This kills the mussels, so cook them immediately.)

3. Place the mussels in a large pot and cover with cool, fresh water by about 2 inches (5 cm). Agitate the mussels with your hand in the water in a washing machine motion.

4. Drain and discard the water.

5. Repeat several times until the water is clear.

6. Drain once more and keep the mussels cool until you're ready to use them.

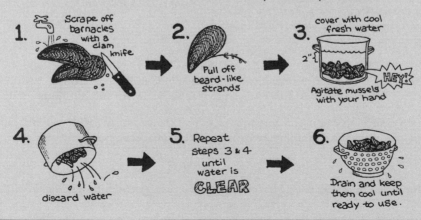

Gazpacho

Gazpacho, a puree of raw vegetables with citric accents, is a staple of the pool party set, and no two recipes are ever the same. At home, making gazpacho in a food processor or blender is a cinch. Don't overblend, though, because you want the soup to have a pulpy texture. If you like your gazpacho spicier, simply add more jalapeño pepper to taste. Lemon or lime juice adds a refreshing touch.

Whenever you make a cold soup, be sure to use only the freshest, ripest vegetables or fruits. Gazpacho is an excellent choice as a summer soup when juicy, locally grown tomatoes are abundant.

Fresh Tomato Gazpacho

Tools: *Chef's knife, paring knife, vegetable peeler, food processor or blender, medium bowl*

Preparation time: *About 30 minutes*

Cooking time: *A few seconds to puree and about 1 hour to chill*

6 cups (1.5 L) peeled, seeded, and chopped ripe tomatoes, about 3 pounds (1.5 kg)

1 cup (250 mL) peeled and chopped onion, about 1 large onion

1 cup (250 mL) cored, seeded, and chopped sweet red pepper, about 1 large pepper

1 tablespoon (15 mL) peeled and chopped garlic, about 3 large cloves

2 teaspoons (10 mL) seeded and chopped jalapeño pepper, or to taste, about 1 small pepper

6 tablespoons (90 mL) coarsely chopped fresh coriander

¹/₄ cup (50 mL) olive oil

3 tablespoons (45 mL) red wine vinegar

3 tablespoons (45 mL) fresh lime or lemon juice

Salt and freshly ground pepper to taste

1 cup (250 mL) peeled and seeded cucumber, about 1 medium cucumber, cut into ¹/₄-inch (6-mm) cubes

1 Combine all ingredients except for 2 tablespoons (30 mL) of the coriander and the cucumbers in a food processor or blender. Blend to a semicoarse (still chunky) texture. Pour and scrape the mixture into a bowl. Cover with plastic wrap and refrigerate until cold.

2 Just before serving, stir in the cucumbers, adjust the seasoning with salt and pepper, and sprinkle with the remaining 2 tablespoons (30 mL) coriander.

Yield: *About 7 cups (1.75 L), or 6 appetizer servings.*

To remove the seeds from a cucumber, cut the cucumber in half lengthwise and scrape away the layer of seeds with a spoon.

If you want to get fancy with gazpacho, you can add a pound (500 g) or so of cooked lump crab meat, shrimp, or pieces of lobster with the cucumber in step 2. The acid in the soup works well with rich shellfish.

If you use shrimp, place about 2 pounds (1 kg) in a pot, cover with cold water, and add onion, a clove, thyme, a bay leaf, and black pepper. Bring the water to a boil and then turn off the heat. Remove the shrimp, peel, devein (see Chapter 12 for illustrated instructions), and slice before adding to the soup.

If you use lobster, boil the lobster and let it cool before picking out the meat. Steam crabs with some shellfish seasonings, which you can find in grocery stores.

Dressing Up Your Soups

You can make soup look sensational in many ways. A successful garnish complements a soup without masking its basic character. There's only one cardinal rule never to break: Complex-tasting soups that have lots of flavor call for simple garnishes, and simple soups call for complex garnishes.

Try chopped fresh herbs, a slice of lemon or lime (see Figure 9-1), a dollop of sour cream, a grating of Parmesan, a sprig of watercress, chopped scallions, hard-cooked egg, steamed shrimp, or assorted chopped wild mushrooms.

You also can try these garnishes:

- **Julienned vegetables:** Thinly sliced and parboiled root vegetables, such as carrots and parsnips. In a *brunoise* garnish, the same thin strips are cut into small cubes.

- **Chiffonade:** Roll spinach or sorrel leaves lengthwise like a cigar and slice into thin, lacy strands. Drop into clear broths just before serving.

- **Croutons:** Season toasted bread cubes with garlic and smother with grated cheese before dropping into hot soups. (See the following recipe for Garlic Croutons.)

Figure 9-1:
A simple garnish can make a bowl of soup look festive and inviting.

- ✔ **Gremolata:** Toss together chopped garlic, chopped parsley, and grated lemon peel — also wonderful on broiled steak, chicken, or pork.

- ✔ **Pistou:** Similar to pesto sauce, but with tomatoes. Pound fresh basil leaves, cloves of garlic, chopped tomatoes, Parmesan cheese, and olive oil into a creamy paste.

- ✔ **Spaetzle:** Thin pieces of boiled dough made from flour, eggs, and milk that float on the surface of a flavored broth.

- ✔ **Salsa:** Chopped fresh tomatoes, garlic, onion, and hot chili peppers. (See the Salsa recipe earlier in this chapter.) Endless variations exist.

- ✔ **Fancy garnishes:** Carve a little man out of a carrot and place him on a tarragon leaf "surfboard." Blow to make waves in the soup.

Many soups benefit from tasty little croutons. Anyone who wastes money buying croutons in the grocery — they are nothing but seasoned, dry bread — should be sentenced to a weekend of watching the Weather Channel. Homemade croutons are much better than store-bought ones, and you can make them in minutes.

Garlic Croutons

Tools: *Serrated knife, chef's knife, wooden cutting board, skillet, pancake turner*

Preparation time: *About 5 minutes*

Cooking time: *About 3 minutes*

4 slices white, whole wheat, or pumpernickel bread

2 large cloves garlic, peeled

¹/₄ cup (50 mL) oil

Freshly ground pepper to taste (optional)

1 Stack the bread slices and use a serrated knife to trim off the crusts. Cut the slices into ¹/₄-inch (6-mm) cubes. You should have about 2 cups (500 mL).

2 Set the garlic cloves on a wooden cutting board and use the side of a chef's knife to press or crush the cloves flat.

3 Heat the oil in a large skillet over medium-high heat. Add the crushed garlic and cook for about 1 minute or until very lightly browned. (Do not let it burn.) Add the bread and cook for about another 2 minutes, using a pancake turner to toss the cubes so that they brown on all sides. Remove from the skillet and drain on paper towels. Season with freshly ground pepper, if desired.

Yield: *6 servings.*

Chapter 10

Salads

● ●

In This Chapter

▶ Making vinaigrettes and creamy dressings

▶ Checking out oils and vinegars

▶ Foraging for greens

▶ Ten quick and easy salads

● ●

*T*ossing together a salad is easy if you have fresh ingredients; what you put *on* the salad makes the difference. For simplicity's sake, we break down dressings into two categories: vinaigrette and creamy (or mayonnaise-based). When you're making a salad, the first thing to consider is which kind of dressing you want.

Gentlemen, Choose Your Dressing: The Two Types

Vinaigrette goes with all sorts of salad greens and grilled vegetables. A cream-based dressing can enhance various greens as well as cold shellfish, meat, and poultry. Both types are simple to prepare. The advantage of vinaigrette-based dressing is that you can make a large quantity and store it, sealed, in an old wine bottle or mason jar. Mayonnaise-based dressings should be used within a week or so. Cream-based dressings have a similar shelf life and are usually high in calories and saturated fats.

Following are two basic dressing recipes and suggestions for varying them.

Vinaigrette Dressing

Tools: *Small bowl, wire whisk*

Preparation time: *Less than 5 minutes*

2 tablespoons (30 mL) red or white wine vinegar

1 teaspoon (5 mL) Dijon-style mustard

¹/₃ cup (75 mL) olive oil

Salt and freshly ground pepper to taste

Place the vinegar and mustard in a bowl. Whisk to blend well. Add the olive oil in a stream while whisking. Season with salt and pepper to taste.

Yield: *4 to 6 servings.*

Following are some variations on this basic vinaigrette:

- ✔ Substitute 2 tablespoons (30 mL) walnut oil for 2 tablespoons (30 mL) of the olive oil to give the vinaigrette a distinctive, nutty flavor. Serve with mixed green salads or salads with grilled poultry.

- ✔ Substitute 2 tablespoons (30 mL) peanut oil for 2 tablespoons (30 mL) of the olive oil. Add 2 tablespoons (30 mL) sesame seeds, 2 tablespoons (30 mL) sherry or *mirin* (Japanese sweet wine), and 1 tablespoon (15 mL) soy sauce. This Oriental sauce is wonderful with grilled vegetables or poultry.

- ✔ Add 1 teaspoon (5 mL) drained capers and 1 tablespoon (15 mL) chopped fresh chervil, tarragon, basil, or lemon thyme. This herby vinaigrette really enlivens a cold pasta salad.

- ✔ Specialty shops and even supermarkets sell all kinds of flavored vinegars. Tarragon and other herb vinegars add a nice touch to salads; if you want something sweeter, try raspberry vinegar — but in moderation.

- ✔ Place one quartered, ripe tomato in a blender or food processor container with the rest of the dressing and blend well.

- ✔ To thicken the vinaigrette, combine it in a blender with a tablespoon or two (15 or 30 mL) of ricotta cheese. Lowfat ricotta enriches just like cream.

- ✔ Substitute 2 tablespoons (30 mL) lemon juice for the vinegar to make a lemon-flavored dressing.

We add sour cream to the following mayonnaise dressing because it adds a nice, sharp edge. You can use all mayonnaise if you prefer.

Herbed Mayonnaise Dressing

Tools: *Chef's knife, bowl, juicer, wire whisk*

Preparation time: *About 5 minutes*

¹/₃ cup (75 mL) mayonnaise

3 tablespoons (45 mL) sour cream (substitute lowfat sour cream if desired)

2 tablespoons (30 mL) minced fresh chives

2 tablespoons (30 mL) minced fresh parsley

1¹/₂ tablespoons (22 mL) fresh lemon juice, about half a lemon

Salt and freshly ground pepper to taste

Combine all ingredients in a bowl and whisk well. Taste for seasoning.

Try jazzing up this dressing in any of the following ways:

- ✔ For a seafood salad, add 1 tablespoon (15 mL) drained capers and 1 table-spoon (15 mL) (or to taste) minced fresh tarragon leaves, or 1 teaspoon (5 mL) dried.

- ✔ For a cold meat dish, chicken salad, or perhaps shrimp, make a curry dressing by eliminating the tarragon from the preceding variation and adding 1 teaspoon (5 mL) curry powder (or to taste).

- ✔ For cold vegetable salad, crumble ¹/₂ cup (125 mL) or more bleu cheese or Roquefort and blend it with the dressing.

- ✔ For cold meats, add 1 teaspoon (5 mL) horseradish (or to taste) and mix well.

Every chef has his or her secret when it comes to making salad dressings. "Use a flavored oil and a good quality vinegar," recommends Annie Somerville, chef of Greens Restaurant, a famous vegetarian restaurant in San Francisco, "and don't use too much oil in proportion to the vinegar. Our standard at the restaurant is one part vinegar to three parts oil, unless the vinegar is balsamic — then you can use a little more vinegar because it's sweeter."

Olive and Other Salad Oils

Buying olive oil in the supermarket has become as confusing as choosing a computer, what with all the nationalities and fancy labels and terminology in baffling languages. The most important thing to look for in olive oil is its *grade*, which is usually printed right on the front of the bottle. In ascending order of quality, you'll find *pure, virgin,* and *extra-virgin.*

The grade has to do with the oleic acid content of the oil, with the finest oils having the least acidity. All the preceding varieties come from the olive's first *pressing* (the crushing process that releases the oil from the olives), but extra virgin is the highest quality. Extra-virgin olive oil usually has the richest aroma and strongest flavor. Pure olive oil can come from both the first and second pressing of the tree-ripened olives and may be blended with 5 to 10 percent virgin olive oil to enrich its flavor. It is usually sold in cans that look as though they belong at a service station.

Don't be misled by olive oil sold as "light." The "light" refers to its pale color and extremely bland flavor, a result of the way it's processed. One tablespoon (15 mL) of any oil contains the same 120 calories.

Other salad oils include walnut, sesame, corn, peanut, safflower, soy, and avocado. The neutral flavors of corn, peanut, and safflower oils can be mixed with equal amounts of olive or nut oils.

Fancy food markets and gourmet shops are increasingly stocking oils flavored with herbs, lemon, peppercorns, and sun-dried tomatoes. These oils can add just the right seasoning touch to a tossed green salad, and they are delicious drizzled over pizza, French bread, goat cheese or Brie, roasted vegetables, or toasted croutons.

The shelf life of oil depends on its variety. Olive oils should keep for up to a year if tightly capped and stored out of the sun in a cool, dark place. But nut oils last only a few months, so purchase them in small quantities.

Vinegars

Oil in a salad dressing needs an acidic counterpoint — a tart ingredient that stimulates the palate and cuts through the smoothness of oil. In most cases, vinegar is the choice, but fresh lemon juice and mustard also carry a pungent bite.

Although red or white wine is the most common liquid base, anything that ferments can be used to make vinegar:

- **Cider vinegar:** Made from apples, this strong, clear, brown vinegar holds up well with pungent greens and is especially good sprinkled in meat, fish, or fruit salads. Also excellent with ginger or curry dressings.

- **White vinegar:** Colorless and sharp, white vinegar is distilled from assorted grains, and it's terrific in cold rice or pasta salads.

- ✔ **Red wine vinegar:** Made from any number of red wines, this vinegar is full bodied and perfect for dressing pungent, dark greens.

- ✔ **Rice vinegar:** Common to Japan and China, rice vinegars are less tart than white vinegars and combine well with sesame oils. They are also good in seafood salads.

Homemade flavored vinegar

You can lace white wine vinegar with fruits like raspberries or lemon, garlic, herbs, peppercorns, honey, or edible flower petals. Herb vinegars are easy to produce at home. For a lemon-herb vinegar, add a long strip of lemon peel, a well-washed sprig of fresh herbs (dill, tarragon, or marjoram will do), and a clove of garlic to a clean, decorative bottle fitted with a lid or cork. Fill the bottle with good quality cider or white wine vinegar, cap, and refrigerate for about three days before using. This vinegar is excellent in a vinaigrette for greens, chicken salad, or marinated vegetables. (See Figure 10-1.)

Figure 10-1:
Homemade flavored vinegars are simple to make and are an excellent complement to many salads.

Balsamic: the world's most expensive vinegar

Balsamic vinegar is a dark, sweet, syrupy, aged liquid that is worth its weight in gold. The real thing is made in the area around Modena, Italy, and nowhere else. Virtually all those large bottles of balsamic vinegar you see in supermarkets are imitations — some aged, some not — made to look like the real thing. This "fake" balsamic vinegar is not necessarily bad, just different.

Recognizing real balsamic vinegar is easy: You start to hyperventilate upon seeing the price. Real balsamic vinegar is sold only in little bulb-shaped bottles — it looks like perfume. It is usually more than 25 years old and costs $100 and up for a tiny portion. Such rarefied vinegar is not to be tossed around in salads. Italians use it for sauces or just drizzle some on fresh fruit (strawberries are best).

Salad Days: Vinaigrette-Based Recipes

A delicious, lowfat potato salad hinges on a good vinaigrette. The following version is relatively lean but flavorful and is delicious warm or chilled.

French Potato Salad

Tools: *Chef's knife, medium saucepan, small mixing bowl, serving bowl*

Preparation time: *About 15 minutes*

Cooking time: *About 30 minutes*

2 pounds (1 kg) red potatoes, well scrubbed

Salt to taste

6 tablespoons (90 mL) olive oil

1 tablespoon (15 mL) white vinegar

$^1/_2$ cup (125 mL) peeled and chopped red onion, about 1 small red onion

$^1/_4$ cup (50 mL) finely chopped parsley

1 teaspoon (5 mL) peeled and finely chopped garlic, about 1 large clove

Freshly ground pepper to taste

$^1/_4$ cup (50 mL) dry white wine at room temperature

1 In a medium saucepan, cover the potatoes with lightly salted water and bring to a boil. Boil for 20 minutes or until the potatoes are tender when pierced with a knife, but not until they fall apart. Drain and let stand until cool enough to handle. (You should make the salad while the potatoes are still hot or warm.)

2 As the potatoes cook, make the dressing by combining the oil, vinegar, red onion, parsley, garlic, and salt and pepper to taste in a small mixing bowl.

3 Peel the cooked potatoes and cut them into $^1/_4$-inch-thick (6-mm) slices. (Or leave the skins on for more color.) You should have about 5 cups (1.25 L). Put the slices in a shallow serving bowl, sprinkling the wine between the layers.

4 Pour the dressing over the potatoes and toss to blend well. If you let the salad stand, stir from the bottom before serving.

Yield: *4 to 6 servings.*

This potato salad is a natural for picnics because it doesn't spoil in heat. Serve with sandwiches, gazpacho (see Chapter 9), or spicy shrimp (see Chapter 15).

Add ¹⁄₄ cup (50 mL) minced scallions; 2 tablespoons (30 mL) chopped fresh herbs like rosemary, chervil, or basil; or 1 cup (250 mL) diced, roasted sweet peppers (see Chapter 6 for a roasted pepper recipe).

Cold pasta salads are handy to have around for quick lunches or for entertaining. You can make them with just about any ingredients that go into hot pasta. In the following recipe, note that you cook the pasta in the same broth as the vegetables for extra flavor (and nutrition).

Bow-Tie Pasta Salad with Fresh Mussels

Tools: *Small mixing bowl, wire whisk, chef's knife, large saucepan or pot, colander, slotted spoon*

Preparation time: *About 30 minutes*

Cooking time: *About 20 minutes*

2 tablespoons (30 mL) red or white wine vinegar

1 tablespoon (15 mL) Dijon-style mustard

Salt and freshly ground pepper to taste

³⁄₄ cup (175 mL) olive oil

3 tablespoons (45 mL) finely chopped shallots or scallions

2 teaspoons (10 mL) peeled and finely chopped garlic, about 2 large cloves

Pinch of cayenne pepper

3 pounds (1.5 kg) mussels, well scrubbed, with beards and barnacles removed (see Chapter 9 for illustrated instructions)

¹⁄₂ cup (125 mL) dry white wine

2 quarts (2 L) water

2 small zucchini, about ³⁄₄ pound (375 g), cut into ¹⁄₂-inch (12-mm) rounds (optional)

¹⁄₂ pound (250 g) farfalle pasta (bow-ties)

2 ripe tomatoes, about ³⁄₄ pound (375 g), peeled and cut into ¹⁄₂-inch (12-mm) cubes

¹⁄₂ cup (125 mL) coarsely chopped fresh basil leaves or Italian parsley

1 Combine the vinegar, mustard, and salt and pepper in a mixing bowl. Beat the mixture with a wire whisk while slowly adding the oil a few drops at a time at first and then in a slow drizzle. After all the oil is incorporated, add the shallots or scallions, garlic, and cayenne pepper and blend well. Set aside.

2 Place the mussels in a large saucepan and add the wine. Cover and cook over high heat, gently shaking the pan occasionally to redistribute the mussels, for about 4 minutes or until all the mussels open.

3 Remove the mussels with a slotted spoon and set them aside to cool. Pour the cooking liquid into a colander that is lined with a paper towel and set over a large bowl to strain and reserve the broth. When the mussels are cool enough to handle, remove the meat and discard the shells.

(continued)

4 Place the strained broth and the 2 quarts (2 L) water in a large saucepan or pot. Bring to a boil and add the zucchini. Cook for 3 minutes and then remove the zucchini with a slotted spoon.

5 Add the pasta to the pot, stir, and bring to a boil. Cook for about 10 to 12 minutes or according to package instructions until the pasta is tender but still firm (al dente). Drain well and let cool slightly.

6 Place the zucchini, tomatoes, pasta, and mussels in a large bowl. Add the dressing and basil and toss well. Adjust the seasoning with more salt and pepper, if desired. Serve chilled or at room temperature.

Yield: 4 servings.

Cold pasta is best served with other cold items, like Avocado and Tomato Salad (see Chapter 15).

You can vary this recipe in many ways:

- ✔ Use different pastas, such as shells, penne, fusilli, or tortellini. (See Chapter 11 for explanations of the different types of pastas.)

- ✔ Toss cold pasta with al dente-cooked vegetables tossed in vinaigrette, perhaps with fresh herbs.

- ✔ Substitute little-neck clams for the mussels.

- ✔ Roast three types of peppers — red, green, and yellow — and cut them into ¼-inch (6-mm) cubes. Dress the pasta with herb vinaigrette and toss in the peppers.

The following colorful salad combines the pungency of watercress and endive with sweet orange, a refreshing combination. You also can add black olives or Nicoise-style olives for a salty flavor.

Watercress, Endive, and Orange Salad

Tools: *Chef's knife, salad or mixing bowl, wire whisk*

Preparation time: *About 25 minutes*

1 bunch watercress, washed and drained

2 Belgian endives

2 teaspoons (10 mL) Dijon-style mustard

2 tablespoons (30 mL) red wine vinegar (or to taste)

¹/₄ cup (50 mL) olive, vegetable, or corn oil

Salt and freshly ground pepper to taste

¹/₂ cup (125 mL) peeled and chopped red onion, about 1 small red onion

1 medium navel orange, peeled and sectioned (see following Essential Skill icon)

2 tablespoons (30 mL) chopped fresh parsley

1 Trim and discard the stems of the watercress and endives. Cut the endives crosswise into 2-inch (5-cm) lengths.

2 To make the dressing, put the mustard in a salad or mixing bowl. Add the vinegar. Start beating with a wire whisk while adding the oil. Add salt and pepper and the chopped red onion. Blend well.

3 Add the watercress, endive, orange sections, and parsley. Toss well and serve.

Yield: *4 servings.*

The sweetness of orange makes this salad especially good with Mustard-Brushed Barbecued Chicken Breasts (see Chapter 6).

 To section an orange, use a sharp knife to first peel the fruit and then divide the sections along the membranes. If you want to eliminate the stringy, white membrane that holds each section in place, cut along each side of the membrane, working the knife beneath the membrane and down toward the center of the fruit. (See Figure 10-2.)

 Adding orange, lemon, or lime zest is a simple way to dramatically alter the flavor of a salad dressing. Grate the fruit against the smallest holes of a hand grater, taking care to remove only the colored portion of the skin. The white, underneath layer, though perfectly edible, tends to be slightly bitter.

Sectioning an Orange to Eliminate Membranes

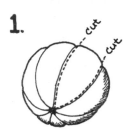

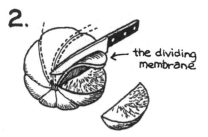

← the dividing membrane

Figure 10-2:
Sectioning
an orange.

Roasted Pepper and Snow Pea Salad

Tools: *Baking sheet, paper bag, chef's knife, paring knife, colander, large skillet, wire whisk, small bowl*

Preparation time: *About 20 minutes*

Cooking time: *About 30 minutes*

2 red sweet peppers, about ³/₄ pound (375 g), cored

³/₄ pound (375 g) snow peas, rinsed and trimmed

Salt to taste

1 small red onion, peeled, halved, and cut into thin slices

2 tablespoons (30 mL) red wine vinegar

1 tablespoon (15 mL) Dijon-style mustard

¹/₂ teaspoon (2 mL) ground cumin

Freshly ground pepper to taste

¹/₄ cup (50 mL) olive oil

¹/₄ cup (50 mL) finely chopped fresh parsley

8 leaves Bibb or Boston lettuce, rinsed and dried

1 Preheat the broiler. Place the peppers on a baking sheet and place under the broiler, 4 to 6 inches (10 to 15 cm) from the heat. As one side of each pepper blackens, rotate away from the heat until all sides of the peppers are blackened. Remove the peppers from the broiler and place in a closed paper bag for about 5 minutes to loosen the skin.

2 Remove the peppers from the bag and peel away the skin with a paring knife. Slice the peppers lengthwise into ¹/₄-inch (6-mm) strips, discarding the seeds.

3 Trim the snow peas by snapping off the stem end and pulling off the string that runs across the top of the pod. Bring a skillet or pot that contains about 2 inches of lightly salted water to a boil. Add the snow peas and cook for 2 minutes. Drain. Run cold water briefly over the peas to cool them quickly and drain again. Put the snow peas, pepper strips, and red onion in a salad bowl.

(continued)

4 Combine the vinegar, mustard, and cumin in a small bowl and add salt and pepper. Beat vigorously with a whisk while slowly adding the oil. Stir in the parsley. Pour the dressing over the vegetables and toss. Place 2 lettuce leaves on each of 4 serving plates and spoon equal portions of the salad in the center.

Yield: 4 servings.

This colorful salad is wonderful with Grilled Flank Steak with Rosemary and Sage (see Chapter 15) or Grilled Swordfish Steaks with Lemon and Thyme (see Chapter 6).

Try varying this recipe in any of the following ways:

- ✔ Use different-colored peppers.
- ✔ Place around the plate halved cherry tomatoes and thinly sliced fresh *fennel,* a faintly licorice-tasting root vegetable.
- ✔ Garnish with cooked asparagus spears.
- ✔ Place cooked pasta shells, tossed in herbed vinaigrette, in the center of the salad under the peppers and snow peas.

Warm Shrimp Salad with Spinach

Tools: Shrimp deveiner, chef's knife, large nonstick skillet

Preparation time: About 25 minutes

Cooking time: About 4 minutes

1¹/₄ pounds (625 g) large shrimp, about 28 shrimp

4 cups (1 L) loosely packed fresh spinach leaves

4 thin, peeled slices of red onion, broken into rings

6 tablespoons (90 mL) olive oil

2 sweet red peppers, cored, seeded, and cut into ¹/₂-inch (12-mm) cubes

Salt and freshly ground pepper to taste

2 teaspoons (10 mL) peeled and finely chopped garlic, about 2 large cloves

3 tablespoons (45 mL) red wine vinegar

¹/₂ cup (125 mL) chopped fresh basil leaves or parsley

¹/₂ teaspoon (2 mL) grated lemon peel

1 Peel and devein the shrimp and set aside. (Turn to Chapter 12 for instructions.)

2 Trim off any tough stems of the spinach leaves. Rinse well and pat dry. Arrange the spinach leaves on 4 dinner plates.

(continued)

3 Arrange an equal portion of the onion rings in the center of each plate.

4 Heat the oil in a large skillet (nonstick if possible) over medium-high heat. Add the shrimp, red peppers, and salt and pepper. Cook, stirring, for about 2 minutes. Add the garlic and cook, stirring, for 1 minute more. (Do not let the garlic brown.) Add the vinegar; cook and stir for 45 seconds. Remove from the heat.

5 Add half the basil and all the lemon peel and toss well. Spoon the shrimp and sauce equally over the onion rings and spinach. Sprinkle with the remaining basil. Taste for seasoning, adding more salt and pepper if desired. Serve immediately.

Yield: 4 servings.

Warm salads are usually served alone with bread. You can, though, follow this salad with Broiled Skirt Steak, Cajun Style (see Chapter 15) or Grilled Brochettes of Pork with Rosemary (see Chapter 6).

A Glossary of Greens

A salad demands the freshest greens and herbs and the tastiest vegetables you can find. If at all possible, buy produce that is in season, and then speed home with your lights flashing.

Greens range in taste from mild to pungent and even bitter. Mild greens like iceberg, Boston, and Bibb lettuce should be used as a base for more assertive, full-strength ingredients and seasonings. Use greens like radicchio, arugula, and escarole sparingly as a contrasting accent. Composing a salad of tart radicchio with a sharp vinaigrette is like catching baseballs without a glove — you can do it, but ouch! Counterbalance pungent greens with cream-style dressings.

Supermarkets and produce markets carry an array of greens 12 months of the year, allowing you to combine different types in one bowl. Don't limit yourself to a boring salad of iceberg lettuce. The more variety of greens in the bowl, the better.

Don't overdress

A common mistake is overdressing salads, which is just as bad as overdressing for dinner. Drizzle just enough dressing over the greens to cover them when tossed well. And when you toss, really toss. Don't just phlegmatically move the greens around the bowl. Pretend that you're conducting the Boston Pops and go to it.

Our favorite salad greens, some of which are pictured in Figure 10-3, include the following.

Mild greens

- **Bibb (or limestone lettuce):** Tender, rippled leaves form a small, compact head. Bibb has the mildness of Boston lettuce, but more crunch. It tends to be expensive, but a little makes a big impression.

- **Boston:** Buttery textured, this lettuce looks like a green rose. Mixes well with all varieties and stands well alone topped with ripe, sliced summer tomatoes.

- **Iceberg:** The white bread of the salad world, iceberg is common to salad bars and political banquets. Iceberg has more texture than flavor, and, if wrapped, can be used for foul-shot practice. To remove the core, smash the head on a cutting board or countertop, with the core side facing down. The hard core should then twist out easily.

- **Loose-leaf lettuce:** Also called red-leaf or green-leaf lettuce, depending on its color. Its long, curly leaves are buttery and almost sweet. Add the red-leaf variety to green salad for an elegant contrast or mix red and green leaf together in one bowl.

- **Romaine:** The emperor green of Caesar salad, romaine has dark-green exterior leaves with a pale-yellow core. Mixes well with other greens. One advantage of romaine is that it keeps well for up to a week in the refrigerator. Like other dark, leafy greens, romaine is a good source of vitamin A.

- **Red oakleaf lettuce:** Named for the oak tree leaves it resembles, this green is sweet and colorful. Good mixed with Boston or Bibb lettuce. Also makes a pretty plate garnish.

Pungent greens

- **Arugula:** You can practically taste the iron in arugula's dark green leaves. Mix with any mild lettuce or toss with grilled, sliced portobello mushrooms, red onions, and a lemon vinaigrette.

- **Belgian endive:** Its pale yellow and white leaves are packed tightly together, resembling a thick cigar. This green has lots of crunch and a slightly bitter taste. Pull the leaves away from the base and tear them into pieces in green salads, or use an entire leaf as a serving base for various cheese and vegetable spreads and fillings.

- **Cabbage:** Red or green, cabbage is a great salad addition and amazingly inexpensive. Tear or shred leaves with a knife and toss with other greens to add color and texture. A long-storage vegetable and a good source of vitamin C.

- **Curly endive (sometimes called chicory):** Similar to escarole in flavor, but with very curly leaves.

- **Dandelion:** A green that you can probably harvest off your front lawn (if you don't have dogs), dandelion leaves arrive on the market in the spring. Italians cherish its bitter, crunchy qualities. Toss in a mixed green salad with chopped, hard-cooked eggs and a vinaigrette dressing. A good source of vitamin C and calcium.

- **Escarole:** A green that you can consume raw in salad or sauté in olive oil and garlic. A member of the endive family, escarole is also rather tart and stands up to strong-flavored dressings.

- **Frisée:** Mildly bitter, this pale-yellow green also has prickly-shaped leaves. Mix it sparingly with other greens for contrasting texture and taste.

- **Mesclun (pronounced *mess-clān*):** A salad mix that usually contains frisée, arugula, radicchio, red and oak leaf lettuces, mustard, and other delicate greens. Mesclun is very expensive, from $9 to $12 a pound. Purchase only if it appears very fresh, or the greens will wilt before you get home. It's best to buy a small amount to mix with other less expensive salad greens.

- **Radicchio:** A small, tightly wound head with deep magenta leaves that can add brilliant splashes of color to a bowl of greens. Radicchio is extremely pungent and comparatively expensive. Use it sparingly. Keeps well in the refrigerator (up to two weeks), especially if wrapped in moist paper towels. Like cabbage, radicchio also may be grilled, baked, or sautéed.

- **Spinach:** Deep green, slightly crumpled leaves that are full of iron. Slice off and discard the thick stems. The leaves of baby spinach are smaller, oval shaped, smooth, and buttery. Rinse all spinach thoroughly to rid the leaves of sand. Dry well. Mix with milder greens like Boston, Bibb, or loose-leaf.

- **Watercress:** Its clover-shaped leaves lend crunch to any salad. Snap off and discard the tough stems and be sure to rinse well. Watercress makes a pretty soup or plate garnish.

Depending on where you live, different greens are better than others at different times of the year. If you see dark green arugula leaves in the market, try mixing them with other greens like romaine, red leaf, or chicory (curly endive). Arugula has a nice, tart snap that enlivens any salad. It can be sandy, so rinse it well.

Figure 10-3:
Our favorite salad greens.

Here is a simple, well-balanced salad combining snappy arugula and mild Boston or red-leaf lettuce.

Mixed Green Salad with Red Onion

Tools: *Large pot, salad spinner or paper towels, chef's knife, small mixing bowl*

Preparation time: *About 20 minutes*

4 cups (1 L) Boston or red-leaf lettuce leaves

3 cups (750 mL) arugula

1/3 cup (75 mL) peeled and coarsely chopped red onion

2 tablespoons (30 mL) finely chopped fresh parsley

1 1/2 tablespoons (22 mL) red or white wine vinegar

Salt and freshly ground pepper to taste

1/4 cup (50 mL) olive oil

1 Rinse the greens in a large pot of cold water. (Change the water several times, rinsing until no sand remains and the greens are thoroughly cleaned.) Pick over the leaves, removing tough stems. Spin the greens in a salad spinner or lay them flat on paper towels and pat dry. (Greens may be washed and dried ahead of serving time and stored in plastic bags in the refrigerator.)

2 Tear the washed and dried greens into bite-sized pieces and put them in a salad bowl; then add the onion and parsley.

3 Put the vinegar in a small mixing bowl and add salt and pepper. Start beating while gradually adding the oil. Pour the dressing over the salad and toss to blend well.

Yield: *4 servings.*

This salad is a fine all-around first course.

The following variations to this recipe are tasty, too:

- Substitute balsamic vinegar for the red wine vinegar.
- Whisk 2 teaspoons (10 mL) Dijon-style mustard into the vinaigrette.
- Add 2 teaspoons (10 mL) mayonnaise, yogurt, or sour cream for a creamy vinaigrette.
- Mix up the lettuce, adding romaine, Bibb, or radicchio.
- Add a tablespoon (15 mL) of minced garlic.

- ✔ Add minced fresh herbs, such as tarragon, thyme, basil, chervil, sage, or savory, to taste.
- ✔ Add a tablespoon (15 mL) of capers.
- ✔ Crumble goat cheese or bleu cheese over the greens.
- ✔ Make garlic croutons (see recipe in Chapter 9) and sprinkle them over the greens.

Buying and Storing Greens

When buying greens, avoid those that are wilted, limp, or lying on the floor. A fresh head of romaine should look like a bouquet of green leaves, clumped tightly together without any rust-colored edges or signs of decay. Pass up the watercress if its leaves are yellowing. Brown spots on iceberg lettuce indicate rot. Greens sold in bunches, such as arugula and dandelion, are especially delicate and prone to quick decay; consume them within a few days of purchase. And don't believe (just because you watched your mother do it) that wilted greens revive when plunged into cold water.

Store rinsed and dried greens in the extra-cold crisper drawer of the refrigerator, wrapped in damp paper towels. You can place bunches of watercress, arugula, parsley, and other fresh herbs in a full glass of water, stem ends down, like fresh-cut flowers. Greens are not long-storage items, so consume them within a week of purchase.

Now that prebuttered rolls and pregrilled chicken are commonly available at supermarkets, you should not be surprised to find prepackaged salad greens complete with dressings, croutons, and other "instant" salad ingredients. Although these bagged salads save you time, they are comparatively expensive and do not offer, in our opinion, the same fresh taste of loose greens.

Washing and drying lettuce

Did you ever fall asleep at the beach with your mouth open and the wind blowing sand in your direction? Well, that's what unwashed salad can taste like. To make sure that you get all the sand out of lettuce, remove the leaves and soak them briefly in cold water, shaking occasionally. Then run them under the tap, being careful to rinse the root ends thoroughly.

Drying lettuce completely is also critical, or else the dressing slides right off. Towel-drying works, but it's a nuisance. The easiest method is to use a salad spinner (see Chapter 2) that dries with centrifugal force. Or you can practice this simple trick of our friend, who tosses his greens into a bag of loose nylon netting and then whirls them until dry in the spin cycle of his washing machine.

Ten Quick Salads . . . So Easy You Don't Need a Recipe

Simply follow the advice of your taste buds to create your own salads from these simple combinations:

- **Tomato, red onion, and basil salad:** Slice ripe, red tomatoes ¹/₄ inch (6 mm) thick and layer on a platter with diced red onion and 4 or 5 large chopped fresh basil leaves. Drizzle with oil and vinegar and season with salt and pepper.

- **Red and green pepper rice salad:** Combine about 3 cups (750 mL) cooked white rice with 1 cup (250 mL) cooked green peas and 2 cups (500 mL) seeded, cored, and chopped red, green, or yellow peppers (or any combination of colors). Toss with enough herb-vinaigrette dressing to moisten the ingredients sufficiently, add salt and pepper to taste, and chill before serving.

- **Cucumber-dill salad:** Toss peeled, sliced, and seeded cucumbers in a dill-flavored vinaigrette.

- **Cherry tomato and feta cheese salad:** Toss 1 pint (500 mL) cherry tomatoes, rinsed and sliced in half, with 4 ounces (125 g) crumbled feta cheese and ¹/₂ cup (125 mL) sliced, pitted black olives. Season with vinaigrette dressing to taste.

- **Orzo medley salad:** Combine about 2 cups (500 mL) cooked orzo (a rice-shaped pasta) with ¹/₂ cup (125 mL) chopped sun-dried tomatoes. Season lightly with oil, vinegar, and freshly ground pepper to taste.

- **Garbanzo bean toss:** Combine 1 can (13 ounces/398 mL) drained garbanzo beans, ¹/₂ cup (125 mL) chopped red onion, 1 or 2 cloves crushed garlic, and the grated peel of 1 lemon. Toss with lemon-vinaigrette dressing.

- **Layered cheese and vegetable salad:** Arrange alternating thin slices of ripe tomatoes and mozzarella cheese on a round platter. Fill the center with slices of avocado sprinkled with fresh lemon juice to prevent discoloration. Drizzle with olive oil and lemon juice; garnish with fresh basil.

- **Grilled vegetable platter with fresh pesto:** Arrange any assortment of grilled vegetables (see Chapter 6) on a platter. Serve with spoonfuls of fresh pesto (see Chapter 7).

- **Fruit salsa:** Combine 1 ripe, peeled, seeded, and chopped avocado, 2 ripe, peeled, seeded, and chopped papayas, ¹/₂ cup (125 mL) chopped red onion, and 1 teaspoon (5 mL) seeded, chopped jalapeño pepper with a dressing of 1 tablespoon (15 mL) honey and the grated peel and juice of 1 lemon. Serve as a side salad with broiled hamburgers, chicken, or fish.

- **Three-berry dessert salad:** Combine 2 pints (1 L) rinsed and hulled strawberries, 1 pint (500 mL) rinsed blueberries, and 1 pint (500 mL) rinsed raspberries in a bowl. Toss with a dressing of ¹/₂ cup (125 mL) heavy cream sweetened with confectioners' sugar to taste.

Chapter 11

Pastamania

*N*o man can be wise on an empty stomach.

— George Eliot

Ancient Greeks ate foods that resembled today's pasta, and so did the Romans. In the late 13th century, Marco Polo returned from China toting a variety of noodles, although it's a wonder that he didn't scarf them down with tomato sauce on the long trek home. Today, people in dozens of nations eat pasta of one kind or another. Few people argue, though, that the Italians would take home the gold in a pasta Olympics.

Pasta is a complex carbohydrate, which means that the human body can draw upon the energy in it readily and for a long period. Simple carbohydrates, such as sugar and honey, shoot energy but not nutrients into our systems. Put it this way: If you're on a diet high in simple carbohydrates, stick to short-distance sprints. The pasta guys can run the distances. Moreover, 2 ounces (56 g) of pasta contains only 211 calories and about 1 gram of fat. One big ladleful of Alfredo sauce can easily destroy that, but don't blame us.

Dried Pasta versus Fresh Pasta

America's attics and closets must be jammed with pasta-making machines. In the late 1970s and early 1980s, anyone who knew how to boil water wanted to make fresh pasta. Somehow — maybe through a conspiracy of glossy food magazines — people started believing that if you didn't roll your own pasta, you were somehow unpatriotic. Young couples spent weeknights in the kitchen with flour flying all over, eggs spilling, and dough falling on the floor. They cranked and cranked and cranked some more. Then they hung the pasta overnight to dry on chairs, books, tables, and lampshades.

This trend didn't last long. But you can always spot the lapsed pastamaniacs — they're the ones who always remark in Italian restaurants, "Oooh, fresh pasta. We love making fresh pasta, but the kids like dried."

The truth is that fresh pasta is not inherently better than dried; it's just different. Many fine dried pastas are sold on the market, and the choice between fresh and dried is really a matter of personal taste. Homemade pasta — that is, well-made homemade pasta — is definitely lighter and more delicate. Dried pasta tastes more substantial — and because a wide range of flours are used, flavors vary. The better dried pastas use semolina flour, made from nutritious durum wheat. (Homemade pasta is usually made from plain white flour.) Look on the box to find out what type of flour is used.

Interviews with several of the finest Italian chefs in the country produced the following list of their favorite imported and domestic brands of pastas. Imported pastas that are available throughout the U.S. included De Cecco, Delverde, and Barilla. American pastas cited for excellence were Antoine's and Al Dente. Many excellent domestic pastas are available only locally.

Delis and gourmet markets sell fresh pasta in the refrigerator section. Fresh pasta is good, but you pay a premium. For purposes of this chapter, we concentrate on dried pasta because it is widely available. In any case, the sauce is what really elevates pasta from ordinary to sublime.

Is the Pasta Ready Yet?

Al dente is not the name of an Italian orthodontist. It is a sacred term in Italy that means "to the tooth" or "to the bite." In cooking, al dente means slightly firm to the bite. Almost all nations outside Italy cook pasta longer. When pasta cooks too long, it absorbs more water and becomes mushy.

The time-tested method for checking pasta is still the best: Scoop out a strand or two with a fork, take the pasta in hand, jump around and toss the scorching pasta in the air, and then taste it. (You don't really have to toss it in the air, but it makes the process more fun.)

Some people say that pasta is cooked if you throw it at the refrigerator door and it sticks. We have found this hypothesis to be flawed, owing to children's finger smudges and sundry food smears that mitigate the door's adhesiveness. An alternate test is to toss a strand at the television screen. If it forms a humorous mustache on one of the actors, it's done; if it just hangs there vertically, however, cook it for 3 more minutes or so.

Ten tips for cooking pasta

✔ **Use a lot of water and an 8-quart (8-L) pot: 5 to 6 quarts (5 to 6 L) of water for a pound (500 g) of pasta.** Pasta, like tango dancers, needs room to move. If you don't have a pot large enough to hold that much water and still be three-fourths full or less, splitting pasta into two pots of boiling water is better than overloading one pot. An overloaded pot will splash boiling water all over the stovetop.

✔ **Salt the water to add flavor and to help the pasta absorb the sauce.** As a rule of thumb, 4 quarts (4 L) of water takes about 2 teaspoons (10 mL) of salt, and 6 quarts (6 L) calls for 1 tablespoon (15 mL).

✔ **Oil is for salads, not pasta water.** You don't need to add oil to the water if you use enough water and stir occasionally to prevent sticking. *Be sure to stir the pasta strands or macaroni shapes immediately and thoroughly* after adding them to the water.

✔ **Cover the pot to hasten heat recovery.** After you add pasta to the water, the water ceases to boil. When the water begins boiling again, remove the lid and finish cooking.

✔ **Test pasta after about 7 minutes.** If it is still stiff, resist the temptation to chew on it (your dental work costs too much to risk it). Imported pastas are generally more dense and take longer to cook than commercial American pastas. In any case, don't go more than three rooms away from the boiling pot. (To find out your pasta's average cooking time, check out Tables 11-1 through 11-5.)

✔ **Save 2 cups (500 mL) of the cooking liquid when the pasta is done.** You can use the liquid to add moisture to the sauce. The starch in the water binds the sauce, helping it adhere to the pasta.

✔ **Do not rinse pasta.** When the pasta is al dente (tender but firm), pour it gradually into a colander. *Do not rinse!* You want starch on the pasta to help the sauce adhere to it. The only exception is if you are making a cold pasta salad.

✔ **After draining it, place the pasta in the pan in which the sauce is cooking and stir well.** This method coats the pasta better than spooning the sauce on top. Serve from the saucepan.

✔ **Never combine two types or sizes of pasta in the same pot of water.** Fishing out the type that is done first is a real nuisance.

✔ **Don't try to speak broken Italian when you serve your pasta.** "Bonissimo! Perfectamente mia amigas, Mangia, Mangia!" You will sound silly and irritate your guests.

Making Perfect Pasta and Sauce

The basic principles of making sauce for pasta are the same as those for making the other kinds of sauces described in Chapter 7. The main difference is that the quantities for the pasta sauces in this chapter are often larger.

Piero Selvaggio, owner of the famous Valentino in Los Angeles, offers these general tips for cooking perfect pasta: "Use a wooden, not a metal spoon, to stir the pasta right after it's dropped into the boiling water. Add the pasta to the water all at once and don't break up long pasta strands — it's a sin! If you absolutely cannot have salt, add a little lemon juice to the cooking water. It adds a pleasant little tartness."

Timing is everything: Adding the sauce

Cooked pasta needs to be sauced immediately after it's drained or it becomes stiff and gluey. So always have the sauce ready and waiting before the pasta is cooked. Then all you need to do is drain the pasta, add the sauce, toss well, and serve.

Note: In many of the recipes in this chapter, we have you work on the sauce as the water for the pasta boils or the pasta cooks. This way, you can ensure that your pasta and sauce will be ready at about the same time.

Choosing the right amount and type of sauce

"The pasta sauce must be the right consistency, neither too thin, nor too thick, so it coats all of the pasta, leaving it perfectly moist. Too much sauce, and the pasta is mushy. Too little, and it is dry," says Lidia Bastianich, owner of Felidia restaurant in New York City.

Bastianich recommends changing pasta sauces to suit the seasons of the year:

- In the spring, serve pasta with fresh herbs and tender vegetables.
- In the summer, serve pasta with light fish sauces.
- In the fall, serve pasta with wild mushrooms or meat.
- In the winter, serve pasta with root vegetables or meat.

When pulling together a pasta sauce, always think in terms of a hierarchy of flavors. By *hierarchy,* we mean that one assertive ingredient should dominate; the dominant ingredient should not have to duke it out with other ingredients. Other elements of sauce should enhance and complement that main ingredient.

For example, if you have beautiful wild mushrooms in the fall, combining them in a sauce with powerful gorgonzola is a folly. The cheese you use, if any, should be mild and smoky to support the mushroom's flavor.

Picking perfect tomatoes

Nothing can compare with a vine-ripened summer tomato. But locally grown summer tomatoes are available only a few months of the year in most parts of the U.S. One alternative is the hot-house varieties that are picked green, gassed to a pale shade of pink, and then marketed by commercial growers from far away. For making most soups, sauces, and stews, canned Italian plum tomatoes are far superior to these anemic imitations. If a recipe calls for fresh tomatoes when regular tomatoes are not good, look for plum or Italian tomatoes. Named for the fruit they resemble, plum tomatoes ripen fully within a day or two and are perfect for quick skillet sauces laced with fresh basil and garlic.

Increasingly, imported tomatoes from Israel and Holland are appearing in markets. These tomatoes are worth the extravagant price tag when you use them to garnish a salad of mixed winter greens. Less pricey cherry tomatoes, though not suitable for marinara sauce, are also excellent tossed into salads and are usually ripe and juicy even during the winter season. Figure 11-1 shows a few tomato varieties.

The best way to ripen tomatoes is to place several in a brown paper bag for one or two days, thereby trapping their natural ripening gases. To hasten the ripening even more, place a banana in the bag. For a quick lesson on peeling and seeding tomatoes, turn to the recipe for Spaghetti with Quick Fresh Tomato Sauce, later in this chapter.

Figure 11-1:
The right tomatoes can make ordinary pasta taste delicious.

Name That Pasta: Pasta Types and Cooking Times

Italian pasta comes in two basic forms: macaroni and spaghetti.

Macaroni has distinctive shapes, hollows, and curves. *Spaghetti,* which means "a length of string," is pasta cut into delicate strands. Sometimes linguine and fettuccine noodles are identified apart from spaghetti because their strands are flattened. Figure 11-2 depicts some common pasta shapes, also described in the following sections.

Macaroni

Also known as *tubular pasta,* macaroni is served with thick, rich sauces. Table 11-1 describes the different types of tubular pastas and tells you how to cook and sauce them.

Table 11-1	The Macaroni Family	
Italian Name	*Translation*	*Description and Approximate Cooking Time*
Cannelloni	"Large reeds"	Stuffed with meat or cheese and baked smothered in sauce. Cooks in 7 to 9 minutes.
Ditali	"Thimbles"	Smooth and long. Cooks in 8 to 10 minutes.
Penne	"Quills"	Best coated all over with rich sauces. Cooks in 10 to 12 minutes.
Rigatoni	"Large grooves"	Large, wide tube that is excellent with tomato, meat, and vegetable sauces. Cooks in 10 to 12 minutes.
Ziti	"Bridegrooms"	Narrow tube shape that is excellent in rich, baked casseroles with thick tomato sauces. Cooks in 10 to 12 minutes.

Strand pasta

Strand pasta is best served with thin, flavorful sauces that are rich in oil, which keep the very thin pasta from sticking together. Table 11-2 shows the best way to cook each type of strand pasta.

Table 11-2	The Spaghetti Family	
Italian Name	*Translation*	*Description and Approximate Cooking Time*
Capelli d'angelo	"Angel hair"	The thinnest pasta of all. Excellent with thin cream or tomato sauces. Cooks quickly in 3 to 4 minutes.
Cappellini	"Little hairs"	Slightly thicker than angel hair. Cooks in 4 to 5 minutes.
Fusilli	"Twists"	Corkscrew shaped and good with chunky sauces. Cooks in 10 to 12 minutes.
Spaghetti	"Length of string"	Delicate strands. Cooks in 10 to 12 minutes.
Vermicelli	"Little worms"	Thin strands. Cooks in 5 to 6 minutes.

Flat ribbon pasta

Flat ribbon pasta is excellent with rich, creamy sauces such as Alfredo or simple butter sauces with fresh sautéed vegetables. To find out the best way to cook different types of flat ribbon pasta, see Table 11-3.

Table 11-3	Flat Ribbon Pastas	
Italian Name	*Translation*	*Description and Approximate Cooking Time*
Fettuccine	"Small ribbons"	Flat strands of egg noodles. Cooks in 8 to 10 minutes.
Linguine	"Little tongues"	Long, thin ribbons. Cooks in 8 to 10 minutes.
Tagliatelle	"Small ribbons"	Like fettuccine, but a bit wider. Cooks in 7 to 8 minutes.

Stuffed pasta

Filled with meat, cheese, fish, or vegetables, stuffed pastas are best coated with simple tomato or light cream-based sauces. The dough is often flavored and tinted with spinach, tomato, mushrooms, or *saffron,* a fragrant spice. Table 11-4 gives the cooking times for stuffed pastas.

Table 11-4	Stuffed Pastas	
Italian Name	*Translation*	*Stuffing and Approximate Cooking Time*
Agnolotti	"Half-moon shaped"	Stuffed with meat or cheese. Cooks in 7 to 9 minutes.
Ravioli	"Little square pillows"	Stuffed with meat, cheese, fish, or vegetables. Cooks in 7 to 9 minutes.
Tortellini	"Ring-shaped little twists"	Stuffed with meat or cheese. Cooks in 10 to 12 minutes.

Sundry other shapes

Table 11-5 lists a grab bag of other pastas that don't quite fit into any of the other categories.

Table 11-5	Miscellaneous-Shaped Pastas	
Italian Name	*Translation*	*Great Accompaniments and Approximate Cooking Time*
Conchiglie	"Conch shells"	Wonderful with a simple butter-basil sauce and a grating of Parmesan cheese. Cooks in 10 to 12 minutes.
Farfalle	"Butterflies"	Pretty tossed into cold salads with fresh vegetables. Cooks in 10 to 12 minutes.
Orecchiette	"Little ears"	Wonderful in chicken soups and clear broths. Cooks in 7 to 9 minutes.
Orzo	"Rice-shaped"	Good cold in chicken and sun-dried tomato salad with vinaigrette. Cooks in 8 to 10 minutes.
Rotelle	"Small wheels"	Fun-shaped favorite of children. Cooks in 8 to 10 minutes.

Pasta Sauces You Should Know About

Italian pasta sauces are as inventive and varied as macaroni shapes. We briefly describe the classic ones, so the next time you dine at an expensive trattoria where the puttanesca is $24 a plate, you'll know what you're paying for.

- **Ragù or Bolognese:** A long-simmered sauce of meat (usually ground beef, veal, or pork) and tomatoes, named for the city of Bologna, where it was invented. For a true ragù, you brown the meat lightly and then cook it in a small amount of milk and wine before adding tomatoes.

- **Primavera:** A mixture of sautéed spring vegetables, such as sweet red pepper, tomatoes, asparagus, and snow peas, and fresh herbs and spices.

- **Fettuccine all'Alfredo:** A rich sauce of cream, butter, Parmesan cheese, and freshly ground black pepper tossed over fettuccine.

- **Carbonara:** Crisply cooked bacon (usually Italian bacon or pancetta) combined with garlic, eggs, Parmesan cheese, and light cream.

- **Spaghetti alle Vongole:** Spaghetti tossed with clams, olive oil, white wine, and herbs and spices.

- **Puttanesca:** A pungent sauce of anchovies, garlic, tomatoes, capers, and black olives.

- **Pesto:** Fresh basil leaves, pine nuts, garlic, Parmesan cheese, and olive oil blended to a fine paste.

Getting Started with Pasta

Following are some simple pasta recipes that you can vary after you feel more confident.

Pasta sauce 101

You can use this à la minute sauce as the foundation for endless enhancements with herbs, vegetables, meat, and more.

Spaghetti with Quick Fresh Tomato Sauce

Tools: *Paring knife, chef's knife, large pot, colander, saucepan or skillet, grater*

Preparation time: *About 15 minutes*

Cooking time: *About 15 minutes*

(continued)

5 to 6 ripe plum tomatoes, about 1¹/₂ pounds (750 g)

Water

Salt to taste

³/₄ pound (375 g) spaghetti or pasta of your choice

3 tablespoons (45 mL) olive oil

2 teaspoons (10 mL) peeled and minced garlic, about 2 large cloves

Freshly ground pepper to taste

3 tablespoons (45 mL) grated Parmesan cheese

2 tablespoons (30 mL) coarsely chopped fresh basil leaves, about 12 leaves

1 Core the tomatoes and peel them by dropping into boiling water for about 10 to 15 seconds. Remove with a slotted spoon and plunge into a bowl of ice water to cool them quickly. After the tomatoes are cool enough to handle, peel them with a paring knife. Cut them into ¹/₂-inch (6-mm) cubes. You should have about 2 cups (500 mL). (See Figure 11-3 for an illustration of this procedure.)

2 Bring 4 to 5 quarts (4 to 5 L) lightly salted water to a boil over high heat in a large, covered pot. Add the spaghetti, stir with a long fork, and cook, uncovered, for about 8 minutes or just until al dente.

3 While the spaghetti cooks, heat the oil in a saucepan or skillet over medium heat. Add the garlic. Cook and stir briefly with a wooden spoon. Do not brown the garlic. Add the cubed tomatoes and salt and pepper to taste. Cook, crushing the tomatoes with a fork and stirring, for about 3 minutes.

(continued)

How to Peel, Seed, and Chop Tomatoes

Figure 11-3: Dropping tomatoes in boiling water for a few seconds makes peeling them much easier.

4 Just before the pasta is done, carefully scoop out and reserve ¹/₄ cup (50 mL) of the cooking liquid. When the pasta is ready, drain it and return it to the large pot. Add the tomato sauce, cheese, basil, and ¹/₄ cup (50 mL) reserved cooking liquid to the pasta. Toss well over low heat for a few seconds. Serve immediately.

Yield: 4 servings.

You can omit the Parmesan cheese and add a small can of drained, flaked tuna. Or keep the cheese and toss in some sliced black olives and cooked artichoke hearts. A few sautéed shrimp and asparagus spears, or even sautéed chicken livers, also work with this classic sauce.

A saucy freeze-for-all

You can make this slow-cooked, intensely flavored marinara sauce in large quantities and freeze it for later use. Omit perishables like cheese, shrimp, and asparagus until you thaw the sauce base.

Marinara Sauce

Tools: *Chef's knife, heavy saucepan, wooden spoon, food processor or blender, grater*

Preparation time: *About 15 minutes*

Cooking time: *About 1 hour*

1 cup (250 mL) peeled and minced onion, about 1 large onion

1 tablespoon (15 mL) peeled and minced garlic, about 3 large cloves

¹/₄ cup (50 mL) olive oil

35-ounce can (or 2 pounds, 3 ounces or 910 mL) Italian plum tomatoes

6-ounce (156-mL) can tomato paste

¹/₃ cup (75 mL) dry red wine

¹/₂ cup (125 mL) water

Salt and freshly ground pepper to taste

2 teaspoons (10 mL) chopped fresh thyme, or 1 teaspoon (5 mL) dried

2 teaspoons (10 mL) chopped fresh oregano, or 1 teaspoon (5 mL) dried

¹/₃ cup (75 mL) grated Parmesan or romano cheese

1 In a heavy saucepan over medium heat, sauté the onion and garlic in the olive oil until wilted, about 3 to 4 minutes, stirring frequently. (Do not let the garlic brown.) Add all remaining ingredients except the cheese and simmer, partially covered, for about 1 hour, stirring occasionally.

(continued)

2 Carefully transfer the sauce to the container of an electric blender or food processor, secure the lid tightly, and puree until semismooth. (Leave the sauce a little grainy.)

3 Return the sauce to the saucepan and keep it warm over very low heat. Taste for seasoning, adding cheese to the sauce now or at the table.

Yield: *About 5 cups (1.25 L).*

Note: *Calling for Italian plum tomatoes should not be taken as an unpatriotic act. It's just that Italian tomatoes have more flavor.*

A large pot of boiling water is one of the most dangerous elements in any kitchen. Use a pot with short handles that cannot be tipped easily and set it to boil on a back burner, away from small and curious hands.

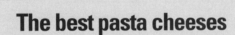

The best pasta cheeses

Parmesan: This is one of Italy's finest pasta cheeses. Parmesan is made from the milk of Parma cows, but only between April 15 and November 15, when the grazing grass in northern Italy is at its peak. True Parmesan is carefully aged at least two years before it's sold. A good one is pale yellow and has a pleasant, salty taste. We do not recommend using pre-grated Parmesan, as it does not hold its flavor. Keep the cheese tightly wrapped in the refrigerator and grate the exact amount called for in the recipe.

Romano: A bit stronger and more salty than Parmesan, this cheese is produced from the milk of sheep, so it's sometimes sold as *pecorino* (all sheep's milk cheeses are known as pecorino in Italy).

Romano's strength makes it suitable for pasta with hot, spicy sauces and hearty meats, but not for more delicate dishes.

Fontina: This semisoft cheese is the finest produced in northern Italy's Val d'Aosta region.

Fontina is wonderful grated into creamy white sauces and for stuffed pastas and lasagna.

Mozzarella: Another semisoft cheese, most often used as a topping for pizzas or in lasagna, but also terrific diced and tossed into just about any type of tomato or vegetable sauce for pasta. You can bake chunks of mozzarella in a casserole of penne, tomato sauce, and roasted eggplant. Many small specialty markets offer freshly made buffalo milk mozzarella that is far superior to most commercial brands.

Chèvres: Most chèvres are made from goat's milk, but a few blend in cow's milk to produce a softer, creamier texture. Mix chunks of chèvre into pasta with grilled vegetables or pesto sauces. Or add a little chèvre to a lasagna casserole along with ricotta.

Feta: Don't confuse this cheese with any of the chèvres. Feta is made from sheep's milk and therefore is more salty and much less creamy than goat cheese. Known primarily as the principal

(continued)

(continued)

ingredient in a Greek salad, feta can be an interesting addition to pasta. Add small chunks of feta to pasta sauces of fresh tomatoes and shrimp or to a quick sauce of scallions, olive oil, and roasted red peppers. Feta is intensely flavorful, yet it has less fat and fewer calories than most other cheeses.

Ricotta: Creamy, slightly grainy ricotta has a multitude of uses in dishes that range from savory to sweet. In pasta, ricotta is an essential ingredient in baked casseroles like lasagna, but it can also be the foundation of a quick and delicious sauce for spaghetti or linguine. Toss heaping spoonfuls of ricotta into steaming pasta along with grated Parmesan and pepper. To dress up pasta a little more, add cooked broccoli florets or cut-up asparagus. You also can use ricotta to bind (or thicken) sauces finished in an electric blender.

Pasta on the run

Sometimes you can forgo a formal sauce and just whip together a quick cheese garnish for pasta, as in the following recipe.

Penne with Cheese

Tools: *Large pot, chef's knife, grater, colander*

Preparation time: *About 10 minutes*

Cooking time: *About 20 minutes*

Water

Salt to taste

$^1/_2$ pound (250 g) penne (Italian tube pasta)

2 tablespoons (30 mL) olive oil

1 tablespoon (15 mL) butter

$^1/_4$ cup (50 mL) grated Parmesan or romano cheese

$^1/_4$ cup (50 mL) chopped fresh basil or Italian parsley

$^1/_8$ teaspoon (0.5 mL) freshly grated or ground nutmeg

Freshly ground pepper to taste

1 Bring 3 to 4 quarts (3 to 4 L) lightly salted water to a boil in a large, covered pot over high heat. Add the penne, stir, and bring to a boil again. Cook, uncovered, for about 10 minutes or until the pasta is al dente.

2 Just before the penne is done, carefully scoop out $^1/_4$ cup (50 mL) of the cooking liquid. When the penne is ready, drain it and return it to the pot. Add the olive oil, butter, cheese, basil, nutmeg, pepper, and the reserved cooking liquid.

(continued)

3 Toss and blend over medium-high heat for 30 seconds. Serve immediately.

Yield: *3 to 4 servings.*

A briny combination

Pasta with clam sauce is an all-time favorite. If you have access to fresh clams, particularly cherrystones, chop up the meat and use all the clam juice (or brine) in the sauce. Canned clams are very good, too.

Spaghetti with Clam Sauce

Tools: *Chef's knife, clam knife (if shucking clams yourself), large pot, large saucepan, colander, grater*

Preparation time: *About 15 minutes (more for shucking clams)*

Cooking time: *About 25 minutes*

18 cherrystone clams, shucked, with clam juice reserved, about 2 cups (500 mL), or three 6¹/₂-ounce (184-g) cans minced clams

Water

Salt to taste

2 tablespoons (30 mL) olive oil

1 tablespoon (15 mL) peeled and finely chopped garlic, about 3 large cloves

5 ripe plum tomatoes, about 1¹/₂ pounds (750 g), cored and cut into ¹/₂-inch (6-mm) cubes

Juice of half a lemon, about 1¹/₂ tablespoons (22 mL)

¹/₈ teaspoon (0.5 mL) red pepper flakes

Freshly ground pepper to taste

1 pound (500 g) spaghetti

¹/₂ cup (125 mL) coarsely chopped fresh basil leaves or Italian parsley

Freshly grated romano or Parmesan cheese (optional)

1 If using fresh clams, shuck them and chop the meat coarsely, reserving all brine (or clam juice) in a separate cup — you should have about 1 cup (250 mL) of brine. If using canned clams, strain the clams from the juice, reserving both the juice and the clams.

2 Bring 5 to 6 quarts (5 to 6 L) lightly salted water to a boil in a large, covered pot over high heat.

(continued)

3 Meanwhile, heat the oil in a large saucepan over medium heat. Add the garlic and cook briefly for about 1 minute, stirring, without browning. Add the tomatoes, lemon juice, red pepper flakes, pepper, and reserved clam juice. Simmer, stirring, for about 10 to 15 minutes or until the mixture reduces to about 2 cups (500 mL) total. Remove from heat.

4 When the water boils, add the spaghetti, stir, and boil, uncovered. Check for doneness after about 6 minutes, or when the pasta is still a bit firm. (The pasta finishes cooking in the sauce.)

5 Drain the pasta in a colander and transfer it to the saucepan holding the tomato mixture. Bring all to a simmer. Cook until the spaghetti is al dente, stirring often, about 2 to 3 minutes. Add the clams and basil, toss, and cook about 1 to 2 minutes more. (Do not boil.) Serve immediately with romano or Parmesan cheese, if desired.

Yield: *4 servings.*

Shuck those clams

Follow these steps to shuck clams:

1. Hold the clam in one hand with the clam's *hinge,* or pointed side, toward your palm.

2. Work a clam knife into the thin opening between the top and bottom shell as shown.

3. Run the knife along the upper shell as shown. As you move toward the hinge, work the knife up and down.

4. When the upper shell is loose, scrape away any edible meat clinging to it. Remove the upper shell and discard. (A muscle holds the meat to the bottom shell. If possible, do not sever that muscle until the last moment, or the meat begins to shrivel.)

Raw clams that are alive and well have shells that are tightly shut. Discard any clams that are not shut tightly. Also discard any clams that do not open after you cook them.

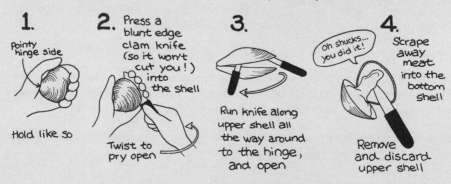

Branching out

After you can make basic pasta dishes with relative ease, you can begin experimenting with different ingredients. Before you dash down to the store and buy Virginia ham and starfruit to toss into the pan, think first about food pairings. You don't want a single sauce ingredient to bully all the others — turnips, for example, overpower any combination. Think of it this way: If you can imagine the ingredients combined and served as part of a nonpasta dinner, then they probably work in a pasta sauce.

Eggplant and summer squash

Following is an example of a vegetable pasta that harmonizes flavors. Eggplant has a distinctive texture and a slightly tart but sweet flavor. Let the eggplant be the dominant ingredient. Subtle summer squash adds lovely color, enhanced by sweet tomatoes.

Rigatoni with Eggplant and Summer Squash

Tools: *Chef's knife, grater, large pot, 2 large saucepans or sauté pans, colander*

Preparation time: *About 25 minutes*

Cooking time: *About 30 minutes*

4 tablespoons (60 mL) olive oil

2 teaspoons (10 mL) peeled and finely chopped garlic, about 2 large cloves

1½ pounds (750 g) ripe tomatoes, cored, peeled, and chopped, or 28-ounce can (about 796 mL) crushed tomatoes

¼ cup (50 mL) chopped fresh Italian parsley

2 teaspoons (10 mL) dried oregano

½ teaspoon (2 mL) sugar

½ teaspoon (2 mL) red pepper flakes (optional)

Salt and freshly ground pepper to taste

1 pound (500 g) eggplant, ends trimmed, peeled, and cut into 1-inch (2.5-cm) cubes, about 1 medium eggplant (see Figure 11-4 for illustrated instructions for dicing)

½ pound (250 g) yellow summer squash or zucchini, ends trimmed, cut into ½-inch (12-mm) thick rounds and then into semicircles

Water

1 pound (500 g) rigatoni, ziti, fusilli, or shells

¼ cup (50 mL) coarsely chopped fresh basil

⅓ cup (75 mL) grated Parmesan cheese

(continued)

1 Heat 1 tablespoon (15 mL) of the olive oil in a large saucepan or sauté pan over medium heat and then add the garlic. Cook, stirring constantly, for about 1 minute, without browning the garlic. Add the tomatoes, parsley, oregano, sugar, pepper flakes (if desired), and salt and pepper. Stir to blend, bring to a boil, reduce heat, and simmer for 15 minutes, partially covered.

2 As the sauce simmers, heat the remaining 3 tablespoons (45 mL) olive oil over high heat in a separate large pan. When the oil is very hot, add the eggplant, squash, and salt and pepper to taste. Cook over medium heat, tossing, about 5 to 7 minutes or until nicely browned and tender. After the tomato sauce simmers for 15 minutes, stir in the eggplant and zucchini mixture and simmer for 15 minutes more.

3 Meanwhile, bring a large, covered pot with 5 quarts (5 L) lightly salted water to a boil over high heat.

4 Add the pasta to the boiling water, stir, and cook according to package instructions or until al dente. Just before draining the pasta, use a measuring cup to carefully scoop out ¹/₂ cup (125 mL) of the cooking liquid and add it to the sauce.

5 When it's ready, drain the cooked pasta and return it to the large pot. Add the sauce, basil, and Parmesan cheese. Toss and serve hot with extra cheese.

Yield: *4 to 6 servings.*

Dicing an Eggplant

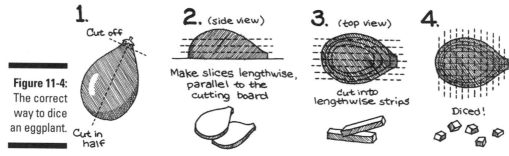

Figure 11-4:
The correct
way to dice
an eggplant.

This thick and hearty sauce stands up to the addition of a savory meat like sweet Italian sausage or ground pork. For example, you can coarsely chop and then cook in a small skillet ¹/₂ pound (250 g) sweet Italian sausage. Add the cooked sausage to the tomato sauce along with the eggplant and squash mixture. For roasted flavor, brush the eggplant and summer squash pieces with oil and grill them, or roast them in the oven until tender and then add to the tomato sauce.

Broccoli rape, tomatoes, and red peppers

Broccoli rape (pronounced RAH-pay), shown in Figure 11-5, is a staple with pasta in Italy. Its slightly bitter flavor contrasts beautifully with heady garlic and aromatic olive oil. The following pasta dish takes advantage of the sharp, almost peppery quality of broccoli rape, which complements the sweet crushed tomatoes and sweet red peppers. Rosemary and oregano give the sauce an extra dimension. (If you cannot find fresh herbs, use one-third to one-half the quantity of dried herbs, which are more potent.) You can make this light, delicious sauce in minutes and refrigerate or freeze it if necessary.

Figure 11-5:
Broccoli rape works well in a garlic-flavored sauce.

Many people confuse broccoli rape with turnip greens. Unlike turnip greens, though, broccoli rape has distinctive little buds, which you consume along with the tender leaves and stalks. One thing broccoli rape has in common with turnip and mustard greens is that it is a powerhouse of vitamins and minerals, particularly vitamin C and iron. Save the vitamin-loaded cooking water and use it for making chicken or vegetable soup.

In the following dish, tart broccoli rape is the dominant flavor and texture. Tomatoes and red peppers soften the sauce's flavor.

Broccoli Rape with Pasta

Tools: *Large pot, tongs or slotted spoon, large saucepan or sauté pan, chef's knife, grater, colander*

Preparation time: *About 25 minutes*

Cooking time: *About 25 minutes*

Water

Salt to taste

1 pound (500 g) broccoli rape, washed, trimmed, and cut into 2-inch (5-cm) pieces (see following note)

³/₄ pound (375 g) penne or rigatoni

4 tablespoons (50 mL) olive oil

1 tablespoon (15 mL) peeled and finely chopped garlic, about 3 large cloves

1 large sweet red pepper, cored, seeded, and cut into ¹/₂-inch (12-mm) cubes

1 teaspoon (5 mL) chopped fresh rosemary, or ¹/₂ teaspoon (2 mL) dried

1 teaspoon (5 mL) chopped fresh oregano, or ¹/₂ teaspoon (2 mL) dried

¹/₂ teaspoon (2 mL) red pepper flakes, or to taste

2 cups (500 mL) cored and diced ripe plum tomatoes, about 4 large plum tomatoes

Freshly ground pepper to taste

¹/₄ cup (50 mL) grated Parmesan cheese

1 Add 4 to 5 quarts (4 to 5 L) lightly salted water to a large pot over high heat. Add the broccoli rape, cover, and cook until crisp-tender, or about 2 to 3 minutes after the water begins to boil. Do not overcook. Remove the broccoli rape with tongs or a slotted spoon to a small bowl and set aside. Reserve the cooking water.

2 Bring the cooking water to a boil again. Add the pasta and cook for about 8 to 10 minutes (depending on the pasta) or until al dente.

3 As the pasta cooks, heat 2 tablespoons (30 mL) of the olive oil over medium heat in a large saucepan or sauté pan and add the garlic. Cook for only a few seconds, without browning. Add the sweet pepper, rosemary, oregano, and red pepper flakes and cook for about 2 minutes, stirring. Stir in the diced plum tomatoes and salt and pepper to taste. Cover and cook over medium heat, about 5 to 6 minutes, stirring occasionally.

4 Just before the pasta is done, scoop out and reserve ¹/₂ cup (125 mL) of the cooking water. When it's ready, drain the cooked pasta and return it to the large pot.

5 To assemble the dish, add the broccoli rape, tomato-pepper sauce, remaining 2 tablespoons (30 mL) olive oil, Parmesan cheese, and half the reserved cooking water to the drained pasta. Cook over low heat, stirring and tossing, for just a few seconds. If the sauce needs more moisture, add the rest of the cooking water. Check for seasoning, adding more salt and pepper if necessary, and serve immediately.

(continued)

Yield: *4 servings.*

Note: *Trim about 3 inches (8 cm) off the bottom of the stems of the broccoli rape before rinsing in cold water. As you cut the broccoli into bite-sized pieces, be sure to leave the little buds intact.*

Goat cheese and asparagus

Fresh goat cheese has a lovely, creamy texture and a faint, tangy aftertaste. It pairs naturally with pasta and fresh vegetables.

Fettuccine with Goat Cheese and Asparagus

Tools: *Large pot, large skillet, colander, grater*

Preparation time: *About 15 minutes*

Cooking time: *About 20 minutes*

Water

Salt to taste

$1^{1}/_{4}$ pounds (625 g) fresh asparagus

4 ripe plum tomatoes

$^{3}/_{4}$ pound (375 g) fettuccine

2 tablespoons (30 mL) olive oil

2 tablespoons (30 mL) butter

2 teaspoons (10 mL) peeled and finely chopped garlic, about 2 large cloves

$^{1}/_{4}$ pound (125 g) soft goat cheese

$^{1}/_{4}$ cup (50 mL) coarsely chopped fresh basil leaves

Freshly ground pepper to taste

Freshly grated Parmesan cheese (optional)

1 Bring 4 to 5 quarts (4 to 5 L) lightly salted water to a boil in a large, covered pot over high heat.

2 Meanwhile, remove the woody base of the asparagus with a knife or by snapping at the natural breaking point (about 2 inches/5 cm) from the thick, woody end). Slice the spears diagonally, creating $^{1}/_{2}$-inch (12-mm) pieces. Rinse and drain well.

3 When the water boils, carefully drop in the tomatoes for 10 to 20 seconds. Remove them from the water with a slotted spoon. (You are cooking them only long enough to loosen the skins.) When they are cool enough to handle, peel off the skins with a paring knife. Remove the core and seeds. (Refer to Figure 11-3 for illustrated instructions.) Chop the tomatoes coarsely and set aside.

(continued)

4 Bring the water to a boil again and add the fettuccine. Stir thoroughly to separate the strands and cook, uncovered, for about 8 minutes or just until al dente.

5 As the pasta cooks, heat the oil and butter in a large skillet and add the asparagus, tomatoes, and garlic. Cook over medium heat for 4 to 5 minutes, stirring, until the asparagus is crisp-tender. Reduce heat to very low to keep warm.

6 Before draining the pasta, use a measuring cup to carefully scoop out and reserve ¹/₄ cup (50 mL) of the cooking liquid. When it's ready, drain the pasta and return it to the large pot.

7 Add the vegetable mixture, goat cheese, basil, and salt and pepper to the pasta. Toss well over medium heat just until warmed through. If the sauce needs extra liquid, pour in some of the reserved cooking water. Serve immediately with Parmesan cheese on the side, if desired.

Yield: 4 servings.

Seafood

Seafood and pasta are an enduring and blissful marriage. Be careful not to overcook the seafood, which you usually add toward the end of the sauce-making.

This recipe, as with most others calling for seafood, can be made with different fish. For example, you can swap the halibut for monkfish, swordfish, or any other firm-fleshed white fish. If you try to make pasta with a delicate fish, like sole or flounder, it may fall apart in the sauce.

Ziti with Fresh Halibut in Tomato-Tarragon Sauce

Tools: *Chef's knife, large pot, two large saucepans or sauté pans, colander*

Preparation time: *About 20 minutes*

Cooking time: *About 20 minutes*

$^1/_4$ cup (50 mL) plus 1 tablespoon (15 mL) olive oil

$^1/_2$ cup (125 mL) peeled and finely chopped onion, about 1 medium onion

2 tablespoons (30 mL) peeled and chopped shallots, about 2 medium shallots

$^1/_2$ teaspoon (2 mL) peeled and finely minced garlic, about 1 small clove

$^1/_2$ cup (125 mL) dry white wine

$^1/_2$ cup (125 mL) crushed canned tomatoes (or fresh if in season and ripe)

2 teaspoons (10 mL) minced fresh tarragon, or 1 teaspoon (5 mL) dried

$^1/_4$ teaspoon (1 mL) red pepper flakes

Salt and freshly ground pepper to taste

Water

$^3/_4$ pound (375 g) ziti

1 pound (500 g) halibut fillets, cut into roughly 1-inch (2.5-cm) cubes

$^1/_4$ cup (50 mL) finely chopped fresh parsley

1 In a large saucepan, heat $^1/_4$ cup (50 mL) of the olive oil over medium-high heat for about 1 minute. Add the onion, shallots, and garlic. Cook, stirring, for about 3 minutes. Do not brown the garlic.

2 Add the wine, tomatoes, tarragon, pepper flakes, and salt and pepper. Bring the sauce to a boil and then remove from the heat.

3 Fill a large pot with 4 to 5 quarts (4 to 5 L) lightly salted water, cover, and bring to a boil over high heat. Add the pasta and cook, uncovered, stirring often, for about 10 minutes or just until al dente.

4 As pasta cooks, add the remaining tablespoon (15 mL) of oil to a large saucepan or sauté pan and add the halibut. Cook briefly for about 1 minute, stirring, and then add the sauce. Cook for about 4 to 5 minutes more over medium-low heat, stirring very gently. Remove from the heat.

(continued)

5 Just before the cooked pasta has finished cooking, use a measuring cup to scoop out and reserve about ¹/₂ cup (125 mL) of the cooking water. When it's ready, drain the cooked pasta and add it to the sauce. If the sauce needs more moisture, add some or all of the reserved cooking water. Stir gently and taste for seasoning. Sprinkle with parsley and serve.

Yield: *4 servings.*

Oriental seasonings

Now you can get daring. Oriental seasonings have pervaded Western cooking in recent years as chefs discover how vibrant (and healthful) they are. Ginger root is one such ingredient. Its snappy flavor is invigorating with shrimp. Thus shrimp and ginger are the dominant flavors in this recipe.

Fresh ginger root (see Figure 11-6), sold in the produce departments of most supermarkets and all Asian produce stores, tastes nothing like ground ginger. You cannot substitute one for the other. Look for ginger root that has no signs of softness or decay. Use a vegetable peeler to remove the root's thin layer of skin before chopping or grating. Ginger root should be wrapped in plastic wrap and stored in the refrigerator, where it keeps for a week to ten days.

Figure 11-6:
Fresh
ginger root.

In this recipe, ginger root gives the pasta a pleasant bite. After you trim and cut the vegetables, assembling this recipe is easy.

Fettuccine with Ginger Shrimp

Tools: *Pasta pot, chef's knife, large skillet or sauté pan, colander*

Preparation time: *About 15 minutes (25 minutes if cleaning shrimp)*

Cooking time: *About 25 minutes*

Water

Salt to taste

$^1/_2$ pound (250 g) fettuccine

4 tablespoons (50 mL) olive oil

1 cup (250 mL) peeled and coarsely chopped red onion, about 1 medium onion

1 pound (500 g) small zucchini, rinsed, trimmed, and cut into $^1/_2$-inch (12-mm) cubes

2 medium sweet red peppers, cored, seeded, and cut into $^1/_2$-inch (12-mm) cubes

Freshly ground pepper to taste

$1^1/_4$ pounds (625 g) medium shrimp, peeled and deveined (see instructions in Chapter 12)

6 ripe plum tomatoes, cored and cut into $^1/_2$-inch (12-mm) cubes

1 tablespoon (15 mL) peeled and finely chopped garlic, about 3 large cloves

1 tablespoon (15 mL) peeled and finely chopped fresh ginger root

$^1/_4$ teaspoon (1 mL) red pepper flakes

$^1/_4$ cup (50 mL) chopped fresh basil

1 tablespoon (15 mL) red wine vinegar

1 Bring 4 to 5 quarts (4 to 5 L) lightly salted water to a boil in a large, covered pot over high heat. Add the fettuccine, stir, and cook, uncovered, according to package instructions. The pasta should be al dente.

2 Start to make the sauce as the water boils. Heat 2 tablespoons (30 mL) of the olive oil in a large skillet or sauté pan. Add the onion, zucchini, red peppers, and salt and pepper. Cook, stirring, over medium-high heat until the vegetables wilt, about 3 to 4 minutes. Add the shrimp, tomatoes, garlic, ginger root, and red pepper flakes. Cook and stir about 3 to 4 minutes longer, or just until the shrimp are pink and cooked through. Add the remaining 2 tablespoons (30 mL) olive oil, basil, and vinegar and stir to blend well.

3 Just before draining the pasta, use a measuring cup to carefully scoop out and reserve $^1/_4$ cup (50 mL) of the cooking liquid. When it's ready, drain the pasta and return it to the large pot. Add the shrimp-tomato sauce to the pasta and toss well. If the sauce needs more moisture, add the reserved cooking liquid. Serve immediately.

Yield: *4 servings.*

Family cooking

Here's a lasagna with a little bit of everything: cheese, meat, and a fresh tomato sauce redolent with onions, zucchini, and red pepper flakes. It lacks mozzarella cheese, one ingredient always found in more traditional lasagna. If you must have your lasagna with mozzarella, sprinkle it, cubed, between the layers of ricotta, sauce, and noodles.

You can make this recipe the day before, refrigerate it, and then bake it for about 1 hour before serving.

Lasagna with Fresh Tomato and Zucchini Sauce

Tools: *Chef's knife, blender or food processor, large skillet, large pot, large nonstick skillet, colander, lasagna pan, wooden spoon*

Preparation time: *About 30 minutes*

Cooking time: *About 1 hour, plus 10 minutes standing time*

3 pounds (1.5 k) ripe plum tomatoes or 5 cups (1.25 L) canned, crushed tomatoes

4 tablespoons (60 mL) olive oil

1 medium zucchini, trimmed and finely chopped, about 1 pound (500 g)

1 cup (250 mL) peeled and finely chopped onion, about 1 large onion

1 tablespoon (15 mL) peeled and finely chopped garlic, about 3 large cloves

2 teaspoons (10 mL) chopped fresh oregano, or 1 teaspoon (5 mL) dried

$^1/_2$ teaspoon (2 mL) red pepper flakes, or to taste

Salt and freshly ground pepper to taste

Water

$^1/_2$ pound (250 g) freshly ground pork

$^1/_2$ pound (250 g) freshly ground veal or beef

$^1/_2$ cup (125 mL) dry red wine or beef broth

1 teaspoon (5 mL) Italian seasoning

2 tablespoons (30 mL) tomato paste

12 lasagna noodles

16 ounces or 2 cups (500 g) ricotta cheese (use reduced-fat variety, if desired)

$^1/_4$ cup (50 mL) hot water

1 cup (250 mL) grated Parmesan or romano cheese

2 tablespoons (30 mL) chopped fresh parsley

(continued)

1 To make the sauce, core the tomatoes (if fresh) and cut them into cubes. Place the tomatoes in a food processor or blender container and puree until coarsely chopped. You should have about 5 cups (1.25 L).

2 Heat 3 tablespoons (45 mL) of the oil in a large skillet over medium heat. Add the zucchini, onion, and garlic and cook for about 5 minutes or until the onion wilts, stirring often. Add the chopped tomatoes, oregano, red pepper flakes, and salt and pepper to taste. Bring to a boil, reduce heat, and simmer for 10 to 15 minutes.

3 Preheat the oven to 350° F (180° C).

4 Bring an 8-quart (8-L) pot filled with about 6 quarts (6 L) of lightly salted water to a boil over high heat.

5 Continue preparing the sauce. Heat the remaining 1 tablespoon (15 mL) oil in a large nonstick skillet. Add the ground meats. Cook until lightly browned, stirring to break up the particles of meat. Carefully pour off all the fat into a metal can (not down the sink!). Let the fat harden in the can and then discard it.

6 Stir the wine or broth and the Italian seasoning into the browned meat. Bring to a boil over high heat and cook until the liquid evaporates. Stir the meat and tomato paste into the tomato-zucchini mixture. Adjust the seasoning with salt and pepper to taste. Bring to a boil; then reduce the heat and simmer for 5 minutes.

7 When the water is boiling, add the lasagna noodles one at a time. Cook, uncovered, according to package instructions until tender but not so soft that they tear easily.

8 As the noodles cook, mix the ricotta and ¼ cup (50 mL) hot water (you can take it from the boiling pot of lasagna noodles) in a bowl with a wooden spoon until smooth and spreadable. Add the grated Parmesan and chopped parsley. Season with salt and pepper to taste.

9 When they are cooked, gently drain the noodles in a colander in the sink. Run cold water over them and then stretch them out flat on a clean dish towel.

10 To assemble the lasagna, spread a heaping cup (250 mL) of the sauce on the bottom of a 12 x 9 x 2½-inch (30 x 20 x 6-cm) ovenproof lasagna pan. Place 3 noodles over the sauce so that they completely cover the bottom of the pan. Spread one-third of the ricotta mixture evenly over the noodles. Spread another heaping cup of the sauce over this layer.

11 Continue making layers, ending with a layer of sauce. Bake in the preheated oven for 25 minutes. Cover with aluminum foil and bake another 10 minutes or until the lasagna is piping hot. Remove and let stand for 10 to 15 minutes before slicing into squares.

Yield: 6 to 8 servings.

Buying shrimp

Unless you live within eyeshot of fishing boats, you can be sure that almost all shrimp sold in your supermarket is frozen.

Much shrimp comes from the Gulf states or the Deep South. Flash-frozen shrimp (which is plunged into a super-deep freeze upon harvest) is excellent when handled and stored properly. Its shelf life is about six months when well wrapped.

Always buy shrimp in the shell and not pre-cooked. After you remove the shell, pick out the thin, blackish vein that runs down the back, which has a bitter flavor. Turn to the sidebar in Chapter 12 for detailed instructions on cleaning and deveining shrimp. (Or ask your fish merchant to devein your shrimp when you purchase it.)

Chapter 12

One-Pot Meals

▶ Casseroles for crazed lives

▶ Shepherd cuisine

▶ Memory lane: meat loaf, pot pie, and macaroni and cheese

*W*hy use two pots when one will do? For families, singles, and party animals, one-pot meals can be a lifesaver. Every culture has its own one-pot specialties: pot-au-feu (chicken in a pot with vegetables) in France, the seafood stews of Spain, the squab pies of Morocco, and even the jambalaya of Louisiana.

Why Casserole Dishes Are for You

Casseroles may seem as fashionable as an unzipped fly, but they come in handy. Here are some reasons why:

- ✔ **Casseroles take advantage of the economies of scale.** Two pounds of black beans cost little more than one pound. Go ahead, invite the neighbors!

- ✔ **Casseroles save time and effort.** You can drink and chat and drink some more with your dinner guests and then coolly saunter into the kitchen. Five minutes later, voilà! Dinner.

- ✔ **Casseroles make great leftovers.** If you come home late and ravenous, you can excavate a casserole and zap it in the microwave. (Resist the temptation to eat it out of the casserole dish, at least while it's still in the refrigerator.)

- ✔ **Casseroles are classics.** You can boast that your one-pot meal is an old family recipe, even if you got the recipe from a Kraft box.

Strata: Rock Formation or Family Meal?

A *strata* is essentially a custard baked around layers of different ingredients, including bread, vegetables, cheese, and seasoning. If you don't have old, stale bread on hand, dry fresh slices in a 175° F (80° C) oven for about 15 minutes.

Stratas need to "set" a few minutes before baking so that the bread can absorb the custard mixture. If it's convenient, prepare and refrigerate the dish before heading out for work in the morning. Then just place the casserole in a pre-heated 350° F (180° C) oven about half an hour before you're ready to eat.

 You can vary a strata almost as much as an omelet filling. Substitute cooked, ground meat or ham for the bacon. Use slices of challah (an egg-enriched bread) for the Italian bread. Omit the spinach and add ¹/₂ cup (125 mL) cooked broccoli florets, chopped onion, or sautéed mushrooms.

A strata is also great for Sunday brunch.

Bacon and Cheese Strata

Tools: *2-quart (2-L) shallow baking dish, mixing bowl, chef's knife, skillet*

Preparation time: *About 25 minutes, plus 15 minutes standing time*

Baking time: *About 35 minutes*

Butter for greasing baking dish

8-ounce (250-g) loaf of Italian bread

¹/₄ pound (125 g) bacon (6 slices)

1¹/₂ cups (375 mL) grated Gouda, Gruyère, or Italian fontina cheese

¹/₃ cup (75 mL) rinsed, chopped spinach or sorrel leaves

5 large eggs

2 cups (500 mL) milk

2 tablespoons (30 mL) tomato-based salsa

Salt and freshly ground pepper to taste

1 Butter the bottom and sides of a 2-quart (2-L) shallow baking dish.

2 Trim and discard the ends off the loaf of bread and cut it into about 16 slices. If the bread is fresh, dry the slices in a 175° F (80° C) oven for about 15 minutes. Arrange the slices in the baking dish, overlapping the edges. (See Figure 12-1.)

3 Sauté the bacon in a skillet (or cook on paper towels in the microwave) until crisp. Drain on paper towels. When it's cool enough to handle, crumble it into small pieces.

(continued)

Figure 12-1:
The right
way to layer
bread for a
strata.

4 Sprinkle the crumbled bacon over the bread slices and top with the grated cheese and chopped spinach or sorrel leaves.

5 In a medium mixing bowl, beat together the eggs, milk, salsa, and salt and pepper. Pour the mixture over the layers of bread, bacon, cheese, and spinach. Using a fork, press the bread slices down to submerge them in the egg mixture. Let it set for about 15 minutes.

6 Preheat the oven to 350° F (180° C).

7 Bake on the middle oven rack, about 35 minutes or until the custard mixture is firm and lightly browned. Do not overbake. Remove from the oven and serve immediately, cutting into squares.

Yield: *4 to 6 servings.*

Serve this rich dish with bread and a simple salad like the Mixed Green Salad with Red Onion in Chapter 10.

Shepherd's Pie

In Ireland, the classic Shepherd's Pie is made with beef, not lamb. We prefer the more distinctive flavor of lamb, so we're giving you the following lamb recipe. If you want to try it with beef, simply substitute the same amount of meat.

This dish is so good that you may want to have leg of lamb every week just to generate enough leftovers for a pie. Some people like to add sliced carrots, leeks, or other vegetables. Try this version first and see what you think.

Shepherd's Pie

Tools: *Chef's knife, large pot, potato masher or ricer, large skillet, ovenproof dish*

Preparation time: *About 45 minutes*

Baking time: *About 35 minutes*

2¹/₂ pounds (1.25 kg) baking potatoes

4 tablespoons (60 mL) butter

About 1 cup (250 mL) milk

Salt and freshly ground pepper to taste

1 tablespoon (15 mL) vegetable oil

¹/₂ cup (125 mL) peeled and chopped onion, about 1 medium onion

2 teaspoons (10 mL) peeled and chopped garlic, about 2 large cloves

1¹/₂ pounds (750 g) cooked, chopped lamb (or raw, ground lamb)

1 tablespoon (15 mL) flour

¹/₂ cup (125 mL) beef or chicken stock

1 tablespoon (15 mL) chopped fresh thyme or sage, or 1 teaspoon (5 mL) dried

1 tablespoon (15 mL) chopped fresh rosemary leaves, or 1 teaspoon (5 mL) dried

Dash of nutmeg

1 Preheat the oven to 350° F (180° C).

2 Peel and quarter the potatoes. Bring a large pot of lightly salted water to a boil. Add the potatoes and cook, covered, until potatoes are tender, about 20 minutes. Drain well and return the potatoes to the pot.

3 Mash the potatoes with a masher or ricer along with 2 tablespoons (30 mL) of the butter and enough milk to make them smooth and fluffy. Season with salt and pepper and set aside.

4 Heat the oil in a large skillet over medium-low heat. Add the onion and garlic and cook, stirring, until the onion is soft and wilted. (Be careful not to let the garlic brown.) Turn up the heat to medium and add the lamb. Cook about 5 minutes, stirring. (If using raw, ground lamb, cook 10 to 15 minutes or until it is rare.) Pour off and discard any fat in the pan.

5 Add the flour and cook, stirring, for about 2 to 3 minutes. Add the stock, thyme, rosemary, nutmeg, and salt and pepper. Reduce the heat to low and simmer, stirring occasionally, for about 15 minutes. Remove from the heat and let cool slightly.

6 Transfer the lamb mixture to an oval gratin dish (about 9 inches/23 cm long) or a pie plate. Spread the mashed potatoes over everything. Dot with the remaining 2 tablespoons (30 mL) butter (which simply means to break up the butter into several small pieces and distribute it evenly) and bake for 35 minutes or until nicely browned. Let cool for 5 minutes before serving.

Yield: *4 to 6 servings.*

This dish needs only a salad, like the Tomato, Red Onion, and Basil Salad in Chapter 10.

Meat Loaf

This slightly untraditional meat loaf (made with turkey to cut down on fat) can be a jumping-off point for other creations. If you like, try mixing in a little ground pork or ground veal instead of turkey. Lamb is a nice addition, too. The essential technique is the same for any ground meat.

Beef and Turkey Meat Loaf

Tools: Chef's knife, medium skillet, large mixing bowl, 5- to 6-cup (1.25- to 1.5-L) loaf pan

Preparation time: About 30 minutes

Baking time: About 1 ½ hours, plus 10 minutes standing time

2 tablespoons (30 mL) olive oil

1 cup (250 mL) peeled and chopped onion, about 1 large onion

1 tablespoon (15 mL) peeled and finely chopped garlic, about 3 large cloves

³/₄ cup (175 ml) milk

2 eggs

1¹/₂ cups (375 mL) fresh bread crumbs

1 pound (500 g) ground turkey

1 pound (500 g) lean ground beef

2 tablespoons (30 mL) chopped fresh thyme, or 2 teaspoons (10 mL) dried

2 tablespoons (30 mL) chopped fresh savory, or 2 teaspoons (10 mL) dried

2 tablespoons (30 mL) finely chopped fresh parsley

¹/₄ teaspoon (1 mL) ground nutmeg

Salt and freshly ground pepper to taste

1 Preheat the oven to 350° F (180° C).

2 Heat the oil in a medium skillet over medium heat. Add the onion and cook, stirring, for about 3 minutes or until the onion begins to wilt. Add the garlic and cook, stirring, about 2 minutes more. Do not let the garlic brown. Remove the pan from the heat and set aside.

3 In a large bowl, beat together the milk and eggs; stir in the bread crumbs and let stand for 5 minutes. Add the remaining ingredients and the sautéed onion and garlic. Combine the mixture thoroughly by using your hands or a wooden spoon.

4 Mold the mixture into a 5- to 6-cup (1.25- to 1.5-L) loaf pan. Bake, uncovered, about 1¹/₂ hours, draining off any excess grease every 30 minutes. Let the meat loaf stand for about 10 minutes at room temperature before slicing from the pan.

Yield: 6 servings.

(continued)

You can serve this meat loaf with a quick tomato sauce, spicy salsa, mustard sauce, or even a jazzed-up sauce of ketchup flavored with Tabasco sauce and Worcestershire sauce. Side dishes might include Grilled Summer Vegetables with Basil Marinade (see Chapter 6) or Braised Cabbage with Apple and Caraway (see Chapter 15).

Chicken Pot Pie

In Colonial America, many foods, such as game, birds, and poultry, were served in pies. Pies were hearty one-dish meals that were easy to re-serve. The recipe hasn't changed much, unless you go to some hip new-American restaurant, where they may put fennel or fiddlehead ferns in it.

The following recipe, although not difficult to execute, takes time to make right. Steps include poaching the chicken, making a white sauce, chopping vegetables, and rolling out fresh biscuits for the pie's top. But the result is worth it.

Chicken and Biscuit Pot Pie

Tools: Chef's knife, 4-quart pot with lid, colander, small saucepan, mixing bowl, 2-quart shallow baking dish, wire whisk, rolling pin

Preparation time: About 30 minutes

Cooking time: About 40 minutes

Baking time: About 25 minutes

2 to 2¼ pounds (1 to 1.125 kg) raw chicken breasts with skin and bones

3 cups (750 mL) canned or fresh chicken stock

1 medium onion, peeled and halved

1 celery stalk, trimmed of leaves and sliced into 2-inch (5-cm) pieces

2 cloves garlic, peeled

Water (if necessary)

3 carrots, trimmed, scraped, and sliced into 2-inch (5-cm) pieces

1 medium boiling potato, peeled and quartered

6 tablespoons (90 mL) butter

3 tablespoons (45 mL) flour

¼ cup (50 mL) heavy cream

¼ teaspoon (1 mL) grated nutmeg

Salt and freshly ground pepper to taste

1 cup (250 mL) fresh or frozen peas

1 tablespoon (15 mL) sherry (optional)

1½ cups (375 mL) packaged dry biscuit mix, plus additional mix for dusting work surface

½ cup (125 mL) milk

(continued)

1 Combine the chicken breasts, stock, onion, celery, and garlic in a 4-quart (4-L) pot. Add additional water to just cover the chicken and vegetables. Cover the pot and bring to a boil. Uncover, reduce heat, and simmer for 15 minutes.

2 Add the carrots and potato. Bring the stock back to a boil and then lower the heat and simmer 15 minutes more or until the chicken and vegetables are just tender. Let cool for about 5 minutes in the liquid.

3 Slowly and carefully, pour the broth with the chicken and vegetables into a large colander set over a larger pot to catch and reserve the chicken-vegetable stock. Let cool for about 10 minutes, or until the chicken is cool enough to handle.

4 Remove the meat from the chicken and slice it into bite-sized pieces. Discard the skin and bones, celery, and garlic. Coarsely cube the remaining vegetables into $1/2$-inch (12-mm) pieces and set them aside.

5 Skim the fat from the reserved stock. Pour 2 cups (500 mL) of stock into a glass measuring cup. (Reserve any remaining stock for other uses, or if necessary add additional water to make 2 cups/500 mL.) Heat the measured stock to just below the point of boiling in a small saucepan.

6 Melt 3 tablespoons (45 mL) of the butter in a pot or saucepan over medium heat. (You can use the same pot that you used to make the stock.) Add the flour and cook, whisking constantly, for about 1 minute. Stir in the 2 cups (500 mL) of hot stock, whisking occasionally and cooking about 2 to 3 minutes until the sauce comes to a boil and thickens. Add the cream and nutmeg. Adjust the seasoning with salt and pepper.

7 Stir the chicken, diced vegetables, peas, and, if desired, 1 tablespoon (15 mL) sherry into the sauce. Spoon the mixture into a buttered, 2-quart (2-L) shallow baking dish.

8 Preheat the oven to 425° F (220° C).

The Pastry

1 Combine the biscuit mix and the remaining 3 tablespoons (45 mL) butter in a medium mixing bowl. Using a fork or your fingers, blend the butter into the biscuit mix until the mixture resembles coarse crumbs.

2 Stir in the milk and blend the mixture into a soft dough. Transfer the dough to a well-floured wooden board or countertop. The dough should be very soft. Before you attempt to roll or press out the dough with your hands, add more dry biscuit mix to your work surface and sprinkle the mound of dough with a little more dry mix. Also, dust your hands and the rolling pin (if you are using one) with the dry mix. You want to make the dough just firm enough to roll or press out into a square about $1/2$ inch (12 mm) thick.

3 Using a butter knife, carefully cut the dough into 9 or 10 triangles or rounds. Arrange the dough shapes on top of the chicken mixture and bake for about 25 minutes, or until the biscuits are lightly browned. Serve immediately.

(continued)

Yield: 6 servings.

This is a meal in itself, perhaps served with the Cucumber-Dill Salad in Chapter 10.

This recipe has more variations than spaghetti with meatballs. To start, you can replace the chicken with cooked turkey, a good choice especially at Thanksgiving time. Or add a few mushrooms, sautéed leeks, or even frozen mixed vegetables to the sauce. The seasonings are rather mild and classic, but you can spice it up with cayenne or seeded and chopped jalapeño pepper. For an easier topping, cover the filling with store-bought, ready-made pastry. Or follow the directions on a small box of corn bread mix, spreading the prepared batter over the top of the casserole about 15 minutes before it's finished baking.

Let's Party: Shrimp Appetizers

Shrimp make great party food. You can serve this irresistible preparation as an appetizer or a meal along with rice, noodles, or a vegetable. (See Chapter 3 for rice and vegetable recipes.)

Shrimp are sized and priced according to how many shrimp are in a pound. Although the number can vary from one market to the next, medium shrimp usually contain about 40 to 50 per pound, large shrimp about 30 to 35, extra-large 25 to 30, jumbo 20 to 25, and colossal 15 to 18 per pound. The price of shrimp generally increases with its size, with colossal the most expensive and medium the most reasonable. For this recipe, you want shrimp that are big enough to hold a fair amount of the stuffing.

Baked Shrimp with Scallion Bread Crumbs

Tools: Shrimp deveiner, paring knife, chef's knife, medium skillet, baking sheet, pastry brush for basting

Preparation time: About 30 minutes

Baking time: About 12 minutes

1 pound (500 g) large or jumbo shrimp, shelled and deveined, about 24 shrimp

1¹/₂ tablespoons (22 mL) butter

¹/₂ cup (125 mL) finely chopped scallions

¹/₄ cup (50 ml) finely chopped sweet red pepper

¹/₄ cup (50 mL) finely chopped celery

(continued)

2 teaspoons (10 mL) peeled and finely chopped garlic, about 2 large cloves

³/₄ cup (175 mL) fresh bread crumbs (see following sidebar)

2 teaspoons (10 mL) fresh lemon juice

1 teaspoon (5 mL) chopped fresh marjoram or chervil, or ¹/₂ teaspoon (2 mL) dried

1 teaspoon (5 mL) chopped fresh thyme, or ¹/₂ teaspoon (2 mL) dried

¹/₂ teaspoon (2 mL) paprika

Salt and freshly ground pepper to taste

1 tablespoon (15 mL) olive oil

4 lemon wedges

1 Preheat the oven to 500° F (260° C).

2 Butterfly the shrimp by slicing them with a paring knife from head to tail end along the inside so that they open up like a butterfly.

3 In a medium skillet, melt the butter over medium heat. Add the scallions, red pepper, celery, and garlic. Cook, stirring, over medium heat until the vegetables begin to wilt. Add the bread crumbs, lemon juice, marjoram, thyme, and paprika. Blend well, remove from the heat, and season with salt and pepper.

4 On a lightly oiled baking sheet, lay the shrimp in rows, split side up. Spoon equal amounts of the stuffing into the crevice of each shrimp. Press down lightly to smooth it. (The shrimp coil around the stuffing as they bake.)

5 Brush the stuffing mixture lightly with the tablespoon (15 mL) of olive oil. Bake for about 8 minutes. Serve immediately with the lemon wedges.

Yield: *3 to 4 servings.*

Any of the following would complement this dish: Orzo Medley (see Chapter 10), Converted Rice (see Chapter 3), or Garlic and Goat Cheese Tartines (see Chapter 15).

Cleaning and Deveining Shrimp

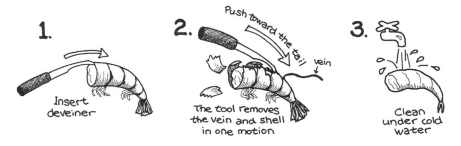

1. Insert deveiner

2. Push toward the tail — vein — The tool removes the vein and shell in one motion

3. Clean under cold water

Making fresh bread crumbs

You don't need to waste your money by buying bread crumbs. Instead, make your own and store them in an airtight jar.

Lightly toast six slices of bread. Tear the bread into pieces and place in a food processor or blender; then blend to the consistency of coarse crumbs.

Variation: Add dried herbs of choice to the blender, or rub the slices with three cloves of peeled garlic before whirling them into crumbs.

Pasta Paradise

This next recipe is a plain and simple version of macaroni and cheese, and you can alter it in many ways. You can substitute all kinds of pasta for the elbow macaroni, such as penne, ziti, or shells. Mozzarella or Gruyère can replace the fontina or cheddar, or you can use the cheeses in any combination. You can make a spicy version by adding more Tabasco sauce or even crushed red pepper flakes. Add sautéed onion and sweet red pepper or cooked broccoli florets and mushrooms to the cheese sauce for a vegetable version. Or sprinkle the top with cooked, crumbled bacon, shredded ham, or Parmesan cheese instead of the bread crumbs.

American Macaroni and Cheese

Tools: *4- or 5-quart (4- or 5-L) pot, two saucepans, wire whisk, grater, colander, chef's knife, 2-quart (2-L) casserole dish with lid*

Preparation time: *About 25 minutes*

Baking time: *About 25 minutes*

Water

Salt to taste

2 cups (500 mL) elbow macaroni

2¹/₂ cups (625 mL) milk

5 tablespoons (75 mL) butter

3 tablespoons (45 mL) flour

¹/₂ teaspoon (2 mL) paprika

Generous dash Tabasco pepper sauce, or to taste

2 cups (500 mL) grated sharp cheddar cheese

Freshly ground pepper to taste

¹/₂ cup (125 mL) cubed Italian fontina cheese

1 cup (250 mL) fresh white bread crumbs (see preceding sidebar)

(continued)

1 Preheat the oven to 350° F (180° C).

2 Bring a 4- or 5-quart (4- or 5-L) pot of lightly salted water to a boil. Add the elbow macaroni and cook for about 6 to 8 minutes or until just tender. (Be careful not to overcook. The macaroni softens even more when it's baked.)

3 As macaroni cooks, make the cheese sauce. Heat the milk almost to the boiling point in a small saucepan.

4 Melt 3 tablespoons (45 mL) of the butter in a medium saucepan over medium heat. Add the flour and whisk over low heat for 1 to 2 minutes. Do not let it brown.

5 Gradually whisk in the hot milk, and then add the paprika and Tabasco sauce. Cook over medium heat for 2 to 3 minutes or until the sauce thickens, whisking occasionally. Stir in the grated cheddar cheese and remove from the heat. Season with salt and pepper to taste.

6 Drain the elbow macaroni as soon as it is done and add it to the cheese sauce. Add the cubes of fontina and stir well to blend. (If the macaroni cooks before you finish making the sauce, drain and set it aside.)

7 Use 1 tablespoon (15 mL) butter to grease a deep, 2-quart (2-L) casserole dish fitted with a lid. Add the macaroni and cheese mixture. Cover and bake for 20 to 25 minutes until hot.

8 As the casserole bakes, melt the remaining tablespoon (15 mL) of butter in a small skillet. Add the bread crumbs and sauté over low heat, stirring constantly, until they are moistened but not browned.

9 Carefully remove the casserole from the oven. Raise the oven temperature to broil; spread the bread crumbs evenly over the macaroni and cheese. Return the casserole to the oven, uncovered, and broil for 1 to 2 minutes, or until the crumbs are crisp and browned. Serve immediately.

Yield: 4 servings.

All this dish needs is a colorful salad, like the Roasted Red Pepper and Snow Pea Salad in Chapter 10.

Pasta on the Internet

The National Pasta Association has its own Web site with lots of information about shapes, frequently asked questions about pasta, nutrition facts, and, of course, recipes. You can find this information and more at `http://www.ilovepasta.org.`

Part IV
Now You're Cooking! Real Menus for Real Life

The 5th Wave   By Rich Tennant

IT'S FRICASSEE OF PYTHON WITH FRIED ANTS AND CRISPY GRASSHOPPERS.

YOU'RE GETTING RECIPES OFF THE INTERNET AGAIN, AREN'T YOU?

In this part . . .

Contrary to what most cookbooks assume, cooking is not done in a vacuum — that is, you may have to contend with limited time, ringing phones, leaking washing machines, traumatized tots, and begging dogs.

We don't offer any help with the dogs or the washing machine, but we do address the critical element of time. Recipes in this part are designed for real-life situations: when you're cooking for only yourself after a long day's work or when you have guests coming in an hour and need to put together a meal, for example. We also offer some tips for becoming a savvy shopper so that you can make a good meal from what you have on hand — both quickly and inexpensively.

Chapter 13

The Bare Necessities: A Pantry List

In This Chapter

▶ Stocking up on spices, condiments, and canned and bottled goods

▶ Storing vegetables, fruits, and meats

▶ Making great meals from the cupboard

*Y*ou could probably survive for quite some time on a diet of peanut butter, canned tuna, and saltines, but eventually you would get bored. This chapter helps to alleviate the boredom of stocking your pantry. Shopping thoughtfully not only cuts down on trips to the market, but it also saves you money — those 8 p.m. dashes to 7-Eleven for grated cheese add up quickly. And when you don't have time to make it to the market, what's for dinner often depends on the ingredients you have in the fridge and cupboard.

Following are a series of checklists of pantry basics. Foods such as milk, cheese, eggs, and bread are obvious items to keep stocked. Less common staples such as sun-dried tomatoes, fruit chutney, dry sherry, anchovies, and artichoke hearts are important, too, because they can instantly impart flavor and dress up everyday dishes like tossed salads, omelets, and pasta.

Dry Goods

You will probably consume these foods at least once a week, so buy them in bulk to save on packaging costs:

- ✔ **Assorted coffees:** You can freeze ground or whole beans for long storage.

- ✔ **Cold and hot cereals:** Always tightly reseal cereal boxes after opening to keep them fresh.

- ✓ **Assorted breads and English muffins:** All breads can be frozen. Yeast breads freeze well for 6 to 8 months. Quick breads (baked with baking powder or soda) freeze without losing flavor for 2 to 4 months.

- ✓ **Dry beans and grains:** See Chapter 14 for more information about the various types.

- ✓ **Herbal and regular teas:** Store in a sealed canister in a cool, dry place.

- ✓ **Macaroni and pasta:** See Chapter 11 for a complete pasta chart.

- ✓ **White and brown rice, wild rice, and Arborio (an Italian rice used for making risotto):** See Chapter 3 for more information about the various types of rice.

Dry Herbs, Spices, and Seasonings

Herbs and spices are essential flavoring ingredients. Herbs are produced from the leaves and stems of a variety of plants; spices can come from a plant's roots, seeds, bark, buds, or berries. See Chapter 5 for a complete herb and spice chart. Here are the herbs, spices, and seasonings you should stock regularly:

- ✓ **Dry herbs:** Basil, bay leaves, chervil, dill, marjoram, oregano, rosemary, sage, tarragon, thyme, and parsley

- ✓ **Salt and pepper:** Table salt, black peppercorns, whole or ground white pepper, and red pepper flakes

- ✓ **Spices:** Allspice, chili powder, cinnamon, cloves, ground cumin, curry powder, ginger, dry mustard, nutmeg, and paprika

Purchase dried herbs and spices in small quantities. After a year or so of storage, their potency diminishes drastically. Keep all dried herbs and spices tightly sealed and away from direct heat (don't store them near the stove) and sunlight.

To get the most flavor from dried herbs, crush them briefly between your fingers before adding them to a dish. Whole spices, such as peppercorns and nutmeg, have much more aroma and flavor than those sold pre-ground, so try grinding or grating them yourself.

Bottled and Canned Goods

Obvious items include canned tuna, jellies and jams, peanut butter, and assorted canned soups. Always stock the following essentials:

- **Assorted oils and vinegars:** See Chapter 10 for a complete list.

- **Tomato paste:** Buy it in cans or the more convenient tube (which you can store in the refrigerator after opening). For flavoring stews and sauces.

- **Wines:** A dry white and a dry red wine, for adding to sauces, stews, and long-simmering casseroles and soups. Dry sherry, port, and Madeira are nice to have, too.

Following are other items that can help make your cooking more inspired:

- **Anchovies:** For salad dressings and simple sauces, anchovies can lend subtle depth of flavor. They also enhance store-bought Boboli and pizza. (See Chapter 15 for more information about anchovies.)

- **Artichoke hearts marinated in olive oil:** Great tossed into green salads or other marinated vegetable salads.

- **Beans:** Kidney, garbanzo, and baked beans for soups, salads, and quick side dishes. Refried beans for tacos, burritos, nachos, omelet fillings, and side dishes come in handy, too.

- **Canned broth:** For when you run out of your own. Purchase beef and chicken (or vegetable for vegetarians), preferably salt free.

- **Canned clams and clam juice:** For quick pasta sauce (see Chapter 11) or as a substitute for homemade fish stock.

- **Capers (pickled flower buds of the caper bush):** For making quick, tangy sauces for meats and poultry. See Chapter 7 for a recipe.

- **Cranberry sauce:** Serve with grilled meats and poultry or use as a basting sauce.

- **Hoisin sauce:** A favorite of Chinese cuisine that is made from soybeans, garlic, chile peppers, and spices. Terrific in marinades and with spareribs, roast duck, or poultry.

- **Olives:** Green, black, and stuffed for appetizers and slicing into salads and pasta dishes. (See the Mediterranean Pasta recipe, later in this chapter.)

- **Roasted bottled peppers:** For adding to marinated vegetables, tossed green salads, and creamy dips.

- **Tomatoes:** Italian plum tomatoes and crushed tomatoes for making pasta sauces when fresh tomatoes are pale and tasteless.

Condiments

Having quality, commercially prepared condiments and sauces — mustards, chutneys, salsas, hot sauces, barbecue sauce, and more — in the pantry or refrigerator is always wise. Make sure to stock the following:

- **Dijon-style mustard:** Good for adding to salad dressings, dips, and sauces and for garnishing hot or cold meats and sandwiches. To produce a flavored mustard, add herbs or spices, citrus juice or zest, or a little honey to the Dijon base.

- **Ketchup:** For hamburgers and as an ingredient in fish and barbecue sauces and baked beans.

- **Mayonnaise:** Because you can't always make your own. (You can find a recipe in Chapter 7.)

These items are handy to keep on hand, too.

- **A good bottle of mango or tomato chutney:** Chutney is a sweetened fruit condiment for broiled chicken, lamb, pork, or duck. Try using it as a basting sauce for roasting meats or poultry or for spreading on cold sandwiches of hard-cooked eggs, tuna, chicken, or turkey. Also good in yogurt-based dips and in omelet fillings.

- **Assorted relishes:** Relishes such as corn, tomato, cranberry, and onion are good for spreading on cold sandwiches and grilled and roasted meats.

- **Dill and sweet pickles:** For serving with sandwiches and also for chopping into potato, chicken, and egg salads. *Cornichons* are crisp, tiny pickles made from small gherkin cucumbers. Serve them with cheeses, roasted meats, and pâtés, or chop them into vinaigrettes or creamy dressings.

- **Horseradish:** For sandwiches, salad dressings, roast beef, ham sandwiches, raw oysters and clams, and certain cream and tomato-based sauces.

- **Jars of pesto or frozen, homemade pesto:** For pasta, grilled meats, fish, poultry, or vegetables.

- **Salsa:** With grilled meats and fish, omelets and other egg dishes, salads, and traditional Mexican foods.

- **Soy sauce (dark and light, Chinese and Japanese):** For marinades, salad dressings, stir-fries, sushi, and sauces. Chinese soy sauce is stronger and saltier than the Japanese variety. Light soy sauces are for seasoning shrimp, fish, and vegetables, such as stir-fried snow peas or broccoli. Dark soy sauce, flavored with caramel, is delicious with broiled meats.

- **Sun-dried tomatoes in olive oil:** Enhance sauces (especially for pasta), tossed salads, and dressings.

- **Tabasco sauce:** For adding flavor and heat to savory dishes. Use in omelets, on steaks and French fries, and in marinades, soups, stews, and casseroles.

✔ **Worcestershire sauce:** For hamburgers, steak, marinades, sauces, baked clams, and Bloody Marys.

Condiments such as relishes, jellies, pickles, mayonnaise, mustard, and jars of salsa keep for months in the refrigerator after you open them. Ketchup, steak sauce, peanut butter, oil, vinegar, honey, and syrup do not require refrigeration after you open them and can be stored on a shelf or in a cool cabinet for months, away from heat and sunlight.

Baking Items

No one expects you to bake a cake when you get home from work at 7:30 p.m. But sometimes you need a quick dessert or sweet and have the zeal to do it yourself. Having the ingredients on hand makes it so much easier. Always keep these items in stock:

✔ **All-purpose flour (5-pound/2.5 kg bag):** For dredging meats, fish, and poultry, and for pancakes, biscuits, and waffles, as well as baking. Store flour in a tightly covered canister, where it stays fresh for months.

✔ **Baking powder:** A leavening agent used in some cake, cookie, and quick bread recipes to lighten texture and increase volume. Check the sell-by date to ensure that the powder is fresh before buying. (Baking powder loses its effectiveness sitting on the shelf.) Buy a small container and keep it tightly sealed. To test whether powder is still potent, mix 1 teaspoon (10 mL) baking powder with $1/3$ cup (75 mL) warm water. The solution fizzes if the powder is good.

✔ **Baking soda:** Used as a leavening agent in baked goods and batters that contain an acidic ingredient such as molasses, vinegar, or buttermilk. Also good for putting out grease fires and flare-ups in the oven or on the grill. Keep an open box in the refrigerator to absorb odors. (Change the box every 6 months, or it may become one of the foul odors.)

✔ **Granulated sugar (5-pound/2.5 kg bag):** An all-purpose sweetener. Store in a canister with a tight-fitting lid.

Having the following items increases your range of possibilities:

✔ **Chocolate:** Unsweetened and bittersweet squares, semisweet chips, and cocoa powder for chocolate sauces, chocolate chip cookies, and hot chocolate. (Recipes for chocolate sauces are in Chapter 7.)

When the temperature climbs above 78° F (26° C), chocolate begins to melt, causing the cocoa butter to separate and rise to the surface. If the cocoa butter separates, the chocolate produces a whitish exterior called *bloom*. Though it looks a little chalky, bloomed chocolate is perfectly safe to eat. To prevent bloom on chocolate, store it in a cool, dry place (not the refrigerator), tightly wrapped.

✔ **Confectioner's sugar (l-pound/500-g box):** For sprinkling over baked goods and cookies or for quick frostings.

✔ **Cornmeal:** Yellow or white for corn muffins and quick bread toppings for stews and baked casseroles. Keep in a canister or tightly sealed bag.

✔ **Cream of tartar:** For stabilizing egg whites.

✔ **Dark and light brown sugars:** For baking and making barbecue sauces and glazes for ham and pork. Dark brown is more intense in flavor than light. To keep brown sugar soft after you open it, store the whole box in a tightly sealed plastic bag. If it hardens, place half an apple in the bag for several hours or overnight and then remove the apple.

✔ **Gelatin:** Unflavored and powdered for molded salads and cold dessert mousses.

✔ **Honey:** For sweet glazes, dressings, and syrups. To thin crystallized honey, set the bottle in a pan of hot tap water.

✔ **Maple syrup:** For pancakes and waffles.

✔ **Muffin mixes in assorted flavors:** For when you don't have time to make them from scratch.

✔ **Vanilla and almond extract:** For flavoring whipped cream, desserts, and baked goods. (Other handy extracts include orange, lemon, and hazelnut.) Don't buy imitation vanilla extract. It's a poor substitute for the real thing.

✔ **Vanilla bean:** For dessert sauces and vanilla sugar. (See the Vanilla Sauce recipe in Chapter 7.)

Refrigerated and Frozen Staples

Following are a few essential items to stock in the refrigerator or freezer:

✔ **Eggs:** Never be without them for omelets, breakfast foods, and quick dinners. (See Chapter 8 for handy egg recipes and other egg tips.) Store in the shipping carton to keep them from picking up odors and flavors from other refrigerated foods. Raw eggs keep in refrigerator for at least 4 weeks beyond their pack date.

✔ **Milk:** We make our recipes with whole milk, which has about 3.5 percent butterfat. If you prefer, use 1 percent or 2 percent lowfat milk or skim (nonfat) milk, with the understanding that the recipe may not have as creamy a consistency. Whole milk keeps for about a week after the store expiration date. Skim milk has a shorter shelf life. Some markets sell sterilized milk in vacuum packages that last for months unrefrigerated. After you break the seal, however, vacuum-packed milk is just like any other milk.

✔ **Pastas:** Stock various stuffed pastas like ravioli in the freezer for quick dinners. You can wrap fresh pasta in freezer bags and store it for 6 to 8 months. Do not defrost before cooking. Simply drop frozen pasta into boiling water and cook until al dente.

✔ **Sweet (unsalted) butter:** Use sweet butter in all recipes so that you can control the amount of salt. Butter has a refrigerator shelf life of about 2 to 3 weeks and can be frozen for 8 to 12 months.

These items are nice to have, too:

✔ **Bagels and other specialty breads:** For breakfasts and sandwiches. All bread products can be frozen in freezer bags. Thaw on the counter, in the microwave, or in the oven at 300° F (150° C).

✔ **Cottage cheese, ricotta, and cream cheese:** For adding to dressings and dips, snacking, spreading on bagels or toast, and for cheesecakes. Store in the original, covered container or foil wrapping and consume within 1 to 2 weeks.

✔ **Hard and semihard cheeses:** Mozzarella, Parmesan, cheddar, and bleu for salads, casseroles, omelets, white sauces, and sandwiches, to grate into pasta, and just to eat. (See the sidebar "Cheese: Milk gone to heaven" for more cheese choices.)

Wrap all cheese in foil or plastic wrap after opening. Trim off any mold that grows on the outside edges of hard cheeses. Depending on its variety, cheese keeps in the refrigerator for several weeks to months.

Don't buy pre-grated Parmesan or romano cheese. It quickly loses its potency and absorbs the odors of other refrigerated foods. Instead, keep a piece of cheese for grating in the fridge to use as needed.

✔ **Heavy cream, light cream, or half and half:** For making quick pan sauces for fish, poultry, and pasta. Use within a week of purchase or freeze for longer storage.

✔ **Ice cream or frozen yogurt:** Instant dessert; for gorging on in bed at midnight. After you open it, you should eat ice cream within 2 weeks. You can freeze unopened containers for up to 2 months.

✔ **Pie crusts:** Keep frozen shells in the freezer for up to 6 to 8 months to fill with fresh fruits and pudding fillings when you need a dessert in a hurry, or to make a quick quiche. (See Chapter 16 for a recipe for Classic Quiche Lorraine.)

✔ **Sour cream:** You can use standard (18 percent fat), lowfat, and nonfat interchangeably in recipes. As with all dairy products, buy the container with the latest store expiration date. Sour cream should keep for about 2 weeks.

✔ **Yogurt:** Good for quick dips and lowfat sauces, especially if mixed with dry mustard and various herbs. Also makes pancake batters lighter. Use within a week of purchase.

Cheese: Milk gone to heaven

Compared to most European countries, America is not a major cheese consumer. That is, cheese is not routinely part of a meal, either in addition to or in place of dessert. But if you get to know your cheeses, eating it can be a tantalizing change of pace.

Cheese is a perfect after-dinner course, especially if you don't have time to fuss with dessert. Serve it with fruit or with neutral crackers that don't interfere with the flavor. Let cheese reach room temperature before serving.

Trying to define which cheeses are best for dessert is sort of like saying which cars are best for driving to the supermarket — most of them can do the job; it's just that some do it with more style. Foremost, think of what is harmonious with the meal. For example, you don't want to serve a very potent bleu cheese after a subtle dinner of grilled chicken breasts and summer vegetables.

Wine also is a consideration. For example, sharp cheddars and similar cheeses go best with assertive red wines (Bordeaux, California Cabernet Sauvignons, Zinfandels, ports, and even bitter beer). You want a wine that can stand up to the potent cheese. Light cheeses like Gouda, Havarti, California Jack, and Muenster call for equally delicate wines so that you have a balanced taste: Beaujolais, lighter Côtes-du-Rhône, and Barbarescos. For more information about wines, see *Wine For Dummies*.

When buying cheese, remember that there's a big difference between aged cheese and old cheese. Old cheese looks fatigued, has discoloration, maybe a cracked rind, and signs of overdryness. Old cheese makes your car smell like the Notre Dame locker room after the Michigan game. If cheddars look darker around the periphery than at the center, they probably are dried out. Many stores cover cheese tightly in plastic wrap, which is not the best way to let it age naturally. Inspect these cheeses extra carefully. Your best bet is to go to a store that sells a lot of cheese because its selection is probably better and fresher.

- **Boursin:** French. Rich, savory, often coated with herbs. A lovely dessert cheese with a medium-bodied red wine.

- **Brie:** Almost a cliché because it was the first "gourmet" cheese for many American palates, spawning wine-and-cheese cocktail parties across the land. This soft, creamy cheese is generally mild tasting and goes well with most light red wines.

- **Camembert:** French, from Normandy. A creamy cheese not unlike Brie. When ripe, oozes luxuriously.

- **Cheddar:** One of the world's most popular cheeses. Made all over the world, the flavor of this semifirm cheese ranges from rich and nutty to extremely sharp.

- **Fontina Val d'Aosta:** Italian cow's milk cheese, semifirm, subtle, nutty, and rich.

- **Goat cheese (*chèvres* in France):** Goat cheese ranges from mild and tart when young to sharp and crumbly when aged. Choose wines accordingly.

- **Gorgonzola:** From the Lombardy region of Italy. This blue-veined cheese is extremely popular in the U.S. Gorgonzola is rich and creamy yet pleasantly pungent. Creamier than Roquefort.

- **Gruyère:** Sort of a more gutsy version of Swiss cheese, from Switzerland. Faint nuttiness. Excellent in cooking.

- **Mascarpone:** An Italian cow's milk cheese that has the consistency of clotted cream. Often used in cooking but can be seasoned with fresh herbs and used as a delicious dip.

✔ **Monterey Jack:** A California cow's milk cheese in the cheddar family that is semi-soft, smooth, and very mild when young, and sharper when aged.

✔ **Mozzarella:** Familiar to all from pizza and lasagna fame. Mozzarella is often breaded and fried for an appetizer, called *Mozzarella in Carozza.*

✔ **Pecorino romano (or romano):** A sheep's milk Italian cheese (all sheep's milk cheese in Italy is called pecorino). Pecorino romano is

soft and mild when young with a touch of tartness. Quite tart when older, mostly grated over pasta.

✔ **Roquefort:** Made from ewe's milk and aged in the famous caves of Roquefort, France. Roquefort is among the most intense of all blue-veined cheeses. Has a creamy texture at its best.

✔ **Taleggio:** A semisoft cow's milk cheese from Lombardy. Very mild with touch of sharpness that increases with age.

Kiwi Anyone? Storing Fruits and Vegetables

Have on hand potatoes, onions, garlic, carrots, salad greens, parsley, and a few other fresh herbs like basil and dill. You also may want to stock cucumbers, scallions, assorted citrus, mushrooms, red and green peppers, and celery for slicing and eating raw or for flavoring sauces, soups, salads, and stews. Keep an assortment of fresh fruits — apples, oranges, grapes, bananas, or whatever is in season — for snacking, slicing into cereals, or making quick dessert sauces.

It's best to keep unripe melons and tree fruits like pears, peaches, and nectarines at room temperature so that they can ripen and grow sweeter. Once fully ripe, they can be stored in the refrigerator for several more days. Fruits like cherries and berries are quite perishable and should always be refrigerated. For best flavor, consume them the same day you purchase them.

✔ Bananas can go in the refrigerator to slow down their ripening. Their peel continues to darken, but not their flesh.

✔ Tomatoes have more flavor at room temperature. Keep in a cool, dark place or in a paper bag to ripen fully. Refrigerate them after they ripen to keep them from spoiling. Then return to room temperature before eating. (See Chapter 11 for more information about tomatoes.)

✔ Citrus fruits, such as lemons, grapefruits, kiwis, and oranges, do not ripen further after they are picked and are relatively long-storage fruits. They keep for up to 3 weeks or more if refrigerated.

✔ Avocados, papayas, and mangoes should be kept at room temperature until fully ripened and then refrigerated to keep for several more days.

✓ Most vegetables are quite perishable and require refrigeration, with the exception of onions, white potatoes, garlic, shallots, and hard-shelled squash, which keep at room temperature for several weeks to a month. Keep garlic and shallots in a small bowl within reach of your food preparation area. Store onions, potatoes, and winter squash in a cool, dry, dark drawer or bin.

Here are some storage tips for specific fresh fruits and vegetables:

✓ **Apples:** Refrigerate or store in a cool, dark place. Keep for several weeks.

✓ **Artichokes and asparagus:** Refrigerate and use within 2 to 3 days of purchase.

✓ **Beans:** Refrigerate and use within 3 to 4 days of purchase.

✓ **Broccoli and cauliflower:** Refrigerate and consume within a week.

✓ **Cabbage:** Keeps for 1 to 2 weeks in the refrigerator.

✓ **Carrots:** Keep in the refrigerator for several weeks.

✓ **Celery:** Keeps for 1 to 2 weeks in the refrigerator.

✓ **Corn:** Refrigerate and use the same day of purchase. After corn is picked, its sugar immediately converts to starch, diminishing its sweetness.

✓ **Cucumbers and eggplant:** Keep for 1 week in the cold crisper drawer of the refrigerator.

✓ **Grapes:** Keep in the refrigerator for up to a week.

✓ **Leaf greens (beet tops, collards, kale, mustard greens, and so on):** Very perishable. Refrigerate and consume within 1 to 2 days.

✓ **Mushrooms:** Store in a paper bag or plastic container in the refrigerator. Use within a week.

✓ **Pineapple:** Does not ripen after it's picked. Cut up, place in a plastic bag or sealed container, and refrigerate until ready to serve.

✓ **Salad greens:** Store completely dry in plastic bags in the refrigerator crisper drawer. Keep for 3 to 4 days. (See Chapter 10 for more information.)

✓ **Sweet bell peppers:** Store in the refrigerator for up to 2 weeks.

✓ **Spinach:** Store completely dry in the refrigerator for 2 to 3 days.

✓ **Summer squash (zucchini and yellow squash):** Store in the refrigerator for up to a week.

Buying and Storing Meat, Poultry, and Fish

Meat, poultry, and fish are highly perishable foods that need to be stored in the coldest part of your refrigerator. Keep them tightly wrapped, preferably in their own drawer, to prevent their juices from dripping onto other foods.

Always check expiration dates and choose items that are dated furthest from the day of purchase. Avoid items that are older than your car's last oil change, in other words. And never allow meat, poultry, or fish to thaw at room temperature, where bacteria can have a field day.

Beef

Beef is rated according to the animal's age, the amount of fat, or *marbling,* in the cut (the more marbling, the more tender), and its color and texture. *Prime* meat is the highest grade and the most expensive. In general, the most tender and flavorful meat falls under this category. But aging has a lot to do with it. Years ago, all beef aged "on the hoof," or the whole carcass, before it was shipped. Today, most meat is cut up and shipped in eerie-looking vacuum-sealed Cry-O-Vac containers. The aging takes place in the box. Try to buy from independent butchers in your area who still age their own beef. You pay a little more, but it's worth the price. Aged meat is more tender and has more flavor.

Choice is the second tier of meat grading, leaner than prime. *Select* meats are best for stewing and braising.

The more tender cuts of meat include steaks such as porterhouse, sirloin, shell, New York strip, delmonico, and filet mignon and roasts like rib, rib eye, and tenderloin. Tender meats are usually cooked by the dry heat methods of roasting, broiling, grilling, and sautéing. (See Chapter 6 for roasting, broiling, and grilling recipes and Chapter 4 for sautéing recipes.)

Less tender cuts that have more muscle tissue and less fat are usually cooked by moist heat methods like braising and stewing. (See Chapter 5 for braising and stewing recipes.) Tougher cuts include brisket, chuck, shoulder, rump, and bottom round. Figure 13-1 illustrates where the various cuts come from.

Look beyond ratings to judge the meat you buy. Meat should look bright red, never dull or gray. Excess juice in the package may indicate that the meat was previously frozen and thawed — do not purchase it. Boneless, well-trimmed cuts are slightly more expensive per pound but have more edible meat than untrimmed cuts.

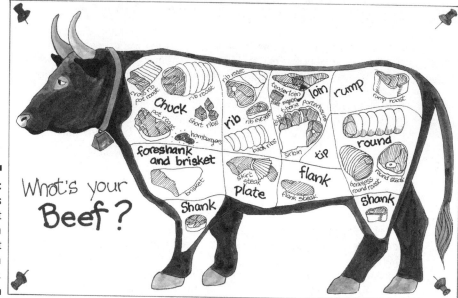

Figure 13-1: Various cuts of meat come from different parts of a steer.

Store meat in the meat compartment or the coldest part of the refrigerator. Keep raw meat away from ready-to-eat foods. To freeze, rewrap in aluminum foil, heavy-duty plastic wrap, or freezer bags, pressing out as much air as possible and dating all packages. Freeze ground meat for a maximum of 3 months; freeze other cuts for up to 6 months. Defrost in the refrigerator or microwave.

Chicken

The tenderness and flavor of fresh poultry vary greatly from one commercial producer to the next, so you should buy and taste a few different brands to determine which you like. Grade A poultry is the most economical because it has the most meat in proportion to bone. Skin color is not an indication of quality or fat content. A chicken's skin ranges from white to deep yellow, depending on its diet.

Most supermarkets carry five kinds of chicken:

- **Broiler/fryer:** A 7- to 9-week-old bird weighing between 2 and 4 pounds (1 to 2 kg). Flavorful meat that is best for broiling, frying, sautéing, or roasting. A whole broiler/fryer is always less expensive than a precut one.

- **Roaster or pullet:** From 3 to 7 months old and between 3 and 7 pounds (1.5 and 3.5 kg). Very meaty, with high fat content under the skin, which makes for excellent roasting.

How free is free range?

Compared to cooped-up, hormone-blasted, sun-shine-deprived regular chickens, free-range chickens have a pretty cozy life. But *free range* is a bit of exaggeration in most cases. These privileged chickens do not pack lunches and take daily outings across the vast countryside, stopping for a couple of pecks in fields of clover on the way home. Most free-range chickens are enclosed in fenced areas with very limited room to maneuver. They do get some sunshine, at least, and a little exercise. And in most cases, they are chemical free.

- **Capon:** A 6- to 9-pound (3- to 4.5-kg) castrated male chicken. Excellent as a roasting chicken because of its abundance of fat. Just to be sure, pour off or scoop out excess melted fat as the chicken roasts — especially if you do not have an exhaust fan — or your kitchen will resemble the *Towering Inferno.*

- **Stewing chicken:** From 3 to 7 pounds (1.5 to 3.5 kg) and at least 1 year old. Needs slow, moist cooking to tenderize. Makes the best soups and stews.

- **Rock Cornish game hen:** A smaller breed of chicken weighing 1 to 2 pounds (500 g to 1 kg). Meaty, moist, and flavorful for roasting.

Remove the package of giblets (the neck, heart, gizzard, and liver) in the cavity of a whole bird and then rinse under running cold water before cooking it. Also trim away excess fat. After preparing poultry, wash your hands and work surfaces (counters and cutting boards) with soap and water to avoid bacteria.

You should consume whole or cut-up poultry within 1 to 2 days of purchase. A whole, raw chicken may be wrapped and frozen for up to 12 months; parts can be frozen for up to 9 months. Defrost in the refrigerator, never at room temperature. Be sure to place the thawing package in a pan or on a plate to catch any dripping juices. A 4-pound chicken takes 24 hours to thaw in the refrigerator; cut-up parts between 3 and 6 hours. If you use your microwave to defrost poultry, be sure to cook the poultry immediately after thawing it.

Fish

Fish can be placed into two broad categories: lean and oily. Lean fish include light-fleshed, mild-tasting sole, flounder, snapper, cod, halibut, and haddock. Oily fish have more intense flavor and darker flesh and include bluefish, mackerel, salmon, swordfish, and tuna. In general, you should purchase fillets of oily fish with the skin intact. That way, the fish holds together better during cooking. Purchase lean fish skinless.

Here are some of the more reasonably priced types of fish that you can try in lieu of expensive gray sole, swordfish, and the like. Always ask you fish dealer what is the most fresh and local fish that day. Prices may dip during peak season.

- **Bluefish:** Rich, mild flavor, especially when fresh and under 2 pounds (1 kg). Bake or broil.

- **Catfish:** Dense, strong-flavored fish. Usually cooked in a strong sauce or deep-fried.

- **Cod:** Mild-flavored, white, firm flesh. Can be broiled, baked, fried, or braised.

- **Haddock:** Meaty, white flesh, mild flavor. Good pan-fried or braised.

- **Mako shark:** Assertive, swordfish-like flavor and oily, dark flesh. Best broiled or grilled.

- **Porgy:** Firm, lowfat, white-fleshed fish with delicate flavor. Excellent grilled or broiled. (See Chapter 15 for a recipe for Broiled Porgies with Rosemary Oil.)

- **Whiting (Silver Hake):** Fine, semifirm white flesh. Subtle and delicious when broiled or pan-fried.

Freshness is the single most important factor in purchasing fish. Learn to recognize it. In a whole fish, the eyes should be bright and clear, not cloudy. The gills of fresh fish are deep red, not pink or brownish. The skin should be clear and bright with no trace of slime. Fish get slimy if they are not properly iced.

How do you tell whether the fish is fresh? "Put your nose close to the fish to find out," says Eric Ripert, executive chef of Le Bernardin in New York. "Fresh fish doesn't smell like fish. It might smell like the ocean, but it will never smell fishy."

If possible, have your fishmonger cut fresh fillets from whole fish while you wait. Purchase precut fillets only if they are displayed on a bed of ice, not sealed under plastic, which can trap bacteria and foul odors. Fillets should look moist and lay flat, with no curling at the edges. Fresh fish and seafood should be consumed as soon as possible and ideally on the day of purchase. Freshly caught and cleaned fish may be frozen for 2 to 3 months if wrapped well in 2 layers of freezer paper. Never refreeze fish after thawing it.

Shellfish should be firmly closed and odorless when purchased. If clams or mussels do not close immediately when heated, toss them. Eat fresh clams, oysters, and mussels as soon as possible after purchase. Store for no more than 24 hours in the refrigerator in a plastic bag poked with small holes, allowing air to circulate. Purchase shrimp only in the shell. Precooked shrimp is tough and lacks flavor. Eat shrimp the same day you purchase it. Most of all, never overcook shellfish because it gets rubbery.

Cooking in a Well-Stocked Kitchen

The payoff for keeping a well-stocked kitchen — with only enough perishables that you can eat in a week — is that you can whip up satisfying meals on short notice. Here are just a few dishes to get you started.

Onion Soup

Tools: *Chef's knife, heavy-bottom saucepan or pot, wooden spoon, grater*

Preparation time: *About 15 minutes*

Cooking time: *About 1 hour*

3 tablespoons (45 mL) butter

1 pound (500 g) onions, peeled and thinly sliced, about 3 medium onions

2 tablespoons (30 mL) flour

2 cups (500 mL) canned or fresh beef (or chicken or vegetable) broth

2 cups (500 mL) water

Salt and freshly ground pepper to taste

4 slices French bread, toasted

$^1/_2$ cup (125 mL) grated Gruyère or Parmesan cheese

1 Melt the butter in a heavy-bottom saucepan or pot over medium heat. Add the onions and cook for about 5 minutes or until the onions wilt, stirring often. Reduce the heat to low and cook for about 20 to 25 minutes or until the onions are well browned, stirring often.

2 Sprinkle the flour over the onions and cook for about 2 minutes, stirring constantly and scraping the bottom of the pan with a wooden spoon.

3 Gradually stir in the broth and water. Cover the pan and bring to a boil over high heat. Reduce the heat and simmer for 30 minutes, stirring occasionally. Taste and adjust seasoning with salt and pepper, if desired.

4 Ladle the soup into a *tureen* (a large soup serving bowl) or 4 individual soup bowls. Float the toasted bread slices in the hot soup and sprinkle each bowl evenly with the cheese.

Yield: *4 servings.*

This dish, tomatoes stuffed with an herbed egg mixture, makes a perfect Sunday brunch or supper.

Tomatoes Stuffed with Eggs and Sweet Peppers

Tools: *Baking dish, paring knife, chef's knife, colander, blender or food processor, saucepan, large mixing bowl*

Preparation time: *About 25 minutes*

Baking time: *About 1 hour*

Butter for greasing baking dish

4 firm, medium tomatoes

Salt to taste

2 tablespoons (30 mL) olive oil

2 tablespoons (30 mL) peeled and diced shallots or onions

1 teaspoon (5 mL) peeled and chopped garlic, about 1 large clove

1/4 cup (50 mL) seeded, cored, and diced sweet red pepper

3/4 teaspoon (3 mL) chopped fresh tarragon, or 1/4 teaspoon (1 mL) dried

3/4 teaspoon (3 mL) chopped fresh thyme, or 1/4 teaspoon (1 mL) dried

1 teaspoon (5 mL) chopped fresh basil, or 1/4 teaspoon (1 mL) dried

4 large eggs

1/3 cup (75 mL) heavy cream or half and half

1 1/2 teaspoons (7 mL) tomato paste

1/4 cup (50 mL) fresh bread crumbs

Freshly ground pepper to taste

1 Preheat oven to 350° F (180° C). Butter a shallow baking dish.

2 Core each tomato and scoop out the pulp with a spoon, reserving it. (Be careful not to puncture the tomato shells.) Sprinkle salt inside the shells and place them upside down in a colander to drain.

3 Strain the juice from the tomato pulp and remove as many seeds as possible. Chop the pulp coarsely, reserving 2/3 cup (150 mL).

4 In a medium saucepan, heat 1 tablespoon (15 mL) of the olive oil over medium heat. Add the tomato pulp, cooking and stirring for about 1 minute. Using a rubber spatula, scrape the mixture into the container of a blender or food processor.

5 In the same saucepan, heat the remaining tablespoon (15 mL) of olive oil. Add the shallots or onions, garlic, and peppers and cook until they are soft but not brown, about 2 minutes. Stir in the tarragon, thyme, and basil and add the mixture to the food processor or blender with the tomato pulp. Blend smooth.

(continued)

6 Beat the eggs, heavy cream, or half and half and the tomato paste in a large mixing bowl. Stir in the bread crumbs and the pureed tomato mixture. Season with salt and pepper to taste.

7 Place the tomato shells in the greased baking dish. Pour the tomato-egg mixture into them evenly. Bake for about 1 hour or until the egg mixture is firm. If desired, serve with toasted corn muffins and a mixed green salad. (See Chapter 10 for salad recipes.)

Yield: 4 servings.

If you follow our pantry-stocking instructions, you can turn out the following two pasta recipes without leaving the house.

Mediterranean Spaghetti

Tools: Chef's knife, large pot, large saucepan or sauté pan, colander

Preparation time: About 20 minutes

Cooking time: About 15 minutes

1 pound (500 g) spaghetti

Salt to taste

¹/₄ cup (50 mL) olive oil

¹/₂ cup (125 mL) peeled and diced onion, about 1 small onion

4 anchovy fillets packed in olive oil, drained and chopped (optional)

1 tablespoon (15 mL) peeled and chopped garlic, about 3 large cloves

¹/₄ teaspoon (1 mL) red pepper flakes, or to taste

28-ounce can (about 796 mL) Italian plum tomatoes, drained and diced

12 pitted black olives

2 tablespoons (30 mL) capers, rinsed and drained

¹/₄ teaspoon (1 mL) dried thyme

¹/₂ cup (125 mL) chopped fresh parsley

1 Bring 5 quarts (5 L) lightly salted water to boil in a large pot over high heat. Add the spaghetti and cook according to package directions, or just until al dente.

2 As the pasta cooks, heat the oil in a large saucepan or sauté pan over medium heat. Add the onion, anchovies (if desired), garlic, and red pepper flakes. Cook for 1 to 2 minutes or until the garlic is golden, stirring often. Do not let the garlic brown.

(continued)

3 Add the tomatoes, olives, capers, and thyme to the pan. Stir to blend well. Bring to a boil; then reduce the heat and simmer, partially covered, for about 5 minutes. Stir in the parsley and set aside.

4 Just before the pasta is done, carefully scoop out and reserve ¹/₂ cup (125 mL) of the cooking liquid. Then drain the pasta, returning it to the same pot. Add the sauce and toss well, adding a little of the reserved cooking liquid to moisten the mixture, if necessary.

Yield: *4 to 6 servings.*

TOQUE TIP

Francesco Antonucci, cookbook author and exuberant chef of Remi Restaurant in New York City, says that his mother used to make the following recipe for dinner whenever she was running late and had no time to visit the market. "I also make this dish after a long day in the restaurant because it is so practical and delicious — not to mention that it reminds me of my youth in Venice," says Antonucci. From the ingredients you have on hand, you can make this dish, too.

Francesco Antonucci's Spaghetti with Tuna

Tools: *Large pot, grater, small bowl, colander*

Preparation time: *About 5 minutes*

Cooking time: *About 15 minutes*

Salt and freshly ground pepper to taste

8 ounces (500 g) spaghetti

6¹/₂-ounce (184-g) can tuna packed in olive oil

2 tablespoons (30 mL) freshly grated Parmesan cheese

2 tablespoons (30 mL) extra-virgin olive oil

2 teaspoons (10 mL) butter

1 Bring 4 quarts (4 L) lightly salted water to boil in a large pot over high heat. Add the spaghetti and cook according to package directions, just until al dente.

2. As the pasta cooks, drain the can of tuna. Mash the tuna in a small bowl with a fork to break it into small pieces.

3 Before draining the pasta, scoop out and reserve about ¹/₄ cup (50 mL) cooking liquid. When it's ready, drain the pasta and return it to the large pot.

(continued)

4 Add the tuna, Parmesan, olive oil, butter, and just enough of the reserved cooking liquid to moisten the pasta. Toss well, check for seasonings, and serve immediately.

Yield: 3 to 4 servings.

 A boiling pot of water is one of the most dangerous elements in any kitchen. Use pots with short handles that cannot be easily tipped and set them to boil on back burners, away from small and curious hands.

Cuban and much of South American cuisine is built around highly seasoned rice dishes — from *arroz y pollo* (chicken and rice) and black bean and rice dishes of Brazil to the fish and rice casseroles of the Mexican coast. If you have long-grain rice in the pantry (converted is the easiest to cook, as Chapter 3 explains), you can turn out dozens of spontaneous, economical dishes like the following one.

Red Beans and Rice

Tools: *Chef's knife, large sauté pan with lid*

Preparation time: *About 20 minutes*

Cooking time: *About 20 minutes*

1 tablespoon (15 mL) olive oil

4 slices bacon, coarsely chopped

³/₄ cup (175 mL) peeled and diced onion, about 1 medium onion

2 teaspoons (10 mL) peeled and chopped garlic, about 2 large cloves

1¹/₂ cups (375 mL) uncooked converted white rice

¹/₂ teaspoon (2 mL) turmeric

¹/₂ teaspoon (2 mL) ground coriander

8-ounce can (250 mL) diced tomatoes

2¹/₂ cups (625 mL) fresh or canned chicken broth

14-ounce can (398 mL) red kidney beans, drained

1 bay leaf

¹/₄ teaspoon (1mL) red pepper flakes

2 tablespoons (30 mL) dry sherry (optional)

2 tablespoons (30 mL) chopped fresh parsley (optional)

(continued)

1 Heat the olive oil in a sauté pan over medium heat. Add the bacon and onion and cook for 2 to 3 minutes or until the bacon is crisp, stirring often. Add the garlic and cook for 1 minute, stirring. Do not let the garlic brown.

2 Add the rice, turmeric, and ground coriander, stirring to coat the rice grains with the oil. Add the tomatoes with their juice, chicken broth, beans, bay leaf, and red pepper flakes. Stir well.

3 Bring to a boil. Cover and simmer over low heat for about 17 minutes or until most of the liquid is absorbed. (If adding sherry, stir it into the rice mixture about 2 minutes before the rice is tender.) Before serving, remove the bay leaf and sprinkle with the chopped parsley.

Yield: *4 servings.*

Other ways to season rice include the following:

✔ **Pilaf:** Melt butter in a pan, add chopped onion and garlic, and cook, stirring. Add the rice and stir to coat grains in the oil; then add the broth, parsley, thyme, salt and pepper, and a bay leaf. Bring to a boil, cover, and simmer for about 17 minutes or until the rice is tender.

Note: For most of the following variations, the technique is the same as pilaf; you simply change the seasoning as indicated.

✔ **Turmeric rice:** Add chopped onion, minced garlic, turmeric, rice, chicken stock, thyme, and a bay leaf.

✔ **Sweet rice:** Add chopped onion, minced garlic, raisins, rice, broth, and pine nuts or almonds just before serving.

✔ **Creole rice:** Cook the rice and set aside. Place butter and chopped onion in a sauté pan and cook until the onion wilts. Add diced tomatoes and salt and pepper, cooking and stirring for 1 to 2 minutes. Add the cooked rice to the tomato mixture with chopped fresh basil, 1 tablespoon (15 mL) fresh lemon juice, and ¹/₂ teaspoon (2 mL) grated lemon peel.

✔ **Curried rice:** Cook chopped onions in butter in a skillet. Add the rice and chicken or vegetable broth, 2 teaspoons (10 mL) curry powder (or to taste), salt and pepper, and ¹/₂ cup (125 mL) raisins, if desired. Cover and cook until done.

Potatoes are one of four or five vegetables that no kitchen should be without. You can almost make a meal of this simple potato side dish — it's that rich and satisfying. If you like the mellow, nutty taste of baked garlic, add a few more crushed cloves.

Potatoes Layered in Cream and Cheese

Tools: *Chef's knife, shallow baking dish, grater, mixing bowl*

Preparation time: *About 20 minutes*

Baking time: *About 1 hour and 15 minutes*

Butter for greasing baking dish	*$1/8$ teaspoon (0.5 mL) nutmeg (optional)*
2 large cloves garlic, peeled	*Salt and freshly ground pepper to taste*
$1^1/4$ cups (300 mL) light cream or half and half	*4 medium baking potatoes, about $1^1/2$ pounds (750 g)*
$1/8$ teaspoon (0.5 mL) cayenne pepper, or to taste	*1 cup (250 mL) grated, tightly packed Swiss or Gruyère cheese*

1 Preheat oven to 350° F (180° C).

2 Butter the sides and bottom of a $2^1/2$-quart (2.5-L) shallow baking dish.

3 Place a garlic clove on a wooden cutting board or other firm surface and use the broad side of a chef's knife to crush or press the clove flat. Repeat with the second clove.

4 Combine the garlic cloves, cream, cayenne, nutmeg, and salt and pepper in a mixing bowl or measuring cup. Set aside.

5 Peel and slice the potatoes thinly. They should be about $1/4$ inch (6 mm) thick or slightly less.

6 Place a layer of potato slices on the bottom of the baking dish so that their edges overlap slightly. Pour over about half the cream mixture and then sprinkle about half the cheese on top. Repeat with another layer of potatoes, cream mixture, and cheese.

7 Bake for l hour and 15 minutes or until the potatoes are tender and the top is golden brown.

Yield: 4 servings.

You can serve this rich and creamy potato side dish with a simple piece of grilled chicken (see Chapter 6) and a steamed green vegetable like broccoli or brussels sprouts (see Chapter 3) or with scrambled eggs (see Chapter 8).

Here are a few more suggestions for dishes you can make from your pantry:

- Omelet with Herbs, Frittata with Sweet Peppers and Potatoes, or Gruyère Soufflé (see Chapter 8)
- Spaghetti with Quick Fresh Tomato Sauce (substitute canned tomatoes for fresh — see Chapter 11)
- Penne with Cheese (see Chapter 11)
- Spaghetti with Clam Sauce (see Chapter 11)
- American Macaroni and Cheese (see Chapter 12)
- Bacon and Cheese Strata (see Chapter 12)

Inspiration from eGG

Maybe your sole purpose in buying this book is to master the two-egg omelet. Maybe you just want to be able to talk the talk and throw around words like *al dente* and *remoulade*. But the best thing about nailing the basics of cooking is that a whole new world of flavors and creativity opens up to you, and you're no longer limited by what Chef Boyardee decides to put in a can.

The best way to stimulate both your imagination and your skill level is to investigate what other people are trying. Read new recipes; flip through magazines. (Never mind that those Thanksgiving-issue turkeys are gorgeously glazed with shoe polish!) A foray onto the Information Superhighway yields a wealth of suggestions. Recipes abound, as do interviews with famous chefs, tips on techniques, and, of course, opportunities to buy: cookbooks, cookware, and specialty foods.

A great site where you can find all these things in one place is the electronic Gourmet Guide, an Internet magazine that has constantly changing articles and information, plus forums where readers can discuss interests, ask questions, and offer advice. eGG also explores wine and beer with links to several excellent sources for food and wine combining information. They've got interviews with winemakers and professional chefs, ideas for entertaining, polls of readers on subjects like the "worst fast-food burger" and the "best airplane food," illustrated how-tos, and even a Recipe of the Day.

To access eGG, type in keyword **eGG** on America Online, or use eGG's World Wide Web address: http://www.2way.com/food/egg.

Chapter 14

Champagne Meals on a Beer Budget

∙ ∙

In This Chapter

▶ Tell them it's filet mignon: Delicious meals from tough cuts

▶ Beans, greens, and cheap proteins

▶ Thrifty cooking made easy

∙ ∙

*T*o understand how much money the average shopper wastes every week, just stand around any supermarket checkout counter. Instead of flipping through the intellectual journals on sale ("Liz to Marry an Alien; Honeymoon on Pluto"), take an inventory of customers' shopping carts. Even discounting the usual fatty snack food, you'll find that the average cart is loaded with high-priced frozen dinners, sugared-up prepared sauces, prebuttered bread, precut vegetables, frozen pizzas, boxed croutons (stale bread!), and more.

In an experiment done several years ago, a Tennessee newspaper gave $10 to noted chef and cookbook author Jacques Pépin and asked him to prepare a dinner for four. Not only did he pull off the stunt, but he served beef and came back with 35 cents in change. The meal consisted of salad; flank steak (pounded and seared) in red wine sauce; sautéed cabbage; mashed potatoes; and poached pear with orange sauce — and yes, he bought the bottle of wine.

Of course, preparing that meal takes great skill. But by rethinking your shopping habits and getting acquainted with less common cuts of meat, poultry, and fish — and with beans, legumes, and seasonal fresh vegetables — you can approximate this economic approach and eat better, too.

Remember, frugality is no reason to forgo elegance, as the recipes in this chapter demonstrate.

Big Dishes for Small Bucks

Whether you're using inexpensive cuts of beef, dirt-cheap chicken legs, or a weekly special at the supermarket, a little attention to detail and presentation can make any meal fit for a, well, family.

All the main dish recipes in this section are designed to transform into delicious leftovers — a blessing for busy cooks. Consider the following advice from Jacques Pépin:

"A good cook never apologizes about leftovers. The common mistake is to try to re-serve them in their original form. A roasted chicken is good only when fresh. Reheated, it tastes like a leftover, with all the word's pejorative connotations. But if it is served in a hash or in a cream sauce or is transformed into a salad, it will taste as it should — like a freshly made dish."

Chili

Few words spark gastronomic brouhaha like chili, whether it is rich Texas-style chili con carne, fiery Arizona-style chili, or one of the myriad variations in between. Maybe it's not a glamorous meal, but chili is a real crowd-pleaser, and you'd be surprised how festive you can make it look with some thought to presentation. And with a good batch, you can impress your whole football team for about ten bucks.

Chili is generally agreed to have originated in Texas more than 100 years ago, in the days of cowboys. Chili made sense for these hard-riding buckaroos because it was quick, filled with protein, and cheap — beef was not exactly scarce for the herders. The degree of fire in the form of hot peppers became a matter of cowboy competition.

In New Mexico, another state famous for chili, it was made with lamb or mutton rather than beef, and red beans were popular.

You can make endless variations on chili. Many champion chilis in competitions around the U.S. combine beef and pork, one for flavor and the other for texture, as in the following recipe. If you like, you can add lamb, too. Vegetarians can increase the amount of vegetables and skip the meat altogether.

Stoke the chili as much as you want with extra red pepper flakes and chili powder. Be careful, though, because pepper flakes tend to intensify as they cook.

If the chili cooks too rapidly and needs more liquid, add a little more beef broth or water, or even some liquid from the canned kidney beans.

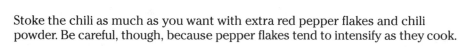

Southwestern Chili

Tools: *Chef's knife, deep pot or pan, wooden spoon*

Preparation time: *About 25 minutes*

Cooking time: *About 35 minutes*

1 tablespoon (15 mL) olive oil

1 cup (250 mL) peeled and finely chopped onion, about 1 large onion

$^1/_2$ cup (125 mL) seeded, cored, and finely chopped green pepper, about 1 small pepper

2 teaspoons (10 mL) peeled and finely chopped garlic, about 2 large cloves

$^1/_2$ pound (250 g) lean ground beef

$^1/_2$ pound (250 g) lean ground pork

1 tablespoon (15 mL) chili powder, or to taste

1 teaspoon (5 mL) ground cumin

$^1/_2$ teaspoon (2 mL) ground coriander

$1^1/_2$ cups (375 mL) ripe, diced tomatoes, or $14^1/_2$-ounce (398-mL) can diced tomatoes

$^3/_4$ cup (175 mL) canned or fresh beef broth

$^1/_2$ cup (125 mL) red wine or water

2 teaspoons (10 mL) tomato paste

$^1/_4$ teaspoon (1 mL) red pepper flakes, or to taste

Salt and freshly ground pepper to taste

15-ounce (398-mL) can red kidney beans, drained

Sour cream or chopped fresh cilantro or parsley for garnish (optional)

1 Heat the oil in a large, deep pot or pan. Add the onion, pepper, and garlic and cook for 2 to 3 minutes over medium heat, stirring occasionally.

2 Add the ground meat and cook for another 3 minutes or until browned, stirring to break up any lumps. Add the chili powder, cumin, and coriander. Stir well.

3 Stir in the tomatoes, beef broth, wine (or water), tomato paste, red pepper flakes, and salt and pepper to taste. Bring to a boil, reduce heat to a simmer, and then cook for 25 minutes, stirring often. Add the drained kidney beans and cook 5 minutes more. Serve over rice (see Chapter 3), garnished with sour cream and chopped cilantro or parsley.

Yield: *4 servings.*

Note: *If you have a plastic ketchup bottle (available in restaurant supply stores), you can squirt flavored sour cream in the shape of Texas. Clumps of fresh herbs could be major cities, too. You can really get carried away with this idea.*

Chili calls for colorful side dishes like Grilled Peppers (see Chapter 6), Avocado and Tomato Salad (see Chapter 15), or Watercress, Endive, and Orange Salad (see Chapter 10).

Chicken

Following is an inexpensive chicken dish with sunny mediterranean flavors of garlic, green olives, and tomatoes.

Mediterranean-Style Chicken

Tools: *Chef's knife, large sauté pan, tongs*

Preparation time: *About 25 minutes*

Cooking time: *About 40 minutes*

3¹/₂-pound (1.75-kg) chicken, cut into serving pieces and trimmed of excess fat

Salt and freshly ground pepper to taste

2 tablespoons (30 mL) olive oil

1 cup (250 mL) finely chopped onion, about 1 large onion

2 teaspoons (10 mL) peeled and finely minced garlic, about 2 large cloves

1 tablespoon (15 mL) flour

1¹/₂ cups (375 mL) fresh or canned chicken broth

¹/₂ cup (125 mL) dry white wine or water

2 cups (500 mL) cored, seeded, and coarsely chopped sweet peppers, preferably red, about 2 medium peppers

1¹/₂ cups (375 mL) coarsely chopped ripe or canned tomatoes, about 2 medium tomatoes

1 tablespoon (15 mL) tomato paste

1¹/₂ teaspoons (7 mL) dried rosemary leaves, crushed

¹/₄ teaspoon (1 mL) hot red pepper flakes

1 bay leaf

2 small zucchini, ends trimmed and cut into ¹/₂-inch (12-mm) rounds

16 small, pitted green olives (optional)

1 Rinse chicken pieces and pat dry with paper towel. Season pieces on all sides with salt and pepper. Heat the oil in a large sauté pan. Add the chicken pieces, skin side down, and cook over medium-high heat, about 10 minutes or until browned all over, turning frequently with tongs.

2 Remove the chicken from the pan and drain on paper towels. Spoon off all but 1 tablespoon (15 mL) of fat from the pan. Add the onion and garlic and cook for 2 to 3 minutes over medium heat, stirring. Add the flour and cook for 1 minute, stirring and scraping the bottom of the pan.

(continued)

3 Gradually pour in the chicken broth and wine or water. Raise the heat and bring to a boil, stirring constantly. Add the red peppers, tomatoes, tomato paste, rosemary, red pepper flakes, and bay leaf.

4 Return chicken pieces to the skillet. Cover, reduce heat, and simmer for about 10 minutes. Add the zucchini and olives (if desired), cover, and cook for about 5 minutes. Uncover and cook for about 10 minutes more or until the chicken and zucchini are tender. Season with salt and pepper to taste. Remove the bay leaf before serving.

Yield: *4 servings.*

The herby broth here is terrific with Couscous with Yellow Squash (see following recipe) or any kind of rice (see Chapter 3).

Super Sidekicks

Fancy-sounding side dishes are another great way to dress up your meals. Following are some inexpensive but tasty recipes.

Couscous

If you have never tried couscous, this recipe will be an eye-opener. Couscous is a wonderful alternative to rice or noodles.

Couscous, which is really semolina (coarse durum wheat) grains, originated in North Africa and is especially popular in Morocco, Algeria, and Tunisia. Traditional couscous is steamed over simmering meats and vegetables in a two-tier utensil called a *couscoussière.*

Precooked couscous, available in supermarkets, is quite good, too, and it saves a lot of time. Couscous is a fine alternative to rice or noodles with many foods, simply seasoned with butter and salt and pepper. It is exceptionally tasty when you cook it in a flavorful stock, stirring well to keep the grains fluffy. We add onions, garlic, yellow squash, and coriander. Zucchini and eggplant are fine substitutes for the yellow squash.

Couscous with Yellow Squash

Tools: Chef's knife, medium saucepan or pot fitted with a lid

Preparation time: About 15 minutes

Cooking time: About 10 minutes

1 tablespoon (15 mL) butter

1 tablespoon (15 mL) olive oil

1/3 cup (75 mL) peeled and finely chopped onion, about 1 small onion

1 teaspoon (5 mL) peeled and finely chopped garlic, about 1 large clove

1 cup (250 mL) diced yellow squash, cut into 1/4-inch (6-mm) cubes, about 1 small squash

2 cups (500 mL) fresh or canned chicken or vegetable broth

1 cup (250 mL) precooked couscous

1/4 cup (50 mL) coarsely chopped fresh coriander

Salt and freshly ground pepper to taste

1 Heat the butter and oil in a medium saucepan over medium heat. Add the onion, garlic, and squash. Cook, stirring, over medium heat until the onion wilts, about 2 to 3 minutes.

2 Add the chicken or vegetable broth and bring to a boil. Add the couscous and blend well. Cover tightly, remove from the heat, and let stand for 5 minutes. Stir in the coriander with a fork. Season to taste with salt and pepper, if desired.

Yield: 4 servings.

This type of couscous goes best with dishes that have a lot of juice or sauce, such as Mediterranean-Style Chicken (earlier in this chapter), Osso Buco (see Chapter 15), or Mediterranean Seafood Stew (see Chapter 5).

You can substitute 1 cup (250 mL) fresh or frozen cooked corn kernels or peas for the yellow squash.

Cumin-flavored carrots

Cumin, a spice most often associated with Middle Eastern and Indian cooking, has an affinity with sweet carrots, as the following recipe demonstrates. These exotic-tasting carrots are best paired with a mild-flavored dish, such as Broiled Porgies with Rosemary Oil (see Chapter 15) or Roasted Chicken (see Chapter 6).

Baby Carrots in Cumin Butter

Tools: *Chef's knife, medium saucepan*

Preparation time: *About 10 minutes*

Cooking time: *About 15 minutes*

1 pound (500 g) carrots

Salt to taste

2 tablespoons (30 mL) butter

¹/₄ teaspoon (1 mL) ground cumin

2 tablespoons (30 mL) chopped fresh coriander or parsley, or 2 teaspoons (10 mL) dried

1 Scrape the carrots, trim off the ends, and slice into 1-inch (2.5-cm) pieces.

2 Put the carrots in a saucepan and add water to cover, along with salt to taste. Bring to a boil and simmer until the carrots are tender, about 15 minutes.

3 Drain the carrots; add the butter, cumin, and coriander or parsley and toss well. Serve immediately.

Yield: *4 to 6 servings.*

Beans

We find it rather amazing that Americans don't cook more with dried beans, which are so inexpensive, healthful, and delicious. You can use dried beans in a side dish, as in the following recipe, or as part of a main course. Whether or not you are cooking on a tight budget, becoming familiar with all kinds of legumes, each of which has a special texture and flavor, is definitely worthwhile. Table 14-1 lists several common types of dried beans.

Before cooking dried beans, sort and rinse them. Look over the beans carefully, picking out and discarding any that are withered. Rinse them thoroughly in cold water until the water runs clear, removing any beans or other substances that float to the surface.

White Beans with Tomato and Thyme

Tools: *Chef's knife, large pot, large skillet or sauté pan, colander or strainer*

Preparation time: *About 20 minutes, plus time to soak beans*

Cooking time: *About 50 minutes*

1 cup (250 mL) dried white beans (such as Great Northern or baby limas), rinsed

2 medium onions

1 quart (1 L) water

2 whole cloves

3 strips bacon

1 large carrot, scraped, trimmed, and cut in half lengthwise

2 sprigs fresh thyme, or ¹/₂ teaspoon (2 mL) dried

1 bay leaf

Salt and freshly ground pepper to taste

2 teaspoons (10 mL) butter or oil

1 teaspoon (5 mL) peeled and minced garlic, about 1 large clove

1 teaspoon (5 mL) chopped fresh thyme, or ¹/₂ teaspoon (2 mL) dried

14¹/₂-ounce (398-mL) can peeled tomatoes, drained and chopped

2 tablespoons (30 mL) chopped fresh parsley

1 Place the beans in a large pot and add water to cover by about 1 inch (2.5 cm). Soak overnight or boil for 2 minutes and then let stand for 1 hour. (See note at the end of this recipe.)

2 Peel the onions. Stick the cloves into one onion, and chop the other onion finely.

3 Drain the beans and return them to the pot. Add 1 quart (1 L) water, the onion stuck with cloves, the bacon, carrot, thyme, bay leaf, and salt and pepper to taste. Bring to a boil and simmer for 45 minutes to 1 hour or until the beans are tender. (Different varieties require different cooking times.)

4 Remove the bacon strips and chop them into small pieces.

5 Melt the butter or oil in a large skillet or sauté pan and sauté the chopped bacon over medium heat until golden brown, stirring. Add the chopped onion, garlic, and thyme and cook for about 2 to 3 minutes or until the onions wilt. Add the tomatoes and cook for 2 to 3 minutes, stirring frequently. Remove from the heat.

6 When the beans are tender, remove and discard the carrot, onion with cloves, and bay leaf. Carefully scoop out and reserve ¹/₂ cup (125 mL) of the bean liquid and drain the beans. Add the beans to the tomato mixture and stir gently. If the mixture seems dry, add a little of the reserved liquid. Adjust seasoning with salt and pepper. Serve the beans hot, sprinkled with the chopped parsley.

Yield: *4 to 5 servings.*

(continued)

Note: *You soak most dried beans before cooking to shorten the cooking time, which is important if you cook them with other ingredients. If you don't have time to soak the beans overnight, use this shortcut: Place the beans in a deep pot covered with lots of water. Bring to a boil and cook for 2 minutes. Remove pot from the heat, cover, and let stand for 1 hour.*

Pair these aromatic beans with dishes like Mustard-Brushed Barbecued Chicken Breasts (see Chapter 6), Grilled Flank Steak with Rosemary and Sage (see Chapter 15), or Salmon Marinated with Ginger and Coriander (see Chapter 15).

Table 14-1	Dried Beans
Bean	*Description*
Black beans	Often used in South American and Caribbean dishes and mixed with rice and spices. Sweetish flavor.
Black-eyed peas	Traditional ingredient in the cooking of the American South — black-eyed peas and collard greens, black-eyed peas with ham. Earthy.
Borlotto beans	Large, speckled beans. Mostly pureed and turned into creamy dips.
Boston beans	See "White beans (Boston beans), small."
Chickpeas	Large, semifirm beans sold dried and canned. Used in casseroles, soups, and stews. Pureed and seasoned in Middle Eastern cuisine. Also known as *garbanzo beans.*
Kidney beans/red beans	The traditional beans used in chili and other earthy casserole dishes and soups. A white kidney bean, called *cannellini,* is used in many northern Italian dishes. A staple in Mexican cooking as well. Faintly sweet.
Lentils	Boiled with vegetables and other seasonings for side dishes, soups, and stews. No soaking is required before cooking.
Lima beans	Eaten as a side dish with mild seasonings. Also good in casseroles, especially with ham. Sweet flavor.
Pinto beans	The base of Mexican refried beans. Frequently used in highly spiced dishes. Earthy, mild flavor.
Split peas	Often used in soups, especially with ham. Sweet. Like lentils, no soaking is required.

(continued)

Table 14-1 *(continued)*

Bean	Description
White beans, large	Used in stews and casseroles. Often simmered with ham bones or other flavorful stocks. Neutral flavor.
White beans (Boston beans), small	Foundation of Boston baked beans and the French *cassoulet*. Neutral flavor.

The sweet edge of the balsamic vinegar performs magic on the nutty flavored lentils in the following recipe. Unlike other dried beans, lentils don't require soaking and boil tender in 20 to 25 minutes.

Lentils with Balsamic Vinegar

Tools: *Chef's knife, large pot or saucepan, large sauté pan*

Preparation time: *About 20 minutes*

Cooking time: *About 30 minutes*

$1^1/_2$ *cups (375 mL) lentils, rinsed*

4 cups (1 L) water

Salt to taste

2 small onions, peeled

2 cloves

1 bay leaf

2 sprigs fresh thyme, or $^1/_2$ teaspoon (2 mL) dried

1 tablespoon (15 mL) butter

1 tablespoon (15 mL) olive oil

$^3/_4$ *cup (175 mL) scraped and finely diced carrot, about 1 large carrot*

1 teaspoon (5 mL) peeled and finely chopped garlic, about 1 large clove

1 tablespoon (15 mL) balsamic (or red wine) vinegar

Freshly ground pepper to taste

1 Put the lentils in a large pot or saucepan. Add the water and salt to taste. Bring to a boil over high heat. Stick the cloves into one onion and chop the other onion finely. Add the onion with cloves to the saucepan with the bay leaf and thyme. Cover, reduce heat, and simmer for about 20 minutes or until the lentils are tender.

2 Before draining the lentils, carefully scoop out and reserve $^1/_2$ cup (125 mL) of the cooking liquid. Drain the lentils. Remove and discard the onion with cloves.

3 Heat the butter and olive oil in a large sauté pan over medium heat. Add the carrot, chopped onion, and garlic. Cook, stirring, until the onion wilts, about 3 to 4 minutes. (Do not brown the garlic.) Add the vinegar and the reserved $^1/_2$ cup (125 mL) cooking liquid. Cover, reduce heat, and simmer for about 5 minutes or until the vegetables are tender.

(continued)

4 Add the lentils to the vegetable-vinegar mixture, cover, and simmer for about 2 minutes more, just to blend flavors. Remove the bay leaf and sprigs of thyme. Season with salt and pepper and serve.

Yield: *4 servings.*

Lentils are ideal with Grilled Brochettes of Pork with Rosemary (see Chapter 6) or Chicken Breasts with Garlic and Capers (see Chapter 7).

Seasonal vegetables

Most seasonal vegetables tend to be a relative bargain (except for exotic and imported produce), and certain types are incredibly cheap. And like the less expensive cuts of meat, vegetables are terrific when prepared properly. Kale, a hearty, iron-packed member of the cabbage family that is available year-round, is one of those vegetables. Others include collard greens, mustard greens, squashes of all kinds, turnips, rutabagas, cabbage, and zucchini (in season).

Following is a down-home recipe for kale, which Southerners traditionally combine with some kind of sausage or bacon.

Homestyle Kale

Tools: *Chef's knife, sauté pan*

Preparation time: *About 15 minutes*

Cooking time: *About 15 minutes*

2 pounds (1 kg) kale

2 slices bacon, diced

¹/₂ cup (125 mL) peeled and finely chopped onion, about 1 medium onion

1 tablespoon (15 mL) peeled and minced garlic, about 3 large cloves

¹/₂ cup (125 mL) water

1 bay leaf

¹/₄ teaspoon (1 mL) ground cumin

Salt and freshly ground pepper to taste

4 lemon wedges

1 Wash the kale thoroughly. Strip the leaves from the tough center ribs (discarding the ribs) and cut out any blemished areas.

(continued)

2 In a sauté pan, cook the bacon over medium heat for about 4 to 5 minutes or until lightly browned. Add the onion, garlic, kale leaves, water, bay leaf, cumin, and salt and pepper. Cover and simmer for 15 minutes or until tender, stirring occasionally. Discard the bay leaf and serve with lemon wedges.

Yield: 4 servings.

Try this dish with Beef Braised in Beaujolais (see Chapter 7) or Roasted Duck with Honey Glaze (see Chapter 6).

Desserts: Standing Ovation

The best way to turn a simple meal or a one-pot dish into a menu with pizzazz is to add a dessert. If you're thinking about champagne and truffles, think again: A dessert can be elegant without costing the earth.

The following is an inexpensive dessert that will dazzle 'em. You can prepare the sweet base ahead of time and, before serving, fold in the egg whites and pop the soufflés in the oven. Because timing is critical (and you may be occupied in entertaining guests by making shadow animals on the wall), designating someone as the official timer — maybe one of your children, preferably one who is fast at short-distance running — is a good idea. Then you know that the soufflé will come out on time and make it to the table at its peak of puffy pulchritude.

Flourless Orange Soufflés with Grand Marnier Sauce

Tools: Wire whisk or electric mixer, four 1¹/₂-cup (375-mL) soufflé dishes, grater, juicer, two large mixing bowls, rubber spatula, baking sheet, small saucepan

Preparation time: About 30 minutes

Baking time: About 12 minutes

1 tablespoon (15 mL) butter for greasing soufflé dishes

5 eggs, separated (see Chapter 8 for illustrated instructions)

¹/₃ cup (75 mL) plus 3 tablespoons (45 mL) sugar

¹/₃ cup (75 mL) orange juice with pulp, from a large navel orange

3 teaspoons (15 mL) grated orange peel from a navel orange

Orange sections from a second navel orange (see Chapter 10 for illustrated sectioning instructions)

3 tablespoons (45 mL) orange marmalade

1 tablespoon (15 mL) Grand Marnier or other orange-flavored liqueur (optional)

(continued)

1 Preheat the oven to 425° F (220° C).

2 Butter four 1¹/₂-cup (375-mL) soufflé dishes. Place them in the refrigerator to chill.

3 Place the 5 egg yolks, ¹/₃ cup (75 mL) sugar, orange juice, and 2 teaspoons (10 mL) of the orange peel in a large mixing bowl.

4 Place the egg whites and the remaining 3 tablespoons (45 mL) sugar in another large mixing bowl (preferably copper).

5 Use a wire whisk or electric mixer to beat the egg yolk mixture until lemon-colored. Whip the egg whites and sugar until they form stiff peaks. (For illustrated instructions, see Chapter 8.)

6 Blend about one-quarter of the beaten egg whites into the yolk mixture, stirring gently with a rubber spatula. Fold in the remaining whites. (For illustrated instructions, see Chapter 8.)

7 Fill the chilled soufflé dishes with the mixture. Smooth the tops slightly with a spatula. With your thumb, create a channel around the periphery of the dish to allow for expansion. Place the dishes on a baking sheet and bake for 12 to 13 minutes or until the soufflés are well risen and firm.

8 As the soufflés bake, combine the remaining teaspoon (5 mL) of grated orange peel, orange sections, marmalade, and Grand Marnier or other orange-flavored liqueur (if desired) in a small saucepan. Heat until warmed.

9 Remove the baked soufflés when done and, using the back of a spoon, make a hole in the middle of each. Pour in some sauce and serve immediately.

Yield: 4 servings.

A good, flexible alternative is a home-baked pie. (See Chapter 15 for a recipe.) Pastry is easy and economical, and pies let you take advantage of low prices on fresh seasonal fruit. Or if you're pinching pennies *and* pressed for time, try a fruit sauce over ice cream (see Chapter 7).

Money-saving kitchen tips

Being economical in the kitchen has nothing to do with cutting quality — in fact, just the contrary. Making every ounce count takes skill and respect for food. Here are some ways to begin:

✔ **Don't let leftovers ossify in the refrigerator.** Think ahead and use them the next day in omelets (see Chapter 8), chili, soups (see Chapter 9), stir-fries, casseroles like macaroni and cheese (see Chapter 12), and salads (see Chapter 10).

✔ **Develop knife skills.** Cutting up your own chicken and boning your own meat saves considerable money. Plus, you have bones for making stock. Whole vegetables are cheaper than cut-up ones, too.

✔ **Develop delicious recipes with high-protein dried beans and less-expensive vegetables like squash, kale, collard greens, and potatoes.**

✔ **Use your freezer intelligently.** Take advantage of supermarket sales. Buy in bulk ground meat, chicken cutlets, poultry parts, steaks, and chops. Wrap and save leftovers from large casseroles such as baked lasagna (see Chapter 11), meat from a roasted leg of lamb (see Chapter 6), or a baked ham. And date everything you put in the freezer.

✔ **If possible, grow an herb garden, even if in a window box.** So many packaged fresh herbs go to waste because you don't use them often enough.

✔ **Make your own versions of foods that you routinely buy in the supermarket.** You'll spend less money and get better quality. Examples include croutons (see Chapter 9), salad dressings (see Chapter 10), garlic bread, and herb vinegar (see Chapter 10).

✔ **Buy less-expensive cuts of meat and learn to tenderize them by braising and stewing.** (See Chapter 5.)

✔ **Experiment with less expensive types of fish.** Examples include mako shark and porgies (see Chapter 15).

✔ **Discourage children from bringing friends home for dinner.** And visit friends and relatives around mealtime and compliment them on how delicious the kitchen smells.

Chapter 15

The Clock Is Ticking ... and the Guests Are on Their Way!

. . . .

In This Chapter

▶ Leisurely menu planning: When you have all day
▶ When the guests are coming in one hour
▶ When the guests are coming in 30 minutes

. . . .

*N*oncooks think it's silly to invest two hours' work in two minutes' enjoyment; but if cooking is evanescent, well, so is the ballet.

— Julia Child

Picture yourself in this situation: In a foolish moment of bravado at an office cocktail party, you invite two couples to dinner Friday evening a week hence, 7:30 p.m. When the dreaded day arrives, you dart out of the office at 5:45 with no idea what to prepare for dinner. In fact, you become so agitated that you're not even sure where you live. After running several red lights on the way to the grocery store — all the while thinking, "I'll get inspired by what looks good in the market" — you arrive to find that the lettuce looks as if it has been used for batting practice and the only items left in the picked-over meat section are beef tongue and tripe.

So you frantically buy boxes of pasta, tomato paste, sweet peppers, garlic, broccoli, leeks, a turnip, prewashed lettuce, Ben and Jerry's Ambulance Vanilla ice cream, and some beef tongue — just in case.

Judging by the traffic on your way home, you would think that the Superbowl had been transferred to your suburb this evening. You listen to a talk show on the radio. The topic: "The Joys of Summer Entertaining." After what seems like an eternity, you pull into the driveway only to see a strange car parked there. Even more disturbing, people outside the house are looking into your windows.

"What the heck do you think you're doing?" you shout, realizing in mid-sentence that the suspected burglars are, in fact, your guests. Yikes!

This little scene goes to show that cooking is not always done under ideal conditions. Even Julia Child's washing machine sometimes goes haywire right in the middle of a stuffed goose recipe.

Cooking by the Clock

When you plan a vacation, what is the first consideration: Cost? Distance? Exoticism? Not at all. The first consideration is *time*. If you have only one week, doing a flora tour of Australia's outback hardly makes sense — the flight alone takes five days (well, almost).

The same philosophy applies to cooking for company. Think about how much time you realistically have. If you are lucky enough to have all day Saturday to prepare for a dinner party, indulge in it. We give you some great ideas for that luxury.

But if you have only one hour — or less — the type of foods you prepare by necessity are totally different, which does not mean that they are not as good. Rather than making a braised shoulder of pork that takes three hours to cook, for example, you might serve Mustard-Brushed Barbecued Chicken Breasts, which take about 20 minutes. (See Chapter 6 for the recipe.)

Regardless of how much time you have, the important thing is to use it well. With the right scheduling strategies and planning, you can whip up a dinner party in whatever time's available and still be sane when your guests arrive. The trick is in getting the techniques down and then planning your menus accordingly.

If You Have All Day

If you have all day, then — heck, you have all day. Relax. Enjoy yourself. Try something different. But don't lose track of the clock. The danger with having plenty of time on your hands is forgetting that you still have a schedule and a deadline (the guests *are* going to show up eventually). Go ahead and run errands while the main dish roasts, but don't forget to be back in time to adjust that oven temperature or stir that side dish. And make a list before you start so that you don't find yourself at the end of a day's happy cooking without a crucial part of your menu that you forgot all about. If you plan your day's cooking, at least roughly, before you get started, you'll be sure to have a leisurely day in the kitchen, and everything you want to serve will be ready by dinnertime.

One nice menu planning option, if you have lots of time, is to start your meal with an appetizer that requires marinating, such as the spectacular salmon infused with ginger and coriander in the following recipe.

Marinating fish is tricky business. The acid in the marinade — which comes from the lime and vinegar — actually "cooks" the fish. Be sure not to leave it in the marinade too long. (This marinade does not have the same effect on dense cuts of meat or poultry.) This dish calls for marinating for four to five hours, so you can put everything together in the early afternoon and have it for dinner. You know if you overmarinate the fish: It turns the color of well-trod cement and falls apart to the touch.

Salmon Marinated in Ginger and Coriander

Tools: *Chef's knife, grater, large mixing bowl*

Preparation time: *About 25 minutes*

Marinating time: *4 to 5 hours*

2 pounds (1 kg) skinless salmon fillets (have your fishmonger remove the skin)

¹/₂ cup (125 mL) fresh lime juice

1 cup (250 mL) peeled and thinly sliced onion, about 1 large onion

2 tablespoons (30 mL) white wine vinegar

2 tablespoons (30 mL) olive oil

1 tablespoon (15 mL) chopped fresh coriander

1 tablespoon (15 mL) grated fresh ginger

¹/₄ teaspoon (1 mL) hot red pepper flakes

Salt and freshly ground pepper to taste

Lettuce for garnish

1 Slice salmon thinly (¹/₄ inch/6 mm or less) widthwise, leaving strips about 2 inches (5 cm) long. Place the strips in a large mixing bowl.

2 Add the lime juice, onion, vinegar, oil, coriander, ginger, red pepper flakes, and salt and pepper. Stir gently and cover with plastic wrap. Refrigerate for 4 to 5 hours. Taste for seasoning. (You may need more salt; if so, blend it in thoroughly.)

3 Line small serving plates with lettuce of your choice and place a serving of salmon over the lettuce.

Yield: *6 servings.*

In some cases, we give a dried substitute for a fresh herb. However, substitutions don't work with a few ingredients. You cannot substitute dried coriander for fresh, or powdered ginger for fresh ginger root. The fresh ingredient tastes entirely different from the dried one. Dried parsley is another herb that has its limitations. Always use fresh, chopped parsley, never dried, when sprinkling it on a dish as a garnish.

Other starter dishes

Another way to go if you have the luxury of time is to start the meal with a light vegetable soup. This type of vegetable soup — and you can vary the cast of characters as you like — is a perfect prelude to the hearty main course of Osso Buco that we tackle next. You don't want to serve a full-bodied soup like black bean or cheesy onion before a lusty main course (unless you are cooking in a lumberjack camp).

Notice how the *pistou,* a French recipe that mixes chopped tomatoes, basil, garlic, and olive oil, first sits and marinates a bit before you stir it into the simmering soup. You may want to accompany this dish with a loaf of hot and crusty French bread.

Spring Vegetable Soup

Tools: Medium pot or saucepan, chef's knife, paring knife, vegetable peeler, small bowl

Preparation time: About 45 minutes

Cooking time: About 35 minutes

1 tablespoon (15 mL) vegetable oil

1 large onion, peeled and diced, about 1 cup (250 mL)

1 large carrot, scraped and diced, about $^1/_2$ cup (125 mL)

4 cups (1 L) water

2 cups (500 mL) chicken or vegetable broth

2 medium baking potatoes, peeled and diced

1 large leek (white and light green parts only), washed and diced

1 small zucchini, rinsed, trimmed of ends, and diced

1 cup (250 mL) green beans, trimmed and cut into $^1/_2$-inch (12-mm) pieces

2 large ripe tomatoes, peeled, seeded, and chopped, about 2 cups (500 mL)

2 tablespoons (30 mL) finely chopped basil

2 teaspoons (10 mL) peeled and minced garlic, about 2 medium cloves

1 tablespoon (15 mL) olive oil

$1^1/_2$ teaspoons (7 mL) salt, or to taste

Freshly ground white (or black) pepper to taste

(continued)

1 Heat the vegetable oil in a medium (4-quart/4-L) pot or saucepan over medium heat. Add the onion and cook for about 3 minutes, stirring occasionally.

2 Stir in the carrot and cook for 1 minute. Stir in the water and chicken or vegetable broth. Raise the heat and bring to a boil; then reduce the heat to low and simmer for 10 minutes, uncovered.

3 Add the potatoes, leek, zucchini, and green beans. Cover, raise the heat to high, and bring to a boil. Then uncover, reduce the heat to low, and simmer 25 minutes (you may want to set your kitchen timer at this point), skimming the surface when necessary to remove any foam.

4 While the soup simmers, place the chopped tomatoes in a small bowl. Stir in the basil, garlic, and olive oil. Set aside.

5 One minute before the soup finishes cooking, stir in the tomato-basil mixture and the salt and pepper. Serve hot or at room temperature.

Yield: About 8 cups (2 L), or enough for 6 main course or 8 first course servings.

You can make a pasta and vegetable version of this soup by omitting the two potatoes and adding $^1/_2$ cup (125 mL) small-shaped macaroni (elbows or shells) 6 to 7 minutes before the soup finishes cooking. Replace the green beans with $1^1/_2$ cups (375 mL) of coarsely chopped cabbage for cabbage-flavored broth.

If you have all day, you also can try one of these first courses:

- ✔ Grilled Peppers (see Chapter 6)
- ✔ Gazpacho (see Chapter 9)
- ✔ Black Bean Soup (see Chapter 9)
- ✔ Cream of Leek Soup (see Chapter 9)
- ✔ Warm Shrimp Salad with Spinach (see Chapter 10)
- ✔ Bow-Tie Pasta Salad with Fresh Mussels (see Chapter 10)
- ✔ Spaghetti with Clam Sauce (see Chapter 11)

Main dish choices

One of the long-cooked main courses we recommend for entertaining is Osso Buco, a glorious dish of braised veal shank with garlic, tomato, and other ingredients. Osso Buco is one of the greatest gifts from northern Italy since Michelangelo. The meat on the shank is exceptionally succulent, and the sauce that simmers in the meat juices is packed with herbal flavors and a touch of lemon.

Many cooks don't know it, but one traditional ingredient in Osso Buco is anchovies. Their intense saltiness, when added in moderation, adds a special flavor. If you are one of those people who pick anchovies off pizza, simply omit them from the recipe.

Ideally, Osso Buco should be made a day or two in advance, chilled, and then reheated — the flavors meld and intensify that way. Because you have all day to make this meal, you can prepare it at midday, cool it, and then serve it for a dinner party.

TOQUE TIP

Anchovies

On the culinary hit parade, anchovies fall somewhere at the bottom, between brussels sprouts and tripe. A staple of Mediterranean cooking, anchovies have never had widespread appeal among American home cooks — although professional chefs use them frequently.

Fresh anchovies, which are superb when grilled over charcoal, are rarely available in the U.S. Typically, they are sold salted in jars or cans, yielding a product that has little relation to fresh anchovies, although you can put the salted ones to good use in many ways.

In French cuisine, anchovies add a lovely saline touch to dishes like *tapenade* (a spread made with desalted anchovies, black olives, and herbs)

and *pissaladiere,* a specialty of Nice in which a garlic-seasoned flan filled with onions is garnished with fresh anchovy fillets and black olives. Anchovy paste, sold commercially in tubes, can add a distinctive touch to all sorts of dishes, from pasta sauces to vinaigrettes.

Todd English, chef and owner of Olives restaurant in Charlestown, Massachusetts, says, "There are many interesting ways to season a dish. I use anchovies a lot. . . . I know that lots of people don't like them, but they add an element, a depth of flavor that tastes nothing like an anchovy. Often, you can't even tell they are in the dish."

Osso Buco

Tools: *Chef's knife, grater, Dutch oven (cast-iron is best)*

Preparation time: *About 40 minutes*

Cooking time: *1 hour and 30 minutes*

4 meaty slices of veal shanks cut across the marrow bones (each about 2 inches/ 5 cm thick), about 3¹/₂ pounds (1.75 kg) total

Salt and freshly ground pepper to taste

¹/₂ cup (125 mL) flour for dredging

2 tablespoons (30 mL) olive oil

1 cup (250 mL) peeled and finely chopped onion, about 1 large onion

¹/₂ cup (125 mL) chopped celery, about 1 stalk

1 cup (250 mL) scraped and chopped carrots, about 2 to 3 large carrots

1 tablespoon (15 mL) peeled and finely chopped garlic, about 3 large cloves

4 canned anchovy fillets, drained and mashed with a fork (optional)

¹/₂ teaspoon (2 mL) dried marjoram

2 sprigs fresh thyme, or 1 teaspoon (5 mL) dried

1 cup (250 mL) dry white wine

1¹/₂ cups (375 mL) crushed tomatoes

1 bay leaf

1 teaspoon (5 mL) finely grated lemon peel

1 teaspoon (5 mL) finely grated orange peel

¹/₄ cup (50 mL) finely chopped fresh parsley

1 Sprinkle the veal shanks with salt and pepper to taste and then roll them in the flour to give them a light coating. (This technique is called *dredging.*)

2 Heat the oil over medium-high heat in a heavy Dutch oven large enough to hold the veal shanks in one layer with the bones upright. Brown the veal all around, turning often, about 10 minutes. Remove shanks from the pan and reserve them on a plate.

3 Lower the heat to medium and add the onions, celery, and carrots to the pan. Cook, stirring, until the onions wilt, about 2 or 3 minutes. Add the garlic, mashed anchovies (if desired), marjoram, and thyme. Stir and add the wine, tomatoes, bay leaf, and salt and pepper to taste. Return the veal shanks to the pan. Cover, reduce heat to low, and simmer for about 1 hour or until meat is tender. (The meat should easily separate from the bone when prodded with a fork.)

(continued)

4 Sprinkle the orange and lemon peel over the veal and stir to blend. Cover and cook about 15 minutes more. Remove bay leaf and sprinkle with chopped parsley.

Yield: *4 servings.*

You can serve this dish with garlic mashed potatoes, buttered rice (see Chapter 3), or couscous (see Chapter 14).

Following is another stick-to-the-ribs style of cooking that is perfect for entertaining. In this ancient French country recipe (also found in the Spanish repertoire), you first brown a loin of pork on the stovetop to sear in the moisture and then braise it slowly in sweet onions and milk for three hours. The milk gives the pork a rich and velvety texture that is out of this world. You set aside the pan juices to form the base of a gravy and then finish the roast in the oven.

Pork Loin Braised with Milk and Onions

Tools: *Chef's knife, Dutch oven, roasting pan, strainer or sieve, small saucepan*

Preparation time: *About 20 minutes*

Cooking time: *About 2 hours and 50 minutes*

3-pound (1.5-kg) boneless loin of pork

Salt and freshly ground pepper to taste

1 tablespoon (15 mL) olive oil

12 small white onions, peeled, about 1 pound (500 g)

1 quart (1 L) milk

¹/₄ cup (50 mL) heavy cream or half and half (optional)

1 Rub the pork with salt and pepper.

2 Heat the oil in a Dutch oven over medium heat until hot, about 1 minute. Brown the pork well in the oil on all sides for about 10 minutes. Remove the meat to a platter. Add the onions to the Dutch oven. Stir and brown them for about 5 minutes.

3 Carefully drain off all the fat. Return the pork to the Dutch oven, pushing the onions to the sides. Add the milk and cover. Raise the heat to high and bring to a boil. Reduce the heat to low and simmer for 1 hour, turning the roast over after 30 minutes.

4 Remove the lid and simmer over medium-low heat for another 1¹/₂ hours (turning the roast every 30 minutes), or until about 2 cups (500 mL) of the simmering liquid remains in the pan.

(continued)

5 Preheat the oven to 425° F (220° C).

6 Place the roast on a lightly oiled roasting pan and cook about 10 minutes until brown.

7 As the pork cooks in the oven, strain the sauce into a saucepan. (Discard the solids left in the strainer.) Add the cream, if desired, to the sauce and heat just to a simmer.

8 Slice the pork and serve, spooning 2 to 3 tablespoons (30 to 45 mL) of sauce over each slice.

Yield: *6 servings and about 1¹/₃ cups (325 mL) sauce.*

 You tie butcher's string around a boned roast to preserve its shape. Remove the string with a sharp knife or kitchen shears just before slicing.

If you have all day, you also can try any of these main dishes:

- ✔ Poached Salmon Steaks with Herbed Vinaigrette Sauce (see Chapter 3)
- ✔ Old-Fashioned Beef Stew (see Chapter 5)
- ✔ Braised Lamb with White Beans (see Chapter 5)
- ✔ Pot Roast with Vegetables (see Chapter 5)
- ✔ Mediterranean Seafood Stew (see Chapter 5)
- ✔ Any of the roasting recipes from Chapter 6
- ✔ Beef Braised in Beaujolais (see Chapter 7)
- ✔ Fettuccine with Ginger Shrimp (see Chapter 11)
- ✔ Lasagna with Fresh Tomato and Zucchini Sauce (see Chapter 11)
- ✔ Chicken and Biscuit Pot Pie (see Chapter 12)
- ✔ Shepherd's Pie (see Chapter 12)

Orange and lemon peel

You may notice that many braising dishes call for a little lemon or orange peel, or *zest*. These magical ingredients add a barely perceptible perfume to long-cooked dishes that you may not detect immediately but that you will enjoy. When grating, remove just the orange or yellow zest and not the bitter white pith underneath.

Side dishes

A perfect side dish for all roasts is mashed potatoes — chefs today like to call them "pureed potatoes," as if they are something more sophisticated. But how can you improve on something so basic and so delicious? Serve mashed potatoes with baked garlic, found in Chapter 3. And mashed potatoes can be enhanced in many ways. You can add mashed parsnips, carrots, or turnips or chopped scallions, onions, or fresh herbs.

The slight crunch of cabbage and its sweet-sour flavor also go particularly well with roasted pork. You can make cabbage ahead of time and reheat it before serving. The following recipe brings the lowly cabbage to life, giving it a sweet personality with apples and a bit of spice with caraway. If you want to get more exotic, try crushed coriander seed.

Braised Cabbage with Apple and Caraway

Tools: *Chef's knife, paring knife, large saucepan or sauté pan with cover, wooden spoon*

Preparation time: *About 25 minutes*

Cooking time: *About 25 minutes*

3 tablespoons (45 mL) vegetable oil

1 cup (250 mL) peeled and coarsely chopped onion, about 1 medium onion

1 teaspoon (5 mL) peeled and minced garlic, about 1 large clove

1 small head cabbage, about 2 pounds (1 kg), coarsely shredded, about 5 cups (1.25 L)

1 medium apple, peeled, cored, and cut into thin slices

1 tablespoon (15 mL) white vinegar

1 teaspoon (5 mL) caraway seeds

¹/₂ cup (125 mL) fresh or canned chicken or vegetable broth

Salt and freshly ground pepper to taste

1 Over medium setting, heat the oil in a large saucepan or sauté pan and add the onion and garlic. Cook, stirring, until the onion is wilted. (Do not brown the garlic.) Add the cabbage, apple, vinegar, caraway seeds, chicken or vegetable broth, and salt and pepper.

2 Raise the heat to high and bring to a boil. Cover, reduce the heat to low, and simmer for 15 to 20 minutes or until the cabbage is crisp-tender, stirring occasionally. Uncover. If a lot of liquid is still in the pan, raise heat to high and cook, stirring, for about 1 to 2 minutes or until most of the liquid is evaporated.

Yield: *4 servings.*

Or try any of these side dishes if you have all day:

- ✔ Basic Wild Rice (see Chapter 3)
- ✔ Flavored Brown Rice (see Chapter 3)
- ✔ Risotto (see Chapter 3)
- ✔ Roasted Winter Vegetables (see Chapter 6)
- ✔ Sautéed Cubed Potatoes (see Chapter 4)
- ✔ Creamed Spinach (see Chapter 7)
- ✔ Grilled Summer Vegetables with Basil Marinade (see Chapter 6)

Desserts

Okay, dessert time. Without getting involved in stratified layer cakes or chocolate concoctions that resemble a nuclear power plant, you can make plenty of intriguing desserts that are suitable for entertaining. Knowing how to make a basic sweet pastry crust is always a good idea. Make the recipe over and over again until you can make it in your sleep. Then when fresh fruit is in season, or when you want to make a lemon or chocolate mousse pie, all you have to concentrate on is the filling. And that's a cinch.

All you have to know about a basic pastry crust is that butter makes it sweet and shortening (like Crisco) makes it flaky. Many cooks split it down the middle and use equal amounts of butter and lard to make the dough.

"Typical pie dough pastry calls for you to cut the butter and shortening into the flour with a pastry blender until the mixture resembles coarse corn meal, but we do it just the opposite at Campanile," says Nancy Silverton, owner and chef of this famous Los Angeles bakery-restaurant. "We've found the texture of the pastry to be lighter and flakier when the butter and shortening are first creamed together and then the dry ingredients are worked in.

"We also bake our pies in a very hot, preheated 450° F (230° C) oven for about 15 minutes and then turn the heat to 350° F (180° C) for the remainder of the baking time," says Chef Silverton. "The hot oven helps to 'set' the crust and gives it a nice brown color.

"Be sure to use really cold water, chilled with ice cubes, to hold together the dough," she says.

See how you like this pastry dough and then modify it, if you want, with suggestions that follow this recipe.

Basic Pastry Crust

Tools: *Food processor or electronic mixer, wire pastry blender (if making by hand), rolling pin, 9-inch (23-cm) pie pan*

Preparation time: *About 1¹/₂ hours (includes time to chill dough)*

¹/₃ cup (75 mL) plus 1 tablespoon (15 mL) cold, unsalted butter

¹/₃ cup (75 mL) plus 1 tablespoon (15 mL) vegetable shortening (like Crisco or margarine)

2 cups (500 mL) all-purpose flour

³/₄ teaspoon (3 mL) salt

4 to 5 tablespoons (60 to 75 mL) ice water

1 In the bowl of a food processor, cream the butter and shortening. Add the flour and salt and process just a few seconds until the dough resembles coarse corn meal. With the motor running, add the cold water a little at a time, just enough to hold together the dry ingredients. (The exact amount of water required depends on the humidity of the day.) Do not overblend or the dough will get tough. Shape the dough into a ball.

To make the dough without a food processor, as shown in Figure 15-1, cream the butter and shortening in a large bowl by using an electric mixer. Add the flour and salt. Using a pastry blender or your fingers, work the flour mixture into the butter and shortening, making a dough that resembles coarse corn meal. Sprinkle enough water to form soft but not sticky dough. Shape the dough into a loose ball.

2 Divide the dough into two equal halves, wrap both in plastic, and refrigerate for at least 1 hour. (As the dough is chilling, prepare the filling from the following Apple Pie recipe.)

3 When ready to make your pie, preheat the oven to 450° F (230° C).

4 Lightly flour a large cutting board or counter and roll out one dough ball into a circle that is a few inches larger in diameter than the pie plate — that is, about 11 inches (28 cm). (See Figure 15-2 for illustrated rolling instructions.)

5 Loosely drape the dough around the rolling pin and transfer it to the pie plate. Unroll the dough flat on the bottom and flush against the sides. Trim off any excess dough with a knife and crimp it by pressing the tines of a fork around the edges. Lightly press any excess dough into the remaining ball. (Fill or bake crust as recipe directs. For an apple pie filling, see the following recipe.)

(continued)

6 Roll out the second ball of dough the same way and lay it over the filled bottom crust, leaving an overhang of about ¹/₂ inch (12 mm). Tuck the overhang under to form a neat edge, crimp firmly, and prick the top a few times with a fork before baking. (See the following Apple Pie recipe for baking instructions.)

Yield: Enough pastry for a 9-inch (23-cm) double-crust pie.

Making Pie Dough by Hand

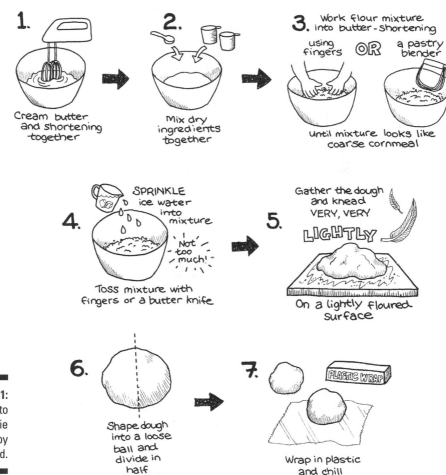

1. Cream butter and shortening together

2. Mix dry ingredients together

3. Work flour mixture into butter-shortening using fingers **OR** a pastry blender until mixture looks like coarse cornmeal

4. SPRINKLE ice water into mixture "Not too much!" Toss mixture with fingers or a butter knife

5. Gather the dough and knead VERY, VERY **LIGHTLY** On a lightly floured surface

6. Shape dough into a loose ball and divide in half

7. PLASTIC WRAP Wrap in plastic and chill

Figure 15-1: How to make pie dough by hand.

How to Roll Dough

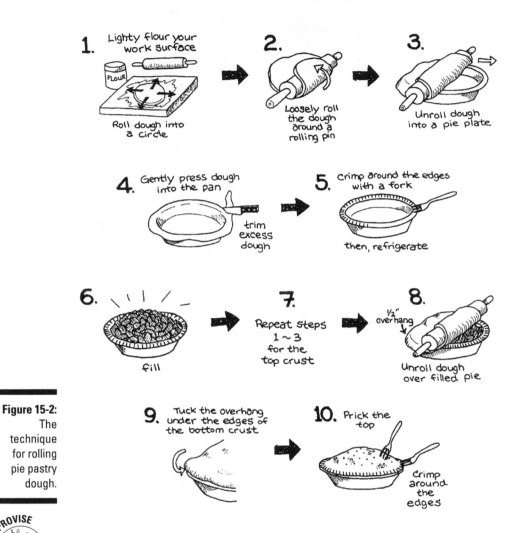

1. Lightly flour your work surface

Roll dough into a circle

2. Loosely roll the dough around a rolling pin

3. Unroll dough into a pie plate

4. Gently press dough into the pan

trim excess dough

5. Crimp around the edges with a fork

then, refrigerate

6. fill

7. Repeat steps 1~3 for the top crust

8. ½" overhang

Unroll dough over filled pie

9. Tuck the overhang under the edges of the bottom crust

10. Prick the top

Crimp around the edges

Figure 15-2:
The technique for rolling pie pastry dough.

Variations to this pastry crust include the following:

- **Nuts:** Add ¼ cup (50 mL) ground pecans, hazelnuts, or walnuts to the flour mixture before you process or blend by hand.

- **Spice:** Add some cinnamon, allspice, or ginger to the flour.

- **Citrus:** Add 2 teaspoons (10 mL) of lemon or orange zest to the flour.

- **Sweet:** Add 1 tablespoon (15 mL) sugar to the flour-salt mixture.

✔ **Single-crust pie:** If you are making a pie without a top crust, cover the pie shell with aluminum foil and pour dried beans or other weights inside, as shown in Figure 15-3. Bake the crust for 15 minutes in a 400° F (200° C) oven; then lower the heat to 350° F (180° C) and bake another 10 minutes. Be careful that the crust does not get too brown.

For a Single Crust

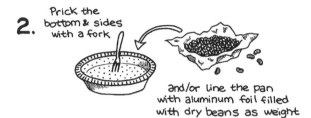

Figure 15-3: Preparing dough for a single crust.

1. Follow "How to Roll Dough," steps 1 ~ 5

2. Prick the bottom & sides with a fork and/or line the pan with aluminum foil filled with dry beans as weight

Remember these tips for rolling pastry dough:

✔ Work on a lightly floured counter or board. Dust the rolling pin and your dough *lightly* with flour, using a little more flour *only* if the dough sticks to the counter or the pin.

✔ Roll the dough from its center out to the edges and turn it frequently (about one quarter turn) to keep it from sticking to the counter.

✔ Try to work quickly so that the dough remains chilled. Room temperature dough is more difficult to roll.

✔ Run a long metal spatula under the dough to loosen it from the counter if necessary.

✔ Do not stretch the dough when transferring it from the counter to the pie plate.

Rolling dough is a skill that demands practice. Don't be discouraged if your pie crust looks like a relief map of Antarctica after your first try.

If your pastry starts to break apart as you roll it out, overlap and then roll over the edges to bring them together, moistening the edges first with a drop of water. If that doesn't work, reshape the pastry into a ball and roll again. But remember, the more you handle the pastry dough, the tougher it becomes.

The taste and texture of a homemade crust is superior to any packaged mix. But when you don't have the time to make the pastry yourself, using a box of pie crust mix or frozen pie shells is better than having no pie at all.

Apple Pie

Tools: *Paring knife, large bowl, 9-inch (23-cm) pie plate*

Preparation time: *About 30 minutes, plus time to prepare pie crust dough*

Cooking time: *About 1 hour*

6 medium apples (tart style is best), peeled, cored, and sliced about $^1/_2$-inch (12-mm) thick (see Figure 15-4)

$^3/_4$ cup (175 mL) sugar

2 tablespoons (30 mL) flour

1 tablespoon (15 mL) fresh lemon juice

$^1/_2$ teaspoon (2 mL) grated lemon peel

$^3/_4$ teaspoon (1 mL) cinnamon

$^1/_8$ teaspoon (0.5 mL) nutmeg

9-inch (23-cm) pie plate covered with pastry dough plus 1 uncooked sheet of pastry dough, about 11 inches (28 cm) in diameter (see preceding recipe)

1 tablespoon (15 mL) butter

2 tablespoons (30 mL) (more or less) milk or water (optional)

1 teaspoon (5 mL) (more or less) sugar (optional)

1 Preheat oven to 450° F (230° C).

2 Combine apples, sugar, flour, lemon juice, lemon peel, cinnamon, and nutmeg in a large bowl. Toss gently to coat apples with sugar and seasonings.

3 Fill the uncooked pie shell with the apple mixture. Dot the butter over the filling in small pieces. Fit the top crust over the apples, trim off excess, and crimp edges firmly, as in Figure 15-2. (You may want to lightly brush the bottom rim first with water, which helps to keep the edges tightly sealed as the pie bakes.)

4 Prick the top crust several times with a fork to provide a vent for steam to escape. (For a shiny crust, use a pastry brush to brush the crust lightly with milk or water and then sprinkle 1 teaspoon/5 mL sugar over it.)

5 Bake for 15 minutes. Reduce heat to 350° F (180° C) and bake another 45 minutes or until the pie is brown and bubbly. Cool the pie for at least 20 minutes before serving.

Yield: *6 to 8 servings.*

Peeling and Coring an Apple

Figure 15-4: You peel and core apples before slicing them into a pie.

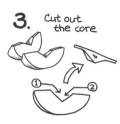

You can replicate the basic filling technique for this apple pie with other fruits, such as peaches, strawberries, apricots, and berries. You may want to vary the seasonings, but the idea is essentially the same. Pick a fruit and think about how to enhance it. For example, you may want to toss peaches with sugar, vanilla extract, and maybe a touch of rum. For pears, you can use sugar, cinnamon, maybe clove, and, if you like, vanilla extract. A dash of rum or brandy doesn't hurt, either. Adding $1/4$ cup (50 mL) brown sugar gives the filling a slightly caramelized flavor.

You also can use the basic pie crust for individual ramekins (single-serving, porcelain baking dishes) and fill them with fruits. The cooking time is less, of course — approximately half the cooking time for a 9-inch (23-cm) pie.

If You Have One Hour

One hour is actually a good chunk of time in which to put together a meal — that is, if you are organized, have all the shopping done, and can focus without interruptions. One phone call can throw off your pace.

Which apples are best for baking?

Tart, crisp apples that hold their shape are best for pie-making. Fall or early winter is the ideal time to bake an apple pie because the apple crop is fresh. With the exception of Granny Smiths (tart, green apples from Australia and New Zealand that are available all year), apples found in markets in the spring and summer have been stored since the fall harvest and do not have the same taste or texture as fresh apples.

The following varieties are among the best for baking in pies: Baldwin, Cortland, Granny Smith, Gravenstein, Jonathan, Macoun, Newtown Pippin, Northern Spy, Rhode Island Greening, Rome Beauty, and Winesap.

So don't be tempted to run out to the mailbox, and do think in advance about how long each dish needs at each stage so that one doesn't burn while another is still cold, and they all make it to the table on cue.

To help you concentrate on the task at hand and bring that meal down the runway within 60 minutes, here are a few tips:

- ✔ Ignore howling kids trying to get your attention (unless excessive bleeding is evident).
- ✔ Don't try to channel surf while you cook.
- ✔ Eschew any "Honey, I'm home!" chitchat with your significant other. Tell him or her that you'll be able to chat over dinner.
- ✔ Ignore pesky neighbors, no matter how many times they rap on your windows. You don't have time for idle socializing.
- ✔ Don't try to be doubly efficient by trying to cook and do laundry at the same time. You're apt to toss a shirt into your soup and a pork loin in the dryer.

Starter dishes

You can take a lot of heat off the situation by starting with a good mixed salad. A balanced vinaigrette is the fuel that energizes a salad, as in the following recipe.

Mixed Summer Salad with Balsamic Vinegar Dressing

Tools: *Chef's knife, small mixing bowl*

Preparation time: *About 25 minutes, plus 1 hour (more or less) to let dressing stand*

Dressing

¹/₂ cup (125 mL) olive oil

3 tablespoons (45mL) balsamic vinegar (Imitation balsamic vinegar is fine.)

¹/₃ cup (75 mL) peeled and finely chopped shallots

1 clove garlic, peeled and cut crosswise in half

Salt and freshly ground pepper to taste

Prepare the salad dressing at least 1 hour in advance and let stand at room temperature. Combine the oil, vinegar, shallots, garlic pieces, and salt and pepper in a bowl. Cover and let stand. Before serving, discard the garlic pieces. Covered leftover salad dressing keeps in the refrigerator for weeks.

(continued)

Salad

This slightly tart combination of endive and radicchio is a refreshing starter. You can jazz it up with other lettuce or roasted sweet peppers.

20 Belgian endive leaves, rinsed and dried

4 radicchio leaves, rinsed and dried

4 cups (1 L) rinsed, dried, loosely packed arugula or corn-salad leaves

1 Arrange 5 endive lettuce leaves, spoke-fashion, on each of 4 large dinner plates. Arrange 1 radicchio leaf in the center of each plate.

2 Put equal portions of arugula or corn-salad leaves in the center of the radicchio leaves. Spoon as much salad dressing as desired over the leaves and serve.

Yield: 4 servings.

Coarsely chop 1 large ripe tomato and divide among the plates, or add 4 to 5 cooked shrimp to each serving.

Here's another simple, colorful salad that you can serve if you have one hour to prepare a meal.

Avocado and Tomato Salad

Tools: *Chef's knife, paring knife, salad bowl*

Preparation time: *About 25 minutes*

Cooking time: *About 15 minutes (to hard-cook eggs)*

2 ripe avocados

4 ripe plum tomatoes

2 hard-cooked eggs, peeled and quartered (see Chapter 8 for recipe)

1 small red onion, peeled and cut into thin slices

¹/₄ cup (50 mL) coarsely chopped fresh coriander

2 teaspoons (10 mL) peeled and finely chopped garlic, about 2 large cloves

6 tablespoons (90 mL) olive oil

2 tablespoons (30 mL) red wine vinegar

¹/₂ teaspoon (2 mL) ground cumin

Salt and freshly ground pepper to taste

1 Peel the avocados and cut them in half. Discard the pit and cut each half into 4 lengthwise slices. Cut the slices into large cubes.

(continued)

2 Core the tomatoes and cut them into 1-inch (2.5-cm) cubes.

3 Toss the cubes of avocado and tomato with all the remaining ingredients in a salad bowl and serve.

Yield: 4 servings.

Or you may want to try one of these starter dishes if you have an hour:

- Garlic-Grilled Mushrooms (see Chapter 6)
- Smoked Trout with Watercress Sauce (see Chapter 7)
- Carrot Soup with Dill (see Chapter 9)
- Baked Shrimp with Scallion Bread Crumbs (see Chapter 12)

Main dish choices

You use either of the French aperitifs Ricard and Pernod, based on anise, in the following recipe to give the sauce a refreshing lift.

Making and storing dressings

To save the time and effort of making a vinaigrette every time you need one, try making a large batch and storing it in empty wine bottles. Start with 2 tablespoons (30 mL) or more of Dijon-style mustard and lots of salt and freshly ground pepper in a mixing bowl. Add olive oil in a slow stream while whisking. Every once in a while, whisk in vinegar (roughly a 5-to-2 ratio of oil to vinegar). Taste constantly. When you like the results, pour the dressing into the bottle with a funnel. If you like, add fresh herbs or minced garlic to the bottle. Shake, seal with a cork, and refrigerate.

The exotic flavors of anise, turmeric, and fennel

Anise, which tastes something like licorice, is one of those flavors that people either love or find cloying, like candy. When used in moderation, anise can add a lovely Provençale accent to dishes made with tomato. Anise extract comes from the anise plant, which is popular in Italy and parts of France.

Turmeric is technically a member of the ginger family, although it must be the black sheep of that clan, for it tastes nothing like ginger — it is somewhat pungent but otherwise not distinctive. In ancient times, turmeric was used as a dye as well as a spice. Today, turmeric is used for flavor as well as to color (it has a wonderful orange-yellow hue). Turmeric is often added to dishes with saffron for color purposes.

With its tall, pale stalks, fennel looks something like celery, except that its base is a beautiful round bulb. Trim away the pale green stalks. Eat only the delicious licorice-like bulb — raw, boiled, sautéed, or braised.

Snapper Fillets with Tomatoes and Anise

Tools: *Chef's knife, paring knife, medium saucepan, sauté pan with lid*

Preparation time: *About 30 minutes*

Cooking time: *About 15 minutes*

2 tablespoons (30 mL) olive oil

2 cups (500 mL) peeled and chopped fresh plum tomatoes, about 5 tomatoes

1 large leek, white part only, finely chopped, about 1 cup (250 mL)

1/2 cup (125 mL) rinsed and chopped fennel

2 teaspoons (10 mL) peeled and finely chopped garlic, about 2 large cloves

1 teaspoon (5 mL) turmeric

Salt and freshly ground pepper to taste

1/2 cup (125 mL) dry white wine

1/2 cup (125 mL) fish broth or bottled clam juice

1 bay leaf

4 sprigs fresh thyme, or 1 teaspoon (5 mL) dried

1/8 teaspoon (0.5 mL) Tabasco sauce

4 snapper fillets with skin on, or other firm, white-fleshed fish, about 6 ounces (168 g) each

2 tablespoons (30 mL) Ricard, Pernod, or anise-flavored liquor

2 tablespoons (30 mL) chopped fresh basil or parsley

1 In a medium saucepan over medium heat, combine 1 tablespoon (15 mL) of the olive oil and the tomatoes, leeks, fennel, garlic, and turmeric. Season with salt and pepper to taste. Cook, stirring, about 3 minutes. Add the wine, broth, bay leaf, thyme, and Tabasco. Bring to a boil and simmer for 5 minutes.

(continued)

2 In a large sauté pan, add the remaining tablespoon (15 mL) of oil and arrange the fillets of fish in one layer, skin side down. Season with salt and pepper. Pour the leek-tomato mixture evenly over the fish fillets. Sprinkle the Ricard or Pernod, cover, and cook over medium heat for about 5 minutes until the fish is done. (The exact cooking time depends on the thickness of the fillets.) Discard bay leaf and sprinkle with basil or parsley before serving.

Yield: 4 servings.

If you have a barbecue grill, you can cook the following herb-perfumed steak over charcoal. We admit to cheating a little with this next recipe, asking you to (ideally) marinate this meat for eight hours or overnight. But if you are really time-pressed, marinate the steak for as much time as you have; you still get some of the marinade's flavor. The rest of the recipe is really quick.

Grilled Flank Steak with Rosemary and Sage

Tools: *Chef's knife, large bowl or roasting pan, oven broiler or grill*

Preparation time: *About 20 minutes, plus marinating time*

Cooking time: *About 10 minutes*

¹/₂ cup (125 mL) red wine

¹/₂ cup (125 mL) olive oil

¹/₂ cup (125 mL) minced fresh sage leaves

¹/₃ cup (75 mL) minced fresh rosemary leaves

2 cloves peeled and minced garlic

Grated peel of one large orange

1 tablespoon (15 mL) whole black peppercorns, crushed (see Chapter 4 for instructions)

Salt to taste

2 pounds (1 kg) flank steak, trimmed for grilling

1 In a large bowl or high-sided roasting pan, combine all the ingredients except the meat. Add the flank steak, turning the meat in the marinade to coat both sides. Cover with plastic wrap and marinate in the refrigerator overnight, or for about 8 hours.

2 Before cooking, preheat your grill or broiler. If grilling, cook for about 4 to 5 minutes per side for medium rare (depends on thickness). If broiling, place meat about 6 inches (15 cm) from the heat source and broil about 4 to 5 minutes per side and then check. Let the steak rest for 5 minutes before slicing.

Yield: 4 to 6 servings.

ESSENTIAL SKILL

Buying flank steak

Flank steak, according to our butcher, is "the fibrous muscle located on the inside wall of the whole beef flank." All you really need to know is that flank steak is short and on the thick side with a little fat on both sides. Have your butcher trim it. Flank steaks are particularly juicy and best when marinated and grilled or broiled. Do not buy flank steaks that are elongated and thin — these are as tough as a leather chair and have little flavor.

This zesty skirt steak dish is an alternative to flank steak. Adjust the seasonings to taste.

Broiled Skirt Steak, Cajun Style

Tools: *Chef's knife, mixing bowl, broiler or grill*

Preparation time: *About 35 minutes, including marinating time*

Cooking time: *About 10 minutes, including standing time*

4 skirt steaks, $^1/_2$ pound (250 g) each	$^1/_2$ teaspoon (2 mL) dried thyme
Salt to taste	$^1/_4$ teaspoon (1 mL) cayenne pepper
2 tablespoons (30 mL) olive oil	$^1/_4$ teaspoon (1 mL) freshly ground pepper
1 teaspoon (5 mL) chili powder	2 tablespoons (30 mL) butter
$^1/_2$ teaspoon (2 mL) ground cumin	2 tablespoons (30 mL) finely chopped fresh parsley

1 Half an hour before broiling or grilling, sprinkle the steaks with salt. Blend well the oil, chili powder, cumin, thyme, cayenne, and pepper in a bowl. Brush this mixture all over the steaks. Cover the steaks with plastic wrap but do not refrigerate.

2 Preheat the broiler to high or preheat the grill.

(continued)

3 If broiling, arrange the steaks on a rack and place under the broiler about 6 inches (15 cm) from the heat source. Broil for 3 minutes with the door partly open. Turn the steaks and continue broiling, leaving the door partly open. Broil for about 3 minutes more or to the desired degree of doneness.

If grilling, put the steaks on a very hot grill and cover. Cook for 3 minutes. Turn the steaks, cover, and cook about 3 minutes more or to the desired degree of doneness.

4 Transfer the steaks to a hot platter and dot with butter. Let them stand in a warm place for 5 minutes to redistribute the internal juices, which accumulate as the steaks stand.

5 Sprinkle with parsley and serve with the accumulated butter sauce.

Yield: 4 servings.

Skirt steak

Skirt steak, formerly unknown to home cooks and now a fashionable cut of meat in restaurants, goes by many names, including hanger steak, oyster steak, and butcher steak. The last name arose because butchers traditionally kept these exceptionally juicy and flavorful cuts for themselves.

If you know how to cook a skirt steak, it can be delicious and far less expensive (and leaner) than sirloins or fillets. The skirt steak comes from the pad of muscle that runs from the rib cage toward the loin (see beef chart in Chapter 13). It is usually sold in sections of about 12 ounces (375 g) each and has a thin, silvery membrane that the butcher should remove.

Because skirt steak contains a lot of moisture, it should be cooked very fast over high heat to sear. For that reason, you should let the steak reach room temperature before broiling or grilling. Also let the cooked steak sit for several minutes before slicing, so the juices can settle. Cut the steak on a bias across the fibrous muscle on a cutting board that can catch the runoff. *(Cutting on a bias* means slicing the meat at about a 45-degree angle to the cutting board — not perpendicular to the board as you would with a loaf of bread. Cutting on a bias gives you a larger, thinner slice for each portion.) Pour the juice back over the steak when serving, or use it in your sauce.

When you are trying to get everything together within an hour, you may want to serve a dish that finishes in the oven while you are doing other things, like panicking.

You also can try one of these main dishes if you have an hour:

- ✔ Braised Chicken Legs in Red Wine (see Chapter 5)
- ✔ Grilled Brochettes of Pork with Rosemary (see Chapter 6)
- ✔ Frittata with Sweet Peppers and Potatoes (see Chapter 8)
- ✔ Fettuccine with Goat Cheese and Asparagus (see Chapter 11)
- ✔ Rigatoni with Eggplant and Summer Squash (see Chapter 11)

Side dishes

The following colorful combination goes perfectly with steak. The dish is so easy and appealing that it could tempt anyone to flirt with vegetarianism. You can substitute summer squash, or even thin slices of eggplant, for the zucchini.

Roasted Zucchini and Tomatoes with Summer Herbs

Tools: *Chef's knife, medium saucepan or skillet, shallow ovenproof baking dish with lid*

Preparation time: *About 25 minutes*

Cooking time: *About 40 minutes*

3 tablespoons (45 mL) olive oil

1 large onion, peeled and thinly sliced

1 tablespoon (15 mL) peeled and minced garlic, about 3 large cloves

1 tablespoon (15 mL) chopped fresh sage, or 1 teaspoon (5 mL) dried

1 tablespoon (15 mL) chopped fresh rosemary leaves, or 1 teaspoon (5 mL) dried

2 teaspoons (10 mL) chopped fresh basil leaves, or 1 teaspoon (5 mL) dried

1¹/₂ pounds (750 g) zucchini, trimmed and sliced into ¹/₄-inch (6-mm) rounds

Salt and freshly ground pepper to taste

3 ripe red tomatoes, sliced ¹/₄-inch (6-mm) thick

¹/₃ cup (75 mL) grated Parmesan cheese

1 Preheat oven to 375° F (190° C).

2 In a medium saucepan or skillet over medium heat, add 2 tablespoons (30 mL) of the olive oil, the onion, garlic, and half the herbs. Cook, stirring, for about 3 minutes (do not let the garlic brown). Remove the onions and garlic to a shallow ovenproof baking dish.

(continued)

3 In the same skillet, add the remaining tablespoon (15 mL) of olive oil, the zucchini, remaining herbs, and salt and pepper. Cook, stirring, for about 5 minutes.

4 Place the zucchini in the baking dish and blend well with the onions. Lay the tomatoes over the zucchini in a decorative fashion. Sprinkle the Parmesan cheese over everything.

5 Cover and bake for about 20 minutes. Remove cover and bake 10 minutes more.

Yield: 4 servings.

This exotic-tasting rice goes well with any steak or poultry dish as long as the sauce does not contain the same seasonings.

Ginger Rice with Fresh Coriander

Tools: Chef's knife, medium saucepan or sauté pan, grater

Preparation time: About 15 minutes

Cooking time: About 20 minutes

2 tablespoons (30 mL) butter

$^1/_4$ cup (50 mL) peeled and finely chopped onion

1 teaspoon (5 mL) peeled and grated fresh ginger

$^1/_4$ teaspoon (1 mL) red pepper flakes, or to taste

1 cup (250 mL) converted rice

$1^3/_4$ cups (425 mL) fresh or canned chicken or vegetable broth, heated to just below boiling

Salt to taste, if desired

3 tablespoons (45 mL) finely chopped fresh coriander leaves

1 Heat the butter in a saucepan over medium heat. Add the onion and cook, stirring, until the onion is wilted. Add the ginger and pepper flakes. Cook, stirring, for about 30 seconds. Stir in the rice. Carefully add the hot chicken broth. Season with salt, if desired.

2 Cover and simmer 20 minutes or until the rice is tender. Stir in coriander just before serving.

Yield: 3 to 4 servings.

If you have one hour, you also can try any of the side dishes listed in the "If You Have All Day" section.

Desserts

A warm sauce to go over ice cream, puddings, pastries, or even a simple pound cake is a quick but elegant dessert. This basic technique works for all fresh berries.

Warm Blueberry Sauce

Tools: *Paring knife, saucepan, wire whisk*

Preparation time: *About 10 minutes*

Cooking time: *About 7 minutes*

¹/₃ cup (75 mL) granulated sugar

1 tablespoon (15 mL) cornstarch

Pinch of salt

³/₄ cup (175 mL) water

2 teaspoons (10 mL) fresh lemon juice

1 cup (250 mL) ripe blueberries, rinsed and stems removed

2 tablespoons (30 mL) unsalted butter, softened

¹/₄ teaspoon (2 mL) ground cinnamon, or to taste

1 In a saucepan, combine well the sugar, cornstarch, and salt. Add the water and lemon juice and cook over medium-high heat, stirring, until the mixture thickens, about 5 minutes. (Whisk, if necessary, to break up any lumps.)

2 Add the blueberries and lower the heat to medium, stirring frequently for 1 minute. Remove the pan from the heat and add the butter and cinnamon. Stir well. Keep warm in a double boiler or over very low heat until served. Stir well before serving.

Yield: *About 1 cup.*

If You Have 30 Minutes

What can you do in 30 minutes? Half an aerobics class? Almost wash the car? Watch the first part of *60 Minutes?* Not much fun, huh? But you can prepare a meal in this time if you follow our approach.

The good news is that you don't have to worry too much about orchestrating your time; the bad news is that's because you'll be doing everything at once. Before you dive in, give some thought to what tasks, if any, you can combine. Chop all the vegetables together, for example. Do two of your dishes call for celery? Prepare enough for both at one time. Another key time-saver is to have all your materials out and ready before you begin so that you don't get thrown off track mid-menu trying to locate the darn marjoram.

Putting a meal on the table in 30 minutes also often means that you have to rely on certain store-bought goods for help and gives your timesaving gadgets in the kitchen a real workout. But in the end, you have a real meal.

The following recipes are meant to steer you into a certain way of thinking when the clock's incessant ticking is following you all over the house and your guests will be arriving in no time.

Starter dishes

In France, tartines are open-faced sandwiches that can be topped with cheese, meats, fish, or whatever. This tasty version calls for goat cheese and olive oil and couldn't be easier. These tidbits are superb with red wine. (See *Wine For Dummies* for more information about pairing food with wine.)

Garlic and Goat Cheese Tartines

Tools: *Toaster oven (optional), bread knife*

Preparation time: *About 10 minutes*

Cooking time: *Less than a minute*

¹/₂ loaf French or Italian bread, sliced into ¹/₄-inch (6-mm) pieces

3 cloves garlic, peeled and split

¹/₄ cup (50 mL) olive oil (about)

Salt and freshly ground pepper to taste

8 ounces (250 g) fresh goat cheese

3 sprigs fresh rosemary, thyme, or sage, coarsely chopped

1 In a toaster oven or preheated 400° F (220° C) oven, toast the bread slices until they just begin to turn golden, no more. Let the bread cool.

(continued)

2 Rub the bread on both sides with the garlic. Drizzle about ¹/₂ teaspoon (2 mL) olive oil over one side of each slice. Lightly salt and pepper the same side.

3 Spread goat cheese over the slices and garnish with chopped fresh herbs.

Yield: 6 to 8 servings.

And with a little practice, you can knock off any of these appetizers in minutes:

- ✔ **White fish bites:** Serve store-bought white fish salad on toasted bagel chips topped with sprig of fresh dill or chopped black olives.

- ✔ **Hummus dip:** Whirl in a blender until smooth a 16-ounce (398 mL) can of drained chickpeas, 1 clove garlic, ¹/₄ cup (50 mL) sesame seeds, the juice and grated peel of 1 lemon, and ¹/₂ cup (125 mL) water, and salt and freshly ground pepper to taste. Serve on triangles of toasted pita or with assorted vegetable crudités.

- ✔ **Sweet mustard chicken kebobs:** Thread thin strips of boneless chicken and cherry tomatoes on skewers (if skewers are wooden, soak them first for half an hour in water); grill or broil about 2 minutes a side or until done, brushing at the last minute with store-bought honey mustard. Serve hot.

- ✔ **Guacamole:** Mash in a small bowl the flesh from two medium, ripe avocados. Add 1 small, finely chopped onion, 1 ripe finely chopped tomato, 2 tablespoons (30 mL) chopped coriander leaves, half a jalapeño chili, seeded and minced, and the juice and grated peel of half a lemon. Season with salt and pepper and serve with blue or white corn chips.

- ✔ **Sun-dried tomato spread:** Whirl sun-dried tomatoes, garlic, and onions in a food processor or blender container with enough oil to moisten into a coarse spread. Season with white pepper. Serve on Melba toast rounds.

- ✔ **Spicy shrimp:** Marinate boiled or grilled shrimp for about 30 minutes in a lemon-vinaigrette dressing spiced with red pepper flakes, Tabasco sauce, or Szechuan-style hot and spicy oil.

- ✔ **Shrimp poached in beer and dill:** Combine in a pot enough beer to cover your shrimp. Add fresh dill, garlic, dried thyme, and salt and pepper. Bring to a boil and cook the shelled and deveined shrimp for about 45 seconds or until done. Drain and serve with melted dill butter.

- ✔ **Smoked chicken slices with coriander sauce:** You can buy smoked chicken and slice it into bite-sized strips, serving the strips over thin slices of French or Italian bread. Brush with a basic vinaigrette seasoned with fresh chopped coriander, and, if you like, a dash of Tabasco sauce.

Main dish choices

Grilling fish makes sense when you have only minutes to prepare dinner for guests. Maybe we're cheating a little, but this dish of broiled porgies calls for herbed olive oil instead of a time-consuming sauce. Making herbed oils at home is easy. All you do is put fresh stalks of herbs plus a few cloves of peeled garlic and peppercorns in a bottle. If you don't have a bottle, pour olive oil into a mixing bowl along with the seasoning ingredients. Let them stand all day or for as much time as you have. Store any leftover herb-flavored oil in the refrigerator.

The oil called for in this next recipe is flavored with rosemary (see Figure 15-5), although most any fresh herb oil will do. To fully release the flavor of the herb, crush the rosemary leaves between your fingers before adding them to the oil. The rosemary doesn't take long to perfume the oil with its distinctive flavor. This dish is simple, elegant, and above all, *fast.*

Figure 15-5:
A cruet of
rosemary
oil.

Broiled Porgies with Rosemary Olive Oil

Tools: *Chef's knife, broiler*

Preparation time: *About 15 minutes, plus time to make rosemary oil*

Cooking time: *About 10 minutes*

4 fillets of fresh porgies, sea bass, tilefish, snapper, or other firm, white-fleshed fish, each fillet about 6 ounces (168 g)

Salt and freshly ground pepper to taste

Rosemary oil (see preceding text for instructions)

4 lemon wedges

4 sprigs fresh rosemary for garnish

(continued)

1 Preheat the broiler.

2 Sprinkle the fillets with salt and pepper and brush them on both sides with rosemary oil.

3 Place the fillets on a broiler tray, skin side down, about 4 to 5 inches (10 to 13 cm) from the heat source. Broil for about 4 minutes or until lightly browned. Flip the fish gently, brush again with the oil, and cook another 4 to 5 minutes, or until done. Serve with lemon wedges and a cruet (or small bottle) of the rosemary oil for those who want more oil. Garnish with sprigs of fresh rosemary.

Yield: 4 servings.

Shop and platter: The art of antipasto

When you barely have time to shop, much less prepare a full meal, knowing how to buy and assemble prepared foods into an attractive spread is an invaluable skill. As a source of inspiration, we recommend an Italian approach that calls for serving an array of cheeses, meats, breads, olives, and vegetables on a large platter.

Assembling an Italian *antipasto* is 90 percent presentation. Think about how the tastes and colors contrast. Antipasto is traditionally served as the appetizer course, but there's no reason you can't make a meal of it. Here is an incomplete list of choices for an antipasto platter that you can purchase just minutes before your guests arrive — that is, if you catch all the green lights on the way home from the market.

✔ Mozzarella, provolone, fontina, Parmesan, or goat cheese (cubed or thinly sliced)

✔ Thinly sliced ham, prosciutto, and Genoa salami

✔ Rounds of pepperoni or sopressata salami

✔ Thin slices of *mortadella* (a garlic-flavored bologna) or *capicola* (made from cured pork)

✔ Cooked shrimp (best if tossed in a vinaigrette dressing)

✔ Canned anchovies, sardines, or tuna packed in olive oil

✔ Canned chickpeas tossed in vinaigrette dressing (you need to make the dressing)

✔ Sun-dried tomatoes in oil

✔ Marinated artichoke hearts, roasted red peppers, and capers

✔ Assorted black and green olives

✔ Assorted fresh vegetables like radishes with tops; carrot, celery, cucumber, and pepper sticks; pieces of fennel; scallions; and whole red or yellow cherry tomatoes

✔ Arugula, basil leaves, and radicchio for garnishing

✔ Sliced ripe pears, melon, figs, or small bunches of grapes

✔ Flavored breads, breadsticks, flatbreads, and warmed Boboli (a flat bread that resembles a thick pizza crust)

(continued)

(continued)

If you have only about 30 minutes, you also can try any of these main dishes:

- Salmon Steaks with Sweet Red Pepper Sauce (see Chapter 4)
- Sea Scallops Provençale (see Chapter 4)
- Sautéed Chicken Breasts with Tomatoes and Thyme (see Chapter 4)
- Mustard-Brushed Barbecued Chicken Breasts (see Chapter 6)
- Chicken Breasts with Garlic and Capers (see Chapter 7)
- Omelets or Frittatas (see Chapter 8)
- Spaghetti with Quick Fresh Tomato Sauce (see Chapter 11)
- Bacon and Cheese Strata (see Chapter 12)
- Turkey Burgers with Quick Caper Sauce (see Chapter 16)

Quick sauces

Keeping a few versatile sauces on hand in the refrigerator for last-minute meals or unexpected guests is a good idea. Following is a sauce that is perfect over grilled fish or poultry or cold, poached chicken. Another good choice is the Watercress Sauce in Chapter 7.

Creamy Mustard Sauce

Tools: *Chef's knife, small mixing bowl*

Preparation time: *About 10 minutes*

1 cup (250 mL) plain yogurt or sour cream

1¹/₂ tablespoons (22 mL) Dijon-style mustard

1 tablespoon (15 mL) minced scallions

Salt and freshly ground pepper to taste

Combine all the ingredients in a small bowl and mix to blend well. Cover and chill in the refrigerator. This sauce lasts a week or more.

Yield: *About 1 cup (250 mL).*

Side dishes

If you want to serve a side dish but time is running short, quickly cook frozen corn, which can be quite good. Frozen lima beans are another option. Or if you have someone to help you chop and trim a few vegetables, try the following colorful vegetable sauté that cooks in minutes. You can use this same technique to cook zucchini, green beans, mushrooms, thinly sliced carrots, broccoli florets, or any number of tender vegetables that you find fresh and in season at your market.

Quick Vegetable Sauté

Tools: *Chef's knife, large nonstick skillet*

Preparation time: *About 15 minutes*

Cooking time: *About 6 minutes*

1 pound (500 g) asparagus

1 medium yellow squash

2 tablespoons (30 mL) olive oil

1 small onion, peeled and diced

2 ripe Italian plum tomatoes, cored and cut into wedges

1 clove peeled and thinly sliced garlic

2 tablespoons (30 mL) chopped fresh basil or marjoram, or 2 teaspoons (10 mL) dried

Grated peel and juice of half a lemon

Salt and freshly ground pepper to taste

1 Rinse and trim the asparagus, breaking off the woody stems at their natural snapping point, about 2 inches (5 cm) from the thick end. Slice the spears into 2-inch (5-cm) long pieces.

2 Rinse the squash, trim off the ends, and cut into ¹/₄-inch (6-mm) rounds.

3 Heat the olive oil in a large nonstick skillet over high heat. Add the asparagus, squash, and onion and cook 2 to 3 minutes, stirring often.

4 Add the plum tomatoes, garlic, chopped basil or marjoram, lemon juice, and grated peel and cook 2 to 3 minutes more or until the vegetables are tender but still slightly crisp. Season with salt and pepper before serving.

Yield: *4 servings.*

You also can try one of these quick side dishes:

- ✔ Steamed Broccoli (see Chapter 3)
- ✔ Sautéed Spinach Leaves (see Chapter 4)
- ✔ Mixed Green Salad with Red Onion (see Chapter 10)
- ✔ Any of the ten quick salads from Chapter 10
- ✔ Francesco Antonucci's Spaghetti with Tuna (see Chapter 11)

Desserts

As for dessert, you have little choice aside from fresh fruit and ice cream. You can make a nice, quick ice cream sauce with frozen strawberries (or fresh, of course, if they're in season). See Chapter 7 for a recipe for Fresh Strawberry Sauce. The Caramel Sauce from Chapter 7 is also great with ice cream.

If you have 30 minutes, you also can try sweetened Whipped Cream (see Chapter 7).

Chapter 16

Parties of One: Solo Shopping and Dining

*S**haring food is an intimate act that should not be indulged in lightly.*

— M. F. K. Fisher

Although the esteemed writer M. F. K. Fisher often dined alone by preference, most people dine alone by necessity. Fisher makes solo dining sound like a transcendental experience. To most other people, dining alone is as uplifting as a tax audit.

That feeling arises because many people don't know *how* to enjoy cooking and dining alone, either at home or in a restaurant. This chapter aims to help you overcome that barrier.

The Pitfalls of Eating Alone

Dining alone is often unavoidable. To make your solo dining experience as pleasant and palatable as possible, we offer the following suggestions:

✔ Defrosting a dish of frozen ravioli and eating it while leaning over the sink may be fun the first few times, but before long, your lower back will begin to give out, and worse, you'll start to feel uneasy about eating like a refugee.

✔ Eating enormous quantities of bread may fill you temporarily, but by bedtime, you'll have a cottony, full-but-not-full feeling.

✔ Picking at tuna fish from the can while watching *Family Feud* has nutritional value — that is, if you don't choke on it. Moreover, you'll drive your cat insane.

✔ Wolfing down a big bowl of Wheaties sates hunger pangs. Problem is, the next morning you're not able to face cereal, thus throwing off your pacing for the week.

✔ Frantically rummaging through the freezer tearing open aluminum foil packages is a bad idea. If you have forgotten what they contain, they're probably calcified.

✔ Devouring a pint of Häagen-Dazs in bed is perfectly fine.

But does dining alone need to be so awful? Not really, especially if you learn to enjoy preparing a quick and balanced meal — maybe leaving enough to make a variation the next day.

Spontaneous Cooking for One

The key to successful cooking for one is having an adequately stocked pantry (see Chapter 13). That way, you can pick up a main ingredient on the way home (chicken, steak, fish fillets, fresh vegetables, or whatever) and round out the meal from your kitchen provisions. Or in a worst-case scenario, when you have no time to shop, you can always throw together something civilized from items on hand.

Walk through a typical scenario. You leave work at 5:30 p.m. and join some colleagues for cocktails at Ricky's Recovery Room. At about 7 p.m., after your hints that everyone go out to dinner fall on deaf ears, you drive home.

At the front door, you're greeted by Sal, your cat, who is visibly miffed over your preprandial delay. You feed him immediately, envying his modest gastronomic needs. Now what?

Suppose you have chicken breasts left over from the weekend, a little bit of fresh broccoli, and some onions and pasta. You may not realize that you have a fine meal on hand. Here's what you might do:

1. Place a large pot of lightly salted water on high heat and bring to a boil.

2. Sauté one-quarter of an onion (chopped) in 2 tablespoons (30 mL) olive oil in a large skillet or saucepan until it wilts. Add ½ teaspoon (2 mL) dried thyme and salt and pepper. If you have garlic, peel and mince 2 cloves and add that to the onions. Stir and cook for another minute.

3. Open a small can of whole plum tomatoes and place 2 tomatoes and a few tablespoons (15 mL measures) of the packing juice in the pan. Break up the tomatoes in the pan with a fork. Add some broccoli florets (split the stems first so they cook faster). Cook, covered, over low heat for 5 minutes, stirring occasionally. If the sauce gets too dry, open a can of chicken or vegetable stock and add ¹/₄ cup (50 mL).

4. Cook the pasta in the boiling water until al dente — ¹/₄ or ¹/₃ pound (125 to 167 g) of pasta should suffice, depending on when your last meal was. When the pasta is cooked, drain it and then add it to the saucepan. Toss to coat well and serve.

While the pasta is cooking, slice a chicken breast (actually, one-half of the whole two-sided breast) into ¹/₄-inch (6-mm) strips. Season with salt and pepper and cook in a hot, lightly oiled nonstick pan. Toss until golden brown and cooked through, about 5 minutes. Lay the strips over the pasta.

The technique of sautéing onions and garlic and then adding canned tomatoes lends itself to all kinds of variations:

- Add cut-up cooked vegetables such as fresh asparagus, broccoli rape, mustard greens, arugula, snow peas, wild mushrooms, cauliflower, fennel, green beans, zucchini, or sautéed eggplant after the onions cook.

- Give the sauce a smooth finish by stirring in a few tablespoons (15mL measures) of ricotta cheese at the end of cooking.

- Add cubes of cooked sweet or hot sausage, chicken, turkey, pork, or beef along with the vegetables.

- Add cooked calamari, 10 minutes before finished, or cubes of codfish, swordfish, or any firm-fleshed white fish that holds together in the sauce, 5 minutes before finished.

- To vary the flavor, add hot red pepper flakes, capers, black olives, roasted sweet peppers, or jalapeño peppers after the onions cook.

TV Dinners

Few people have the patience and self-absorption to sit at a dining room table alone and dine, staring at the walls in eerie silence. Most solo diners divert themselves by reading, listening to the radio, doing crossword puzzles, or pretending that they are at the court of Louis XIV trading *bon mots* with counts and countesses. (Most of the latter, however, are hospitalized.)

For many people, television is the balm for solitude, an endless 24-hour smorgasbord of diversion and enlightenment. ("Your question for $500: If your wife were a tight-rope walker, what part of her body would most likely throw her off balance?")

Eating in front of the television, however, is not just a matter of pulling up a tray table and working the clicker. Engaging in these two entertaining activities at the same time requires strategy. It starts with menu planning. Following are a few TV dining tips:

- **Not all foods can be eaten easily while you are looking in another direction — for example, at a TV.** Take spaghetti, which is practically impossible to twirl and bring to your mouth without looking down at what you're doing. If you tried it while watching *Home Improvement,* chances are that most of the spaghetti would land on your lap.

  Other not-for-prime-time dishes include soup of any kind, Chinese stir-fries (especially with chopsticks), dinner salads, soupy stews, lima beans, peas, whole, roasted birds like Cornish hen, grilled pigs' feet, lobster in the shell, and duck à l'orange. Essentially, you should avoid anything that has to be cut, cracked, stabbed, picked, or plucked.

- **Stay away from fragile foods that get cold fast.** It is a scientific fact that those who eat while watching TV consume food more slowly than those sitting at a table.

- **Avoid aggressively spicy foods.** We're talking about Cajun-style fish, Mexican chilies, certain Tex-Mex firecrackers — that kind of stuff. You'll be dashing to the refrigerator for cold drinks every five minutes and miss much of the program.

So what does that leave to eat?

- Risotto (see Chapter 3)
- Salmon Steaks with Sweet Red Pepper Sauce (see Chapter 4)
- Grilled Swordfish Steaks with Lemon and Thyme (see Chapter 6)
- Pork Chops with Chervil Sauce (see Chapter 7)
- Fresh Tomato Gazpacho (see Chapter 9)
- Warm Shrimp Salad with Spinach (see Chapter 10)
- American Macaroni and Cheese (see Chapter 12)
- Beef and Turkey Meat Loaf (see Chapter 12)
- Shepherd's Pie (see Chapter 12)
- Broiled Skirt Steak, Cajun Style (see Chapter 15)

Egg-based dishes work well, too, specifically omelets, frittatas, and quiches. (See Chapter 8 for egg recipes.) Quiche seems to have been relegated to a carry-out food status, but the homemade version, warm from the oven, can be a real treat. This quick version uses a commercial pastry crust, which you can buy in the supermarket. Save any leftover quiche to eat the next day, either cold or reheated in a 325° F (160° C) oven for about 15 minutes.

Classic Quiche Lorraine

Tools: *Chef's knife, skillet, wire whisk, mixing bowl, baking sheet*

Preparation time: *About 20 minutes*

Cooking time: *About 50 minutes*

3 strips bacon

$^1/_4$ cup (50 mL) peeled and diced onion, about 1 small onion

9-inch (23-cm) frozen, commercial pie crust

$^1/_2$ cup (125 mL) cubed Gruyère or Swiss cheese

2 tablespoons (30 mL) grated Parmesan cheese (optional)

3 eggs, lightly beaten

$^1/_2$ cup (175 mL) heavy cream or half and half

$^1/_2$ cup (175 mL) milk

2 tablespoons (30 mL) minced fresh parsley

$^1/_4$ teaspoon (1 mL) grated or ground nutmeg

$^1/_4$ teaspoon (1 mL) salt, or to taste

$^1/_8$ teaspoon (0.5 mL) freshly ground white pepper, or to taste

1 Preheat the oven to 375° F (190° C).

2 Separate the strips of bacon and place in a large, prewarmed skillet over medium heat. Cook for about 3 to 4 minutes or until crisp, turning frequently. Remove and drain on paper towels. Pour off all but 1 tablespoon (15 mL) of fat from the pan. (Pour the fat into a metal can — not down the sink where it can clog the drain.) In the same pan, cook the onions over medium heat until they wilt.

3 Crumble the bacon and sprinkle it over the pie crust along with the onion and the cheese.

4 In a bowl, whisk together the eggs, cream, milk, parsley, nutmeg, and salt and pepper. Pour this mixture over the bacon, onions, and cheese. Place on a baking sheet and bake in the lower third of the oven for 45 to 50 minutes or until firm.

Yield: *4 servings.*

Quiche variations: Instead of bacon, add cooked cubed zucchini, summer squash, okra, chopped spinach, roasted sweet peppers, diced sautéed mushrooms, chopped sautéed leeks, cubed tomatoes sautéed with garlic and onions, cubed sautéed artichoke hearts, or blanched asparagus.

The following quick dish is similar to a hamburger but more flavorful. You can make this recipe with ground turkey, pork, chicken, or any combination of ground meat.

Turkey Burgers with Quick Caper Sauce

Tools: *Chef's knife, medium skillet, mixing bowl*

Preparation time: *About 15 minutes*

Cooking time: *About 15 minutes*

2 teaspoons (10 mL) butter

¹/₄ cup (50 mL) peeled and chopped onion, about 1 small onion

¹/₂ cup (175 mL) fresh bread crumbs

¹/₄ cup (50 mL) chicken broth or water

1 egg yolk (see instructions for separating an egg in Chapter 8)

1 tablespoon (15 mL) chopped fresh parsley, or 1 teaspoon (5 mL) dried

Dash of nutmeg

Salt and freshly ground pepper to taste

¹/₂ pound (250 g) ground turkey

1 tablespoon (15 mL) vegetable oil

Quick Caper Sauce (see following recipe)

1 In a medium skillet, melt the butter over medium heat. Add the onion and cook for 2 to 3 minutes or until wilted, stirring often. Set aside.

2 In a mixing bowl, combine the bread crumbs with the chicken broth. Stir in the cooked onion, egg yolk, parsley, nutmeg, and salt and pepper. Add the ground turkey and blend well with a fork or wooden spoon. Divide and shape the mixture into 2 burger patties.

3 Heat the tablespoon (15 mL) of oil in the skillet over medium heat, add the burgers, and cook on one side for about 6 minutes. Flip and cook another 6 to 7 minutes until done, or until the center of each is no longer pink and the juices run clear. Set aside and cover with aluminum foil to keep warm. Serve with the following Quick Caper Sauce.

Yield: *2 burgers.*

Quick Caper Sauce

Tools: *Small saucepan*

Preparation time: *About 5 minutes*

Cooking time: *About 4 minutes*

1 tablespoon (15 mL) butter

2 tablespoons (30 mL) peeled and finely minced onion

1 tablespoon (15 mL) capers, rinsed and drained

¹/₄ cup (50 mL) chicken broth

Salt and freshly ground pepper to taste

(continued)

1 Melt half the butter over medium heat in a small saucepan; then add the onion. Cook, stirring often, for about 2 to 3 minutes or until the onions wilt.

2 Add the capers. Stir and cook for a few seconds and then add the chicken broth. Raise the heat to high and cook for a few seconds, stirring, to reduce the amount of liquid slightly.

3 Remove the pan from the heat and swirl in the remaining butter. Adjust the seasoning with salt and pepper to taste and pour over the burgers.

Yield: Enough for 2 burgers.

The Solo Shopper

To whip together tasty meals for one, you must know how to shop for one. Shopping for one is not like being a housewife with three kids, who just pirouettes down the aisles taking one of everything. Solo shoppers must be more discriminating. The first rule: Don't look for one portion of everything, like one lamb chop, one small box of cereal, one yogurt, one carrot, or one garlic clove. Not only would you look pathetic on the checkout line, but you also would constantly be running to the store to replenish.

The world is, to a large extent, designed for two or more: hotel rooms, restaurant tables, cars, couches, cantaloupe, love seats, badminton sets, Ferris wheel seats, and so on. So, too, is food packaging. Solo shoppers should take advantage of this and buy for a minimum of two people. That way, you always have usable leftovers. If you buy meat, you may want to cook only half the portion, saving the other half for another use in a day or two. You can make pasta sauce in larger quantities and freeze the extra. About the only exception is fish, which you should use immediately.

Surviving the supermarket

Supermarkets are as conspiratorial as any Las Vegas casino. All along those innocent-looking aisles, to the backdrop of piped-in bouncy showtunes, are alimentary ambushes.

The conspiracy starts at the entrance, where you pick up the shopping cart with one stuck wheel. As you head toward the produce section, you may pass bins of *Specials!* like batteries, paper towels, dented tuna fish cans, and other items you may not need but might buy because of the effusive display. In fact, many items in these special displays are relative bargains — but not if you already have two dozen batteries at home.

The last thing a supermarket wants you to do is walk directly to the item or items you need and then leave the store. Supermarket aisles are designed to send you on a sightseeing excursion through the aisles. Say you need all the ingredients for a salad. You go to the lettuce bin first. If supermarkets were based purely on convenience, the salad oils, vinegars, and bottled dressings would be nearby.

Instead, the oil is two, three, or more aisles away. The vinegar is yet farther off, requiring a tour of the store to get your salad provisions. Meat displays are usually at the back of the store to prevent shoppers from dropping in, buying some ground beef, and leaving.

Alert shoppers also notice that brand-name products are generally placed at eye level. Less costly generics — which sometimes are just as good as national brands (but not always) — are less conspicuous. The reason for this is simple: National brands pay extra for good placement on the shelf.

Making a list and checking it twice

One adage among savvy supermarket shoppers is this: Never go to the store hungry. Everything looks tempting, and you may wind up with a groaning cart full of steaks, turkeys, watermelons, cheese wheels, and ice cream sandwiches.

A second rule is to always make a list. It doesn't matter whether the list is on a matchbook cover, a dry cleaner receipt, or the back of your hand. You need a battle plan, or you may wind up with two gallons of Clorox, a six-pack of soda, and a bag of Oreos — and nothing for dinner.

Write down recipe ingredients on your list, too. Nothing is more frustrating than following a recipe and finding at the last minute that you are missing something important, like the main ingredient.

Buying generics

Retailers routinely sell store brands, also called *generics,* at 15 to 25 percent less than national brands, according to national surveys of the industry. At the same time, retailers can increase their profit margin by about 10 percent by selling their own brands.

The reason is fundamental: Generics are cheaper to produce. Manufacturers, often the same companies that make popular national brands, save money either by selling their overproduction as a store brand or by making store brands at times when their plants would otherwise be idle. Another savings for store brand labels is the lack of huge national advertising expenses.

A taste test of house label and national label breakfast cereals several years ago by *The New York Times* found little perceptible difference. When it came to price, however, the differences were startling. Table 16-1 shows a sample of what the *Times* found.

Table 16-1		Prices from *The New York Times*		
Brand	*Per Pound*	*Generic Brand*	*Per Pound*	*Difference*
General Mills Cheerios	$4.04	Private-label Tasteeos	$2.98	$1.06
Kellogg's Corn Flakes	$2.30	Private-label Corn Flakes	$1.49	.81
Kellogg's Frosted Flakes	$3.19	Private-label Frosted Flakes	$2.39	.80
Kellogg's Fruit Loops	$4.26	Private-label Fruit Rings	$3.19	1.07
Kellogg's Rice Krispies	$4.30	Private-label Crispie Rice	$2.82	1.48
Kellogg's Raisin Bran	$3.19	Private-label Raisin Bran	$2.39	.80
Post Bran Flakes	$2.89	Private-label 40 Percent Bran Flakes	$1.99	.90
Nabisco Bite-Size Shredded Wheat	$3.79	Private-label Bite-Size Shredded Wheat	$2.65	1.14
Nabisco Shredded Wheat	$3.82	Private-label Shredded Wheat	$2.86	.96
Quaker Cap'n Crunch	$3.59	Private-label Crisp Crunch	$2.99	.60

Buying survival foods

Survival rations for the solo cook (see Chapter 13 for a more complete list) include the following:

- **Smoked meats (turkey, chicken):** For cold salads, sandwiches, and appetizers
- **Sun-dried tomatoes:** For adding to sauces and salads
- **Chutneys (or jams and jellies):** For enlivening leftover cold meats
- **Frozen bread:** So you don't run out

- ✔ **Aseptically packaged milk (vacuum packed so it does not need refrigeration and lasts indefinitely):** So you don't run out
- ✔ **Dried pasta**
- ✔ **Canned ham and tuna**
- ✔ **Butter:** You can freeze it
- ✔ **Dried tarragon, thyme, oregano, marjoram, ginger, coriander, cumin, black and white pepper, paprika, red pepper flakes, and turmeric** (Turn to Chapter 5 for more information about herbs and spices.)
- ✔ **Eggs:** So you never starve
- ✔ **Chicken or vegetable stock:** For quick sauces
- ✔ **Dry cereals:** In case it gets that bad
- ✔ **Canned tomatoes and tomato paste:** For all kinds of sauces
- ✔ **Rice:** An easy side dish (Chapter 3 includes recipes for making rice.)
- ✔ **Salad dressing, homemade in large quantity and stored in an old wine bottle:** So you don't have to make dressing every time you want a salad (See Chapter 10 for recipes.)
- ✔ **Ice cream or frozen yogurt:** For instant dessert

Coupons

You see them at the checkout counter, shuffling little squares of brightly colored paper and dropping them into the cashier's hand. They are the coupon clippers, semiprofessional discount hunters packing the sharpest scissors this side of Manhattan's Garment District.

Coupon clipping is not for everyone — you have to have the time and the tenacity to harvest them and then remember to use them. Yet many people do use coupons. According to estimates, nearly 115 million Americans clip coupons and redeem them at one time or another during the year. Serious bargain hunters seldom buy anything at the grocery store unless it is discounted. They also plan their shopping around days when stores double their coupons. Even so, the percentage of all coupons in circulation that are clipped is surprisingly low: about 2 percent.

Do coupon clippers know something you don't? Not really. It's just that these people see coupons as a way to beat the system. But companies are making that more difficult every year.

In recent years, virtually all major consumer products companies, including General Mills and Philip Morris, have cut back on their discount coupons offered on brand-name products. In 1995, the number of coupons in circulation dropped by 6 percent. Many companies are beginning to believe that coupons are no longer the best way to promote their products.

Other companies are shortening expiration time for coupons — so you'd better shuffle through that stack and move fast.

Killing time on the checkout line

Following are ten ways for solo shoppers to kill time on the checkout line:

- ✔ Examine the appalling selection of junk in the grocery cart in front of you and concoct a story about the person's life.

- ✔ Take *TV Guide,* write star-ratings next to your favorite shows, and then put it back.

- ✔ Pretend that your finger is caught in the moving checkout belt.

- ✔ Hold a pint of ice cream in one hand for a few minutes and then affectionately caress the cheek of the toddler sitting in the cart behind you.

- ✔ Eat a carton of yogurt, reseal it, and put it back on the checkout belt.

- ✔ While leafing through *The Star,* ponder the consequences for mankind if, as the headline says, "LIZ GIVES BIRTH TO ALIEN."

- ✔ Make a citizen's arrest when a shopper tries to enter the "10 items or less" aisle with 11 or more objects.

Making and Using Leftovers

Leftovers has such an unappetizing ring, conjuring up images of crusty, over-cooked casseroles you had to eat not once but twice because Mom would never throw out anything unless it had a nice, green color. But leftovers don't have to be boring. In fact, single diners should introduce leftovers into their meal plans for a few good reasons:

- ✔ **Leftovers increase your menu choices.** Even a sumo wrestler would be hard-pressed to consume a whole roast beef in one sitting. Roasts and whole birds are automatically passed over for single-serving chops, modest packages of ground meat, or a package of twin chicken thighs. But roast beef or a whole roasted chicken provides opportunities for satisfying, next-day meals — such as shepherd's pie, chicken tacos, stir-fry, baked rice casseroles, curries, creamy noodle casseroles, and spicy Cajun-style sautés.

- ✔ **Buying larger cuts of beef, lamb, and pork or whole chickens saves you money.** The more the butcher has to cut and handle the meat or poultry, the more it costs you per pound. A small roast may be an extravagance if cooked for only one meal. However, dining on cold roast beef sandwiches with Dijon-style mustard the next day blissfully divides the cost in half.

> ✔ **You spend less time in the kitchen.** "Cook once, eat twice" is a nice adage to live by when you're cooking for yourself.
>
> ✔ **Cooking with leftovers is challenging.** You challenge your culinary imagination as you try to think of ways to turn Sunday's delicious roasted chicken into fajitas for Monday and mulligatawny soup for Tuesday.

Making a casserole is a great way to use leftovers. You can use any kind of leftover ham — boiled or baked — in the following casserole that combines layers of sliced potatoes, onions, and ham. Cooked beef, bacon, or sausage or even crumbled pieces of meat loaf also work between the potato layers, as does leftover salmon. For a vegetarian version, omit the meat and add a vegetable, such as corn or lima beans.

Ham and Potato Bake

Tools: Chef's knife, vegetable peeler, colander, small and medium saucepan, mixing bowl, shallow baking dish

Preparation time: About 30 minutes

Cooking time: About 1 hour

Butter for greasing the baking dish

1 pound (500 g) baking potatoes, peeled and washed

1 clove garlic, peeled

1 tablespoon (15 mL) butter

$1/3$ cup (75 mL) peeled and chopped onion, about 1 small onion

$1/2$ cup (175 mL) heavy cream or half and half

2 teaspoons (10 mL) Dijon-style mustard

Freshly ground pepper to taste

$1^1/4$ cups (300 mL) diced boiled or baked ham

1 Preheat the oven to 325° F (160° C). Butter a $2^1/2$-quart (2.5-L) shallow baking dish.

2 Add about 2 quarts (2 L) of water to a medium saucepan; cover and bring to a boil over high heat. Meanwhile, with a sharp knife, cut the potatoes into $1/4$-inch-thick (6-mm) slices. Partially cook the potato slices in the boiling water for about 5 minutes. Drain them well in a colander and set aside.

3 Place the garlic clove on a wooden cutting board and use the broad side of a chef's knife to crush or press the clove flat. Set aside.

(continued)

4 Melt the butter in a small saucepan over medium heat and add the onion. Cook for about 2 minutes or until the onion wilts.

5 Combine the cream, crushed garlic, mustard, and pepper in a mixing bowl. (You don't have to add salt because the ham provides it.)

6 Layer half the potato slices on the bottom of the baking dish. Sprinkle the ham and onions over the potatoes. Add a second layer of potato slices to cover the ham. Pour the cream mixture over everything. Cover with aluminum foil and bake for 15 minutes. Remove the foil and bake for another 45 minutes or until the potatoes are tender.

Yield: *2 to 3 servings.*

Dining with pets

Solo eaters at home who have pets, especially dogs, usually find them underfoot looking up at the table with long, wistful expressions — as if that last morsel of shepherd's pie could mean life or death. Cats look from afar, aloof and disdainful, as if that slop on your plate is the last thing in the world any self-respecting feline would touch. But just watch when you go into the kitchen for another drink — Fluffy flies onto the table in one Olympic leap.

People put up with this behavior because, face it, pets are good company. Pets offer unrequited love, listen to you attentively no matter how silly they think you sound, and never talk back.

A few suggested topics of dinner conversation for dog and cat owners:

- Whatever happened to Millie, the best-selling dog/author in the Bush White House?

- Why do you dogs think that soccer is the greatest of all sports?

- What time is *Wild Kingdom* on TV tonight?

- Okay, I'll put on the *Cats* soundtrack if you show me how you jump onto the chandelier again.

- What does it feel like to age seven years for every year?

Part V
The Part of Tens

The 5th Wave   By Rich Tennant

COOKBOOKS TO AVOID

CLASSIC New England Boiled Desserts

PASTA ON THE GRILL WITH ROLF

HEADCHEESE HEADCHEESE and more HEADCHEESE at the Gilmore Inn

Technique de Manifold

Cooking on your engine block the French way!

In this part . . .

Think of this part as a cheat sheet to use after finishing the course. You can refer to these lists for specific reminders or just for fun. (We had fun writing them, anyway.)

Here, you'll find information about classic cookbooks, presenting food in attractive ways, and, most important, thinking like a chef.

Chapter 17
Ten Classic Cookbooks

*I*n America, cookbooks roll off assembly lines like Buicks. How can a shopper tell which books are good and which are better employed as trunk weights in a snowstorm?

For advice on sorting through the awesomely cluttered cookbook shelves in bookstores today, we asked one of America's authorities, Nach Waxman, owner of Kitchen Arts & Letters (212-876-5550), a wonderful shop dedicated to food and wine books that has become a must-see for food lovers who visit New York City.

We asked Waxman: "How can browsers tell the difference between a mediocre cookbook and a great cookbook?" He said, "It may seem obvious at first, but a good cookbook had better be one that has food in it you like. Big-name authors, chic new ingredients, stylish color photographs — they all mean nothing if you don't see food that you really like. Flip through a book and see how many times in, say 20 pages, you find yourself saying, 'Wow, I'd really enjoy eating that.'

"Second, read a couple of recipes and make sure that you know what the authors are talking about. Do you speak their language?

"Third, make sure the book is not merely a collection of recipes — first do this, then do that — but a source of information and ideas that will let you make decisions on your own and will help your cooking grow. The idea is for you to be in control and not simply a rote follower of someone else's instructions."

This chapter lists ten wide-ranging cookbooks that have stood the test of time. There are lots of great cookbooks out there, but if you own the following books, you'll be set for years.

The American Heritage Cookbook

Edited by Helen McCully and Eleanor Noderer (American Heritage Publishing Co., Inc., updated 1980)

A great armchair read, this book recounts wonderful yarns about America's culinary heritage. The recipes are solid, too: everything from Indian pudding to oysters Rockefeller.

The Art of Cooking

Jacques Pépin, Volumes I and II (Knopf, 1987)

This extensive, technique-oriented book is the follow-up to Pépin's *La Methode* and *La Technique.* The clear color photos and terse writing make this book much easier to follow than his preceding two cookbooks. It's expensive, but no other cookbook offers so many color-illustrated techniques, from boning lamb to making soufflés.

Craig Claiborne's The New York Times Cookbook

Craig Claiborne (Times Books, 1979)

Claiborne, the preeminent food journalist of this generation, compiled this book from his extensive travels and his legendary kitchen sessions at his home in East Hampton, Long Island. His partner, Pierre Franey, helped to ensure that the recipes work and are easy to follow. The book addresses a wide range of international cuisine, although the focus is on French and American cooking.

Essentials of Classic Italian Cooking

Marcella Hazan (Knopf, 1992)

If you buy only one book on Italian cooking, you might well choose this one. Hazan, an easygoing and thorough teacher, covers all the techniques involved in Italian cuisine. The fresh pasta and gnocchi chapters are particularly well done.

James Beard's American Cookery

James Beard (Little, Brown, 1972)

A broad look at American culinary styles through the impish personality of the larger-than-life James Beard. Recipes are traditional and solid.

Joy of Cooking

Irma S. Rombauer and Marion Rombauer Becker (Penguin Books USA, updated 1975)

Some people consider this best-selling classic to be a bit moldy around the edges. Nonetheless, it is an excellent primer for beginning cooks, filled with lucid illustrations and instructions. This book tells you how to make the classic version of a dish — you take it from there.

Larousse Gastronomique

Edited by Jennifer H. Lang (Crown, 1988)

This book is more an encyclopedia of food than a cookbook. Filled with color photos and illustrations, it is the definitive resource for answers to cooking questions. The book does not give recipes per se but rather descriptions of how to make something as if you were telling a friend. Its historical notes are interesting, too.

Mastering the Art of French Cooking, Volumes I and II

Julia Child, Louisette Bertholle, and Simone Beck (Knopf, 1961)

Not an everyday cookbook, this two-volume classic is where you go to learn how to do something the way it was originally intended. If you have a strong interest in French cuisine, this book is indispensable. Particularly interesting are the step-by-step instructions for making pastries, dough, bread, and cakes.

The New Doubleday Cookbook

Jean Anderson and Elaine Hanna (Doubleday, updated 1985)

This amazingly comprehensive book belongs in every cook's kitchen. For a tome of this size (965 pages), it is stylish and light on its feet. Instructions are well written, and illustrations are easy to follow. Every aspect of American and international cooking is covered. Whenever we couldn't find something in other references while researching this book, we found it in the *New Doubleday Cookbook*.

The Silver Palate Cookbook

Julee Rosso and Sheila Lukins (Workman Press, 1979)

The staggering sales of this animated, eclectic book testify to America's wide-ranging tastes. Recipes are attractively presented, stylish, and for the most part well written.

Buying cookbooks via the Internet

A lot of the fun of getting a cookbook is browsing through the books you *don't* buy. There are so many gorgeous books out there, full of pictures of glistening fruit pies and steaming loaves of bread, that were never meant to enter a real-life kitchen! But one great picture can get your taste buds working and your imagination off and running.

You also can buy the books you need to get started without ever leaving the comfort of your own home. One way is through the Internet.

A great source for an enormous selection of books is the Sandcat Inc. Web site at `http://www.fishnet.net/~sandcat/cook`. Sandcat's selection of hundreds of books runs the gamut from classics like *Joy of Cooking* and *Mastering the Art of French Cooking* to commercial publications like *The Bisquick Cookbook* and the *Heinz Recipe Book* (published in the 1950s — now *that's* mom food!). You also can order by phone at 800-696-6111. All your purchases through this company help fund the Easter Seals program.

Chapter 18

Ten Ways to Think Like a Chef

In This Chapter

▶ Sniff your way through the spice rack

▶ Save those chicken bones!

▶ Build dishes from the bottom up

In observing and interviewing many chefs, we found a consensus among them about how to progress as a cook. The ten points in this chapter reflect their thoughts.

Know the Basic Techniques

Cooking is so much more fun — and successful — when you approach it with confidence. Chefs say that confidence arises from knowing your techniques so well that they are second nature.

Use Only the Freshest Ingredients

Use only the freshest ingredients and buy in-season fresh fruits and vegetables. Seasonal produce offers the highest quality and supply and the lowest price. Why make an apple pie in the summer from mealy apples held in storage all year when you can make one with fresh, ripe peaches or juicy plums? Let what's fresh and available at the market help you spontaneously decide what's for dinner.

Get It Together

"So much of cooking, even for the home chef, is about being organized," says Gary Danko, Chef at The Dining Room in San Francisco's Ritz Carlton. "Do all of your preparation — cutting, peeling, dicing — before you start cooking."

The French call this preparation *mise en place,* which translates to "everything in its place." Get the chopping, mincing, deboning, and washing chores out of the way in order to create an even, efficient flow of cooking steps.

That way, when the butter or oil is hot and sizzling in the skillet, you don't need to stop suddenly to peel and mince onions and garlic that are supposed to be sautéed in the hot fat.

With This Basil I Thee Wed

Learn about herbs, both fresh and dried, so that you can season without always relying on a book or recipe. Chefs base some of the world's great cuisines on the combination of a few simple herbs and spices. For example, Italian cooking relies heavily on the flavors of garlic, olive oil, tomatoes, Parmesan cheese, and basil.

The French use a basic seasoning blend called *mirepoix* — a sautéed mixture of chopped onions, carrots, and celery. Many chefs begin their soups, stews, stuffings, and pan sauces with these simple, sautéed ingredients. Louisiana home cooks have their own version, which adds chopped bell pepper and garlic to the mix. You can vary this base by adding bacon, ham, fresh herbs, or even curry. In a perfectly made mirepoix, the vegetables cook slowly for a long time, causing them to caramelize slightly and sweeten.

All the Plate's a Stage

Think of the choreography of food on a plate. People eat with their eyes first. The food should be colorful and attractively arranged, with fresh herbs as a colorful garnish. (See Chapter 19 for ways to make food look great.)

"Try to have an average of four components in every dish," says Frank Brigtsen, chef and owner of Brigtsen's restaurant in New Orleans. According to Brigtsen, four distinct components give a dish complexity without being too fussy. For example, Brigtsen serves at his restaurant a blackened tuna with a smoked corn sauce, a red bean salad, and avocado sour cream, which results in four distinct colors. "Dress up the main element of the dish, whether it's fish, meat, or poultry, with sauces, condiments, and garnishes that add a balance of interest and flavors," he says.

Plan Your Menus in Advance

Before cooking, think about contrasting flavors, textures, and colors. If the appetizer is a salad of grilled portobello mushrooms, then mushrooms in the entree is not an interesting choice. Keep the courses balanced and don't overload yourself. If you serve a time-consuming and complex appetizer, serve a simple entree or one that needs only reheating, like a tasty stew. If your appetizer is cold, be sure that the entree is hot.

Take a good look at the timing of the meal, too. Figure out how much cooking and preparation time are needed so that your diners don't feel they are getting the bum's rush or have to wait too long between courses.

Be Thrifty

Throw out nothing (unless, of course, it's spoiled). Every morsel of food is usable for soups, stocks, salads, and so on. You can sometimes make great meals from leftovers (see Chapter 16 for ideas for using leftovers).

Learn about different cuts of meat and how to cook them so that you don't have to rely on more expensive cuts. Hone your knife skills so that you can save money by purchasing whole chickens, ducks, fish, and so on and then cutting them up yourself.

Don't Be a Slave to Recipes

Use a good, basic recipe that you like as a starting point, but don't consider it written in stone. Say you have a recipe for basic stew. You make it once and decide that it could use more garlic, so the next time you double the amount. Or instead of turnips, you think that the sweet effect of chopped carrots would work, so you substitute one vegetable for the other. With experience and good technique, and by learning how ingredients work together, you can simply glance at a recipe and make adjustments to suit your taste.

Simplify, Simplify

"It's not what you decide to put into a dish that's important, it's what you decide to keep out," says Jan Birnbaum, owner and chef of The Catahoula Restaurant and Saloon in Calistoga, California. Start with a product that's fresh and flavorful and add only those seasonings that complement the food.

Above All, Have Fun

Take a cooking course, buy yourself a cookbook, or make a new dish that you've always wanted to try. Cooking, like golf, should be fun — something you look forward to. So what if you slam one into the rough every now and then? It's all part of the game.

As they say, a mistake is never a lost cause — it's a learning experience. And don't be afraid of cooking. "Cooking is about making decisions — not hesitant ones, but decisive ones. Figure out the results you want, give the situation serious, careful thought, and then go for it," says George Germon, chef at Al Forno in Providence, Rhode Island.

Here's just one example of how you can start at the bottom and climb the learning tree. Cook spaghetti, drain, and toss with olive oil that has been used to cook a sliver of garlic (leave the garlic in the oil). Taste it. Now go one step up the flavor ladder by cooking another small batch of pasta. This time, cook onions with the garlic and olive oil. Taste the sweetness? Now do it again with dried oregano added to the other ingredients. See how the oregano adds a whole new flavor dimension? Now add crushed tomatoes. You have a completely different dish.

This little exercise, aside from producing a lot of leftover spaghetti, is a great exercise in taste discrimination. You can do it with other sauces, mousses, soups, and more. The more you learn about how different herbs and spices taste, the better cook you will be.

Perception is reality

Well, not really. Wearing your own chef's hat and coat doesn't actually make your peanut-butter-and-jelly sandwich taste like caviar on melba toast, but looking the part certainly can't hurt! One place that offers authentic chef gear at affordable prices is Chef Direct. You can call the company at 800-789-CHEF, or check out its Web site (with photos of everything) at http://www.chefdirect.com.

Chapter 19

Ten Ways to Make Everyday Food Look Great

*E*ye-appeal is 50 percent of cooking. The most succulent roast leg of lamb with garlic green beans and mashed potatoes can look like Sunday rations at Sing-Sing if it's unceremoniously plopped on a plate. With just a little thought put into presentation, the same meal can look, as a friend from Maine once put it, "just like downtown." This chapter gives some tips for jazzing up your meal's appearance.

Score Sliced Zucchini and Cucumbers

Make sliced zucchini and cucumbers more attractive by taking a vegetable peeler and slicing off strips of skin lengthwise. Leave one strip bare, one strip with skin, one strip bare, and so on. You also can score the skin with a fork.

Learn to Use a Pastry Bag

Buy a pastry bag and different sized tips (they come in sets). Use this tool for pastry as well as for serving mashed potatoes, vegetable purees, and whipped cream in attractive patterns. A few examples of patterns you can make are parallel squiggles, star patterns, Pike's Peak, Abe Lincoln, and your house.

Make a Tomato Rose

Make a tomato rose by taking a very sharp knife and, starting at the top of the tomato, carving away a 1/2-inch-wide strip around the tomato all the way to the base. Let the strip get larger toward the bottom of the tomato. Cut the long strip at the bottom and coil into a rose form with the thinner end at the center, as shown in Figure 19-1.

Figure 19-1: A tomato rose makes a lovely garnish. Coil into a rose form.

Tomato Rose

Fry Julienned Strips of Carrots or Beets

Using a *mandoline* (a stainless steel slicer), the cutting disk of a food processor, or a sharp knife, cut carrots, parsnips, or beets into *julienne strips* (thin strips about 1/8-inch thick and uniform in length). Heat 2 to 3 inches of vegetable oil to 365° F (185° C) — you need an oil thermometer to measure the temperature — and toss a handful of carrots, parsnips, or beets into the pot. Let them cook, stirring only if they stick to the bottom or sides of the pan. Remove with a slotted spoon when crispy but not too dark and drain on a paper towel. Clumps of these vegetables make wonderful and tasty garnishes. ***Note:*** If you're using beets, dust them with flour before frying them.

Tie Carrot Bundles with a Scallion Green

Make a little woodpile of julienned carrots and tie them with a scallion green. To julienne carrots, peel and slice the carrots into 1/8-inch thick strips and then cut the strips into uniform lengths of about 3 inches, or as long as desired. (See Figure 19-2.)

Figure 19-2:
Julienned
carrots are
both tasty
and
attractive.

Woodpile of Carrots

Decorate with Sauces

Rather than ladle sauce over food, buy plastic ketchup-style bottles at a kitchen equipment store and use them to squirt sauces in decorative styles over plates, atop soups, over vegetables and desserts, and so on, as shown in Figure 19-3.

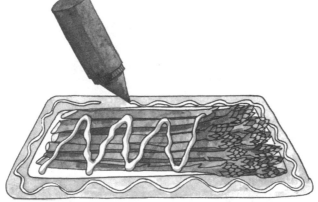

Figure 19-3:
Decorating
with sauces
is a great
way to
dress up
food.

Decorate with Sauces

"Happy Birthday" written on asparagus with hollandaise sauce dissolves before you get it to the table.

Ladle Sauces Attractively

Don't always ladle your sauce all over the main ingredients. Sometimes you can attractively pour it down the middle (as on sautéed fish fillets) or on the plate and then place the food on top.

Don't Always Pile Vegetables on the Side

Instead of always placing vegetables on the side of a main course, use them creatively for color and texture contrast. For example, put mashed potatoes in a pastry bag and ring the main course with piped potatoes. Or place food over vegetables, such as grilled lamb chops or fish over a bed of dark green kale or spinach. Or make a mashed potato replica of the state of Texas.

Garnish with Greens

All kinds of attractive and tasty greens can make a plate look extraordinary. Use your imagination in distributing the greens. Greens that are especially pretty include nasturtium, lamb's lettuce, watercress, arugula, radicchio, frisée, and red oak leaf. (See Chapter 10 for a chart identifying different types of greens.)

Make Colorful Mosaics

Use nickel-sized carrot disks, strips of green scallions, trimmed green beans, pearl onions, strawberries, and the like to make colorful patterns on plates. To produce a flower effect, slice the fruit or vegetable several times from just above the root or base to the tip. If you have very small zucchini, for example, slice 4 to 5 slices lengthwise, starting $1/2$ inch below the top. Lay the slices on a plate spread out like a fan, as shown in Figure 19-4.

Figure 19-4:
Colorful mosaics add eye appeal to a plate.

food mosaic

Slice Meats Creatively

When you serve steak or other meats, slice them on a bias before serving — that means not perpendicular to the cutting board but at about a 45-degree angle. The meat looks much more appetizing that way.

Appendix A

Glossary of 100 (Plus) Common Cooking Terms

● ●

*C*ooking and recipe-writing have their own distinct language. Before you roast a chicken, for example, you need to know what *trussing* means. To make a soufflé that rises above the rim of the dish, you need to understand *whipping* and *folding* egg whites. This appendix gives you a list of basic terms. Most of them are thoroughly described and illustrated elsewhere in the book.

Adjust: To taste the dish before serving and add seasoning (such as salt and pepper), if necessary.

Al dente: An Italian phrase meaning "to the tooth" that describes the tender but still firm texture of perfectly cooked pasta. (See Chapter 11 for pasta recipes.)

Au gratin: A dish, usually topped with buttered bread crumbs, grated cheese, or both, that has been browned in the oven or under the broiler.

Bake: To cook in the dry heat of an oven. (See Chapter 12 for easy baking recipes.)

Barbecue: Any food cooked on a charcoal or gas grill. Also refers to the process of cooking foods in a pit or on a spit for a long time.

Baste: To add flavor and moisture by brushing food with pan drippings, fat, or a seasoned liquid as it cooks.

Batter: An uncooked, semiliquid mixture usually containing beaten eggs, flour, liquid, and a leavening ingredient, such as baking soda or baking powder, that makes the batter rise when cooked.

Beat: To mix ingredients briskly in a circular motion so that they become smooth and creamy. A hundred hand-beaten strokes generally equal one minute with an electric mixer, if you're the type who counts these things. (See Chapter 8 for information about beating egg whites.)

Beurre manié: A butter-flour paste used to thicken soups and stews. (Turn to Chapter 9 for instructions for making this paste.)

Bind: To bring together a liquid mixture, such as a sauce, with a thickening ingredient, such as cream or butter.

Blanch: To plunge vegetables or fruits into boiling water for a short time to loosen its skin or preserve its color. (See Chapter 3.)

Blend: To mix or combine two or more ingredients with a spoon, whisk, spatula, or electric mixer.

Boil: To bring the temperature of a liquid to 212° F (100° C) for water at sea level, causing bubbles to break at the surface. (See Chapter 3.)

Bone (or debone): To remove the bones from meat, fish, or poultry.

Bouquet garni: A package of mixed herbs (often tied in cheesecloth) that is used to season stocks, soups, and stews to impart flavor. A typical combination is parsley, thyme, and bay leaf.

Braise: To brown meat or vegetables in fat and then cook, covered, in a small quantity of liquid over low heat, usually for a long time. The long, slow cooking both tenderizes and flavors the food, especially tough cuts of meat. Braising can take place either on the stovetop or in the oven. (See Chapter 5 for braising and stewing recipes.)

Bread: To coat a piece of food with crackers or bread crumbs to seal in moisture and give it a crisp crust. The piece of fish, poultry, meat, or vegetable is usually first dipped into a liquid, such as beaten egg or milk, to make the crumbs adhere.

Broil: To cook food under a hot oven coil, as opposed to grilling, in which the heat is underneath.

Brown: To cook food briefly over high heat, usually in fat and on top of the stove, to impart a rich brown color to its skin or surface. Food also may be browned in a very hot oven or under the broiler.

Brush: To coat the surface of food with a liquid ingredient such as melted butter, egg, or fruit glaze.

Butterfly: To split food down the center (removing bones if necessary), leaving the two halves joined at the seam so that the food opens flat to resemble a butterfly.

Caramelize: To heat sugar until it melts into a liquid, syrupy state that ranges from golden to dark brown in color (320° F/160° C to 350° F/180° C on a candy thermometer). See Chapter 7 for a recipe for Caramel Sauce. Also to cook onions and other vegetables until they become soft and brown (the sugars they contain carmelize).

Chop: To cut food into small pieces by using a knife or food processor.

Clarify: To make a cloudy liquid clear by removing the impurities. For example, you can clarify a stock or broth by simmering raw egg whites or eggshells for 10 to 15 minutes to attract impurities. You then strain the liquid through a sieve lined with cheesecloth.

Coddle: To cook foods (usually eggs) gently in simmering water.

Core: To cut out the core of a food, usually a fruit or vegetable such as an apple or pepper.

Cream: To beat one ingredient, such as butter, with another, such as sugar, until soft and smooth.

Crimp: To press together with your fingers or a fork and seal the rim of a double-crust pie to form a double thickness of dough that you can then shape into a decorative pattern. (See Chapter 15.)

Crumble: To break up or crush food, such as dried herbs or crackers, into small pieces with your fingers.

Cube: To cut food into ¹/₂-inch (12-mm) square pieces. Cubed food is larger than diced food. See also *dice.*

Cure: To preserve food such as meat or fish by salting, drying, and/or smoking.

Dash: See *pinch.*

Deglaze: To add liquid, usually wine or broth, to a hot skillet or roasting pan and scrape up the browned bits clinging to the bottom of the pan that pieces of sautéed meat, fish, or poultry left behind. You then reduce and season the pan sauce. See Chapter 7 for recipes that use this technique.

Degrease: To skim the fat off the surface of a soup or gravy with a spoon. Also done by chilling the mixture, turning the liquid fat into a solid, which you can then easily lift off the surface.

Demi-glace: A rich, brown sauce made by boiling down meat stock until it's reduced to a thick glaze that can coat a spoon. (See Chapter 7.)

Devein: To remove the vein from shrimp or other shellfish. (See Chapter 12 for illustrated instructions for cleaning shrimp.)

Devil: To season foods with hot and spicy ingredients such as Tabasco sauce, mustard, or red pepper flakes.

Dice: To cut into small ($1/8$-inch to $1/4$-inch/3-mm to 6-mm) cubes.

Dilute: To thin a mixture by adding water or other liquid.

Disjoint: To sever a piece of meat at its joint, as when you separate a chicken leg from its thigh.

Dot: To distribute small portions or pieces of food (such as bits of butter) over the surface of another food.

Drain: To remove the liquid from a food, often in a colander. Also, to pour off liquid fat from a pan after you brown a food (such as bacon or ground meat).

Dredge: To coat the surface of a food by dragging it through flour, cornmeal, or crumbs.

Drizzle: To pour a liquid such as melted butter, sauce, or syrup over a food in a thin, slow steam.

Dust: To give the surface of food a thin coating of flour or confectioner's sugar.

Fillet: To remove the bones from a piece of meat or fish.

Flambé: To ignite food that is drenched in alcohol so that it bursts into a dramatic flame just before serving. (See Chapter 4 for a recipe for Sautéed Peppered Fillet of Beef, which includes a flambé option.)

Flute: To crimp the edge of a pie crust (see Chapter 15 for illustrated instructions) or to cut decorative markings and patterns into vegetables (such as mushrooms) and fruits.

Fold: To combine a lightweight mixture, such as beaten egg whites, with a heavier mixture, such as whipped cream or sugared egg yolks, by using a gentle mixing motion. (See Chapter 8 for illustrated instructions.)

Fricassee: A white stew in which meat or poultry is not browned before cooking. (See Chapter 5.)

Fry: To cook or sauté food in fat over high heat. Deep-fried foods are submerged in hot fat and cooked until crisp.

Fumet: A concentrated meat, fish, or vegetable stock that is used as a flavoring base for sauces.

Garnish: An edible plate adornment, ranging from a simple wedge of lemon to a fancy chocolate leaf. (See Chapter 9 for a list of soup garnishes and Chapter 19 for ten ways to dress up food.)

Glaze: To coat the surface of a food with syrup, melted jelly, an egg wash, or other thin, liquid mixture to give it a glossy shine.

Grate: To rub a large piece of food (such as a block of cheese) against the coarse, serrated holes of a grater.

Grease: To spread a thin layer of fat, usually butter, on the inside of a pan to prevent food from sticking as it cooks.

Gremolata: A mixture of chopped parsley, garlic, and grated lemon peel used to garnish foods like grilled chops, chicken or fish, or osso buco. (See Chapter 15 for an Osso Buco recipe.)

Grill: To cook food over a charcoal or gas grill, or to cook on an iron (or other) grill on the stovetop. (See Chapter 6.)

Hull: To trim strawberries by plucking out their green stems.

Julienne: To cut foods into thin ($^1/_8$ inch/3 mm or less) strips.

Knead: The technique of pushing, folding, and pressing dough for yeast breads and cakes to give it a smooth, elastic texture. You can knead by hand or with an electric mixer equipped with a bread hook or a bread machine.

Marinate: To soak or steep a food such as meat, poultry, fish, or vegetables in a liquid mixture that may be seasoned with spices and herbs in order to impart flavor to the food before it is cooked. (See Chapter 6.) The steeping liquid is called the *marinade.*

Mash: To press food, usually with a potato masher or ricer, into a soft pulp. (See Chapter 3.)

Mince: To cut food into tiny pieces.

Mirepoix: A combination of finely chopped sautéed vegetables, usually carrots, onions, and celery, that is used as a seasoning base for soups, stews, stuffings, and other dishes. (See Chapter 18.)

Parboil: To partially cook foods, such as rice or dense vegetables like carrots and potatoes, by plunging them briefly into boiling water. (See Chapter 3.)

Pare: To remove the skin from fruits or vegetables.

Pickle: To preserve food in a salty brine or vinegar solution.

Pinch or dash: A small amount of any dry ingredient (between $1/8$ and $1/16$ teaspoon/0.5 and 0.25 mL) that can be grasped between the tips of the thumb and forefinger.

Poach: To cook foods in a simmering liquid. (See Chapter 3.)

Pound: To flatten food, especially chicken breasts or meat, with a meat mallet or the flat side of a large knife (such as a cleaver) to make it uniform in thickness. Has some tenderizing effect.

Preheat: To turn on the oven, grill, or broiler before cooking food to set the temperature to the degree required by the recipe.

Puree: To mash or grind food into a paste by forcing through a food mill or sieve or by whirling in a food processor or blender. Finely mashed food also is called a puree.

Ream: To extract the juice from fruit, especially citrus.

Reconstitute: To bring dehydrated food, such as dried milk or juice, back to a liquid state by adding water.

Reduce: The technique of rapidly boiling a liquid mixture, such as wine, stock, or sauce, to decrease its original volume so that it thickens and concentrates in flavor.

Render: To cook a piece of meat over low heat so that its fat melts away.

Roast: To cook in the dry heat of an oven. (See Chapter 6.)

Roux: A cooked paste of flour and fat such as oil or butter that is used to thicken soups, stews, and gumbos. (See Chapter 7.)

Sauté: To cook food quickly in a small amount of fat, usually butter or oil, over very high heat. (See Chapter 4.)

Scald: To heat milk to just below the boiling point when making custards and dessert sauces to shorten the cooking time.

Scallop: A creamy baked dish, sometimes of layered, thinly sliced potatoes, with a bread crumb topping.

Score: To make shallow cuts (often in a crisscross pattern) on the exterior of a food (such as meat, fish, or bread) so that it cooks more evenly.

Sear: To brown quickly in a pan, under the broiler, or in a very hot oven. (See Chapter 4.)

Season: To flavor foods with herbs, spices, salt and pepper, and so on.

Shred: To reduce food to thin strips, usually by rubbing it against a grater.

Shuck: To remove shells from shellfish, such as clams (see Chapter 11 for illustrated instructions), oysters, and mussels or to remove husks from fresh corn.

Sift: To shake dry ingredients, such as flour or confectioner's sugar, through a fine mesh sifter to incorporate air and make them lighter.

Simmer: To gently cook food in a liquid just below the boiling point or just until tiny bubbles begin to break the surface (at about 185° F/85° C). (See Chapter 3.)

Skewer: To thread small pieces of food on long, thin rods made of bamboo or metal to hold meat, fish, or vegetables for grilling or broiling.

Skim: To remove the fat and bits of food that rise to the surface of a soup or stock with a spoon. (See Chapter 3.)

Steam: To cook over a small amount of simmering or boiling water in a covered pan so that the steam trapped in the pan cooks the food. (See Chapter 3.)

Stew: To simmer food for a long time in a tightly covered pot with just enough liquid to cover. The term *stew* also can describe a cooked dish. (See Chapter 5.)

Stir-fry: The Oriental cooking technique of quickly frying small pieces of food in a wok with a small amount of fat over very high heat while constantly tossing and stirring the ingredients. The term *stir-fry* also can refer to a dish prepared this way.

Stock: The strained, flavorful liquid or broth that is produced by cooking meat, fish, poultry, vegetables, seasonings, or other ingredients in water. (See Chapter 3.)

Strain: To separate liquids from solids by passing a mixture through a sieve.

Stuff: To fill a food cavity, such as the inside of chicken, turkey, or tomato, with various types of food.

Tenderize: To soften the connective tissue of meat by pounding or cooking very slowly for a long time. See also *braise*.

Toss: To turn over food a number of times to mix thoroughly, as when a green salad is mixed and coated with dressing.

Truss: To tie meat or poultry with string and/or skewers to maintain its shape during roasting. (See Chapter 6 for illustrated instructions for trussing a chicken.)

Whip: To beat air into ingredients such as eggs or cream with a whisk or electric beater to make them light and fluffy.

Whisk: A handheld wire kitchen utensil used to whip ingredients like eggs, cream, and sauces. When used as a verb, the term *whisk* describes the process of whipping or blending ingredients together with a wire whisk.

Zest: The colored, grated peel of citrus fruit that is used as a flavoring ingredient in dressings, stews, desserts, and so on.

Appendix B
Common Substitutions, Abbreviations, and Equivalents

• •

*S*ay you're making a vinaigrette dressing for a salad and suddenly realize that you're out of vinegar. But you do have lemons, which are an acceptable substitute. How much lemon do you use? Or you may not have whole milk for a gratin dish, but you do have skim milk. Is skim milk okay? Situations like these are what this appendix is all about.

Some ingredients are almost always interchangeable: For example, you can substitute vegetable or olive oil in most cases for butter when sautéing or pan frying, lemon juice for vinegar in salad dressings and marinades, almonds for walnuts in baked breads and muffins, vegetable broth for beef or chicken broth in soups, stews, or sauces, and light cream for half and half.

But sometimes there is no acceptable substitution for an ingredient. Other times, the substitution is very exact and specific. This is most often the case for baked goods, where you need to follow a formula to produce a cake, soufflé, pastry, or bread with the perfect height, density, and texture.

Most of the following substitutions are for emergency situations only — when you have run out of an essential ingredient and need a very specific replacement.

For thickening soups, stews, and sauces:

- ✔ 1 tablespoon (15 mL) cornstarch or potato flour = 2 tablespoons (30 mL) all-purpose flour
- ✔ 1 tablespoon (15 mL) arrowroot = $2^{1}/_{2}$ tablespoons (37 mL) all-purpose flour

For flour:

- ✔ l cup (250 mL) minus 2 tablespoons (30 mL) sifted all-purpose flour = l cup (250 mL) sifted cake flour

- ✔ l cup (250 mL) plus 2 tablespoons (30 mL) sifted cake flour = l cup (250 mL) sifted all-purpose flour

- ✔ l cup (250 mL) sifted self-rising flour = l cup (250 mL) sifted all-purpose flour plus $1\frac{1}{4}$ teaspoons (6 mL) baking powder and a pinch of salt

For leavening agents in baked goods:

- ✔ $\frac{1}{4}$ teaspoon (1 mL) baking soda plus $\frac{1}{2}$ teaspoon (2 mL) cream of tartar = l teaspoon (5 mL) double-acting baking powder

- ✔ $\frac{1}{4}$ teaspoon (1 mL) baking soda plus $\frac{1}{2}$ cup (125 mL) buttermilk or yogurt = l teaspoon (5 mL) double-acting baking powder in liquid mixtures only; reduce liquid in recipe by $\frac{1}{2}$ cup (125 mL)

For dairy products:

- ✔ l cup (250 mL) whole milk = $\frac{1}{2}$ cup (125 mL) unsweetened evaporated milk plus $\frac{1}{2}$ cup (125 mL) water

  or l cup (250 mL) skim milk plus 2 teaspoons (10 mL) melted butter

  or $\frac{1}{4}$ cup (50 mL) powdered milk plus l cup (250 mL) water

  or l cup (250 mL) soy milk

  or l cup (250 mL) buttermilk plus $\frac{1}{2}$ teaspoon (2 mL) baking soda

- ✔ $\frac{3}{4}$ cup (175 mL) whole milk plus $\frac{1}{3}$ cup (75 mL) melted butter = l cup (250 mL) heavy cream (but not for making whipped cream)

- ✔ l cup (250 mL) skim milk = l cup (250 mL) water plus $\frac{1}{4}$ cup (50 mL) nonfat powdered milk, or $\frac{1}{2}$ cup (125 mL) evaporated skim milk plus $\frac{1}{2}$ cup (125 mL) water

- ✔ l cup (250 mL) sour milk = l cup (250 mL) buttermilk or yogurt *or* l cup (250 mL) minus 1 tablespoon (15 mL) milk, plus 1 tablespoon (15 mL) lemon juice or white vinegar after standing 5 to 10 minutes

- ✔ l cup (250 mL) sour cream = l cup (250 mL) plain yogurt

For eggs:

- ✔ 2 egg yolks = l egg for thickening sauces and custards

- ✔ 4 extra-large eggs = 5 large eggs or 6 small eggs

For sweetening:

✔ 1 cup (250 mL) sugar = 1 cup (250 mL) molasses (*or* honey) plus ¹/₂ teaspoon (2 mL) baking soda

✔ 1 cup (250 mL) brown sugar = 1 cup (250 mL) white sugar plus 1¹/₂ tablespoons (22 mL) molasses

Miscellaneous substitutions:

✔ 1 tablespoon (15 mL) prepared mustard = 1 teaspoon (5 mL) dried mustard

✔ 1 cup (250 mL) broth or stock = 1 bouillon cube dissolved in 1 cup (250 mL) boiling water

✔ 1 cup (250 mL) fine bread crumbs = ³/₄ cup (175 mL) cracker crumbs

✔ 1 square (1 ounce/28 g) unsweetened chocolate = 3 tablespoons (45 mL) cocoa plus 1 tablespoon (15 mL) butter, margarine, or vegetable shortening

✔ 1 ounce (28 g) semisweet chocolate = 3 tablespoons (45 mL) cocoa plus 2 tablespoons (30 mL) butter, margarine, or vegetable shortening plus 3 tablespoons (45 mL) sugar

✔ 1-inch (2.5-cm) piece of vanilla bean = 1 teaspoon (5 mL) pure vanilla extract

Although we spell out nonmetric measurements in this book, many cookbooks use abbreviations. Table B-1 lists common abbreviations and what they stand for.

Table B-1	Common Abbreviations
Abbreviation(s)	**What It Stands For**
C, c	cup
g	gram
kg	kilogram
L, l	liter
lb	pound
mL, ml	milliliter
oz	ounce
pt	pint
t, tsp	teaspoon
T, TB, Tbl, Tbsp	tablespoon

TIP

Cookbook writers have a penchant for practical jokes. Just when you are getting the hang of cups and tablespoons, they throw you a recipe in ounces and pounds. Tables B-2 and B-3 list common equivalent measures. All measurements are for level amounts. Note that some metric measurements are approximate.

Table B-2	Conversion Secrets	
This Measurement . . .	*. . . Equals This Measurement*	*. . . Equals This Metric Measurement*
Pinch or dash	less than $\frac{1}{8}$ teaspoon	0.5 mL
3 teaspoons	1 tablespoon	15 mL
2 tablespoons	1 fluid ounce	30 mL
1 jigger	$1\frac{1}{2}$ fluid ounces	45 mL
4 tablespoons	$\frac{1}{4}$ cup	50 mL
5 tablespoons plus 1 teaspoon	$\frac{1}{3}$ cup	75 mL
12 tablespoons	$\frac{3}{4}$ cup	175 mL
16 tablespoons	1 cup	250 mL
1 cup	8 fluid ounces	250 mL
2 cups	1 pint or 16 fluid ounces	500 mL
2 pints	1 quart or 32 fluid ounces	1 L
4 quarts	1 gallon	4 L

Table B-3	Food Equivalents	
This Measurement . . .	*. . . Equals This Measurement*	*. . . Equals This Metric Measurement*
3 medium apples or bananas	approximately 1 pound	500 g
1 ounce baking chocolate	1 square	28 g
2 slices bread	1 cup fresh bread crumbs	250 mL
1 pound brown sugar	$2\frac{1}{4}$ cups packed	550 mL packed
4 tablespoons butter	$\frac{1}{2}$ stick	50 to 60 mL
8 tablespoons butter	1 stick	125 mL
4 sticks butter or margarine	1 pound	454 g
6 ounces chocolate chips	1 cup	250 mL

This Measurement...	... Equals This Measurement	... Equals This Metric Measurement
1 pound confectioners' sugar	4½ cups sifted	1.125 L sifted
1 pound granulated sugar	2 cups	500 mL
½ pound hard cheese (such as cheddar)	approximately 2 cups grated	500 mL grated
1 cup heavy whipping cream	2 cups whipped	500 mL whipped
1 medium lemon	3 tablespoons juice, 2 to 3 teaspoons grated peel	45 mL juice, 10 to 15 mL grated peel
1 pound macaroni	4 cups raw, 8 cups cooked	1 L raw, 2 L cooked
4 ounces nuts	approximately ⅔ cup chopped	150 mL chopped
1 large onion	approximately 1 cup chopped	250 mL chopped
1 cup raw converted rice	4 cups cooked	1 L cooked
1 pint strawberries	approximately 2 cups sliced	500 mL sliced
1 large tomato	approximately ¾ cup chopped	175 mL chopped
3 to 4 tomatoes	approximately 1 pound	500 g
1 pound all-purpose flour	4 cups sifted	1 L sifted
5 large whole eggs	1 cup	250 mL

Index

• *N* •

Sunkist

"COOKING WITH SUNSHINE"

The classic cookbook offered by SUNKIST GROWERS *is now available at a special discount! This 341 page book provides all sorts of delightful ideas for using fresh Sunkist Citrus, from appealing appetizers to luscious desserts.*

Send today! If you are not completely satisfied, return postpaid for a refund on the purchase price. Offer good while supply lasts.

Please send ____ copies of "COOKING WITH SUNSHINE". *Enclosed is* **$9.95** *for each copy ordered, which includes shipping and handling. Do not send cash.*

NAME_____

ADDRESS_____

CITY _____ STATE _____ ZIP _____

MAIL TO: SUNKIST COOKBOOK
Box 4587, OVERLAND PARK, KANSAS 66204   Allow 6 - 8 weeks for delivery   Code # 5157

TABASCO® JALAPEÑO
SAUCE

Pizza, Nachos, Tacos,
Eggs, Hamburgers,
Gumbo, Pork chops,
Stews, Sandwiches,
Baked Potatoes, Chili,
Hotdogs, Chicken,
Salads, Soups, Fish.

Splash It On!

IDG BOOKS WORLDWIDE REGISTRATION CARD

Visit our Web site at http://www.idgbooks.com

ISBN Number: ISBN: 0-7645-5002-0

Title of this book: Cooking For Dummies™

My overall rating of this book: ❏ Very good [1] ❏ Good [2] ❏ Satisfactory [3] ❏ Fair [4] ❏ Poor [5]

How I first heard about this book:

❏ Found in bookstore; name: [6] ❏ Book review: [7]

❏ Advertisement: [8] ❏ Catalog: [9]

❏ Word of mouth; heard about book from friend, co-worker, etc.: [10] ❏ Other: [11]

What I liked most about this book:

What I would change, add, delete, etc., in future editions of this book:

Other comments:

Number of computer books I purchase in a year: ❏ 1 [12] ❏ 2-5 [13] ❏ 6-10 [14] ❏ More than 10 [15]

I would characterize my computer skills as: ❏ Beginner [16] ❏ Intermediate [17] ❏ Advanced [18] ❏ Professional [19]

I use ❏ DOS [20] ❏ Windows [21] ❏ OS/2 [22] ❏ Unix [23] ❏ Macintosh [24] ❏ Other: [25]_____

(please specify)

I would be interested in new books on the following subjects:

(please check all that apply, and use the spaces provided to identify specific software)

❏ Word processing: [26] ❏ Spreadsheets: [27]

❏ Data bases: [28] ❏ Desktop publishing: [29]

❏ File Utilities: [30] ❏ Money management: [31]

❏ Networking: [32] ❏ Programming languages: [33]

❏ Other: [34]

I use a PC at (please check all that apply): ❏ home [35] ❏ work [36] ❏ school [37] ❏ other: [38] _____

The disks I prefer to use are ❏ 5.25 [39] ❏ 3.5 [40] ❏ other: [41]_____

I have a CD ROM: ❏ yes [42] ❏ no [43]

I plan to buy or upgrade computer hardware this year: ❏ yes [44] ❏ no [45]

I plan to buy or upgrade computer software this year: ❏ yes [46] ❏ no [47]

Name: _____ Business title: [48] _____ Type of Business: [49] _____

Address (❏ home [50] ❏ work [51]/Company name: _____)

Street/Suite# _____

City [52]/State [53]/Zip code [54]: _____ Country [55] _____

❏ **I liked this book!** You may quote me by name in future
IDG Books Worldwide promotional materials.

My daytime phone number is _____

IDG BOOKS WORLDWIDE

THE WORLD OF COMPUTER KNOWLEDGE®

❏ YES!

Please keep me informed about IDG Books Worldwide's World of Computer Knowledge. Send me your latest catalog.

BESTSELLING
BOOK SERIES
FROM IDG